LSU LAW

LSU
THE LOUISIANA STATE UNIVERSITY
LAW

LAW SCHOOL FROM 1906 TO 1977

W. LEE HARGRAVE

LOUISIANA STATE UNIVERSITY PRESS
BATON ROUGE

Published by Louisiana State University Press
lsupress.org

Copyright © 2004 by Louisiana State University Press
All rights reserved. Except in the case of brief quotations used in articles
or reviews, no part of this publication may be reproduced or
transmitted in any format or by any means without written
permission of Louisiana State University Press.

Louisiana Paperback Edition, 2023

DESIGNER: Andrew Shurtz
TYPEFACE: Adobe Caslon, Clarendon
TYPESETTER: Coghill Composition Co., Inc.

Cover image courtesy Jim Zietz, LSU University Relations.

LIBRARY OF CONGRESS
CATALOGING-IN-PUBLICATION DATA:

Hargrave, W. Lee.
LSU Law: the Louisiana State University Law School
from 1906 to 1977 / W. Lee Hargrave.

p. cm.
Includes bibliographical references and index.
ISBN 978-0-8071-2914-2 (hardcover : alk. paper)
ISBN 978-0-8071-8039-6 (paperback)

1. Louisiana State University (Baton Rouge, La.). Law School—History.
2. Law Schools—Louisiana—Baton Rouge—History.
I. Title.
KF292.L6674H37   2004
340'.071'176318—DC22
2004003127

for

DEAN PAUL M. HEBERT,
a superb leader

and

PROFESSOR GEORGE W. PUGH,
a great teacher

CONTENTS

Foreword by Carolyn H. Hargrave xi

1. Lawyers in Early Louisiana 1
2. The Beginnings: 1904–1920 8
3. The Semi-Roaring Twenties 41
4. The Extravagant Thirties 59
5. The Forties: World War II and Postwar Challenges 106
6. The Fifties: Return to Normalcy 129
7. The Sixties: Steady Growth 168
8. 1970–1977: Running Hard to Stay in Place 212
9. Ruminations and Conclusions 248

Notes 265

Bibliography 301

Index of Names 315

Subject Index 329

ILLUSTRATIONS

Following page 128

Ira Samuel Flory

Robert Lee Tullis

Harriet S. Daggett

Paul M. Hebert

Wex S. Malone

George W. Pugh

Students and faculty, 1913

Class of 1941

Senior class officers, 1949

Law Faculty, 1953

Phi Delta Phi, 1956

1962 Law Review

Class of 1967

1971 Law Review

1975 Law Review

FOREWORD

Lee Hargrave retired as a professor in the LSU Law School in May 2000. Although he devoted full time for two years to the formal writing of this book, in reality he had been working on and thinking about it since 1964, when he entered the LSU Law School. Upon graduation in 1967, he was appointed to the faculty, serving until his retirement. Throughout this entire period, because of his love for LSU and the Law School, he quietly and continuously collected information with the goal of one day writing a definitive history of the institution. Lee was perfectly situated to write this history, since his education and tenure at the Law School connected him to every generation of the school's faculty. He died November 15, 2002, shortly after Louisiana State University Press had accepted his manuscript for publication.

Lee's book is the first comprehensive history of the Law School. Covering the era from the institution's founding in 1906 to the death of its longtime dean Paul M. Hebert in 1977, it includes all the elements that have given a distinctive mystique to the Law School and to the meaning of a law degree from LSU: the policies and leadership of administrators; the personalities and influence of individual faculty members; the impact of curricular changes; and, of course, the richness of student life in those years.

Lee believed very strongly in the role and importance of the Law School. As the largest and oldest public law school in Louisiana, the LSU Law Center has served generations of citizens. It has been the focus of excellence in legal education, imparting to new lawyers and judges the foundations of the state's legal system and its place in the nation and the world. It has been the custodian of Louisiana's unique civil-law heritage, and it has served as a driver and historical intelligence behind statewide legal reforms. Perhaps most important, it has been a crucible of leadership, combining the talents of law students and others from all walks of life, challenging them to enrich the legal community, guide legislative bodies, and contribute to the body politic as a whole. With a strong work ethic and seriousness of purpose which come from knowing that a degree is not a matter of right, students of the Law School have graduated with a reverence for the school's many outstanding, even legendary, faculty. Many of those graduates have gone on to become the leaders of Louisiana.

As the Law School nears its 100th anniversary in 2006, it is vitally important for those who love it to reflect on its past. Understanding the progress of the Law School in the twentieth century will help ensure its progress in the twenty-first.

Over the two years he devoted to writing this book, Lee spoke often of the many people who helped in so many different ways. On his behalf, I would like to thank Law School staff Gladys Dreher and Susan Davis; Madeline Hebert, Associate Librarian, Hebert Law Center; Mary Hebert Price, University Archivist and Director of the T. Harry Williams Center for Oral History; and Nina Pugh of the Law School's Oral History Project. Faculty colleagues who provided documents and answered questions include Melvin Dakin, Milton Harrison, Robert Pascal, Warren Mengis, Frank Maraist, and George Pugh. I am grateful to them, as well as to all those faculty whose articles, studies, and reports were consulted and to the student editors of the *Law Review*, who inspired and challenged Lee for over thirty years.

I also wish to express my appreciation to those who contributed to bringing the manuscript to publication. From the LSU Press, Les Phillabaum, Gerry Anders, Margaret Hart, and Lee Sioles have been most helpful, as was the freelance copy editor, Margaret Dalrymple; from the Hebert Law Center, Madeline Hebert, Rita Millican, and James Wade; from the LSU Archives, Mary Hebert Price, Barry Cowan, and Jennifer Abraham; from the LSU Office of University Relations, Jim Zietz; and from the Board of Regents, Anthony Monta. Special thanks go also to law colleagues Alston Johnson, Ray Lamonica, Winston Day, and Wendell Holmes, and especially to Katherine Spaht, Lee's *Louisiana Matrimonial Regimes* co-author and close friend, whose dedicated assistance was crucial to completing this book. The outstanding work of Richard Moreno, Class of 1991, in compiling the index is also appreciated. Finally, I wish to thank our daughter, Aleah, and son, Michel, for understanding and supporting their father's commitment of time and effort to writing this important history.

Carolyn H. Hargrave

LSU LAW

1

LAWYERS IN EARLY LOUISIANA

In 1682, when the French explorer Robert Cavelier, the sieur de la Salle, took possession in the name of Louis XIV of the lands drained by the Mississippi River, he and his crew conducted a traditional ceremony at the mouth of the river to comply with existing norms of international law. His proclamation concluded, "I hereby take to witness those who hear me, and demand an act of the notary here present."[1] A notary assigned to an expedition of exploration to authenticate an imperial proclamation issued in such a muddy, marshy venue may well seem a quaint oddity of seventeenth-century imperial protocol, but this gentleman was without a doubt the first lawyer in the territory that was to become Louisiana. It was many years before he was followed by others of his kind.

Commenting on lawyers in the South and Southwest at the beginning of the nineteenth century, Henry S. Foote wrote, "If there were any very learned jurists residing in the city of New Orleans during the first years of the present [i.e., nineteenth] century, their fame has certainly not come down to men of the present generation." Though the colonial Superior Council had two law officers, the attorney general (*procureur-général*) and the registrar (*greffier*), these officers were not professionally trained lawyers. There were some men who were designated notaries who drafted and preserved forms and documents, but "the notarial profession of French North America was not a learned one."[2]

When Louisiana was sold to the United States in 1803, the population of New Orleans was only slightly more than 8,000 people—3,984 whites, 1,335 free blacks, and 2,773 slaves. The colony's population, however, expanded immensely after the Louisiana Purchase. Merchants and lawyers were prominent among the American immigrants. Immigration from St. Domingue (Haiti) after the slave rebellion there in 1804 brought to Louisiana elite planters, merchants, and a number of lawyers of French descent.³ John Henry Wigmore, author of the famed treatise on evidence and dean of the Northwestern University Law School, was more complimentary about the Louisiana bar in the period after statehood:

> But this period was the Augustan age of the bar in Louisiana. The breadth of research which the circumstances forced upon them tended to make and did make jurists of them all. During those twenty years the lawyers drew for their authority upon the Gothic, Spanish, and French codes, the Roman and the civil law, with their attendant cloud of commentators, and, finally, upon the common law of England and its developed form in this country. This keen exercise was not only reserved for the leaders of the bar; it was a matter of daily experience for all. Upon a random page in the reports of cases of that period one may expect with equal probability a citation from Binney or Ulpian, from Lopez or Pothier, from Coke or Vattel. There first in this country, and there only, perhaps it might be added was found at the bar a taste for comparative jurisprudence. The names of the brilliant ones of that day are not often heard now, but Hall, Derbigny, Duponceau, Brown, Lislet, Workman, Mazureau, were eminent names in that creative era.⁴

The 1808 digest of the laws then in effect in Louisiana was a monumental legal work by two extraordinary New Orleans lawyers. James Brown of Virginia had been educated at the predecessor to Washington and Lee University and at William and Mary College, and he practiced law in Kentucky before moving to Louisiana. Louis Moreau-Lislet was a French jurist from St. Domingue who arrived in New Orleans in 1805 and established a law practice with another French lawyer, Pierre Derbigny, who had moved from France to St. Domingue, then to Philadelphia, and finally to New Orleans. Their digest was drafted in response to the failure of Governor William C. C. Claiborne, a native of Virginia who had been admitted to the Tennessee bar, to impose the common law in the Louisiana Territory.⁵

François Xavier Martin, a Marseille native, had emigrated to North Carolina, where he was a printer as well as a lawyer. President James Madison appointed him to the Louisiana territorial court, and he subsequently served on the state supreme court for more than thirty years. Martin was lavishly described as being "Pontifex Maximus in the temple of civil jurisprudence.

He was familiarly acquainted with classical literature and the languages of southern Europe, and he thus had exceptional facilities for acquiring a mastery of the civil law." As John Henry Wigmore described Martin, "his literary vigor was remarkable, and besides a translation of Pothier on Obligations (the first ever published in English) and other legal works, he wrote a history of North Carolina, his first home, and, later, of Louisiana. His solid legal culture brought him into frequent contact with Kent and Story and made him no unequal companion; and in 1841 Harvard University honored him with the degree of LL.D."[6]

When forty-three delegates gathered in New Orleans in November 1811 to draft Louisiana's initial constitution, at least nine of them were lawyers. They were sophisticated experts in legal matters and represented the older Creole elite, the newer foreign French settlers, and the Americans who had immigrated to the new territory. The convention secretary was Eligius Fromentin, a former French Jesuit who had settled in Pennsylvania and Maryland, where he studied law, before moving to Louisiana. Allan Bowie Magruder, who along with Fromentin delivered the document to Washington, was admitted to the Kentucky bar in 1795. Later, he moved to Louisiana and practiced law in Opelousas. He was influential in the convention's decision to use the Kentucky constitution as a model for the constitution of the new state.[7]

One of the first tasks for the new supreme court of the state of Louisiana when it convened in March 1813 was to examine and qualify "gentlemen desirous of licenses to practice and plead." Among the early qualifiers were John B. Prevost, who had previously served for two years as the first and sole judge of the Superior Court of the Territory of Orleans, François Xavier Martin, Edward Livingston, John R. Grymes, Louis Moreau-Lislet, and Etienne Mazureau. Pierre Derbigny, who had practiced in the Territory, became one of the supreme court judges, but it was not until 1820 that he was examined and admitted to practice law. By 1823, ten years after the founding of the state supreme court, sixty-three lawyers had been admitted to practice.[8]

The Louisiana Civil Code of 1825, along with a Code of Practice and a Code of Commerce, was drafted by three prominent attorneys, the aforementioned Louis Moreau-Lislet and Pierre Derbigny of France, along with Edward Livingston. Livingston already had an extraordinary reputation when he moved to Louisiana from New York, which he had represented in Congress. He was also well known for his proposed Louisiana Criminal Code, which won the admiration of Bentham, Macaulay, and Maine.[9] Wigmore wrote of Livingston:

> He is the Bentham of American jurisprudence without the blemishes of that great critic. It was Bentham's misfortune too often to overshoot his mark, perhaps as much by not being thoroughly grounded in the law he criticized as through any other cause. Livingston shared with Bentham his contempt for the rubbish and the useless fictions that disfigured (and in part still disfigure) the common law of England and the United States; but he had moderation and clearer perceptions, and was not only a master of the common law, but was thoroughly acquainted with the civil law and widely read in the continental writers.[10]

Judah Philip Benjamin arrived in New Orleans from South Carolina in 1832 and was admitted to the New Orleans bar. In 1840 the law firm of Slidell, Benjamin, and Conrad was founded, and for several years it produced more than $20,000 annually for each of the partners. Benjamin served in the Confederate cabinet during the Civil War, and after the defeat of the South he moved to England, where he wrote the standard treatise on the law of sales of goods. It was said of him that "the fame of our jurists is necessarily limited by the area in which the system of civil law is cultivated on the continent; but their power in professional contest is demonstrated by the fact that J. P. Benjamin, who was only among the foremost here, leaped into unquestioned primacy at Washington and London."[11]

After the Civil War, a Louisiana lawyer, Thomas Joseph Semmes, was elected president of the American Bar Association in 1886. Born in the District of Columbia, he was a first cousin of Raphael Semmes, the Confederate naval officer. A Harvard law graduate, he studied civil law in New Orleans during 1850 for three months, then began to practice. He served as U.S. attorney, district attorney, and attorney general and participated in the constitutional conventions of 1879 and 1898. He was a faculty member at Tulane, and he delivered a lecture on the civil law in Louisiana before the American Bar Association in 1882.[12]

The expanding bar of the state was noteworthy not only because so many lawyers were trained in other states, but also because most of them were not formally trained in law in educational institutions. Many of them, of course, were literate persons who had attended college and were familiar with the classics, but most of them came to the bar after reading law under the tutelage of practicing lawyers. Judah P. Benjamin, for example, was the son of English Jews, born in St. Croix on August 6, 1811, because the English fleet had blocked traffic to New Orleans. The family later moved to North Carolina, from whence Benjamin attended Yale College for three years and then left without graduating. He arrived in New Orleans in early 1832 and read law in a law office until he was admitted to the bar in December of that year.[13] A. Oakey Hall, best known for his magazine articles collected and published as *The Manhattaner in New Orleans,* was reared in New Orleans and New York. He attended New York University at age fourteen in 1840, then entered Harvard Law School in 1844. He remained there for only one term, then read law in New York and New Orleans. In Louisiana, he studied under John Slidell and was admitted to practice after being examined by a committee that included Judah P. Benjamin.[14]

Colonial Louisiana had not developed strong educational institutions at the advanced level. Little training in law or philosophy was available, and legal training did not develop along a university model. As in the rest of the American colonies and throughout the early national period, legal training developed through a practical apprenticeship system, a system that involved a student's working for a lawyer while obtaining some instruction in the law. Some lawyers were more willing than others to take apprentices, and they developed what can probably be called proprietary law schools. Indeed, the first law programs at Harvard and Yale were formed by absorbing such privately owned institutions. As Robert Stevens put it: "Yale absorbed a local private law school in 1824 by listing the students in its catalog and appointing the 'owner' of the school, Judge David Daggett, to the vacant professorship of law. Harvard reorganized its law offerings in 1829, bringing in Joseph Story for prestige and John Ashmun—from the Northampton Law School—to provide students. When Tulane wanted to establish a law school in 1847, it absorbed the Louisiana Law School, run by the Swedish scholar Gustavus Smith. The University of North Carolina had already made a similar move."[15] Thus it was that the first major American law schools were not the intellectual, theoretical programs typical of European university curricula but more practical endeavors intended to train working lawyers to practice in the conditions of a new and rapidly changing nation.

The Louisiana Law School was a private institution in New Orleans owned by Gustavus Schmidt, a Swedish immigrant. It continued in operation until the University of Louisiana developed its law department in 1847 and absorbed Schmidt's operation. The first graduating class completed its entire course of instruction in six months. The university was renamed Tulane University in 1884 after a large donation from Paul Tulane, but even then the law school was staffed by part-time faculty and "remained small and provincial and was almost constantly in search of a permanent home for itself." The instruction remained "practical," and "lectures, oral examinations, and class schedules went on in the time-honored fashion. In fact, lectures came to be so standardized that a student could buy a copy of last year's lectures from John Westly and thus avoid the necessity of attending this year's class sessions."[16]

Columbia was the nation's leading law school at midcentury, and Harvard became ascendent in the 1870s. At that time, 1,200 students were enrolled in twenty-one law schools across the country. By 1890, there were 4,500 students enrolled in sixty-one law schools. In 1916, it was reported that 4,778 students were enrolled in twenty-four "high entrance standards" law schools, 7,918 in full-time programs at forty-three other schools, and 2,043 in "short course" schools. The market for lawyers had exploded, and there was considerable competition between the higher-quality institutions and the proprietary schools.[17]

Major changes occurred at the Tulane Law School in 1906, when it moved from Canal Street to the uptown campus. The school acquired a new dean and two young assistant professors returning to New Orleans from eastern universities where they had obtained law degrees. Other new faculty were hired, including the department's first full-time professor. Louisiana State University and Agricultural and Mechanical College, the public university up the river in Baton Rouge, founded its own law school in 1906. Loyola University of New Orleans opened its law school in 1914, largely though the efforts of John St. Paul, then a judge of the Orleans Court of Appeals and later associate justice of the Louisiana Supreme Court.[18] Southern University Law School opened in 1947 in Baton Rouge in an attempt to thread the needle between *Plessy v. Ferguson* and *Sweatt v. Painter* and to provide separate but equal legal education for black students.[19] These four institutions remain in operation today.

It was not until 1963, however, that a law school degree was a prerequisite to sitting for the Louisiana bar.[20] Indeed, it was common up to that time for some students to "attend" law school, leave without graduating, and then take the bar exam. Huey P. Long provides the prime example. Financed largely by his brother Julius, who received an LL.B. from Tulane Law School in 1907, Huey left his hometown, Winnfield, with funds for one year in New Orleans. He attended classes at Tulane Law School in 1914–15, studied additional courses on his own that had been recommended by Julius, and was "coached" by lawyer Charles J. Rivet. As T. Harry Williams recounts, Huey "simply went to Chief Justice Frank A. Monroe of the supreme court and asked for an early examination. He was married, he said, and he was poor; he did not have enough money to stay in New Orleans until June, when the bar examinations were scheduled. Monroe was sympathetic and advised him to go to the committee and repeat the request. If the committee passed him, the court would admit him immediately." He passed, and he was admitted.[21]

One wonders why Huey did not choose to study at LSU, where living expenses were cheaper and fees lower. Perhaps it was because Tulane admitted as "special students" persons who had not finished high school and LSU did not.[22] Perhaps Huey simply preferred life in the fast lane.

THE BEGINNINGS: 1904–1920

FOUNDATION IN 1904

In typical Louisiana fashion, when the state began to promote public higher education it adopted a hortatory statement to that effect in the constitution. The 1845 constitution, the state's second, not only specified that a University of Louisiana "shall" be established, but that it be located in New Orleans and that it have four faculties, "One of law, one of medicine, one of the natural sciences, and one of letters." The University of Louisiana floundered until the state transferred it to the supervision of a private board in 1884 and it was renamed Tulane University, but the university had attended to its mandate of establishing a law school by absorbing a proprietary school in 1847.[1]

The State Seminary of Learning, the institution that would become LSU, was founded in 1860 at Pineville. It was mandated to teach "agriculture and the mechanic arts" in order to qualify for federal funds under the Morrill Act of 1862. Legislation adopted in 1877 uniting LSU and the A&M College ("The Louisiana State University and Agricultural and Mechanical College") and relocating the institution to Baton Rouge provided more mandates. Section 4 specified that the University "shall provide special instruction for the purpose of agriculture, the mechanic arts, mining, military science and art, civil engineering, law, medicine, commerce, and navigation." Section 12 of the act repeated the requirement that the University establish "schools of medicine and law." It was not until a quarter century later, however, after the trials of Reconstruction were overcome, that the University was able to fulfill the mandate to establish a law school, the Board of Supervisors doing so in 1904. The "law department" accepted students in 1906 and graduated its first class in 1908. LSU's medical school came much later, in 1930.[2]

When Colonel Thomas D. Boyd became president of LSU in 1896, he led a faculty of nineteen and 140 cadets on a campus north of Baton Rouge near the Pentagon Barracks. Funding was limited, and student morale was low. Boyd began a systematic program of improvements that brought stability, new buildings, and increased funding to the University. He also took "action in liberalizing the military system," thus beginning a new era in military life at the University. The floundering Audubon Sugar School, at an agricultural experiment station in Audubon Park in New Orleans, was relocated to Baton Rouge in 1897 and attracted sixty students. The student newspaper, the *Reveille*, was revived, and a summer "normal" school for teacher training was the forerunner of the summer program at LSU. Alumni were organized, and they assisted in financing the construction program. It was largely through Boyd's efforts that a hesitant Board of Supervisors opened the University to women students in 1905. His daughter, Annie Boyd, was one of the first women to enroll.[3]

Marcus Wilkerson's biography of Boyd noted that "the decade, 1900–1910, was marked by the greatest building program for an educational institution that Louisiana had ever witnessed. A new University, consisting of twenty-two buildings, was erected during this period, replacing the old, poorly equipped structures which the institution had long since outgrown. There was no change in site, no break in the daily routine, as year after year, building after building took its place beside others in the broad space on the south side of the University grounds. Perhaps few realized that a new University in fact was rapidly supplanting the old." During the time, state appropriations grew from $16,000 to $77,100 annually; the faculty doubled from twenty-two to fifty; and the number of courses offered rose from 135 to 336. Enrollment exceeded 400 in the 1901–02 session and reached 458 for the 1904–05 session. Academic departments were reorganized and expanded. Civil engineering was separated from mechanical engineering; a program in commerce was reorganized into a four-year program; premedical studies were offered; and programs in philosophy and education were founded in 1905.[4]

It was during this period of expansion that the Law School was founded. Initial efforts to establish the school were hindered because its financial success hinged on charging tuition fees, which, however, were prohibited by state statute. The legislature refused in 1904 to allow such fees, but the LSU Board of Supervisors nonetheless instructed the administration to prepare a plan for establishing a law school. Students supported the prospect, and the *Reveille* announced in March: "The Louisiana State University is the only school of its kind in the United States that has no law department. Why is this? Surely one is needed badly enough. Is not Louisiana equal to any emergency? Don't the young men of Louisiana need instruction in the legal sciences as well as the young men of other States? Our State University should have a law school."[5]

In May 1906, the Board of Supervisors "approved the recommendations of the President of the Faculty that a professional course in law, requiring two years for completion, be established at once." The student newspaper proudly announced that three professors would be hired and that they would devote their entire time to teaching. It pointed out that Tulane "has a faculty composed entirely of lecturers, and though the ability of these gentlemen cannot for a moment be questioned, they are almost all busy practitioners, and on that account cannot devote a great amount of time to their classes."[6]

CLASSES BEGIN

The first students began classes on September 24, 1906, with little formality, twenty-six of them enrolling as full-time law students and twenty-nine other LSU students taking various law courses. President Boyd met with the class on Monday, lessons were assigned for Tuesday, and the class was dismissed. Subsequently, classes met daily from 2 to 5 P.M., and for each class two hours of preparatory work were required, making the work per day extend over nine hours, according to the *Reveille*, which also stated that "there are several long-established law schools in the United States with smaller attendance."[7]

Although tuition as such was not charged, the University imposed a law-library fee of $20 in addition to the general fee of $5. A 1908 statute allowed the University to charge tuition to law students, but the University *Bulletin* released the following August stated that "this fee will not be charged for the session of 1908–09." In his historical review of the contributions of Louisiana lawyers on the occasion of "Law Day, U.S.A.," Judge John T. Hood Jr. described the first class as composed of a substantial number of mature men: "Among the first students to enroll were: Captain Louis Sorley, who was then Commandant of Cadets at L.S.U., Thomas H. Harris, who at that time was serving as State Superintendent of Education, which position he continued to hold for many years after completing his law course; and Eugene J. Mc-

Givney, who was then serving as Secretary of State for the State of Louisiana." One of the high-ranking younger students was James E. Smitherman, who later served on the LSU Board of Supervisors.[8]

Law students were not required to live on campus or to join the cadet corps. The *Bulletin* advised that "board in the city of Baton Rouge costs from $15 a month upward," but students who opted to board at the University in the military department were charged $121 per session. Most students lived in boardinghouses in town, but according to Hermann Moyse ('12), "there were several of us who remained on the campus in a special building called the Pest House, which at one time had been a pest house, and it was set aside for graduate students or for seniors who were not commissioned. We were allowed to eat in the mess hall and have all of the same privileges as cadets, but we were under no military restrictions except to keep our rooms clean." When Robert Lee Tullis became dean, he emphasized total commitment to law study and discouraged students from participating in the military program and from joining sports teams. Since most law students were not under military restrictions, demerits for class absences were not a viable sanction. Instead, each absence raised the required average to pass a course by one point. That rule was changed in Fall 1910, when students were not allowed to take an examination in a course if they had been absent from one-sixth or more of the class sessions. A variation of that rule remains in effect today.[9]

A campuswide reorganization in 1908–09 established colleges and schools and referred to the "Law School" rather than a law department. The Law School was housed in the Hill Memorial Library, which had been completed in 1903, occupying the ground floor and consisting of a room for the law library, two lecture rooms, and two offices for professors. Heating apparently was not an important priority. Students complained in a *Reveille* editorial about the lack of heat in the lecture rooms and the library, describing a class huddled around one of the "two little toy gas stoves" and a professor on a platform wrapped in an overcoat. In 1908, the Law School moved to three rooms in the "odoriferous basement" of the chemistry building.[10]

The initial announcement of the law program included the holdings of the law library, apparently with some pride. Listed were the *United States Supreme Court Reports, with Rose's Notes;* the entire *Reporter System* of the West Publishing Company from its inauguration; *Lawyers' Reports Annotated; Decisions of the Supreme Court of Louisiana; The American Digest, Century Edi-*

tion and supplementary volumes; *Digest of Louisiana Decisions; The Federal Statutes Annotated; The Statutes of Louisiana;* the *Encyclopedia of Law;* dictionaries and standard treatises on legal subjects; and the leading law journals of the time. Students of that period, however, suggested that the reality was a more humble library, with few treatises and few multiple copies of books. Civil-law treatises were not available, but the law office library of Judge William F. Kernan, who had "quite a collection of French authorities," was sometimes available to lawyers and students.[11]

The law curriculum required two years of resident study for graduation and conformed to the standards of the American Bar Association, adopted in 1897, which merely required a high-school education for admission and two years of study for the LL.B. degree. Though the LSU faculty did not require undergraduate college training, it "recommended a combined curriculum of five years of University study leading to the A.B. and LL.B. degrees." An early *Bulletin* explained to students that the program was designed "to give breadth of view and grasp of principles not easily obtained without a college education." The combined degree program remained in effect well into modern times for LSU undergraduates, and it was not until 1974 that an undergraduate degree (as opposed to ninety hours of college course work) was required for admission to the Law School.[12]

The state supreme court approved the curriculum, and in 1906 it extended the diploma privilege to graduates of LSU, as had been done for graduates of Tulane. Chief Justice Joseph A. Breaux wrote to President Boyd, "the State being interested, that the diplomas granted by the Louisiana State University and Agriculture and Mechanical College to graduates of the Law Department should be given effect and respected accordingly. Consequently, to obtain a license from this Court to practice law in this State no additional examination is deemed necessary."[13]

Graduates of LSU retained the diploma privilege until 1924, when the bar examination requirement was extended to all persons seeking to practice law. As early as 1912, law students were concerned by a report that Dean E. D. Saunders of Tulane's law school urged that law school graduates be required to pass the bar exam. Their argument was that the proposal would favor those who read law and then took the exam and would discourage attendance at law school. Pressure from World War II veterans eager to get into practice as soon as possible led to a temporary return of the diploma privilege, and the bar examination requirement was also suspended during the Korean conflict. A few students, one of them Fred Benton Sr. ('19), took the bar examination before graduation and thus were entitled to practice while still in law school.[14]

PHILOSOPHY OF LEGAL EDUCATION AT LSU

The impetus for the establishment of the LSU Law School was largely an intellectual and academic one. There is little indication of a desire for part-time training or for a trade-school approach, and little use was made of part-time faculty. The organizers and planners were primarily LSU faculty members in political science, history, and commerce. President Boyd saw the Law School as a logical extension of the expansion of the University in all areas of knowledge. The dean and the first faculty members were full-time professors rather than practitioners who taught part-time. Curriculum emphasis was on the theoretical as much as the practical and extended to Roman law and civil law.

This successful evolution of the Law School contrasts with an attempt at about the same time to establish a medical school associated with LSU. Some physicians in New Orleans sensed the desire of the LSU Board of Supervisors to create a medical school, but funding problems could not be overcome. These practitioners therefore established a private institution with the goal of eventual union with LSU. The New Orleans location of the school produced opposition from Tulane University's medical school and from related New Orleans interests. The onset of that debate produced another group of interests that wanted LSU to open a medical school in Shreveport in association with the charity hospital there. Failure to agree on matters led to the closing of the New Orleans school. Not until 1930 during the Huey Long era was LSU's medical school organized and, ironically, located in New Orleans.[15]

The LSU approach to professional full-time legal training also reflected changes that were occurring at Tulane's law school. About the same time, Tulane began to offer a more rigorous professional law program and acquired several full-time professors who had been trained at eastern law schools.[16]

The 1906 LSU *Bulletin* stated that "the Faculty will consist at first of two, later of three, of the ablest teachers of law that can be secured. They will devote their whole time to the work of instruction; and will be assisted by eminent Louisiana practitioners, who will deliver lectures on special subjects."

An important part of the Law School program was its close relationship to other departments of the University. Colonel Arthur T. Prescott, a professor of political science and constitutional law, was the draftsman of the report recommending the establishment of the Law School. He would later assist in teaching some Law School courses. His report summarized the University's approach:

> I heartily endorse the proposition to create a law department in this institution, wherein systematic professional training will prepare students for the bar. If organized with professional teachers, as well as professional lawyers, men as anxious to satisfy the requirements of systematic instruction as to elucidate the principles of legal science, such a department would offer advantages to be had no where else in Louisiana. When we recall the fact that the best law schools in America command the services of men devoted to teaching alone, and that such men, after the great expounders of the law on the bench, have contributed most to the development of the profession, we realize the necessity for exclusive professional teaching. The professor of Political Science and a scholarly lawyer as Professor of Law start the work under favorable auspices. Outsiders could deliver courses of lectures from time to time, as Judge Howe at Yale when he prepared his well known studies in Civil Law. In this connection it would be well to remember that the courses in law now given to our commercial students constitute an important part of the courses prescribed by the Supreme court for applicants to the bar. They are, therefore, an excellent foundation for a professional department.

Dean Paul M. Hebert emphasized in his history of the school, "in keeping with the policy of emphasizing the role of the full-time law teacher, as expressed by President Boyd, the Law Faculty throughout the School's history has been predominantly a faculty of full-time educators devoting substantially all of their time to teaching and research."[17]

The first-year curriculum was a combination of civil- and common-law courses, some taught as lectures and some using casebooks. The curriculum was as follows:

First Year—First Term

The Civil Law: History of the Civil Law; Justinian's Institutes
The Common Law: History of the Common Law

Contracts and Negotiable Paper, with Citations
Partnership; Principal and Agent, with Citations
Insurance, with Citations

First Year—Second Term

The Civil Law: Pothier on Obligations
The Common Law: The Common Law in the United States
Constitutional Law, with Citations
Private Corporations, with Citations
Torts; Bailments and Carriers, with Citations

Second Year—First Term

Civil Code of Louisiana
Code of Practice of Louisiana
Evidence
Crimes and Criminal Procedure
International Law, with Citations

Second Year—Second Term

Civil Code of Louisiana
Admiralty
Equity Jurisprudence and Procedure
Federal Practice
Conflict of Laws

Classes were held six days each week during the two semesters, the students spending three hours per day in three different classes. The school required a full-time commitment, with one class held from 8 to 9 A.M. and the other two classes from 5 to 6 P.M. and 6 to 7 P.M. Law students were also allowed to take courses in other academic departments without charge: "In this way the law student has ample opportunity to study such important subjects as English, History and Economics. The schedule of hours for academic and law classes is so arranged as to permit law students to take academic courses without conflict."[18] The schedule also reflected the heavy demands on the limited classroom space of the growing University.

In addition to the regular courses, the 1906–07 session included two lecture series—twelve lectures on constitutional law by Judge A. A. Gunby of the Monroe bar, and twelve lectures by W. O. Hart of the New Orleans bar. The two were special lecturers again in the 1907–08 term, joined by "Hon. N. C. Blanchard, ex-Governor of Louisiana" and "Judge E. D. Saunders, of the U.S. District Court, Dean of Tulane University Law School." Saunders's similar lectures at Tulane on the civil code were published and are well known. Hart's lectures at LSU were published as *Fragments of Louisiana Jurisprudence; Twelve Lectures Delivered to the Students in the Law Department of the Louisiana State University*. One version of Hart's book contains an addendum advocating the advantages of the civil law over the common law. The added material was based on a letter to the *New Orleans Picayune* written after Judge Saunders was reported to have "advocated the common law in preference to the civil law" in his lectures at LSU. Judge Saunders was shown the letter before publication and "stated that he had not used the expression quoted, and did not intend in his article to make so broad a statement."[19]

Students were also expected to follow a program of directed readings during the summer. The assigned works reflected the emphasis on both civil law and common law: (a) *Holland's Jurisprudence* or *Domat's Civil Law*, and (b) *Blackstone's Commentaries* or Pollock and Maitland's *History of English Law*.[20] The first *Bulletin* also specified the assigned textbooks, including a number of casebooks, indicating that the case method of instruction was adopted even in this early period. Included were *Clark on Criminal Law, Hopkins on Real Property*, and *Ames Cases on Trusts*.

Practical exercises were also assigned, including moot courts, examination of titles, and the drafting of contracts and corporate charters. The moot-court exercises, some civil but mostly criminal trials, were avidly reported by the student newspaper and featured in the yearbook. *Reveille* reporters even then had to publish articles for credit, and reports of moot-court trials were a quick and easy way of garnering column inches. One front-page story reported the classic case of defendants throwing a shipwreck survivor out of a sinking lifeboat; the verdict was guilty of manslaughter after five minutes of deliberation. During the meetings of the Constitutional Convention of 1913, convention president Newton C. Blanchard served as judge of a moot-court criminal trial at the request of Professor Blackshear. Indeed, the 1913 convention was attended by numerous law-student observers. They were reportedly disappointed when a compromise precluded an appearance by Edgar H. Farrar of

New Orleans, former president of the American Bar Association and one of the greatest lawyers in the United States, who had been scheduled to speak on a typically Louisiana "constitutional" question involving the New Orleans Sewerage and Water Board. Louisiana Act 89 of 1914 required the First Circuit Court of Appeals to decide cases in Baton Rouge rather than riding circuit, and it began using the LSU law library for research and for holding conferences, bringing about more contact between students and judges. When a criminal moot-court trial was held in December 1914, "the court room was filled almost to discomfort by interested spectators, among them numerous cadets, from whom the jury was largely selected." The 1915 case of *State v. Hamlet* featured an insanity defense for the murder of Polonius. The jury could not agree, and a mistrial was declared. In time, the "crimes" were actually enacted on campus before the trial, and the *Reveille* would report such events as "Daring Robbery Is Committed in Barracks" and then describe the enactment.[21]

THE FOUNDING FACULTY: KELLY, HENRY, TULLIS

The first dean of the Law School was Joseph Ignatius Kelly; he was the only regular faculty member during the first year, teaching all classes but two. Colonel Arthur T. Prescott, professor of history and political science, taught constitutional law, and Walter Lynwood Fleming, professor of history, taught international law. Kelly's salary was a generous $3,250 per year ($62,500 in Year 2000 dollars).[22]

Kelly had an extraordinarily strong and cosmopolitan background, having earned A.B. and Ph.D. degrees from Fordham University, a C.E. degree from Pennsylvania Military College, and an LL.B. from Chicago College of Law. He had also studied in Germany, at the Polytechnicum in Hanover and the Royal Technical High School in Berlin. He traveled in several foreign countries and eventually became a member of the Illinois bar. "His tastes and accomplishments drew him into the historical as well as the philosophical regions of the science. He planned, and had printed in some tentative fragments, an English translation of the Roman Digest."[23]

Kelly was a lecturer on Roman law at Northwestern University's law school when he became dean at LSU in 1906. Sources state cryptically that after three years in Baton Rouge, he "was obliged by ill health to resign, and returned to Chicago." He began a translation at that time of Enrico Ferri's work on criminal sociology while also engaged in the practice of international and comparative law. Kelly died in 1913, when the translation was half finished, and "American scholarship lost a contributor of brilliant promise." Among his published works are two articles in the *Illinois Law Review*, "The Gaian Fragment" and "The *Titanic* Death Liability." In the latter, he concluded that the corporate owner of the *Titanic* would succeed in limiting its liability only if the negligence of the ship occurred without the privity and knowledge of the corporation.[24]

Dean Kelly is remembered as a staunch champion of the civil law, his interest apparently inspired by his contact with John Henry Wigmore, then dean of the Northwestern University law school.[25] Indeed, the Wigmore/Northwestern/Illinois relationship with LSU will become more apparent as several other professors with those connections become faculty members at LSU over the years. An advertisement for the LSU Law School appeared in the *Alumnus,* a University magazine, in 1909 over Dean Kelly's signature that stated that the school "devotes special attention to Civil Law and Louisiana Jurisprudence." He also "decried the limitations of a two-year program which made coverage of both the common law and civil law systems quite difficult."[26]

The first professor specializing in common-law subjects was Robert Llewellyn Henry Jr., who joined the faculty for the 1907–08 term and remained until 1911. A Chicago native, Henry was only twenty-four when he arrived at LSU after graduating from the University of Chicago (J.D., 1907) and studying as a Rhodes Scholar in Worcester College of Oxford University, where he earned a B.C.L. When Henry spoke to the student body at chapel exercises in November 1907 on his experiences as a Rhodes Scholar, President Boyd introduced him as the youngest member of the University's faculty. Henry married Elaine Goodale Read, a Baton Rouge native, on June 30, 1908. He continued his connection with mid-American law schools after he left LSU: he taught at the University of Illinois (1911–12), was dean at the University of North Dakota (1912–14), and served as professor at the University of Iowa (1914–16). During World War I, Henry served as a captain then major in the U.S. Army and also lectured at Oxford. In 1924, he was appointed a judge of the Mixed Courts of Egypt, serving as a district-court judge until 1941 and on the court of appeals from 1941 until 1949.[27]

It appears that Henry, like Dean Kelly, could also be characterized as cosmopolitan. A 1909 issue of the *Alumnus* reported that Henry and his wife had sailed from New Orleans on a trip to Italy and spent three weeks studying the art of the Florentine School. Their tour took them to the Alps and then to Paris before returning.[28] *Tourisme juridique,* the term popularized by Professor H. Alston Johnson at LSU in the 1970s after René David of the University of Aix–Marseille introduced him to that term for subsidized foreign travel, seems to have been popular at the LSU Law School from earliest times.

Henry had been on the track team for four years at the University of Chicago and remained an athletics enthusiast at LSU. He served on the University Committee on Athletics and wrote a six-page article in the *Alumnus* (1909) on "The Athletic Situation," mentioning his student days as a runner, "so you will not think me a faculty 'fossil' with no appreciation of the needs of the physical man, nor sympathy with the point of view of the student body." Henry began his article with the statement that LSU had won the football championship of the South in 1908, and only later did he mention that "venomous and severe charges have been brought against us." The charges were of course not proved, he said, but Henry did concede, "still, the fact that five members of the team were not native Louisianians, was, we must admit, some grounds for suspicion, though of course not for charges such as were made. We trust we shall never be guilty of such unseemly conduct and ungentlemanly slander if we should have cause to suspect the bona fide character of members of a rival institution." He also admitted, "it is not an unknown thing also for alumni and friends of universities to offer inducements to football players under the mistaken notion that they are helping the universities."[29] Recent graduates of the Law School will note that Professor Dale Bennett's fondness for LSU athletics was foreshadowed at the beginning of the Law School.

Henry entertained law students at tea one Wednesday afternoon in 1910, as the *Reveille* reported, "in the lawyers' lounging room." "This English custom has proven so popular with the students of the Law Department that it bids fair to become a permanent institution. When juniors were entertained, jokes of the popular type held sway. But with seniors, law and politics were the chief topics."[30]

The 1907–08 term also marked the beginning of Robert Lee Tullis's twenty-seven years of service to the Law School that would continue until 1934. He was forty-three when he started, and he died in 1955 at the age of ninety. First designated as the professor of Louisiana jurisprudence, he was designated, after Dean Kelly's resignation, acting dean and professor of civil law, then as permanent dean in 1910. Tullis had attended LSU and Vanderbilt and then obtained his LL.B. from Tulane in 1887. He practiced law in New Orleans until 1908, first with the Denegre, Blair, and Denegre firm, then with McConnell and Tullis, and from 1897 to 1899 he was secretary to the mayor of New Orleans. Dean Paul M. Hebert was one of Tullis's students, and he described Tullis's teaching in the highest terms:

> Dean Tullis had special gifts of exposition and was a master of the legal hypothet which he used with exceptional effectiveness to sharpen the perception of his students in the discussion of legal problems. He was remarkably well versed in the civilian tradition of Louisiana, as derived from its Roman, French and Spanish sources. He worked constantly for the preservation of the civil law, but he was never blind to the desirability of improvement in the law through legislation which could be adapted to the Louisiana legal scene. He did much to influence the Legislature toward adoption of a number of the uniform acts proposed by the National Conference of Commissioners on Uniform State Laws, having served as a commissioner for some thirty-five years.[31]

General Troy H. Middleton, when commandant of cadets, had an office near the Law School and often heard student comments about the law professors. He recalled that "Dean Tullis expected a day's work from his students, and he not only got a day's work but a night's." Tullis was remembered as a "brilliant man with a fantastic memory. I don't think he lost his eyesight until later years"; then "Mrs. Tullis really assisted him greatly, reading to him or grading papers and things of that sort." One student suggested that although Tullis had a keen wit and was a magnificent impromptu speaker, he was "rather boresome when he had a fixed speech to deliver." The LSU alumni were known to have an annual "wet banquet," but around 1910, when Colonel Arthur T. Prescott became secretary of the association, it became a "dry banquet" and attendance decreased. When the wet banquet returned, Tullis was the main speaker, and "he said he was just happy to see this meeting since Prescott, propriety, and prohibition had been overcome." Even while living in Baton Rouge, Tullis kept his membership in the New Orleans Chess Club and the Checkers and Whist Club.[32]

In addition to strong teaching, Tullis began the Law School's emphasis on public service. In 1912, he assisted in organizing a legislative reference bureau to serve the Louisiana legislature. Tullis was later appointed referee in bankruptcy in the Baton Rouge division of the Federal District Court for the Eastern District of Louisiana, succeeding Ben B. Taylor, who resigned to concentrate on his law practice. Tullis published little. Colonel John H. Tucker Jr. ('20), later president of the Louisiana State Law Institute, remarked, "Tullis was not a man that was ever, you might say, put together well. I tried to talk to him many times, afterwards, to write something about the civil code. Never could get him to do it. It's a pity, because he had heart failure. The best mind and the best appreciation on the civil law of Louisiana of any man I've ever known."[33]

Student Phillip S. Gaharan ('24) said that Tullis was tough: "He was a pretty hard . . . a Simon Legree type . . . he taught the freshmen when they first came in." "[I]t was generally understood that a man wasn't going to pass torts the first time around with Dean Tullis. It didn't happen very often." Supreme court justice Frank W. Hawthorne ('24) did not take torts with Tullis: "I dodged it. I went to the University of Texas summer school and took it out there and came back here. . . . He was a brilliant man, though. He could go to the board and write citations up there from memory."[34]

Some students reported that Tullis taught torts out of *Burdick's Casebook* and his own separate textbook, which were written before automobiles were produced. Later, when students had to take the bar examination, they were shocked to see that the exam mostly concerned automobile-negligence law. In later years, Tullis, a native of Tensas Parish, was nicknamed the "Tensas Terror."[35]

The law faculty was an integral part of the University, with Tullis serving on the University's Committee on Candidates for Degrees and Henry serving on the Committee on Athletics and the Committee on Debating.[36] When the second year of operation of the Law School called for additional second-year courses, faculty from other departments were called in to assist in teaching them. Albert G. Reed, professor of English literature and argumentation, and William O. Scroggs, assistant professor of history and economics, joined Professors Prescott and Fleming.

CURRICULUM DEVELOPMENT AND STANDARDS

Dean Kelly's concerns about the shortcomings of a two-year curriculum were expressed with the addition of new degrees to encourage longer programs of study. In addition to the basic two-year LL.B., the school offered the LL.M. to students who successfully pursued a third year of studies, and students with a working knowledge of Latin or French who wanted to specialize in civil law were offered a B.C.L. (Bachelor of Civil Law) for the third year of study. The LL.M. was awarded to Moses C. Scharff in 1909 and to Carroll A. Benoit and Dudley L. Weber in 1910.[37] The numbers of graduate degrees declined, however, after 1911 when the basic LL.B. was converted into a three-year curriculum.

The 1909 *Bulletin* specified in detail what students were expected to do in their civil-code courses:

> Each article is read and discussed in the lecture periods in light of the decisions of the Supreme Court. The student is required to supply himself with the University's own edition of the Code, printed on the margin of loose leaf sheets. On these, the lecture notes and citations are required to be annotated. The student has always before him the text of an article during the discussion of the jurisprudence bearing upon it and thus makes his own annotated Code. Only such leading cases as are necessary for the interpretation of the Code are used. Clearness is attained by avoiding the needless massing of cumulative cases. In this course digest making is neither encouraged nor permitted.

A student's recollection was simpler: "We took the Civil Code article by article." In the 1908–09 academic year, Dean Kelly and Professor Tullis each taught six courses during the academic year, and Professor Henry, the younger man, taught ten courses that year. Six courses were taught by LSU faculty from other departments. The work of the school now filled the day. First-year courses were taught from 8 to 9 and 9 to 10 A.M., and second-year courses were taught from 10 to 11 and 11 to 12. Third-year courses were taught from 4 to 5 and 5 to 6 P.M.[38]

Concern about the state of preparation of entering students led to the rule, published in the 1911 *Bulletin*, that law professors might reject an examination paper for deficiencies in English: "This rule will be strictly enforced by the

Law Faculty; and, in order to make such occurrences rare, [a] test in English will be required. Furthermore, a groundwork in history is essential to a broad comprehension of the law. Applicants who fail to satisfy these requirements will be advised to take up the work of the College of Arts and Sciences in order to fit themselves for the study of law."[39]

More important, the 1911 *Bulletin* also announced the newly imposed requirement of three years of law study to qualify for the LL.B. degree. Candidates for degrees in the 1911–12 term were allowed to graduate under the old rules, but new students were subject to the increased standards. A statement about professional ethics also appeared. Though no special course was provided, students were required to certify that they had read the Canons of Ethics of the ABA, which had been adopted by the Louisiana Bar Association. Also, "illustrative cases dealing with phases of professional conduct therein referred to will be cited to the class, and students will be advised to obtain, for collateral reading, some well-known treatise on professional ethics."[40]

An innovation at the Law School, one responding to concerns about the length of the new three-year curriculum, was the inauguration of a summer-school program to allow students to graduate early. The first summer courses were taught in 1911 (civil code and law of insurance), and students could now complete the LL.B. program in four semesters and three summer terms if they began their law studies in an initial summer session.[41]

By 1912–13, the three-year curriculum was in effect, the changes emphasizing depth of coverage in traditional courses. Sales and negotiable interests became separate courses, and the former course in criminal law and procedure was split into two courses. Evidence also became a separate course, and separate courses in state and federal constitutional law were offered. Partnership and federal procedure also stood alone, as with common-law pleading and equity. Added were courses in admiralty, conflict of laws, and the Commerce Clause and the Fourteenth Amendment. Courses taught by Professors Prescott and Adams in the College of Arts and Sciences were also open to law students. The catalog listed the required texts for most courses and still showed an emphasis on the case method.

In 1916, the faculty and the curriculum remained stable, but an important change was made in admission standards. Law students "must have completed a year of college work of a grade equal to that of the Louisiana State University."[42] LSU undergraduates were still allowed to pursue the combined curriculum, substituting the first-year law courses for their senior undergraduate programs. Those students could obtain a B.A. or B.S. and an LL.B. in six years.

A new section in the 1919 *Bulletin* advised potential law students on undergraduate studies, recommending primarily economics and political-science courses: "Economic Theory; Economic History of the United States; Money and Banking; Public Finance; The Labor Movement; Transportation Economics; General Sociology; History; Comparative Government; Federal Government in the United States; and Commonwealth Government in the United States."[43]

Although an exact measure of the success rate is not available, a general assessment of the enrollment in the four-year period from 1912–13 through 1915–16 discloses that an average of 55 percent of the first-year students were promoted to the second-year program. Admission was relatively easy, but standards for graduation were high.

Year	First-Year Students	Successful	% Promoted
1912–13	26	14	54
1913–14	24	14	58
1914–15	35	18	51
1915–16	29	17	59

The list of law students in the 1916 *Bulletin* showed nineteen third-year students, eighteen second-year, and twenty-nine first-year students. Annotations of that list are marked in ink in the copy of the *Bulletin* available in the law library; they indicated that there would be "14 applicants for degrees," "31 reasonably sure returns," and "15 doubtful."[44]

An important development in raising standards throughout the University was the adoption by the faculty in 1915 of a regulation requiring students to pass a certain number of courses or be dropped from the institution. The student body had also approved the rule by a vote of 296 to 258. The rule, as applied to law students, required passage of six hours of work each semester. It was only after World War I that the rule resulted in the elimination of substantial numbers of students, but it did produce the myth of the "Hog Law," as it was called. Professor Marcus M. Wilkerson wrote: "The 'Hog

Law' soon became a 'bogey-man' to students, particularly freshmen, and at the close of the first term of each session, the campus, especially in the vicinity of the men's dormitories, echoed with the hog calls of playful cadets intent upon reminding their less fortunate classmates of their impending fate. Many upperclassmen became adept at hog calling and rivalry to excel in the art was keen. Just before 'lights-out' the noises emanating from the barracks closely resembled a 'hog calling' contest."[45]

FACULTY CHANGES

When Dean Kelly returned to Illinois at the end of the 1909 term for health reasons, Robert Lee Tullis became acting dean. He and Professor Henry were joined by Edwin Corwin McKeag[46] to complete the three-member faculty of the Law School. In keeping with the school's high academic demands, McKeag had both an LL.B. and a Ph.D. Indeed, after receiving his B.A. from Rutgers in 1896, he pursued a master's degree in higher mathematics and applied astronomy from that institution the following year. His LL.B. was from Columbia University Law School, received in 1900, and he subsequently practiced law in New York and New Jersey. He returned to Columbia as a fellow in the School of Political Science, where his major subject was Roman law and comparative jurisprudence under Professor Munroe Smith. His dissertation, a comparative study of mistake in the law of contracts, was published in 1905. He remained on the LSU faculty only one academic year (1909–10), teaching primarily the common-law courses, before returning to law practice in New Brunswick, New Jersey.[47]

The following term (1911–12) saw the arrival of Thomas Welburn Hughes, who came with an LL.B. and an LL.M. from the University of Michigan. He was fifty-three, had published a 675-page treatise on the law of evidence, and was an experienced law teacher who had been a faculty member at the University of Michigan for six years and at the University of Illinois for twelve years. A Canadian born in Ontario in 1858, he had attended Hamilton and St. Thomas Collegiate Institutes. His publications included *Hughes on Evidence; Hughes' Cases on Evidence; Outline of Criminal Law; Questions on Criminal Law and Procedure;* and *Hughes on Business Law.* When he arrived at LSU, he had nearly completed a textbook on criminal law. He contributed to publications about the LSU Law School, extolling its virtues and its case method in the *Alumnus*. He wrote,

> The chief aim of a law school should be to fit its students for the practice of law. To accomplish this end something more is required than merely to instruct them in the principles of the law. They must be taught to familiarize themselves with legal methods of reasoning and to acquire legal habits of thought that will enable them to apply correctly principles of law to statements of fact. This discipline of the mind is best acquired by a study of well-selected cases. Hence, in the Louisiana State University the law faculty emphasizes the case method of instruction.

He also wrote favorably about the impending change to a three-year course for the LL.B.:

> The machinery of the school is working very smoothly, a happy spirit pervades the entire student body as well as the faculty, and all concerned are taking a deep interest in the work of the school. Moreover, the length of the course is to be increased next year to three years and the change augers greater success.[48]

In the renamed alumni magazine, the *Louisiana State University Quarterly*, Hughes contributed two articles on the law of evidence in an issue devoted entirely to the Law School. These articles, on misapplication of the *res gestae* doctrine and on misapplication of the burden of proof in the insanity defense, illustrate the long-held view that the law professor's mission is to point out errors made by the courts. Students signed a petition in May 1911 asking Hughes not to leave LSU for an offer "made him by one of the large law schools of the country." He stayed for one more year, but in 1912 he left to accept the deanship at the University of Florida Law School.[49]

Professor Robert L. Henry did not remain for the 1911–12 term, and W. Goodwin Williams, M.A., LL.B., became the third full-time member of the faculty for the session. A native of Richmond, Virginia, Williams had studied law at Washington and Lee University under John Randolph Tucker and later in the law school at the University of Virginia. After postgraduate work at the University of Wisconsin, he attended the University of Marburg in Germany. He had practiced law in San Francisco and, according to the *Reveille*, had twice stumped California for William Jennings Bryan and "was a democrat in sympathy."[50]

Williams wrote effusively in the *LSU Quarterly* about the combination of civil- and common-law study: "In the Law School of the State University of Louisiana there are to be found most excellent and complete courses in the Common Law AND in the Civil Law! Here we find both systems of jurisprudence taught daily side by side. . . . Armed with such a course of training, [the graduate] goes forth fully equipped for battle in the forums of Louisiana, or in the tribunals of Massachusetts; before the bench of New York, or in the courts of California." The *Reveille* contained a long, long-winded, and flowery article by Williams that ran for four columns. He argued that lawyers could succeed if they are "efficient and thoroughly equipped." Soon after, the *Reveille* reported that Williams had resigned his chair and that a vacancy existed in the law faculty. No explanation for the resignation was given, and Williams's duties were distributed among other members of the faculty.[51]

A replacement was found shortly in David A. Blackshear, a Natchitoches Parish native who had a B.A. from LSU, attended the University of Virginia, and received the LL.B. from Tulane. He had also attended Harvard Law School from February 1905 to June 1906, then practiced with a leading New Orleans firm, Farrar, Johnson, and Krutschnitt. Health reasons prompted a move in 1909 to El Paso, Texas, where he taught in the high school. Blackshear's eclectic career then led him to Spokane, Washington, where he practiced law from 1910 until 1911. Returning to Louisiana, he served as secretary of the Louisiana Tax Commission under Governor Newton C. Blanchard. He continued in that position under Governor Luther E. Hall, whose administration formulated constitutional amendments to revise the tax system of the state. Blackshear taught at LSU for four academic years (1913–1917), then returned to Harvard to obtain another LL.B. After graduation, he practiced in New York City in the office of Charles Evans Hughes.[52] Later, Blackshear returned to practice law in North Louisiana, and the case reports contain several of his cases involving oil and gas law. He was also a substantial investor in oil and gas properties and prospered.[53]

Blackshear was living in Florida in 1928 when Professor Ira S. Flory wrote a "testimonial to Mr. Blackshear's character and education" to U.S. Attorney General John G. Sargent to support his application for a federal judgeship in Florida. It does not appear that he obtained the judgeship. Blackshear later returned to Louisiana and lived out his life in New Orleans. Apparently his choice to leave academia was a wise one. At least one of his students said, "He was just dull as a yard ax, I thought." Another said, "David Blackshear married into the [Tullis] family and was a very nice fellow. He was a large hulk of a man, with a sort of mumbled speech and little peculiarities of personality. We had criminal law under him for our first year." In October 1942, Blackshear presented a lithographed photograph of Judah P. Benjamin, prominent Confederate statesman and later a lawyer in London, to the Law School.[54]

Ira Samuel Flory began a long career at LSU in the fall of 1912. He was a native of Rockingham County, Virginia, where he was raised on a farm. He held a B.A. from Mount Morris College, where he played left end on the football team, and an LL.B. (1909) from the University of Virginia Law Department. He clerked for a year with a Wall Street law firm, Ledyor and Milburn, whose address was actually 54 Wall Street. He switched to an academic career, teaching arithmetic and algebra at Mount Morris College and then teaching law at the University of Virginia. He came to LSU in 1912 with his wife and three children and remained until 1917, when he left to practice in New York. In 1919 Flory returned to the University and "remained without vacation or leave until the year of his retirement" in 1950.[55] Dean Paul Hebert described Flory in laudatory terms: "The writer had the privilege of attending classes conducted by Professor Flory. He could be classed among the very ablest of classroom teachers. He was especially talented at illuminating complicated technical areas of the law with simple diagrams and in prodding his students into proper application of detailed statutory provisions in such fields as Federal Jurisdiction and Procedure and Negotiable Instruments. He taught many difficult areas of the common law with equal effectiveness." Flory was also remembered as "a fantastic, hard worker; the students were exceedingly fond of him." Typical student comments were that Flory "never got the credit that he was entitled to, but everybody loved him. We could go to him with our problems."[56]

The 1917 *Bulletin* was little changed, but the name of one of the law students listed stands out—Mrs. I. S. Flory of East Baton Rouge. The 1918 *Bulletin*, however, does not include her in the listing of second-year students. Neither does it include Professor Flory in the listing of faculty, because that is when he left to practice law in New York City. Professor Blackshear departed as well. In their place were Professors Carl Crumbie Wheaton and Clarence Milton Updegraff, both of whom came down the Mississippi River to Baton Rouge.

Wheaton taught at LSU for two years, coming from practice in Minnesota and teaching at Macalester College. He had an A.B. from Stanford and an LL.B. from Harvard Law School, and he later continued his distinguished academic career at the University of Cincinnati and Northwestern College of Law, where he was dean. Cincinnati was then one of the oldest law schools in the country, but on leaving LSU, Wheaton said that "we are doing great work." His longest service was at St. Louis University Law School. He specialized in procedure and evidence, and his leading work was *Cases on Federal Procedure.* The copy of that book in the LSU law library was a gift from Ira S. Flory in 1940; it bears Flory's signature and the legend "1921—La. State University." Underlined in the same color ink was the statement in the preface, "Only those portions of the cases which are relevant to the points which are intended to be illustrated by them are set forth."[57]

Clarence Milton Updegraff received an LL.B. in 1916 from the State University of Iowa and practiced for a year in Iowa before coming to LSU for the 1917–18 and 1918–19 academic years. He returned to practice and then continued his academic career after securing an A.B. from George Washington University in 1922 and an S.J.D. from Harvard Law School in 1925. He began teaching at the State University of Iowa in 1926 and continued his long service there. He was a labor-law expert and published three editions of his *Arbitration and Labor Relations.* He ended his legal career, as was common at the time for retired law faculty, by moving on to the Hastings College of the Law in San Francisco. He died in Oakland in 1978, at the age of eighty-five.[58]

Enrollment rose again for the 1918–19 term, with fifty-one students, including twenty-three first-year students. With Wheaton gone, as well as Updegraff, who left to resume his law practice, some stability was gained when Ira S. Flory returned for the Fall 1919 term, the *Reveille* calling him "one of the ablest men in the University faculty from 1912–1917." Flory had served in the army during World War I, enlisting while he was in New York.[59]

Tullis and Flory were joined by George Wilfred Stumberg, B.A., LL.B., B.C.L., who was the product of an LSU undergraduate education, receiving a B.A. in 1909. A native of St. Charles, Missouri, he came down the Mississippi River to LSU, where his brother Charles H. Stumberg was a professor of modern languages from 1895 to 1938. Stumberg's twelve-page senior thesis—"Government in Louisiana During the French and Spanish Regimes"—foreshadowed his interest in law and history. Stumberg's graduation photograph in the 1909 *Gumbo* was accompanied by a caption, "He is forever busy working to keep from working." The commentary added, "Stumberg is one of the laziest men in the Class; however, that does not keep him from making fine grades, since he is endowed with an unusually strong intellect. He has some affinity for ladies and spends some of his time in their company." Stumberg subsequently studied law at Washington University in St. Louis and then obtained an LL.B. in 1912 from Columbia Law School; next, he studied at Oxford University as a Rhodes Scholar and obtained the B.C.L. He taught law at LSU from 1919 to 1923, obtained a doctorate from Yale in 1924, and then returned to LSU to teach for another year. In 1925, he moved to the University of Texas Law School and remained there until his death in 1964.[60]

Stumberg was a leading scholar on conflicts of law, and his hornbook and treatise on the subject were the standard classics in the field. He was also a scholar of French and wrote, in 1931, *A Guide to the Law and Legal Literature of France* for the Library of Congress. He was granted a Sterling Fellowship at Yale to prepare the guide and spent a year in New Haven, Washington, and Paris writing it. His preface contains views typical of a Louisiana academic lawyer:

> One is apt to get the impression that codification arrests legal development. This was perhaps true during the period immediately following the promulgation of the codes, when legal thought was preoccupied with commentary and interpretation. But, as a matter of fact, the French codes, particularly the Civil Code, in stating the law in the form of general principles, left a place for future evolution with the aid of courts and writers. There is here room for thought by American jurists who are attempting to restate our common law. The experience in France—undoubtedly not originally intended—with a pliable and adaptable code, is somewhat comparable with American experience in constitutional interpretation. Recent literature—such as that from the pen of Professor Geny—pertaining to methods of interpretation, is well worth consultation.

Stumberg's connection with France began during the war years, and he was an adviser on French economic affairs to the Foreign Economic Administration. As the *Reveille* put it, Stumberg was an interpreter for the French Red Cross and then, from 1915 to 1918, he was attached to the American Embassy in Paris. "His work there was mostly legal, as it concerned the legal rights of enemy subjects, and was of a very confidential nature." He then served in the U.S. Army and returned to Oxford University for three months before returning to the United States.[61]

STUDENTS

University bulletins listed current students as well as graduates. For the Law School, the 1908–09 list included four students in the third-year class, sixteen in the second year, and fifty-one in the first year. Of the seventy-one students, all but four were from Louisiana, the others coming from Puerto Rico, Pennsylvania, Illinois, and Mississippi. The Louisianians came from throughout the state, with one glaring exception—only one student listed his residence as New Orleans. The school was meeting its mandate to train Louisiana lawyers—but only if they intended to practice outside the state's largest city. Not surprisingly, most of the graduates had Anglo-Saxon rather than French surnames.

The president of the nineteen-member senior class of 1908, the first graduating class, was Eugene J. McGivney, and the class valedictorian was Charles E. Schwing. Schwing was assistant secretary of state in charge of insurance and went on to become general counsel for the Pan American Life Insurance Company. The law students were an integral part of University life, just as the faculty were. William Murray "Buffalo" Lyles, who served as senior class vice-president, was a member of the varsity football team; he would become a district attorney. Marston Arthur Mangham was elected by the seniors to be the Law School representative on the *Reveille* staff; Samuel Stewart Mims, class salutatorian, was on both the *Reveille* and *Gumbo* staffs. LSU had five social fraternities at the time (Kappa Alpha, Kappa Sigma, Sigma Nu, Sigma Alpha Epsilon, and Pi Kappa Alpha), and law students were listed as members of each of them.[62]

A number of law students were members of the short-lived Hockey Club (field hockey). As their photograph in the *Gumbo* showed, they were a ragtag, sloppily dressed group in comparison to the Tennis Club members in their white shirts, long pants, and neckties. Posing with the hockey players were their nattily dressed faculty advisors, Dean Kelly and Professor Henry, whose participation probably explained the interest of law students in the unusual sport. Henry was also listed as an honorary member of the Theta Nu Epsilon Salts, a local interfraternity social club whose group picture showed ten robed students standing around a coffin.[63]

The first graduating class was imbued with respect for the state's civil-law traditions; its "Senior Class History" printed in the 1908 *Gumbo* was effusive: "Our extensive study of the tortuous common law system, or at least what is conceived to be the common law by the respective text writers of the scores of text-books we have studied, makes us have a greater respect than ever for the written law, embodied in our Civil Code, which is acknowledged to be immemorial, certain, fixed, definite, plain, simple and easily accessible to the humblest citizen or law student interested in the study of law. We believe that ultimately, by force of its superiority and simplicity, our Civil Code will win greater admiration and more consideration in the course of study of law in our law school."[64]

The 1909 *Gumbo* featured long descriptions of the students' accomplishments and foibles, along with their photographs. Harry Williams Gueno, "LL.B. and KA" from Crowley, favored "Republican high tariff on rice, but very low on alcohol." His most common failings were "to dress well, drink much, sport, be a dandy, and appear other than he is, to please the girls." Senior class president George Pote Lessley, "LL.B., PiKA" of Carencro, was cited for his common failings—drink and spelling—and that he hoped to reform the spelling—but he also had "power to think, analyze, and talk with logic and force." Henry Rhoderich Macleod was listed as being the only married man in the class, the oldest, and the biggest. The reference to the faculty in the history of the 1909 class suggested that things would be the same after the class was gone: "Dr. Henry will still be modest, that Prof. Tullis will still keep his class over time; and we believe that Dr. Kelly will still hold moot court on Wednesday nights." Also, "Dr. Henry always grins, grins, grins," and "Dr. Tullis wants the exact words of the Code." It was also noted that Istrouma Club members were petitioning Phi Delta Phi, the legal fraternity, for a charter.[65]

Total enrollment for the 1909–10 academic year was sixty-three, and sixteen men graduated in 1909. Fifteen students graduated in 1912. Younger students were attending the Law School at this point. Hermann Moyse, who graduated in May 1912, after first obtaining a B.A. and then completing the two-year law course, had to wait until September to reach the age of twenty-one and qualify for admission to the bar. Cecil Morgan of the Class of 1919 was twenty at the time of his graduation and acted as chief clerk in the East Baton Rouge Parish Clerk of Court Office while waiting for his twenty-first birthday. Asked whether students were always well prepared in class or whether there was some fudging, Moyse said, "they wouldn't have been good candidates for a law degree if they weren't good at fudging." Another member of that class, Amos Ponder, became a justice of the supreme court. Hugo Doré was one of Huey Long's close supporters and chairman of the Finance Committee in the Senate for several years before serving on the court of appeals.[66]

The dress code, if not explicit, was implicit: "You wouldn't have thought of going to school except fully dressed with white shoes and socks."[67] This was at a time when cadets in undergraduate school wore the same type of uniform as West Point cadets and were expected to keep their coats buttoned at all times.

Professor Henry was not above recruiting students through the *Reveille*. He wrote a three-column article titled "Study Law." He commented that, in the past, southerners had to go north to study law, but

> To meet the new situation, two law schools of the highest order have grown up in our State within the last three or four years—one as a branch of the State University in Baton Rouge at which tuition is free to all Louisianians, and the other a making over and transforming of the old Tulane Law School in New Orleans. These institutions have raised their standards to that of the best law school of the country and are already among the leaders in the South.

To undecided students, he said,

> An opportunity such as has never been offered in this State before is knocking at your door. And those of you who may be in doubt as to whether or not a general college education will make you men of greater power: and those of you who don't know what your life occupation will be; and finally those of you who wish to be lawyers, judges and statesmen, can do no better, if you have the necessary qualifications, than to begin right now and take a course of law. STUDY LAW!!!

In response, Frank Long, M.A., secretary of the LSU YMCA, disagreed with the idea that students uncertain about their careers should study law. He wrote that there were already enough "jack leg" lawyers and urged students to take more general liberal-arts courses.[68]

A long, unsigned three-column article appeared in 1911 with the headline "Why Leave Louisiana to Study Law?" The thesis of the article was that Louisiana civil law was different from the common law taught in other states and that the Louisiana student "needs a whole law course." It concluded: "If, then, there are so many differences between the Common Law and the Civil Law as it exists in Louisiana, if lawyers of other states find it necessary to make special preparation to practice in the state, if home schools bend every effort to fit the student for Louisiana practice, and if they lay the foundation of the young lawyer in the Civil Law and in the legal atmosphere in which he will have to make his life's effort, why should a Louisiana boy leave the state to study law?" A special sixty-page Law School edition of the *Louisiana State Law Quarterly* featured articles by Tullis, Henry, and Hughes as well as by Professor Scroggs of political science and history and senior law student Elmo P. Lee.[69]

The 1912 edition of the *Gumbo* was dedicated to Chief Justice of the United States Edward Douglass White, "whom the president of our great and glorious nation has crowned with a most high and well deserved honor in entrusting to him the chief justiceship of the highest tribunal in the world." White was a Louisiana native, born in Lafourche Parish, and had served on the Louisiana Supreme Court from 1891 to 1894. In his honor, law students also formed the Edward Douglass White Law Society, a forensic club to promote extemporaneous speaking. The president was E. J. Elam, vice-president was Hermann Moyse, and secretary-treasurer was H. Magee.[70]

The 1913 *Gumbo*, apparently taking a serious bent, began its Law School section with an article written by Dean Tullis. He pointed out that both LSU and Tulane were requiring three years of law study for the LL.B. and that the state supreme court had amended its rules to require three years of study for all students taking the bar examination without degrees. The dean urged "speedy correction" of the situation in which four separate bar examining committees existed—in New Orleans, Shreveport, Monroe, and Opelousas—with no consistent standards. He was also concerned that men would be encouraged to take the bar exam without attending law school. He stated,

There is, however, one appeal that the Law School can make, more powerful than any other motive of temporary convenience. The association with others in the same pursuit, the mental attention resulting from the constant interchange of ideas in and out of class, afford an exercise for whose value no course of private study can furnish an equivalent. That the training of the Law School has this value will, let us hope, become more and more manifest to the picked men who seek its instruction. By "picked men" it is intended to describe those whose intellectual hardihood fits them for the study of an arduous and exacting profession; and that, as well as physical hardihood, must come from proper preliminary training. That such men are well represented in this year's enrollment, the daily class exercise and the intermediate examinations bear gratifying testimony. Upon them and upon others of their kind the Law School must rely for the fulfillment of its hope to furnish the public not merely with attorneys at law, but with lawyers.

The *Gumbo* also devoted four pages of text to the moot-court program, emphasizing its importance in law education. The senior-class history that year displayed a certain amount of erudition—and arrogance. It was written in French, German, Spanish, Latin, and Italian—but not in English.[71]

The 1914 *Bulletin* indicated that out-of-state student fees at the Law School were $60 per year, but that no tuition was charged to students from Louisiana. All students continued to have to pay a library fee of $20 and a registration fee of $5. The 1915 *Bulletin*, however, displayed a desire to attract out-of-state students, providing that no tuition fees were charged to American citizens. Foreigners were assessed a tuition fee of $100 per year. Law School enrollment was up slightly during the 1914–15 session—sixty-seven students overall, thirty-five in the first year, fourteen in the second, and eighteen in the third. Not one of those students indicated a New Orleans residence.

Law students elected class officers, and seniors chose a class valedictorian from among the top three academic finishers. Elections were routinely reported in the student papers. The senior class in 1914 (Class of 1915) elected as president Leo O'Quin, as vice-president Louis M. Reynaud, and as secretary-treasurer Roland Boatner Howell. "The election was notable for the apparent absence of politics and for perfect harmony." On the other hand, reporting on Mansford T. Hair's marriage after he entered law practice, the *Reveille* recalled that he was active in politics and that his election as senior-class president produced a prolonged controversy: "A strenuous effort was made to declare his election void on the ground that some of his supporters were summer school seniors." Roland Howell was featured in a *Reveille* who's-who profile. Active in athletics while in undergraduate school, he entered the Law School in 1912 while he also served as assistant coach of the football, basketball, and baseball teams. In the summers, he played baseball with the Chattanooga Southern League team and was one of the southern players drafted by the big leagues; he was picked by the Brooklyn Nationals, but his baseball career was short-lived. A front-page *Reveille* story reported that after his marriage in 1915, he and his wife returned from visiting friends in New York, Washington, and Chattanooga to their home in Thibodaux.[72]

In the freshman-class election in 1915, a tie between D. D. Morgan and Hoffman Lewis was decided by a coin toss; Lewis won. A photograph of the coin toss was featured in the window of the official University photographer, Ewing's on Third Street. William Scott Wilkinson was unanimously chosen president of the senior class of 1917. Indeed, there was no competition for any of the offices. Wilkinson had been captain of cadet Company B in 1914–15, president of the senior class that year, and captain of the basketball team.[73]

Two women were graduated from the Law School in the early years, Clift Martin of Caddo Parish and Mary Herron Bird of Baton Rouge. Martin enrolled in 1913, the *Reveille* stating in an editorial that it "congratulates her upon having broken the ice of conventionality and wishes her a pleasant and profitable year."[74] She was graduated in 1916. Bird was graduated in 1919; she had already taken a master's degree at LSU.

Law seniors participated in commencement activities, including the Alumni-Senior Parade in which graduates dressed in the costume of the fields they were entering. Law graduates in 1915 were undecided on a costume; one member of the class suggested the garb of a crook, while another suggested that of an ambulance-chaser. The photograph of the group shows the eventual choice, labeling it "The Law Grads and Their Future Victims," six seated men wearing prisoner's stripes and seven men standing wearing frock coats and stovepipe hats. Also popular during this period were campuswide elections for favorites—faculty as well as students. The winner of the 1916 election for favorite professor was a runaway—Colonel J. W. Nicholson with 299 votes. Second place, with a Law School bloc supporting him, was Ira S. Flory, with 32 votes. Third place went to J. F. Broussard of the language department.[75]

IMPACT OF WORLD WAR I

Colonel John Tucker Jr. recalled that as early as 1915, the war was getting under way in Europe. "Every time you'd go down to a ball in New Orleans, somebody'd try to enlist you for the Coldstream Guards, or something. I felt that we were bound to get into it." The colonel-to-be described himself then, "I didn't know a thing about [the] military." Some two hundred LSU undergraduate students left their studies and entered the service before June 1, 1917, producing the first decline in overall University enrollment since the 1890s. Professor Arthur T. Prescott of the government department, and a Law School lecturer, was president of the local Loyalty League and active in promoting support for the war effort. Red Cross Clubs for coeds were instituted, editorials on patriotism abounded, and a Chautauqua program included a lecturer direct from the French front. Dean Tullis announced that students in his classes who were to enter military training camps would be allowed course credit without the necessity of taking a final examination if they had satisfactory attendance. Professor Wheaton was chairman of the University committee raising money for the Liberty Loan drive, which raised $35,000. Professor David Blackshear left to attend a training camp at Leon Springs, Texas, and was replaced by Carl C. Wheaton. Former professor Robert L. Henry became a captain (and later a major) in the army; Mrs. Henry, a native of Baton Rouge, returned to her hometown while he served in the military.[76]

Lieutenant Hermann Moyse (LL.B. 1912, and a former editor of the *Reveille*) wrote a letter to the student paper that was published in April 1918 in which he described the disorganization of the military in France. Soon after, he was severely injured in the left lung and left foot by German fire, and several of his toes had to be amputated as a consequence. Moyse had led an attack against German machine-gun positions, and a front-page story in September reported that he was awarded the Distinguished Service Cross, the first Baton Rougean thus honored. Later, the *Reveille* featured a photograph of General Pershing presenting the cross to its former editor at Blois, France, on October 12. It also reported that Moyse had been recently awarded the French Croix de Guerre and that he received more distinctions than any other Louisiana soldier in the AEF.[77]

The listing of University committees in the 1918 *Bulletin* included three new ones: War Courses, War Savings, and War Service. Professor Updegraff served on the War Service Committee. A decline in enrollment in the Law School also reflected the war effort: a total of thirty-one law students was enrolled, with only fifteen first-year students. Enrollment was at thirty-three the following term (1918–19), with only ten first-year students.

When Mary Herron Bird graduated from the Law School in 1919, she was admitted to the bar on a Saturday in New Orleans and then left the following Tuesday for New York to take up Red Cross work overseas. The *New Orleans Item* reported that she was presented to the state supreme court by Governor Hall, who stated that there were no more than half a dozen women practicing law in Louisiana. The paper wrote, "Yesterday she was a society girl; today she's a lawyer; and tomorrow she leaves for France as a Red Cross canteen worker."[78] Bird was no doubt a society girl; her father was C. C. Bird, an outstanding lawyer, and her brother Cecil Bird also practiced law in Baton Rouge. Her older brother, Captain Thomas Bird, was serving as a physician in France. She would later marry Paul D. Perkins, and their daughter, Mary Bird Perkins, would graduate from the LSU Law School in the Class of 1950.

Flory returned to the faculty for the 1919 term after he completed his military service, leaving the law faculty with three full-time members, because Wheaton did not continue. Mrs. Flory does not appear to have returned to law studies. Wheaton did leave LSU a memento, however—a fight song called "The Battle Cry," adapted from Stanford's "Bum Bum Song."[79]

With the return of peace came the run of law students, and "once more The Reveille, inc. finds it advisable to nail down chairs, conceal typewriters and negotiate for a Yale lock for the door" to keep the law students away from their offices.[80]

The 1918 *Gumbo* gives some indication of the student perception of Dean Tullis. In a purported report on a moot-court argument, objections abounded and no progress was being made. When Professor Wheaton sustained an objection, loud laughs arose from some student attorneys, "which are quickly checked as Dean Tullis snatches off his glasses and glares at them." Then Tullis is quoted: "A similar question came up in a case that occurred in my practice in New Orleans. One of the attorneys asked that same question and I objected, then—(He begins to talk to himself in an undertone and keeps this up for some time.)" One student asked Tullis to tell more about the case. His response, "It has nothing to do with the matter that we are discussing, nothing whatever, Mr. Applebaum." After another student said he was strictly neutral, Tullis is said to have responded, "Now the origin of that word 'strictly' is very interesting. The 't' is due to the French influence. But of course all of you gentlemen know that, if you know anything about the English language. The lack of knowledge displayed by the average student is appalling—simply appalling. The idea of students at a university being ignorant on the subjects of grammar and spelling! It should be changed, it certainly should! (He looks into space, and his lips move rapidly.)"[81] Later, Professor Wheaton stated that he knew the Minnesota rule on the subject but not the Louisiana rule, and he looked toward Tullis for guidance. Tullis, however, was sleeping soundly, and Wheaton purported to look up the Louisiana law on sleeping in the courtroom.

FACULTY TIMELINE

1906–07	Kelly		
1907–08	Kelly	Tullis	Henry
1908–09	Kelly	Tullis	Henry
1909–10	Tullis	Henry	McKeag
1910–11	Tullis	Henry	Hughes
1911–12	Tullis	Hughes	Williams
1912–13	Tullis	Williams	Flory
1913–14	Tullis	Flory	Blackshear
1914–15	Tullis	Flory	Blackshear
1915–16	Tullis	Flory	Blackshear
1916–17	Tullis	Flory	Blackshear
1917–18	Tullis	Updegraff	Wheaton
1918–19	Tullis	Updegraff	Wheaton
1919–20	Tullis	Flory	Stumberg

ENROLLMENT STATISTICS

Year	Law 1	Law 2	Law 3	Total Law	Law Grads
1906–07	26				
1907–08	16				
1908–09	51	16	4	71	16
1909–10	27	33	3	63	18
1910–11	31	26		57	14
1911–12	30	23		53	15
1912–13	26	9	10	45	7
1913–14	24	14	10	48	6
1914–15	35	14	18	67	14
1915–16	29	18	19	66	16
1916–17	24	17	13	54	11
1917–18	15	9	7	31	6
1918–19	10	13	10	33	8
1919–20	23	14	14	51	14

3

THE SEMI-ROARING TWENTIES

THE GREATER AGRICULTURAL CAMPUS

The Law School vacated the chemistry building in 1922, when the chemists needed more space, and moved to a one-story frame building nearby, which although occupied exclusively by the Law School was less than ideal. There were seven rooms, a library of 3,500 volumes, and a student body of sixty-nine. Some unknown hand looking forward to a new location annotated the description of the building in the *Bulletin:* "with beaver board partitions & trombone radiators." Those references also found their way into Dean Paul M. Hebert's historical sketch of the Law School.[1]

A new location for the University was a realistic prospect at this time. Governor John M. Parker had campaigned on increasing funding for education, and upon taking office he succeeded in passing a severance tax on minerals. Act 31 of 1920 imposed the tax at a rate of 2 percent, pursuant to a "gentleman's agreement" with oil and gas interests, and dedicated the majority of these revenues to LSU. Governor Parker addressed the student body at chapel in October 1920 to celebrate the new era of University development that was beginning. He estimated that LSU would receive more than $12 million over the four years of his administration. The first year's proceeds of the severance tax were $2,315,920.09, and the amount allocated to LSU was $832,920.10. Groundbreaking for the new campus took place on Saturday, April 1, 1922, and a *Reveille* headline proclaimed, "State Will Have College Second to None; Heads of Departments Will Be The Best That Money Can Obtain."[2]

Plans to move the entire University from the Pentagon Barracks site north of Baton Rouge to a new campus to the south were announced in the 1923 *Bulletin* in grandiose terms:

South of Baton Rouge, within two miles of the city limits, the University owns twenty-one hundred and seventy-four acres of land extending from the Mississippi River eastward beyond the highlands. On the highlands, in the edge of the beautiful magnolia grove that has for centuries extended its hospitable shades to those who came for rest and pleasure or who sought to commune with nature where nature is most beautiful, the University is building a new plant that will embody the best in all lines of educational progress. Here the sons and daughters of Louisiana may, in larger numbers and under more favorable conditions than ever before, pursue the studies that will fit them for success in life.[3]

At that time, $200,000 of new work had been done and a million dollars worth of buildings were under construction. A total expenditure of $4 million was anticipated, and it was expected that the University would move to its new campus in 1925–26.

The Law School moved to the new campus in Fall 1925 and was housed in a two-story building next to the Memorial Tower. Later named Thomas D. Boyd Hall, the structure at that time was simply called the Law Building or the North Administration Building. It contained more than 11,000 square feet and was designed in the stucco, red-tile Tuscan style of the original central campus. The first floor included a law library—an oval room on the north end of the building with a capacity of more than 10,000 volumes—a lounging room for law students, two classrooms, and two offices. The second floor divided into five classrooms and four offices.[4]

CURRICULUM AND STANDARDS

Entrance requirements increased for the 1923–24 academic year—two years of college work were now required for admission, in keeping with a new standard "recommended by the American Bar Association." LSU complied early on with that standard, but its application to proprietary schools was controversial. Dean Tullis reported at the end of the decade on an ABA meeting in Memphis at which the section on legal education saw a bitterly contested fight between proprietary law schools and the member schools of the Association of American Law Schools (AALS). The proprietary schools were defeated, and the ABA recommended that they, too, adhere to standards requiring a high-school education and two years of college. The section also recommended that graduates submit to a bar examination, and it opposed basing payment of teachers on numbers of students taught or fees received.[5]

Another major change for Louisiana law students was that graduates after January 1, 1925, were required to pass a state bar examination in order to be licensed to practice, an examination administered by "the Committee of Bar Examiners of the Supreme Court, on such subjects and under such rules and regulations . . . prescribed by the Supreme Court." Applicants who did not present a diploma from an approved law school were required to read law under the supervision of a lawyer for not less than three years. It was not until 1963 that applicants for the Louisiana bar examination were required to be graduates of an approved law school.[6]

Subsequent years saw regular headlines in the student newspaper about LSU's high bar-exam passage rates. The *Reveille* reported in July 1927 that thirteen students took the exam and all passed. It editorialized, "By successfully passing the bar examination last week in New Orleans, the 13 graduates of the L.S.U. law school have added further prestige to their alma mater. The L.S.U. law school has a high rating in the legal world and the success of the 1927 graduates is but a further indication of the high work that Dean Robert L. Tullis and his corps of assistants are doing towards training the future lawyers of the state." The editorial added that Clinton S. Girod made the highest average of all candidates, vindicating his selection as Law School valedictorian. In 1928, the *Reveille* reported, "Congratulations to the faculty upon the third consecutive time that all the law graduates have passed the bar examination upon the first try."[7]

A more important development increasing the Law School's reputation was its admission in 1924 into membership in the AALS. Six schools were admitted that year, increasing total membership to sixty institutions. The inadequacy of the law library had prevented the LSU Law School from being accredited earlier by the AALS, whose standards required 5,000 volumes—LSU had only 3,500. Recognizing the need, Professor Ira S. Flory led a campaign in the summer of 1924 to raise $10,000 to increase the volume count to the AALS's minimum requirements. He gave up a planned vacation in his native Virginia and, between July 4 and September 4, "I drove my car about 4000 miles and traveled about 1500 miles on the train, and saw most of the law alumni in the state." He toured the state at his own expense and without compensation to raise the money. "I drove late at night and early in the morning and exceeded the speed limit many times, but I saw the men." His was no easy or pleasant task. Summer months were not ideal for automobile travel in Louisiana over dusty gravel roads.[8]

The AALS inspection visit was conducted in December 1924 by Dean Henry Craig Jones of the University of Iowa Law School. He found 6,200 volumes in the library. "After a careful examination of the registrar's records, Dean Jones commended the authorities on the strict adherence to the entrance rulings." Tullis, Flory, and Stumberg attended the winter AALS meeting on December 29, 1924, in Chicago when LSU was granted membership. Law students presented Flory a Morris chair and a smoking set in appreciation for his unselfish service, and in the 1924 student-favorites election, Flory placed fourth in the vote for most popular professor, with 65 votes. The first-place winner was Fred C. Frey, a sociologist and later dean and acting president, with 362 votes.[9]

The LSU law faculty became active in the association, attending the annual year-end meetings usually held in Chicago. In 1929, the AALS met in New Orleans in what was seen as a move to encourage raising legal education and bar-admission standards in the South. The LSU Law School was also placed on the approved list of the Council of Legal Education of the American Bar Association. That year, the law library included 7,500 volumes, aided by a sizable donation of some 700 books from William O. Hart, the New Orleans lawyer who had lectured at the Law School when it was first organized.[10]

Tuition still was not charged to citizens of the United States, and the library fee was $45 per regular session. Admission standards were upped slightly: the required two years of undergraduate education now included specific courses. Students were still able to complete a combined curriculum whereby undergraduate and law degrees could be earned in a total of six years, but it appears that most students during this period did not opt for the undergraduate degree and went into law study as soon as possible. Students were also cautioned (again) to perfect their skills in English composition and, "if deficient in such elementary phases of the subject as grammar, spelling, punctuation, sentence structure and paragraphing, should overcome those defects before entering the law school. Failures in this department have sometimes resulted from neglect of this precaution."[11]

Students of the time reported that they obtained excellent preparation for law practice. As Ben R. Miller put it, "With practically no library of consequence, and with just two or three teachers, I think we had a remarkable law school." He credited the determination of the professors and their devotion to the students. The school "was Professor Flory's life. He had no outside interest; it was Dean Flory's life. This was back in the days when things were tough, finances were . . . people didn't squander their time."[12]

The entire University switched to a system of letter grades in 1928 to satisfy the requirements of the American Association of Universities for accreditation by that group. The Law School had been on a numerical grading system, but it too switched to a letter-grade system in which an A was worth 3.0 points. The 1930 *Bulletin* evidenced more flexibility in a student's undergraduate program. Two years of college were still required for admission, but absent were the requirements for specific courses. Instead, "No pre-legal course is prescribed." The *Bulletin* stated, however, that if the work did not indicate that the applicant would be able to do satisfactory work in the Law School, his application might be denied.[13]

FACULTY

Three faculty positions were authorized in the first half of the decade, producing a student-faculty ratio that varied from 16 to 1 to 24 to 1. It was a stable faculty, with Dean Robert Lee Tullis and Professors Ira S. Flory and George W. Stumberg in place. Stumberg took a leave of absence for the 1923–24 term to pursue a J.D. degree at Yale Law School, and his courses were covered by Leslie Clyde Strickland for the year he was gone. Strickland was one of many LSU faculty with a Canadian connection. He had an LL.B. from McGill University and a J.D. from Yale, along with degrees from Boston Tech and Dalhousie University. He was a professor of common law, and he also had practiced law in Montreal and New York. Stumberg returned for the 1924–25 term but resigned after that academic year to accept a position at the University of Texas Law School.[14]

Law faculty participation in the broader aspects of University life continued. Flory served on the Athletic Committee as well as the Commencement Exercises Committee, and Tullis remained on the Candidates for Degrees, Debating, Registration, and Student Welfare committees. Stumberg had served on the Greater University Committee, which was heavily involved in planning for the new campus.[15]

Roy Cletis Gore came to LSU in Fall 1925 as an associate professor to replace Stumberg. He, too, had followed the Mississippi downriver from Illinois. After service during World War I, he had obtained A.B. and LL.B. degrees from the University of Illinois, practiced law for a short period, served as city attorney of Champaign, Illinois, then taught in the Military Department at Iowa State. He obtained an LL.M. in 1929 from Harvard. Gore was liked by the students, who called him "Rabbit" because they could never pin him down on a question. Another student remembered his nickname as "Speedy" because of his lack of speed. He also taught legal bibliography. During Prohibition, Gore taught criminal law, "but he didn't object to a little beer, if he could find out where somebody had a pot cooking. So occasionally he'd be in our apartment." He stayed at LSU through the 1931–32 term.[16]

Odis Herschel Burns received an A.B. from the University of Kansas and was a high-school and college teacher before moving west and obtaining a J.D. from Stanford University in 1925. Upon graduation, he joined the LSU faculty for two terms (1925–1927), taught at Texas during the summer, and then joined the law faculty of the University of Denver in 1928. He was unable to complete the second academic year at LSU because, according to the *Reveille*, he "was forced to resign because of ill health last winter."[17]

With the arrival of Gore and Burns, the law faculty consisted of four full-time law professors for the 1925–26 term, beginning an expansion that would result in five faculty positions by the end of the decade. Professor Arthur Prescott of the government department continued to teach courses cross-listed for second- and third-year law students. Prescott's classes were not held in the law building, and law students walked to the government building near the Hill Memorial Library for his classes. One student referred to him as Colonel Prescott and that taking his constitutional law course was "more or less a formality."[18]

Harriet Spiller Daggett became a Law School faculty member in Fall 1926, and she would remain until her retirement in 1961. Born in rural Springfield, Livingston Parish, she had graduated from the Louisiana State Normal College and taught at Jennings High School. She married DeVan Damon Daggett, a rice farmer, whose crop failure caused the Daggetts to move to Baton Rouge. Her Law School classmate John T. Campbell recalled that Mrs. Daggett and her husband moved to Baton Rouge as abstracters, but when that work shrank she decided to attend law school. A married woman with two children, she was older than most students and attended law school while her two boys attended parochial school nearby. She received an A.B. in government in 1923, the A.M. in 1925, and the LL.B. in 1926. While in law school, she worked as an instructor in the Department of Government. For the 1925–26 term, the *Bulletin* listed three instructors of government courses, Professor Prescott, Associate Professor Charles W. Pipkin (who would later become dean of the Graduate School), and Mrs. Harriet Spiller Daggett, B.A., a fellow. She was listed as assisting Pipkin in three courses—federal government, state government, and local government. The 1925–26 *Bulletin* also listed her as a third-year law student.[19]

In 1926–27, Daggett had a broad range of courses—two civil-code courses as well as municipal corporations, administrative law, and international law. Moreover, her Law School course on constitutional law replaced Prescott's government department course in that subject. Mrs. Daggett also established a pattern for a number of LSU graduates who went on to Yale's law school for "broadening" and then returned to Louisiana to teach. She received her J.S.D. from Yale in 1929 and was promoted to full professor in 1931. She was one of the first female law-faculty members in the country and the first woman to become a full professor at an AALS-ABA–accredited law school in the United States.[20]

Joseph Arthur Loret assisted during the Spring 1925 term, teaching Tullis's class in code of practice and Flory's class in corporations. A 1914 LSU graduate and a member of the Louisiana bar, Loret was fluent in French and Spanish, making him proficient in the study of civil law. He had practiced law in Baton Rouge from 1914 until 1920, serving as city attorney during part of that time, and then became assistant attorney general of Puerto Rico in July 1920, where he served for two and a half years. He returned to Baton Rouge in May 1924, and later he became a member of the Taylor Porter law firm—then known as Taylor, Porter, Loret, and Brooks. Although Loret was listed in the *Bulletin* as an instructor in law, he appears to have been what would now be called an adjunct professor, and his biographical entry in the *AALS Directory of Law Teachers* states that he taught part time at the Law School. His specialty was procedure, and he taught the Louisiana Code of Practice. Known by the students as "Smokey Joe," he attended student dances and "was never seen with a girl over 16 years of age." Another student called him a "dandy," and one suggested that he loved the bottle. He continued his adjunct connection with LSU until 1937.[21]

The faculty listing in the 1927 *Bulletin* continued to demonstrate the stability of the maturing institution, with Professors Tullis, Flory, and Gore remaining and the addition of Newman Freece Baker, a faculty member at the University of Wisconsin who was appointed to succeed Burns for the 1927–28 term. Baker was an authority on municipal corporations and public service who wrote several articles and two books and who had served as special assistant corporation counsel for the City of Chicago. He had a long academic career that covered the length of the Mississippi River. He received an A.B. from Southwestern College in 1917, then moved to the University of Missouri and attained an A.M. and an LL.B. He graduated from the University of Chicago with a J.S.D., and after a short stint of practice in Missouri and Illinois he moved to an academic career. He first taught history and political science, and his first law-teaching stint was at the University of Wisconsin in 1927. He came to LSU for the 1927–28 academic year as an associate professor, moved on down the river to become a professor of law at Tulane for two terms, then found his way upstream again to join the Northwestern University law faculty in 1930. He was the author of *Legal Aspects of Zoning*, in which he acknowledged in the preface that the book contained material from four of his law-review articles. Indeed, he was a prolific writer, and the *Index to Legal Periodicals* contains references to more than twenty-five law journal articles by him published in the 1920s and 1930s. His journal article "Some Legal Aspects of Impeachment in Louisiana" argued that the impeachment of Huey Long was constitutional even though adopted in an extraordinary session of the legislature whose call did not include the subject of impeachment. He also criticized the fifteen senators who had signed the "round robin" for stating that they would acquit *"regardless of the evidence."*[22]

Harold Earl Verrall replaced Baker in 1928. He received his A.B. from the University of Iowa, and the M.A. and LL.B. from the University of Minnesota. He taught for the 1928–29 term at LSU and for the 1929–30 term at Cornell before going to Yale, where he received a J.S.D. in 1931. He was a long-term faculty member at Vanderbilt (1931–1949) and then moved on to UCLA until he too went "over-the-hill" to Hastings. Verrall was an expert on the law of property and was the author of four editions of a casebook on California community property.²³

A more permanent addition to the faculty was James Barclay Smith, B.S., LL.B., with a J.S.D. from Yale. He was promoted to professor and remained at LSU through the 1934–35 academic year. Smith had practiced in New York City and was on leave during 1931–32 to be a valuation attorney at the Interstate Commerce Commission. He was also a valuation expert for the Public Utilities Commission of the District of Columbia. Smith joined the University of Kansas law faculty after leaving LSU and completed his law school career there. He was an expert on constitutional law as well as public utilities.²⁴

While at LSU, Smith was part of a group trying to expand the sphere of research and publications at the University. He published the sixth book in the series of Louisiana State University Studies, *Some Phases of Fair Value and Interstate Rates*. His major publication was *Studies in the Adequacy of the Constitution*. Not only did this high-sounding title suggest a typical law-professorial hubris, the book illustrates the developing trend of publishing articles in law reviews and then combining them into a book. A note indicates that six of the book's seven chapters had appeared originally in the *Temple Law Quarterly*, the *California Law Review*, the *University of Chicago Law Review*, the *Dickinson Law Review*, the *University of Cincinnati Law Review*, and the *Georgetown Law Review*. Smith was also a man with confidence in his views, noting that "most of the materials were prepared before the opinion of the past term of the Supreme Court were announced. The basic soundness of the analysis presented is demonstrated by the fact that the results in those cases were forecast and have fully confirmed the conclusions reached herein." Smith is also given credit for conceiving the idea of establishing the state's law institute.²⁵

Some students recalled that Smith used weird and colorful analogies and hypotheticals, and Leo Gold recalled that Smith's corporations examination was a single question three pages long. Gold said that he went to Smith's office to express his inability to understand the question and complained that all he could do was write down all he knew about corporations. Smith said, "You got it. You passed." Ashton Stewart remembers that Smith did not have a strong voice and was called "Whispering" Smith. He was not very popular, though Stewart remembers, "I recall receiving correspondence from Dr.

James Barclay Smith asking whether it would be possible for him to come back and be made Dean of the Law School." Robert Jennings remembered that Smith was difficult to understand and presented extremely involved hypothetical questions. Clarence Yancey reported that during World War II, when he was on duty with the Judge Advocate General's office in Washington, he found Smith on duty there as well. It appears that a clash of personalities developed between Smith and Gore, which one student reported as nearly resulting in fisticuffs on one occasion.[26]

Scallan Walsh remembered Smith as brilliant and "one of the most sarcastic persons I've ever known." Frank Purvis admitted that he had a low opinion of Smith while in school, but later in life he came to appreciate Smith's methods: "he challenged you, and he made you do the work." Paul Landry recalled that Smith was one of his best professors, and a gentleman. But Jules Landry suggested that Smith had been "shell-shocked."[27]

Professor Flory, described earlier as a no-nonsense money-manager, was not above moonlighting. He taught a course in business law for the Baton Rouge YMCA night school downtown in the Roumain Building. Tuition was $8 per month for a month of twelve classes. One student found Flory a systematic teacher: "If you got five successive examinations from Flory's early classes and studied them, you would do awfully well on the examination." On the other hand, he found Dean Tullis "unsystematic" but "about as quick-witted as anybody you have ever seen or heard of." It was also said that Flory didn't call on the people he thought were good students: "He went back and forth, back and forth over the ones he suspected did not know what they were talking about and made them show off." Robert Roberts said, "Well, to me he was a fine teacher, because he was stimulating. He really was, but there were a lot of people that just did not like him. They did not understand him. As I say, he was not methodical, and you couldn't depend on what you were going to get on an examination."[28]

Tullis and Prescott were also involved in other projects. They were selected by the Constitutional Convention of 1921 to index the new constitution and provide marginal annotations. Tullis was also entertaining political ambitions; he told a *Baton Rouge State-Times* reporter that he would be a candidate in 1922 for the state supreme court vacancy to succeed Justice Provosty. That announcement was followed by a banquet given in his honor in November, with representatives of the three law classes making speeches, but the campaign does not seem to have gone much further. One student recalled that student-dean relationships were rocky at times during this period; he also said that Tullis was a "'prissy little man' who taught all of the codes while they were in law school." The student newspaper reported each year how many faculty members were listed in *Who's Who*—twelve were included in the 1920–21 edition, including Dean Tullis. Tullis, who was now sixty-three years old, was suffering from eye disease. In the summer of 1927, he had surgery in New Orleans to treat secondary glaucoma in addition to a cataract.[29]

Flory apparently chafed under a pay schedule that he found inadequate. As early as 1913, he wrote to President Thomas D. Boyd requesting an increase in salary, arguing that his work load was more demanding since the conversion to a three-year program. He received a $300 increase, to $2,100 per year. After his two-year hiatus and return to LSU, he was paid $2,500 for the 1919–20 term and then in Fall 1920 his salary was increased to $3,500 per year. For Fall 1923, he was paid $4,000 ($39,000 in Year 2000 dollars).[30]

Still, Flory seems to have lacked the security and stability he desired. After his efforts to raise funds for the library were successful, he thought he should have been better rewarded, and it appears that he and Dean Tullis were in a strained relationship at the time. Flory's files do not contain copies of the letters he wrote in January and February of 1925 to friends and professional acquaintances complaining about his treatment, but they do contain some of their responses. A letter from the dean of the University of Virginia Law Department, where Flory had taught earlier, reported no faculty vacancies there, but expressed sympathy: "Ingratitude in Republics is proverbial, but when it is found in an educational institution as you present it, though I can well understand your indignation at the treatment you have received, and your determination to sever your relations with the institution."[31]

Ronald L. Davis, a Monroe attorney, wrote to support Flory, saying, "I cannot understand why Dean Tullis allows himself to receive the credit for the success of Louisiana's entrance to the American Association of Law Schools, when he knows as well as you and I, that he in no way contributed toward the successful conclusion of the enterprise." W. M. Phillips, a Shreveport attorney and friend of both Flory and President Boyd, advised Flory to curb his anger: "I think that probably your trouble has been that you have been overworked and a little dejected by the Dean's indifference." He urged Flory to remain at LSU and suggested that salaries would increase in the next few years. Also, he explained that President Boyd could not conveniently increase Flory's salary at the time, and "you get as high a salary as any professor at the University." Flory took the advice and remained at LSU, and he did get an increase of $300 per academic year.[32]

STUDENT LIFE

National Prohibition had its consequences for law students, and many of the law's opponents were in the student body. Arthur Stelly's in Opelousas was reputed to make the best whiskey in the state: "He had a big underground warehouse. . . . and his house was on top of it, and the whiskey that he made was stored in oak barrels and he would not sell any of it under two years." The same law student recalled, "We didn't have enough money to buy too much of it, but we would go there practically every weekend and get us some." Nor were many other members of the legal profession supportive of Prohibition: "We bought the whiskey for the judges and everybody else, they all got it." And, as stated earlier, Professor Gore, who taught criminal law, sometimes joined his students for home-brewed beer.[33]

Women in small numbers were enrolling in the Law School, and four of them graduated in the decade. Winsome Ware of Rapides Parish ('22) was the first woman to preside over a moot court at LSU. The *Reveille* reported, perhaps surprisingly, that she "presided with a solemn gravity and dignity." She was the daughter of E. O. Ware, president of Louisiana College, and after graduation she returned to Alexandria to practice law. She was killed in an automobile accident in the 1930s. Amelie Ellis Prescott was graduated in 1925, and Harriet Spiller Daggett in 1926. Golda Schill of New Orleans ('28) was the only woman in the LSU Law School in 1928. She ranked second in her class, and according to the *Reveille*, "she believes women should have equal rights with men, and have as much right as men to smoke if they want to."[34]

Moot-court trials were still usually begun with an enactment of the crime. A February 1926 edition of the *Reveille* reported on a robbery that had occurred on campus as though it were a real event, admitting later that the story was fiction. Professor Gore defended the practice: "The purpose of these moot court trials is to give the students experience of the kind they will find after entering the practice of law. These cases are all carried out with the permission of the police department of the city of Baton Rouge."[35]

Law School graduates were rapidly becoming leaders in the political and legal life of the state. Two law seniors, Warren O. Watson of East Baton Rouge Parish and Coleman Lindsey of Allen Parish, were candidates as delegates for the 1921 Constitutional Convention. Watson was a World War I veteran and treasurer of the David Ewing Post of the American Legion. Lindsey was "considered one of the most brilliant men that the Law school has ever turned out, and is destined to a brilliant career." Both candidates promised a short constitution. Lindsey had no opposition in Allen Parish, but Watson had several prominent lawyers as opponents and was not elected. Watson did win another election, however. He was chosen valedictorian of the senior law class by a vote of 10 to 6 over Lindsey. Watson was also business manager of the *Gumbo*. In the campuswide election for favorites, Lindsey was named the Most Intelligent Man. He had 124 votes, and his opponents received a total of 70 votes. Second place went to Fred C. Frey, then president of the campus YMCA and later an LSU professor and administrator.[36]

The twelve graduates in the Class of 1923 included future Congressman Thomas Overton Brooks and future Louisiana Supreme Court chief justice Joe B. Hamiter. Hamiter, who also played varsity baseball, was valedictorian. Fred Johnson was on the track team; indeed, "law students being varsity athletes was almost a tradition back then." Chief Justice Charles A. O'Neill delivered the baccalaureate address at commencement in June 1923 and was also the principal speaker at the installation of the Friars Club into the Delta Kappa Epsilon fraternity.[37]

The 1924 class, also with twelve members, included future justice Frank W. Hawthorne and Thomas Leigh, who became a leader of the Louisiana bar and a member of the LSU Board of Supervisors. John Boone was captain of the baseball team. The 1925 class, the last to graduate from the old campus, included Henry George McMahon, who later became a professor in the Law School, and future bar leaders Robert Roberts Jr., Glen Darsey, and Victor Sachse, as well as future governor Robert F. Kennon. Of McMahon, a classmate said, "He wasn't much of a student. He carried a full time job at Standard Oil Company—a lot of them did." A late-graduating senior was Anthony J. Roy, whom Dean Tullis failed on a final examination, "and we seriously thought he was going to shoot him." But Tullis gave Roy a "condition deficiency," and he was admitted to the bar three months later. "Victor Sachse was the smartest man in our class," according to one contemporary. Robert Roberts was Law School valedictorian and had been voted the most intelligent man at LSU for two years; he was also the librarian of the law library. Also in school at that time were James R. Fuller, called "Yank," who practiced mineral law and was brought into the Taylor Porter and Brooks firm to head their mineral-law department. Charles Austin O'Neill Jr. was the chief justice's son.[38]

Ben R. Miller, graduate of the 1927 class, later boasted that his class of fourteen members was one of the best ever:

> While in the school as student athletes, four of the class played football. That was Ike Carriere, Walter Chandler, Roland Kizer and myself. Another was captain of both the baseball and basketball teams, Robert B. Jones, later Judge Jones. Another, Ike Carriere, played varsity baseball, and still another played both baseball and basketball and that was Roland Kizer. Another was on the track team, Walter B. Chandler; and another was on the golf team, that was Tom Dupree. When they had completed their own varsity eligibility, but while still in school, two served as coaches on the freshman football team, that was Kizer and myself, and one of this class served as an assistant track coach and that was Chandler. After graduation, three of this class became state court judges; that was Carriere, Herget and Bob Jones, and I served for two years by appointment of the supreme court, as a judge. Now two of the class served as state senators; that was Davis Cotton and Fred Blanche; one was a commander in the navy, that was Tom Dupree; one was a former member of the LSU Board of Supervisors on two occasions; that was Ike Carriere. Another served as a president of a bank, and that was Davis Cotton; two served as presidents of the Louisiana Bar Association, and they were Cotton and Blanche; and two were members of the Louisiana Law Institute, Cotton and myself. I was a member of the board of governors of the American Bar Association. One served as city attorney of Baton Rouge for eight years, Roland Kizer. One is a former president of the LSU Alumni Association, W. D. Cotton; and I am a former president of the LSU Law School Alumni Association.[39]

Kizer, representing LSU at the National Collegiate World Court Conference at Princeton, walked out in protest after the election of a "negress" from

Howard University as representative of the South on the Executive Committee. After the withdrawal of southern representatives, the conference adjourned in confusion and without a specific plan to reconvene. A *Reveille* editorial applauded Kizer's act. When the national organization asked LSU to rejoin, President Boyd said that there was nothing to be gained by Kizer's changing his position; he refused to change, and everyone at LSU supported him.[40]

Miller also remembered that his football teams lost to Tulane the three years he played, but that all fourteen LSU law graduates in 1927 passed the bar exam while two graduates from Tulane did not. The 1929 valedictorian was Theo W. Bauer, and dean-to-be Paul Macarius Hebert was elected president of the senior class.

LSU's undergraduate program still reflected its military-school origins during the decade of the 1920s, but Dean Tullis did not approve of law students participating in the military course. W. D. Cotton remembered, however, that he stayed in the military "because it was the only way we could get through school. We stayed in dormitories for about $30 or $40 for three months in those days and would wear the uniform, but Dean Tullis discouraged it every time he was around a student." Oliver Stockwell remembered, "Of course, he was intolerant of people who weren't interested in studying law. I know I was on the LSU track team; and when I started the Law School, he told me, 'Well, you have to turn in your shoes, if you're going to study law and pass the courses' and that's what I did."[41]

The 1926 *Gumbo*, in the section on favorites, featured Harriet S. Daggett as the Most Intelligent Coed. She was formally dressed, with fur-trimmed coat and beret. At the end of the section on fraternities, a page was devoted to the François X. Martin Law Club. Photographs of the members, dressed in white-tie formal dress, included Ben R. Miller, president; Hoye Grafton, vice-president; and John T. Campbell, John T. Carpenter, J. Norman Coon, Caldwell Herget, Robert Hope, Winston K. Joffrion, Orin F. Matthews, and Hugh E. Wilson. In 1927, the club initiated ten new members, added two new pledges, and vowed to "redouble its efforts this term to obtain recognition from the national body of Phi Delta Phi legal fraternity." With the help of Professor Flory, Miller drafted a petition to join Phi Delta Phi and personally presented it to the secretary in Denver. The LSU chapter was accepted and installed in 1928, becoming Martin Inn. Flory and Newman F. Baker were "Fratres in Facultate" of the Inn. Members included J. Denson Smith, Paul Macarius Hebert, and Kemble K. Kennedy.[42]

The Edward Douglass White Law Club became a chapter of Gamma Eta Gamma national fraternity in 1929. Professor Gore was the faculty advisor; J. Vernon Sims was elected vice-president, and Russell E. Gahagan of Coushatta was president. The fraternity sponsored lectures—one by Joseph A. Loret, instructor at the Law School and member of the Taylor, Porter, Loret, and Brooks law firm, and one by H. Payne Breazeale of the Breazeale and Sachse firm.[43]

The 1928 *Gumbo* featured photographs of the first-year law students, including a thin, gaunt John Denson Smith from New Orleans. He was also a member of the debate team that toured four midwestern states and debated at Oklahoma A&M, University of Oklahoma, University of Arkansas, Kansas Agricultural College, University of Kansas, and Texas A&M. "The arguments were put forth in logical and interesting manner, and the rebuttals were particularly bright and witty, bringing forth appreciative applause from the audience."[44]

SUMMARY

By the end of the 1920s, LSU's law program was solidly established with a small but stable and growing faculty that was graduating lawyers who were to become the leaders of the Louisiana bar and the bench outside of Orleans Parish. Its lack of tuition and its low fees were providing the services appropriate for a state institution, though the membership in fraternities and other social activities suggests that the school was also host to a number of the children of the elite.

The school, with no qualitative admission standards, was not selective, and the pattern was set for providing opportunity for law study for a wide range of young persons and then applying demanding standards for graduation. The result was a graduation rate of less than 50 percent of the beginning first-year students.

The small faculty was largely occupied with teaching classes, which meant carrying a heavy course load. Some pressure was taken off the faculty by allowing students to obtain credit for political-science courses, but the course load was nonetheless demanding. The faculty did not publish substantially during this period.

Student morale, at least after the first year, seems to have been high, with a collection of hard-working full-time students. No night program was instituted, and students were ostensibly not allowed to work while law students, though this rule seems to have been overlooked in a number of cases. Few women enrolled in law studies, and the average student was quite young; the typical graduate in law had two or three years of undergraduate study and three years of law study. A number had to wait some time before they became twenty-one and thus eligible to become members of the bar. The success rate continued to show rigorous standards—in the first eight years of the 1920s, 242 students entered the first year and 111 of those students were graduated. That represents a success rate of 46 percent.

Total Law School enrollment was rather static during the period, although the total University enrollment increased more than threefold. Graduate students were fewer than law students until 1926–27, when the trend in graduate student enrollments became sharply higher. Law School enrollment did not share in that trend.

FACULTY TIMELINE

1919–20	Tullis	Flory	Stumberg				
1920–21	Tullis	Flory	Stumberg				
1921–22	Tullis	Flory	Stumberg				
1922–23	Tullis	Flory	Stumberg				
1923–24	Tullis	Flory	Strickland				
1924–25	Tullis	Flory	Stumberg				
1925–26	Tullis	Flory	Burns	Gore			
1926–27	Tullis	Flory	Burns	Gore	Daggett		
1927–28	Tullis	Flory	Gore	Daggett	Baker		
1928–29	Tullis	Flory	Gore	Daggett	Smith, J. B.	Verrall	
1929–30	Tullis	Flory	Gore	Daggett	Smith, J. B.		
1930–31	Tullis	Flory	Gore	Daggett	Smith, J. B.		

ENROLLMENT PATTERNS

Year	Law 1	Law 2	Law 3	Total Law	Law Grads	Total LSU
1920–21	17	18	14	49	9	1,041
1921–22	29	11	21	61	17	1,095
1922–23	45	15	12	72	10	1,156
1923–24	17	29	13	59	11	1,376
1924–25	38	12	23	73	19	1,567
1925–26	34	26	14	74	11	1,661
1926–27	37	29	20	86	15	1,791
1927–28	25	29	23	77	20	1,882
1928–29	22	17	37	76	15	1,879
1929–30	29	20	15	64	10	2,037

4

THE EXTRAVAGANT THIRTIES

THE HUEY P. LONG ERA DAWNS

LSU's new campus was financed as a result of the gentleman's agreement that Governor John M. Parker made with Standard Oil for a 2-percent severance tax on oil and gas, and it was the governor's special solicitude for LSU that led to modest improvement of the University in the 1920s. During Huey Long's losing campaign for governor in 1924, the upstart populist criticized Parker for squandering money on the new campus; his concern was for free schoolbooks in the elementary and high schools. Long attacked the LSU administration and promised to fire a number of deans and professors; the reaction to the attack was hostile, and Huey dropped it. LSU was not an issue in Long's successful 1928 campaign for governor, and other aspects of his programs were on the front burner as he began his term in office.[1]

It was only in November 1930 that Huey intervened in LSU matters, when President Thomas W. Atkinson, successor to President Thomas D. Boyd, who resigned in 1927, suffered a heart attack, contracted influenza, and then resigned. A leading candidate to succeed him was Colonel Campbell B. Hodges, a professional soldier from north Louisiana who was commandant of the U.S. Military Academy at West Point and a man who would continue the military tradition of Sherman and the Boyds. But Hodges was part of an aristocratic planter family, and his brother was one of Huey's leading foes; Huey would not allow such an anti-Long figure to obtain the position. He did not have a particular candidate in mind, and when Atkinson resigned, a member of the Board of Supervisors recommended James Monroe Smith, dean of the College of Education at Southwestern Louisiana Institute in Lafayette. Smith drove to Baton Rouge, had a brief interview with the governor, and was offered the job on the spot, perhaps because he was also a native of

Huey's Winn Parish.[2] A quickly called meeting of the Board of Supervisors was held in the Governor's Mansion, and the Board ratified Huey's choice. A classic story is that Smith was wearing a shabby suit, and Huey handed him a large bill and said, "God damn you, go out and buy a new suit. At least try to look like a president." The story is dubious and is told about several other of Huey's appointees. Smith had respectable academic credentials, including a Ph.D. from Columbia University, and according to historian William Ivy Hair, he "was a good administrator, except for being a thief."[3]

In any event, LSU soon became a special pride of Huey Long, which he referred to as "my university." He would not take criticism from the student newspaper, the *Reveille,* as his pressure to censor it demonstrated,[4] but he did not intervene in the academic heart of the University. Indeed, it was his support of LSU's ambitions that made possible dramatic changes in the University. As Hair put it, "enrollment and academic standards both rose at LSU during the years of Huey's overlordship. From 1,600 students in 1928, enrollment climbed to approximately 4,000 by 1933. Largely because of Long's largess, improvements in facilities and faculty took LSU from mediocrity to the status of a major southern university." The Graduate School, whose leadership was handed to Dean Charles W. Pipkin in Summer 1931, grew from 94 students in 1930 to 505 in 1935.[5]

With funds to hire faculty when the Depression was curtailing recruitment at most other colleges, LSU was able to attract strong faculty members who became the backbone of the school for generations. At a convocation soon after his appointment, President Smith announced expenditures of $1,000,000 for construction. When LSU's funds from the state property tax declined, Long pushed a direct $750,000 appropriation to the University through the legislature in 1934. He also sponsored a constitutional amendment that imposed an insurance tax expected to yield more than $700,000 annually for the University's support. Altogether, the state provided LSU with more than $6 million in capital expenditures between 1931 and 1935.[6]

Huey was a political enemy of President Franklin D. Roosevelt, so LSU did not benefit substantially from federal aid during these years. However, when Richard W. Leche was elected governor in 1936, he reconciled with the national administration, and LSU then benefited from several WPA and PWA buildings. The University grew faster under Leche, who "sought to outdo the Kingfish," than under Huey. The *Southern Review* and the LSU

Press had just been established in 1935, and the LSU Opera was presenting extraordinary performances. The Medical School appeared to be flourishing; its 1931–32 class had attracted 110 first-year students.[7]

That same year, however, total Law School enrollment was only 94. Harriet S. Daggett and James Barclay Smith participated in the LSU research renaissance, writing two of the first six titles published under the LSU Press imprint. However, the Law School program was slow to accelerate at the pace of the rest of the campus. Dean Robert Lee Tullis was now sixty-six years old, frail, and had failing eyesight as the 1930–31 term began. The law faculty consisted of four professors—Tullis, Flory, Smith, and Daggett—along with one associate professor, Gore, and one adjunct, Loret. The curriculum was little changed, although law students were now taking their constitutional law and international law courses with law faculty rather than with government department faculty. Civil and common law courses, along with developing United States statutory law, were provided in one overall curriculum. Nonetheless, it was still just a basic curriculum with few electives. Enrollment was stable, with forty-three students in the first-year class and a total enrollment of eighty-six in 1930–31. Of the students listed in the 1930–31 catalog, all but three were from Louisiana and not a single student was listed with a New Orleans residence. Perhaps the most surprising development was that five women were listed as law students that year.[8]

Tuition was free for all citizens of Louisiana, but residents of other states were now charged $60 for an academic year and citizens of other countries $150. The law library fee remained at $45, and the matriculation fee was $10. The general catalog that year contained a table estimating the total expenses, including room, board, and supplies, that students would incur. The low figure given was $371, the average was $514, and a "liberal" estimate was $689. The catalog also stated, "The policy of the University is to enable the students to secure an education at the lowest possible cost."[9]

The law library volume count was up to ten thousand. Academic regulations were becoming slowly more stringent. For example, in meeting the requirement of two years of college for admission to the Law School, students were limited to a total of two hours of credit in military science and physical education. Law students were required to attain passing grades in at least half of the work undertaken in any semester or they would be excluded during the next regular semester. The curriculum offered little choice, requiring eighty semester hours of credit for graduation, with only three elective courses listed in the catalog. Professor Daggett's course load now included civil-code courses as well as constitutional law and international law. Professor Dale E. Bennett, who arrived in 1933, was perceptive in characterizing the Law School as an institution trying to produce good practitioners: "There were virtually no frills."[10]

The curriculum was as follows:

First-Year Required Courses	Semester Hours	Faculty
Contracts	5	Smith
Agency	3	Gore
Torts	5	Tullis
Sales	2	Daggett
Criminal Law	4	Gore
Common-Law Pleading & Practice	2	Flory
Civil Code of Louisiana	5	Daggett
Civil Code of Louisiana	2	Tullis
Legal Bibliography	1	Gore
Total hours offered	29	

Second-Year Required Courses		
Public Service Law	3	Smith
Real Property	3	Smith
Constitutional Law	4	Daggett
Negotiable Instruments	2	Flory
Equity	3	Gore
Civil Code of Louisiana	3	Tullis
Evidence	4	Flory
Louisiana Code of Practice	4	Loret
Total hours offered	26	

Third-Year Required Courses		
Conflict of Laws	4	Gore
Criminal Procedure	2	Gore
Private Corporations	4	Smith
Bankruptcy	2	Flory
Federal Procedure	3	Flory
Admiralty	2	Flory
Civil Code of Louisiana	5	Tullis
Moot Court	1	Tullis, Gore
Total hours offered	23	

Third-Year Electives		
International Law	2	Daggett
Insurance	2	Daggett
Taxation	2	Smith

THE END OF THE TULLIS ERA

Huey Long, who had attended Tulane Law School, did not show much interest in LSU's law school. Sources suggest that Tullis was conservative and anti-Long, but that fact does not seem to be reflected in any of the actions taken against the dean as the decade opened. Indeed, it was some law students who apparently tried to invoke Long's intervention to make changes at the school. Kemble K. Kennedy, who was president of the LSU student body in 1928–29, was a third-year law student in October 1929 when he helped to form and then became president of a new LSU Law Club. Its purpose was to make "the law student body more of a unit in seeking what they term as 'justifiable concessions' from the faculty and the university." The *Reveille* announced that petitions from students could be handled through the club, "which will function as a union." Ever a student activist, Kennedy was soon elected to represent the law students on the University Student Council, then was elected vice-president of the council and presiding officer of the Honor Court.[11]

Kennedy was described as smart, "quite radical in comparison to the other students; [and] he was older than most." From Farmerville in Union Parish in North Louisiana, he had been injured in an accident and was represented by Huey Long, who secured a workers' compensation settlement for him. Students later remembered that Kennedy lived in the attic of the Governor's Mansion for a while—"typical of Huey Long to take care of needy friends like that."[12]

Kennedy organized a group of law students to call on the governor in December 1929, ostensibly "to complain about Dr. James Barclay Smith, the professor who came down here from Kansas, but my belief has always been that the real reason for the trip to visit Governor Long was to try to give him support from the students to get him to remove Dean Tullis. Dean Tullis had opposed Huey publicly, as I recall."[13] Although Kennedy's motives and those of the other students are not clear, it is not disputed that Huey Long did not intervene at that time. The newspapers reported the students' visit and also that Dean Tullis, who had gone to New Orleans for eye surgery, was reported to have undergone the operation with complete success and returned to Baton Rouge.[14]

Kennedy was reportedly a major participant in the publication of an anonymous humor broadside called the *Whangdoodle*, which criticized and satirized Tullis, "the Tensas Terror," and "Halitosis Smith." The attack on the latter was especially vicious: "Halitosis Smith; his place is in an asylum and not in a law school. While running from the enemy in WWI, he was shell shocked and never recovered. He has never been known to answer a question intelligibly. One of his famous maxims, 'That would be mental masturbation, useless work and no satisfaction.'"[15]

Rumors of misconduct, especially sexual misconduct, about other University officials abounded in the *Whangdoodle*, including a report that the wife of a certain professor received a lover when her husband was in class. Some thought the broadside suggested that Dean Tullis was a drug addict. Though a modern reader might find amusement in the sophomoric, scatological humor, President Atkinson and Dean Tullis did not. They hired a detective, who reported that Kennedy was the probable editor of the *Whangdoodle*. It was approximately a week before Kennedy was to complete his senior-year final exams, and as a classmate described the scene, Kennedy was taking an exam when the "Dean walked in and just picked the pen out of K.K.'s hand

and told him he wouldn't need that anymore. He could go on home; he didn't need to finish the exam; he was expelled." Kennedy's official transcript contains asterisks instead of grades for his last two courses, Law 36 and Law 42, with the notation:

> Suspended for "Having been indicted for publishing and circulating, or causing to be published or circulated an indecent and obscene paper, called the 'Whangdoodle'", containing libelous attacks upon certain officers, faculty members, and employees of the Louisiana State University, as per special order of the President, June 3, 1930.
>
> Executive Order No. 30 . . . was received while Mr. Kennedy was in the process of taking an examination in Law 36. He was estopped by the order from completing the examination.
>
> Law 42 represents Moot Court, in which no examination is required. Executive Order No. 30 estopped the handing in of a grade for the semester in this course.[16]

Huey Long tried to intercede for Kennedy, but he gave way when President Atkinson refused to rescind the expulsion. According to T. Harry Williams, Huey had not read the *Whangdoodle,* and when Atkinson showed it to him, Huey said he could not condone such scurrilous stuff. Student sentiment did not seem to favor Kennedy, because the *Gumbo,* the student yearbook, put him at the head of its list of "Top Ten Jokes of the Year."[17]

Kennedy's more immediate problem was his trial for four counts of criminal libel and circulation of obscene matter: "serious reflection" on a lady; a statement that a professor was a "dope fiend"; allegations that Tullis and R. L. Himes stole University funds; and a blanket charge regarding the circulation of an "indecent sheet." The anti-Long district attorney prosecuted him, and he was found guilty in November 1930. Kennedy did not testify, presented no defense other than one character witness, and was sentenced to one year of imprisonment in the parish prison. He did not name any other participants in publication of the *Whangdoodle.* After serving a week of his sentence, Kennedy was twice granted a reprieve by Governor Long, allowing him to go before the State Pardon Board, composed of the lieutenant governor, the attorney general, and the trial judge. Governor Oscar K. Allen later issued a full pardon. Kennedy had continued his law studies in jail and declared his intention to keep on with the study of law; he also announced that he had started writing a novel about college life.[18]

Kennedy now sought permission to complete his Law School exams, but Tullis remained adamant in his refusal. In 1933, President Smith reported at the spring Board of Supervisors meeting that Tullis, now sixty-nine years old, was incapable of discharging his duties, and he recommended that he be named dean emeritus. Professor Flory was named acting dean of the Law School. Then Smith recommended that Kennedy be granted his degree after taking the required examinations. Kennedy was given a special diploma signed by President Smith and Governor Allen, the latter in his capacity as president *ex officio* of the LSU Board. The diploma was not signed by the dean of the Law School. Kennedy's official transcript contains the entry: "June 5, 1933—BE IT RESOLVED that the Board of Supervisors of the Louisiana State University and Agricultural and Mechanical College does hereby order his reinstatement and directs that he be graduated with the degree of Bachelor of Law as of June 5, 1933." But it was a year and a half before Kennedy received his diploma: "In compliance with this resolution a special diploma conferring the degree of Bachelor of Law, was delivered to Mr. Kennedy on December 10, 1934." The 1977 and 2000 directories of law graduates published by the Alumni Association do not contain an entry for Kennedy.[19]

Kennedy was admitted to the Louisiana bar in March 1935, on his second attempt to pass the exam.[20] That fact was noted in the *New Orleans Item*, with Kennedy identified as the Long crony who was sentenced to imprisonment. Kennedy sued the newspaper for defamation, but the court found the report essentially true, and the Louisiana Supreme Court affirmed.[21] Kennedy ultimately practiced in Baton Rouge and was considered by colleagues as "a good lawyer," "a doggone good lawyer."[22]

As Justice Albert C. Tate recalled the incident, the "elite bar" took up for Tullis, and the Longites thought it was a dirty trick on an underdog to withhold the degree. One student of that period said of Tullis, "I think he was really very hurt. He was a kind of broken man after that; he never was the same." Some uncertainty about the full story surrounding Tullis's retirement exists, one student remembering that Huey "may have given the old dean a shove, but he was practically blind by that time and was in no real condition to continue, and especially to build the law school up as it needed." Another student of that era reports that Tullis "was pretty cantankerous. He and I were on opposite sides for a long time, but after it was all over, he and I and his wife became very good friends." They were on opposite sides "because I thought his effectiveness as dean had got to a low ebb, and I was one of those that went to the Governor then to try to get him to be Dean Emeritus. . . . He found out that I was in the group, and I think he had kind of hard feelings towards me."23

Tullis, then dean emeritus, was presented with a handsome walking cane by the law class of 1933 as a tribute to his years of leadership in the school. The members of the Class of 1934 went to his home after graduation and had him sign their diplomas, in addition to Acting Dean Flory. In Fall 1934, Tullis, described as "recently retired under the University age-limit rule," enrolled in courses in Spanish and chemistry, standing in line with students to have his ID picture taken. Richard E. Gerard, a Law School junior, presented him with a purple-and-gold freshman beanie.24

Meanwhile, the Association of American Law Schools investigated the circumstances surrounding the granting of Kennedy's degree, and the American Bar Association placed the LSU Law School on probation. G. Frank Purvis, a 1935 graduate, recalled that the school did not lose its accreditation as some people believed, and it apparently was not a big issue with the students. Dale Bennett reported that he knew of no instances in which Huey Long tried to control the faculty, but when asked about Tullis's battles with Long, Bennett simply said that those events were before his day.25

FREDERICK K. BEUTEL

Huey Long, a U.S. senator as of January 25, 1932, was not unexpectedly a main actor in recruiting a national figure to head the Law School. Huey's objective was to make LSU's law program nationally recognized. He sought Wayne Morse, then at the University of Oregon Law School and later to become a U.S. senator, "but Morse was influenced by the fact that Huey Long had called him in the middle of the night to ask if he would come here as dean. He didn't give an immediate answer, but later called back and declined on the grounds, as he put it to some of his colleagues, that if he could call me in the middle of the night to hire me, he could call me, also, in the middle of the night to fire me."26

Frederick K. Beutel was named dean in 1935 and remained until 1937. He was a thirty-one-year-old professor at Tulane when President Smith tapped him for the deanship with the hope that he would revolutionize the Law School in the style of LSU's Graduate School and the humanities. Smith offered an outstanding salary under a three-year contract: $6,000 the first year ($75,000 in year 2000 dollars), $6,500 the second, and $7,000 the third.[27] Beutel's tenure was a tempestuous and exciting time, but it only lasted two years.

Beutel, who in 1935 had been a professor at Tulane for seven years, was born in Montgomery, Alabama. With a 1921 A.B. from Cornell, he was the manager of the Beutel Business College and an instructor in business law in 1921 and 1922. He then went to Harvard for the LL.B., which he received in 1925, practiced in Pennsylvania, and then earned an S.J.D. from Harvard in 1928. From there he went to Tulane, where his responsibilities included serving as faculty editor of the reinvigorated *Tulane Law Review*. Tulane's first venture in a legal periodical produced three volumes of the *Southern Law Quarterly* between 1916 and 1918, but the quarterly was discontinued at the outbreak of World War I. A revival of the publication appeared in December 1929 as Volume 4 of what was now called the *Tulane Law Review*, with Beutel as the faculty editor. That first revival issue brought him into contact with the LSU faculty, with Harriet S. Daggett writing a lead article on comparative community property.[28]

Indeed, the Louisiana legal-education community was a small and interconnected group at the time. That same volume of the revived law review published an article on maritime liens by Paul M. Hebert, who was then a Sterling Fellow at Yale Law School. Another Sterling Fellow during that period was Paul Brosman, who would join the Tulane law faculty and later become dean at Tulane. Professor Daggett published an article on separation of property in Volume 5, and Pierre Crabites, the New Orleanian who was a judge of the Mixed Tribunal of Egypt and who would later join the LSU law faculty, also published in that issue. Volume 9 would see the appearance of work by Henry George McMahon, then professor of law at Loyola Law School. Volume 10 introduced to Louisiana the work of Joseph Dainow, a Canadian who had become a professor at Loyola Law School before moving to LSU.[29]

Beutel had become a part of Louisiana's legal elite as well as a national figure. His area of expertise was commercial law, and he assumed the authorship of *Beutel's Brannon's Negotiable Instruments* while at Tulane. When he was named dean of LSU's Law School, the anti-Long *New Orleans Times-Picayune* editorialized, "Dean Beutel is a man of liberal opinions and notably independent disposition. He is the type of man to offset political meddling as much as anyone could." Beutel expressed an interest in the cross-pollination of the civil and common law traditions, suggesting in a leading article that civil-law analogies could be useful in developing a new technique of interpreting the negotiable-instruments law. He concluded, "Surely the science of interpreting written law is the same whether it be French, German, or Anglo-American and the experience of hundreds of years should be used for all the possibilities which it suggests." More important, he was interested in a social-science approach to law and teaching law. One of his early articles was on the pressure of organized interest groups on legislatures. His views on social science and his contentious style are typified in the conclusion of the preface to his 1975 book, *Experimental Jurisprudence and the Scienstate:* "Because this book deprecates the place of religion, the common law, and democracy (the 'sacred cows' of Anglo-American polity) in the proper structure of government, and since it reduces political ideals (values) to their rightful place as unproven hypotheses, it was impossible to get it sponsored in the United States either by endowed university presses or by commercial publishers. It has therefore been necessary to have it published in Germany where the intellectual climate is more favorable to the growth of science."[30]

Beutel detailed his ambitious plans for the LSU Law School at the annual meeting of the Louisiana Bar Association in November 1935. Any good law school, he said, needed three essentials: a library of 60,000 to 400,000 volumes; a faculty of ten to thirty scholars devoted to full-time teaching and research; and a building devoted to legal education with adequate facilities for classrooms, laboratories, research, and perhaps student dormitories. He anticipated meeting those requirements at LSU "through the action of wise administration and a generous legislature, supported by a powerful public opinion which demands education for every man in accordance with his ability." He also stated that revival of the civil law in Louisiana would require substantial investment and research and also that he would soon establish a legal-aid clinic at LSU. He moved quickly on those fronts.[31]

Students at the time considered Beutel a man with a brilliant mind, but he had a contentious personality and liked to argue. He increased the library considerably, "but he just had a most abrasive personality, and he was cocky as unshirted heck." One student said he was an "ornery S.O.B" and that he "wasn't liked by anybody, to tell you frankly."[32]

Grading standards remained high during Beutel's tenure as dean, and the failure rate was more than 50 percent. Paul B. Landry, later a court of appeals judge, was a senior during Beutel's first year, and "to the consternation of the seniors, he revised the curriculum which put a lot of the seniors in a bind, because it affected the possibility or the manner in which we could take the remaining portion of the Civil Code, which we had not had during our first two years." Landry remarked that Beutel had some good ideas and wanted to modernize the school, but students couldn't reason with him. He was dictatorial and arbitrary. Landry commented on Beutel's sudden departure after only two years: "My personal feeling is that that was no great loss." Sam D'Amico was in Beutel's negotiable-instruments class and remembered that he was a "pretty good" professor. Apparently there was friction between Beutel and Flory, who by that time was a sick man with hardening of the arteries.[33]

As Professor Dale E. Bennett later recalled, when Beutel arrived, "I would guess that they doubled the size of the faculty, and they more than doubled the library and the budget; and then they built a new law building. The direction then was more toward trying to establish a national law school, in addition to the Louisiana law school." Bennett, characteristically, was reluctant to criticize Beutel in his oral-history interview, simply saying that "his general approach was not quite like mine would be. He was more interested in painting a broad picture with a broad brush, than in paying attention to day-to-day things." His "theory wasn't quite like mine." Bennett's actions spoke louder than words: he took a leave of absence from LSU and taught at the University of Texas until Beutel left LSU. In 1937, he wrote privately to Paul M. Hebert, "I wanted to let you know of my change of attitude toward returning now that Beutel is gone."[34]

Milton Harrison suggested that Beutel "was a very competent scholar. In his last years of teaching he had a reputation of being a very considerate, kind teacher, and a good teacher at the University of Illinois. He had always had the facility for creating a tempest in a teapot, which he did here and in Nebraska. He was a somewhat bad administrator in the view of the Association of American Law Schools. This was the reputation he had, and I guess, well earned." Wex Malone said that he was a mercurial character, had very distinct ideas of what a law school should be, and was a modernist in every sense of the word: "Under Beutel the school did make phenomenal progress. LSU had been a relatively small Southern, country, law school. But Beutel had great dreams for the institution." Beutel brought with him a coterie of recognized scholars or men who were achieving recognition; "all of them," according to Malone, were "liberal thinkers."[35]

The circumstances of Beutel's resignation after two years in office were altogether tragic and comic, and typically idiosyncratic. When students complained about the lack of civil-code courses to prepare them for the bar exam, Beutel's response was that anyone could pass the civil-code portions of the bar. He said he would have no difficulty, and he registered for the bar exam. Milton Harrison said, "He ended up never studying, and while taking it decided he would not complete the exam because he was flunking, and that was toward the end of his reign." Perhaps the most authoritative explanation of Beutel's bar-exam experiences came from Justice Albert C. Tate, repeating the story told by supreme court justice Amos Lee Ponder: "He took it, but he said, 'I don't need to prepare for this thing.' According to Justice Ponder, they had his paper pulled out and graded quickly after the first day, and they saw he was going to fail it; so they told him you better get sick, and he did." One student penned a poem:

> Tis said by some our boy was ill.
> Perhaps that was the case,
> But I, for one, believe it was true
> That he quit to save his face.[36]

Paul Landry took the bar exam at the same time in the State Capitol. At noon on the second day, the rumor started that Beutel had dropped out because he had become sick. Mel Dakin would explain later in his droll way that "he went in to take it without any special preparation and after a session or so it became apparent that he was failing; it didn't add to his plumage as the dean of the Law School." Frank Craig Jr. commented, "I would have been sick, too, if I had been dean and was failing."[37]

Beutel left before the end of the semester with his resignation, according to public records, effective May 26, 1937. That effective date, however, seems odd since the normal practice would be to finish the term. A confidential letter to Beutel from President Smith dated May 24, 1937, gives additional explanation. In the letter, Smith states: "I have come reluctantly to the point of view that it would not be best for the University or for you to continue your active services for the session 1937–38. I shall, therefore, recommend to the Board that your services be discontinued on June 30, 1937, but that your salary of $7.000.00 be paid for the session 1937–38 in compliance with the terms of your appointment." Beutel submitted his resignation the next day. Smith's letter also suggested that, to avoid embarrassment for all concerned, "I shall be glad to have you submit a request for leave. In any event, your salary for the session 1937–1938 will be paid." A confidential memo to Smith written on the letterhead of Dean of Administration Paul M. Hebert enumerated the reasons for Beutel's dismissal, including Beutel's action in taking the Louisiana bar examination against the advice of the president, resulting in his withdrawal and subjecting the University to extreme embarrassment; his inability to work harmoniously in a cooperative spirit with other major administrative officers of the University; and his failure to develop a program of research in civil law.[38]

Beutel subsequently joined the faculty at William and Mary, and after World War II he became dean of the law school at the University of Nebraska, where he led an ambitious reform like that at LSU. Paul M. Hebert, dean of administration for the University, was named acting, then permanent dean of the Law School. He later summed up Beutel's legacy: "The impact of Dean Beutel's vision and drive affected mightily the level of legal education at LSU. Those who have continued on the Faculty since his time or have followed as new members of the Faculty have all been the beneficiaries of the dynamic change in the Law School's direction which he initiated."[39]

PAUL MACARIUS HEBERT

Paul Macarius Hebert, called Mac by his friends, was an LSU alumnus, with A.B. and LL.B. degrees from the University. He then won a Sterling Fellowship at the Yale Law School and received the J.S.D in 1930. He was a professor at Loyola Law School in New Orleans for a year and moved to LSU for the 1931–32 term with the rank of assistant professor. Loyola called him back the following year to accept a professorship and the deanship of its law school. Hebert was then the youngest dean of an American law school. He returned to LSU in Fall 1936, serving as dean of administration under President James Monroe Smith, holding the second-highest administrative position on the campus. He also had professorial rank on the law faculty. Hebert had signed a five-year contract to serve as law dean at Loyola, but Huey Long asked Father John W. Hynes, S.J., president of Loyola, to release him at the end of his fourth year. Hebert, who was a Baton Rouge native, remained with the University and the Law School, except for brief forays into private practice during the 1950s, until his death in 1977. When Hebert vacated the position of dean of administration, he was replaced by another University stalwart, Troy H. Middleton.[40]

Joseph Dainow later described the period: "When Mac Hebert became Dean [of the Law School] in 1937 there were nine full-time regular faculty and four part-time special lecturers for a total of 150 students. The law library contained 35,000 volumes. The curriculum comprised about 40 courses and 78 semester credits (raised to 80 in 1938) were required for graduation. The dormitory fee was $27 per semester and for $15 a month a student could have all his meals at the Cafeteria Boarding Club." Dale Bennett said that Dean Hebert tried to build the national image that Beutel had envisioned while also cementing relations with the Louisiana bar. Hebert "operated on both fronts. He could lead those of us who wanted to work locally, and he could lead those like Wex [Malone], and others and Mel Dakin, who may have done their work on the national level."[41]

Hebert was called to university administration again at the end of the decade. On June 26, 1939, President James Monroe Smith's resignation was accepted by the Board of Supervisors after he fled to Canada to avoid prosecution for fraud in handling University finances. Hebert was appointed acting president the next day by Governor Earl K. Long, the lieutenant-governor who had succeeded Governor Richard W. Leche when Leche resigned under threat of criminal prosecution. With Hebert gone, Ira S. Flory was again acting dean. He served from July 18, 1939, until June 30, 1941, when Hebert returned to the position.[42]

FRANTIC INNOVATION

Until Robert Lee Tullis's retirement, the Law School had been a dean-led, dean-dominated institution. No formal faculty meetings are recorded, and no minutes are available in the Law School archives. Indeed, with a four- or five-person faculty, informal discussions would likely be the pattern in any event. But, more generally, the entire University was governed in a military tradition, given the long tenure of the Colonels Boyd and the early influence of General Sherman. Also, the long tenure of Dean Tullis reinforced his personal authority. When the survey commission of the American Council of Education reviewed LSU in 1940 after the Louisiana Scandals, it reported a general weakness in faculty governance procedures.[43]

With Beutel's arrival, however, the Law School pattern changed. The faculty minutes of the September 9, 1935, meeting, recorded by the elected faculty secretary, J. Denson Smith, begin, "The first meeting of the Faculty of the Louisiana State University School of Law was called to order . . . by Dean Frederick K. Beutel."[44] The first proposals were a sign of a freer atmosphere and an opportunity to present pent-up ideas that had not found favor previously. The faculty passed a motion by Professor Daggett that graduate students and undergraduate seniors in the social sciences be admitted to courses given in family law, criminal law, and international law. To accommodate Professor J. Denson Smith, separate courses in common-law contracts and civil-law obligations were established; he would teach both. Professor Daggett's successions class became a four-hour course. A course in servitudes was eliminated and, at the request of Professor Flory, the bankruptcy course was increased to three hours. One sign of easing-up appeared; because of the likelihood of student absences on Saturdays because of football games, the criminal-procedure class was changed from Saturday to Thursday, and legal bibliography was moved to Wednesday.

Once the meetings started, they seemed not to stop. Nine more meetings were held before the end of the year, and the attention to minutiae was never-ending. Among the proposals adopted was establishment of the degree of Master of Civil Law. The first student admitted into the program was Robert Anthony Pascal, who graduated in 1940 and later joined the law faculty. Prospects for a doctorate were good until the resignation of President Smith threw the University into turmoil. Three faculty research assistants were hired. An appellate argument competition was proposed, and the Student Moot Court Board was established. A combined curriculum in commerce and law was adopted.[45]

Most significant was the adoption of an alternate curriculum for the LL.B., one that emphasized Dean Beutel's social-science interests. The existing three-year Law School program would be available to students who had completed three years of undergraduate work; however, a new four-year course was to be offered in the 1936–37 term to students who had completed two years of undergraduate work. In either case, a full six years of college were required to obtain a law degree. As the catalog explained the new option, "the growth of administrative law and government regulation of business, together with the increase in legislation on social problems, have greatly widened the activity of the legal profession and complicated the nature of the material which a lawyer must handle to meet the requirements of his practice." To that end, the Law School "will offer a four-year curriculum in law, which closely integrates materials from civil law, comparative law, criminal law and the social sciences such as business organization, government, economics, philosophy and sociology." Courses would be offered by law faculty and faculty members from the Colleges of Commerce and Arts and Sciences, and from the Graduate School. The four-year program contained a dramatically changed first year of courses:

Law 109: Methods of Thinking (3 hours)
Law 121: Sociology of Law (3 hours)
Law 114–115: Comparative Constitutional Theory and Problems (6 hours)
Law 110–111: The Use of Economic and Social Data (6 hours)
Law 102: Torts (5 hours)
Law 101: Contracts (4 hours)
Law 132: History of Legal Institutions (3 hours)

Also adopted was a program that would award a nonprofessional B.S. in Law based on completion of two years of undergraduate study and the first two years of the four-year course. Addressing lawyers in April 1937, Beutel reported that almost one-third of the first-year class was enrolled in the new four-year program, and he expected that to increase. He told the state bar association that a successful lawyer "must be a social engineer who can mold the law to fit the rapidly changing social conditions," and he boasted that LSU offered new courses in sociology of law, jurisprudence, legal analysis and logic, comparative constitutional problems, criminology, and legislation.[46]

The concept of four-year programs was advocated by John Henry Wigmore, who had established such a program at Northwestern University. It was abandoned in 1935. The University of Chicago's optional four-year program began in 1937 and lasted until 1949. The University of Minnesota was most successful with its program; it was begun in 1930 and was not dropped until 1958. Experiments with four-year programs were also tried at Stanford, Washington University, the University of Washington, and Yale.[47]

The experiment at LSU encountered problems in addition to Beutel's resignation. The Curriculum Committee in January 1937 reported difficulty in staffing the new courses and in differentiating them from similar undergraduate courses offered in other departments: "To take an example: if the course in Methods of Thinking consists in the first semester of a straight course in Logic, then we need to ask whether we should not simply require a course in logic to be taken in the colleges and use the additional time thus acquired for some other subject." The Law School had been unable to offer a course in the use of economic and social data. Dean Hebert supported the program, explaining it on LSU's *University Hour* radio program carried throughout the state, but with Beutel no longer there to push the program, Professors Daggett, Hall, and Smith were appointed to a committee to report on the question of retention of the four-year curriculum. The matter was discussed, but not decided, in January, and it was finally abandoned in November 1939.[48]

Beutel announced in Fall 1936 that the Law School had added fifteen new courses and six new professors. The new courses covered fifty-five semester hours, forty-one hours of which were courses in social science and government open to properly qualified upperclass students in the College of Arts and Sciences. Thirteen hours of civil-law courses were offered. He boasted, "With these new faculty members of the law school, LSU now has the largest and strongest law faculty in the South."[49]

Beutel would also boast in May 1937 of a diverse student body consisting of 148 students, 33 of them seniors expected to graduate. The faculty-student ratio was 12 to 1.[50] Beutel said that the current students had prepared for the study of law at thirty-two different undergraduate institutions, and he addressed out-of-state LSU undergraduate students to urge them to consider the LSU Law School, which offered courses that would prepare them to practice law anywhere.

An honors course in civil law was established in 1935. Six students composed the initial class, conducted by Professor Ireland in the first semester and Professor Daggett in the second. It met weekly to discuss written reports on problems related to the civil code. Leonard Greenburg, research assistant in law, presented the French law on a problem, after which Ireland or Daggett would discuss the Roman and Spanish laws. Students were expected to stress the early Louisiana doctrine. Four new courses were added in 1936: Criminal Law Administration and Sales, taught by Jerome Hall; and Civil Law Problems and Mineral Rights, taught by Harriet Daggett.[51]

Beutel and the law faculty had to contend with the repercussions of the law degree granted to K. K. Kennedy by the Board of Supervisors in June 1933 without a recommendation from the law faculty. Three accrediting agencies were involved—the Southern Association of Colleges, which accredited the University,[52] the American Bar Association, and the Association of American Law Schools. However, the matter died quietly after the assassination of Huey Long on September 8, 1935.

LSU had not been placed on probation by the Southern Association of Colleges. A committee dropped its probation proposal after its members decided that alleged political interference at the University had ceased. The SAC met in December 1935 with the Board of Supervisors and the president, and LSU agreed to comply with SAC recommendations, primarily that no degree be awarded except on recommendation of the faculty.[53]

The American Bar Association Section of Legal Education and Admissions to the Bar did place the Law School on probation in May 1935, an action that produced no sanctions but was "intended to be a warning to the school that the Council is dissatisfied with the conditions which prevail there." Dean Beutel appeared before the section in July and spoke of considerable improvement in the situation, but the section took no action at the time. Probation was not lifted at the year-end meeting of the section, provoking an impassioned response by Beutel: "If Louisiana State University Law School is on probation, it presents the grotesque picture of the best equipped and largest law school in the state being given a black eye by standarding associations while the other institutions who have failed to meet our standards remain in unquestioned standing." Speaking to Pi Lambda Beta pre-law fraternity, he said that LSU's standards were as high as those of any law school in the country and that the Law School had more teachers per student than any other school in the country. Even with the Kennedy case, he said, "This, however, does not mean that a law degree from LSU is not recognized as one of the best that can be obtained." The ABA proceedings for the following year, May

1936, simply stated, with little explanation, that LSU was removed from probation and returned to its fully approved status.[54]

The Kennedy affair took on a more political than academic posture when the matter was referred to the Association of American Law Schools. A report of the Executive Committee was presented at the December 1934 meeting, a time when Long was becoming a national figure and a threat to the reelection of FDR. The report did not recommend any sanctions against the Law School other than to inform the successor Executive Committee of the situation. Indeed, the report stated, "It should be said that the law faculty itself has acted with propriety, so far as it has had power to do so. The situation thus far disclosed presents a problem not merely of the law school but of the university of which it is a component part." But in addition to the narrow question of the Kennedy degree, the report referred to other questions relating to "the forced retirement of the dean of the law school," political intercession in other areas of the University, and the passage of a statute creating an integrated bar and thus "giving control over admissions to the bar to a politically elected board." Dean Emeritus Tullis attended the AALS meeting, and in a discussion of Law School–University relations, he said, "May a visitor be heard? I would ask the gentlemen who have just spoken what view they would take if they were forced to the conviction that the law school was absolutely overridden by the president of the university and the Governor of the state?" Also at the meeting was Rufus C. Harris, secretary of the AALS, a member of the Executive Committee and dean of the Tulane Law School.[55]

The denouement of the affair played out at the December 1935 AALS meeting, ironically held in New Orleans rather than in the usual Chicago location. Adding to the irony was the fact that Dean Harris of Tulane was also the president of the AALS and that it was a member of his faculty, Frederick Beutel, who had been named to succeed Tullis as dean. The Executive Committee did not recommend the imposition of sanctions but suggested to the incoming committee that "anxious solicitude" for LSU be maintained, but the matter was not raised in subsequent years. But even after Huey's death, the Executive Committee report contained a two-page recitation of Long's misdeeds, among them exerting "undesirable and far-reaching political influence over the educational institutions of the state," including the high schools and the University's journalism department, and interference with athletics at LSU. With respect to the Law School, it added that "the forced retirement of Dean Tullis, an outspoken opponent of the Long regime, definitely arouses suspicion." Then, for some odd reason, it also found that Long offered the LSU deanship to a certain teacher by long-distance telephone.[56]

The AALS did not debate the report, which imposed no sanctions, but it did debate whether to print the listing of misdeeds in the proceedings. In that debate, Dean Emeritus Tullis spoke, "May I ask a question? Have any of the wrongs that the report of the Executive Committee says have been committed been righted?" The response to that question came from Dean Beutel, who emphasized that no one who investigated the case carefully could find any political influence now—"The marvel is that a man of Long's power at the time he was alive didn't interfere more with the institution." He also stated that Tullis had received complete retirement pay, at more than a third of his former salary.[57]

In any event, the detailed statement was printed and, as one speaker put it, Beutel would not suffer "if it becomes known in the law teaching community that his school had a narrow squeak and got by lucky."[58]

Beutel's resignation did not end the innovations and experimentation at the Law School. In April 1938, President James Monroe Smith announced the establishment at the Law School of a new research organization, the Louisiana State Law Institute. The creation of such a program of legal research and reform and a permanent law-reform agency had been urged earlier by James Barclay Smith, but it was Dean Hebert who pushed it to fruition. Directed by a council composed of law faculty, judges, lawyers, and public officials, one of the institute's primary tasks would be reform of the civil law. It was later made a state agency under the direction of the legislative branch, but members of the law faculty continued to be closely associated with it. Shreveport lawyer John Tucker Jr. was its first president, and he said that the institute would determine the future of the civil law in Louisiana.[59]

LAW FACULTY

Beutel's most important contribution was the enlargement of the faculty between 1935 and 1937 and the extraordinary quality of the faculty members he was able to recruit. The decade opened with five regular faculty members; when Beutel left, the faculty was composed of twelve professors.

The 1933–34 term had seen the arrival of Dale Elmer Bennett as a replacement for Professor Gore. Bennett, who became a criminal-law expert and primary drafter of the Louisiana Criminal Code of 1942, was ironically a native of Crooksville, Ohio. He had an A.B. from Ohio Wesleyan University and a J.D. from the University of Iowa, and he had practiced for a year and a half in Columbus before going to Yale and earning a J.S.D. in 1933. He remained at LSU until his retirement in 1976, except for the two-year break when he taught at the University of Texas. Theo Cangelosi ('34) repeated the view of thousands of students: "Dale Bennett was marvelous." Why did he come to LSU? He said he had two choices in the lean Depression years, LSU and Louisville: "Dean Clark for whom I worked at Yale and who recommended me for the job, suggested that he thought my chances were better in a state school, than a city school. So I came here."[60]

Tullis did not return as a professor for the 1934–35 term, and his slot was filled by another Law School icon, John Denson Smith ('30). Smith had A.B. and LL.B. degrees from LSU and was valedictorian of his law class. He practiced with the Smith, Albritton, and Hardin firm in Baton Rouge from 1930 until 1933. Like Daggett and Hebert, he went to Yale as a Sterling Fellow. He was in residence there from 1933 to 1934 and was awarded his J.S.D. in 1935. His thesis on the impossibility of performance as an excuse in French law was published as a leading article in the *Yale Law Journal* in 1936.[61] Smith was assigned the office that Tullis had reluctantly vacated, and he said it was embarrassing that Tullis wouldn't admit that he did not have the office any more. Smith remained on the faculty until his retirement in 1973, when he was holding an Alumni Professorship. He was known to students as a master of the Socratic method, and he also served as director of the Louisiana State Law Institute. Senator Russell Long said of him upon Smith's retirement, "After I reached the Senate I soon found out that if one could attend the L.S.U. Law School and keep Professor J. Denson Smith from finding out how ignorant he really is, one would have little difficulty as a new Senator in performing the same sort of task in the United States Senate."[62]

James Barclay Smith did not return for the 1935–36 term, but the faculty was enlarged with the addition of Dean Beutel and two experienced teachers he brought with him as full professors, Jerome Hall and Gordon Ireland. Both men had outstanding credentials and Harvard ties, as did Beutel.

Hall held a Jur.Sc.D. from Columbia, a J.D. from the University of Chicago, and an S.J.D. from Harvard. He was especially interested in the relationship of social science and the law, and his book *Theft, Law and Society* had received national acclaim. Hall's initial salary was $5,000 for the academic year ($62,000 in Year 2000 dollars). The senior professor at the time, Ira S. Flory, was paid $5,200. Hall was from Chicago and had been an assistant district attorney in Cook County, a fact he continued to remind his students about, but students complained that he taught little about criminal procedure and that he was "a very poor teacher. Nobody could learn anything about criminal law." He remained at LSU after Beutel's departure, for a total of four years, and he was there when he edited his book *Readings on Jurisprudence*. With 1,183 pages, the readings reflected Hall's social-science approach: "The way these problems present themselves now, we can't depend on the old division of subjects—law, political science, government, philosophy each in its own compartment. The job for educators now is to go through materials available, rework, and integrate them." He left after the 1938–39 term and then completed his career at the Indiana University School of Law.[63]

Ireland had bachelor's, master's, and law degrees from Harvard and a J.S.D. from Yale. He also came at a salary of $5,000 a year. He had an interest in comparative law, focusing on South America, was a contributing editor to the *Tulane Law Review* when Beutel was faculty editor, and was an assistant professor of law at Harvard before he came to LSU. At an earlier time, he had objected to the use of case decisions by United States students of civil law.[64] He left LSU after two years and continued his strong interest in Latin American law, publishing in 1941 a volume on boundary disputes in South America. At that time, he was a professor at Portia Law School, an institution for women only (which became the New England School of Law in 1969). He was co-author of *Divorce in the Americas*, written while he was a visiting professor at the Catholic University of America.[65]

Ireland was assigned to teach obligations, a required senior course. Students stated that he did a very poor job. He gave Paul B. Landry the first failing grade he had ever received, and Ira Flory Jr., who had a straight-A average, made only a B in the course. Of a class of thirty-eight, there were two or three Cs and the rest were Ds and failing grades. Ireland also taught constitutional law, and, as Joe Sanders put it, he was brilliant but "most students found him to be very dry."[66]

Ireland has probably received more credit than he deserved for provoking a debate by publishing an article in the *Tulane Law Review* detailing why

Louisiana should not be considered a civil-law jurisdiction. Actually, Pierre Crabites had said the same thing in a 1928 article in the *Loyola Law Journal*, and Ireland's article was followed by one by Leonard Greenburg, then a research assistant at LSU, which did not dispute Ireland's general findings but urged action to revive civil-law traditions. In a leading article, LSU's civil-law-oriented faculty contested the extent of the decline of the civil law in the state, as did former Dean Tullis.[67]

Dean Beutel recruited five new faculty members for the 1936–37 term: Leavenworth Colby, Thomas Anthony Cowan, Judge Pierre Crabites, Fowler Vincent Harper, and Charles W. Taintor II. They, too, carried extraordinary credentials.

Leavenworth Colby was hired as LSU's first law librarian and also assistant professor of law. He was only thirty years old and came with a B.A. from Stanford, an LL.B and LL.M. from Harvard, and a *Diplome d'Etudes Supérieures du Droit Public et du Droit Privé* from the University of Paris. When Colby arrived, he had funds to make significant acquisitions. After a year, however, he wanted to leave the library position because it had become routine and to become a full-time teaching faculty member. The course load he desired was not feasible, and he left after one year.[68] Alice Daspit was named librarian, and she served from 1938 until 1942, the period of greatest expansion of the library.

Thomas A. Cowan was only thirty-two, but he came with a Ph.D. and LL.B. from the University of Pennsylvania and an S.J.D. from Harvard. He left a position as lecturer in jurisprudence at Catholic University to come to LSU, where he stayed until 1940. His Ph.D. thesis reflected Beutel's concern with social science—"Toward an Experimental Definition of the Criminal Mind." Cowan was an early specialist in administrative law, and in 1937 he compiled a mimeographed 418-page casebook, *Administrative Law in Action*. Two other publications show his eclectic breadth—a short compilation of readings on American jurisprudence and a short collection of essays on torts, including a discussion of interference with academic freedom as a tort, air pollution control, and the merger of contract and tort law. *Time* magazine in March 1937 commented favorably on his article about the elasticity that the U.S. Supreme Court had found in the commerce clause in discussing the Lindbergh Law.[69]

Students recalled that Cowan, who had a long nose and a prominent chin, "would call on you to recite, [and] he would generally come and stand right over you, which was rather intimidating." Cowan and Harriet Daggett "were the type of instructors who would get you to a certain point and then sort of leave it to you to go dig out something," unlike Dean Hebert, who "just laid it out." Frank Craig said, "Cowan made a very strong impression on all of us. He taught torts, I believe, and constitutional law, and had a big chin and would look at you and lick his lips, and you had better watch out when he did that! He was a brilliant fellow, and I think all of us enjoyed him, but were scared to death of him." Judge Alvin B. Rubin was complimentary: "Tom Cowan was one of the best teachers I ever had. He was a very agile person mentally, very quick wit, and I thought he was a very effective teacher who brought to the law another dimension because he had a Ph.D. in philosophy and could move easily from philosophical thought to practical legal thought." Cowan stood out as a casual, even sloppy dresser when the other men on the faculty wore dark suits and hats. He never had handles on the door of his car. One day a student asked him how he got into the car; he took a handle out of his pocket.[70]

Student Milton M. Harrison noted that J. Denson Smith's dignity contrasted with Cowan, who "was a clown who walked around the room and read everybody's notes as he was lecturing, caught flies with his fingers, stole cigarettes from the students who had them out on the desk. He was a typical clown. He taught more constitutional law in torts class than he did torts, and more jurisprudence in constitutional law than he did constitutional law. And I am not sure what he taught in jurisprudence." When Cowan left LSU in 1940, he went to the University of Pennsylvania not as a member of the law faculty but as a member of the philosophy faculty. He later followed Beutel to Nebraska and then found happy situations at Wayne State and then Rutgers, where he was both a law and a philosophy professor.[71]

The elderly Pierre Crabites came to LSU after completion of his service as a judge of the Mixed Tribunal in Egypt. He was a Tulane law graduate who had practiced in New Orleans from 1900 to 1911 and then served on the Egyptian Court from 1911 until 1936. Also on the court during most of that time was Robert L. Henry, one of the first members of the law faculty (1907–11). Crabites had studied at the University of Paris and was given the title of Lecturer in Law at LSU. Students mispronounced his name as "Crab-bites." He remained until 1941, teaching legal history and international law. Frank

Craig and Jean Craighead ('40) were the first names on his roll, and after he called out Craig's name, he would say, "Oh, Mr. Craig, I see you have your head here." He laughed at his joke, and that would have been all right except he made the same little joke every time he called the roll. Crabites was also not impressed with his students. He wrote to the dean, "The results on the whole are distinctly disappointing. I have been impressed by the want of anything approaching scholarship shown by the majority of the candidates. Total ignorance of English is, in certain circumstances, clearly discernible. Men who cannot write English will not lend honor to a LSU degree, however profound may be their knowledge of the law."[72]

Crabites was an irrepressible lecturer, traveling around the state and nation to speak. He addressed the local bar association on Egyptian law; the Newman Club on Louis Pasteur; the Department of Romance Languages on the French influence in Egypt; the American Association of University Professors on education in Egypt; and foreign students on "Mohammed, Champion of Women." He told the *Reveille*, "I am determined to put my heart into my new job, and I am counting on the confidence and teamwork of my students to help me accomplish my aims." He said he was impressed by the prevalent feeling at LSU that "the sky is the limit where the University is concerned." The LSU Press published his book *Unhappy Spain*, which traced Spanish history from the reign of Ferdinand VII to current times, and a British firm published his book *Americans in the Egyptian Army*, a study of American participation in the exploration of the Nile Valley.[73]

Fowler V. Harper was thirty-eight when he came to LSU, having earned an M.A. from the University of Iowa and an S.J.D. from the University of Michigan. He had practiced law and then taught at the universities of North Dakota, Oregon, Indiana, and Texas. He was an expert in torts and taught at LSU during the 1936–37 academic year. His salary for that year was $6,500 ($79,000 in Year 2000 dollars), which included a supplement of $1,000 for serving as director of publications. He returned to Indiana for a decade and then became a professor at the Yale Law School. He published a leading treatise, *Harper on Torts*, later *Harper and James on Torts*. Even as late as 1951, he maintained his contacts with LSU, publishing a book review of a study of Hugo Black's opinions in the *Louisiana Law Review*, commenting in passing, "This is no great shakes of a book by any accepted library or scholarly standards." Harper as a teacher was "splendid," according to student B. B. Taylor Jr.

LSU tried to establish a permanent visiting arrangement with him, but it was scuttled when he was appointed general counsel of the Federal Security Agency in 1939.[74]

Charles W. Taintor II was forty and came with an LL.M. from Harvard and recommendations from Dean Roscoe Pound and Professor Warren A. Seavey. He was hired for a one-year term, Dean Beutel explaining that it was "until we could get an economist." He then went to the University of Nebraska for the 1937–38 term and returned to Harvard in 1938 as a Brandeis Fellow, where he obtained the S.J.D. Then he taught at the University of Mississippi from 1939 to 1942 and at the University of Pittsburgh. He coauthored a casebook, *Conflict of Laws*, with Fowler Harper.[75]

Joseph A. Loret continued as an adjunct during the early part of the decade. He taught the code of practice and assisted with moot court. One student explained, "you almost had to learn [it] by rote anyway. It was more technical than it is today, and I don't think anybody is quite as technical as Joe. I remember he used to advise Porterie in the Attorney General's office." Loret was also remembered as a flashy "dandy."[76]

Four LSU faculty members presented papers at the International Congress of Comparative Law, held in The Hague in the summer of 1937. Daggett read her "Succession on Death"; Hall, "The Maintenance or Abandonment of the Rule Nulla Poena sine Lege"; Harper, "Liability for Damage Done by Chattels"; and Ireland, "Contracts Relating to Publications" and "The Individual as Subject of Private International Law." Hall was appointed a general reporter for the congress, with the task of summarizing and drawing together all the papers submitted on criminal law. Dean Beutel said that no other law school had as many faculty members contributing papers, "a singular recognition of the quality of work being done here." *Tourisme juridique* also expressed itself. Harriet Daggett traveled to Genoa after the conference, meeting her son Jack, who had been on a tour around the world with Graduate School Dean Charles W. Pipkin.[77]

A local committee headed by Mrs. Frances L. Landry ('34) was urging the appointment in 1938 of Harriet Daggett as federal district judge for the Eastern District of Louisiana. Also supporting the move were the Women's Faculty Club and Chi Omega sorority alumnae.[78]

An odd entry in the faculty minutes in 1937 was the decision to participate in an AALS-sponsored poll of faculty members about FDR's court-packing plan. Three of the law faculty were in favor (Cowan, Harper, Ireland) and five were opposed (Daggett, Flory, Hall, Smith, Taintor). There were adequate funds to cover the expenses of faculty members attending the annual meeting of the AALS in Chicago.[79]

Colby, Harper, Ireland, and Taintor left LSU at the end of the 1937 academic year.[80] Added for the 1937–38 term were Henry George McMahon, Elmer E. Hilpert, and Leonard Greenburg.

McMahon held A.B., LL.B. ('25), and A.M. degrees from LSU. A native of New Iberia, he practiced in New Orleans until 1936. His part-time teaching at Loyola blossomed into full-time, and he was an associate of Paul M. Hebert there. He was recruited by Beutel and brought to LSU at the rank of professor, effective July 1, 1937. He specialized in procedure and subsequently studied at Northwestern University Law School from 1940 to 1941 under Robert W. Millar, a noted scholar of procedure, and Dean John Henry Wigmore. When he was hired at LSU, he was expected to organize the legal-clinic program that Beutel wanted to develop. He was the main reporter for the Louisiana Code of Civil Procedure and, in 1963, was named the Law School's first Boyd Professor. He remained at LSU, serving as acting dean and dean, until his death in 1966.[81]

Hilpert was an assistant professor with an A.B. and A.M. from the University of Minnesota and the LL.B. from Western Reserve. He also was finishing a doctorate at Yale and taught real property, equity, procedure, and corporations. He stayed for one year and then returned to Western Reserve University, where he had taught political science. Following him there was Brunette Powers, a cataloger in the law library whom he married soon afterward. Dale E. Bennett, a member of the law faculty from 1933 to 1936, who had left to teach at the University of Texas, returned to LSU as a professor to succeed Hilpert.[82]

Greenburg, who had been one of the first research assistants hired by the Law School in the fall of 1935, was an adjunct who taught a course in legal French. He had an A.B., Phi Beta Kappa, and LL.B. from Tulane, and he married Alice Daspit, who was assistant law librarian. The tenor of the times is perhaps shown by Dean Beutel's letter of recommendation for Greenburg stating, "As you will see, he is a Jew; but without any of the characteristics usually associated with that race."[83]

Joseph Dainow arrived for the 1938–39 term, moving from his faculty post at Loyola Law School at an initial salary of $3,800. A native of Montreal, he held the B.A. and B.C.L. from McGill University and a *Docteur en Droit* from the University of Dijon. He had also studied at Northwestern University under Dean Emeritus John Henry Wigmore and received an S.J.D. in 1938. Dainow was the initial faculty editor of the newly organized law review and specialized in civil-code courses as well as international law and conflict of laws. He also is mentioned in the faculty minutes as urging some action to require that students remedy deficiencies in English grammar, a cause he would maintain throughout his career.[84] He retired from LSU in 1973.

Fall 1939 saw the arrival of another prominent faculty member, Wex Smathers Malone. He had been a friend of Thomas Cowan at Harvard and was also recommended by Newman F. Baker, who had taught at LSU and was then at Northwestern. He was hired to replace Jerome Hall in the criminal-law field, at a salary of $4,000 a year, and he was also a co–faculty editor of the law review. Malone taught criminal law for a year, but when Dale Bennett returned to LSU and was assigned torts, they exchanged courses. Both would become the state's leading experts in their new fields. Malone continued to display high academic credentials, B.A. and J.D. from the University of North Carolina and a Master of Laws from Harvard. He had also practiced law in New York City for several years. Malone became LSU's leading national legal scholar, active in drafting the *Restatement of Torts* with his friend William Prosser and other leading torts scholars. He became national president of the Order of the Coif and president of the Association of American Law Schools. He was named a Boyd Professor in 1966 and retired in 1974. Malone arrived when Hebert was dean but served under Acting Dean Flory while Hebert was acting president of the University. In Flory's recommendation to Hebert that Malone be awarded promotion and tenure, Flory also recommended no salary increase, perhaps revealing more about himself than Malone. Flory wrote, "I do not believe it is good policy to advance young men too rapidly in rank or salary. Besides, Mr. Malone's salary was a little high to start."[85] That salary, of course, had been set by Hebert as law dean. Malone was hired from his teaching position at the University of Mississippi, and he was replaced there by Charles W. Taintor II, who had been at LSU.

Among the more experienced faculty members, Harriet Daggett and Denson Smith were polishing their reputations. Richard Gerard ('36) described them as the faculty who really made students think, because by this time Flory merely lectured and would not tolerate a question: "There was a boy named Molaison who failed the class the previous year and he knew every joke that Flory had ever told." Gerard recalled that James B. Smith was also highly regarded, and Dale Bennett was somewhat like Flory, but he would entertain questions.[86]

Paul Hebert continued teaching negotiable-instruments law while serving as acting university president. The faculty minutes noted that James Bugea ('40) had been asked to sit in on the class and to conduct it when Hebert was absent.[87]

B. B. Taylor remembered, "I would say that the very best teacher I had anywhere anytime from kindergarten through law school was Professor J. Denson Smith. We have had applicants for positions in this firm through the years, and I would ask each one what he thought of Denson Smith, and if he thought well of Denson, that was the right answer."[88]

Milton Harrison of the Class of 1941 summed up the experience:

> At that time the faculty consisted of the following teaching first year courses, and I remember very well what a different variety of techniques the faculty had: Denson Smith for contracts, Tom Cowan for torts, Harriet Daggett for family law, Jerome Hall for criminal law and Judge Pierre Crabites for legal history. You could not have found five more different kind of characters all headed in the same direction and hopefully arriving there, but in completely different manners. This I think was probably the strength of the faculty at that time. Daggett was bombastic. Although Crabites was not a great teacher, he had lots of interesting data and information. Hall was a brilliant scholar, but a very poor teacher.[89]

As prospects of war increased, the *Reveille* printed a letter signed by twenty-eight faculty members supporting a plan to bring refugee students to LSU; they pledged $91 to start a fund to support it. Signers included Jerome Hall, Henry G. McMahon, M. G. Dakin, D. E. Bennett, Joseph Dainow, and Thomas A. Cowan.[90] On the same page, ironically showing the spirit of the times, was a headline, ANOTHER GOLDFISH GULPED BY STUDENT: "Miss Patricia 'Pat' Tucker last night held drugstore visitors and evening diners spellbound while she calmly digested a tropical goldfish."

THE EXTRAVAGANT THIRTIES

LECHE HALL

Dean Frederick K. Beutel told the bar association in November 1935 that any good law school needed three essentials: a library of 60,000 to 400,000 volumes, a faculty of ten to thirty scholars devoted to full-time teaching and research, and a building devoted to legal education with adequate facilities for classrooms, laboratories, research, and perhaps student dormitories. Announcement of plans for a new Law School building came in April 1936. It was to be a scaled-down replica of the United States Supreme Court building and was designed by Leon Weiss of the New Orleans firm of Weiss, Dreyfuss, and Seiferth (the firm that also designed the Louisiana State Capitol). Beutel had toured several schools in the East and North to assist in the planning of the new building.[91]

A bid of $678,913.12 won the contract for Caldwell Brothers and Hart, New Orleans contractors. The groundbreaking was led by Governor Richard W. Leche and LSU president James Monroe Smith, and the entire project was said to cost more than $1 million. It was referred to even then as "Leche Hall." Resembling a block T, with classrooms in front, a courtroom/auditorium in the center, and library and offices in the rear, it was constructed of white limestone and located across the large Parade Ground from the main quadrangle buildings in direct line with the Memorial Tower. It was a startling variation from the rambling, arched, two-story stucco buildings on the main quadrangle. The original campus plan, drawn by Olmsted Brothers of Massachusetts (who had designed a similar plan for Stanford University) and then modified by Theodore Carl Link, was harmonious and modest. But the law building was built in a classical style, complete with decorative friezes and Corinthian columns. The architect was somewhat defensive in justifying his different approach: "The white color of the building will not be in harmony with the light tan stucco exteriors of the other housing units on the campus, but its position and the architecture will be distinctive enough to set it off, rather than cause a clash with the general architectural plan of the University."[92]

Fall 1936 saw construction begin on what was now called the "new" $800,000 law building. The *Bulletin* boasted:

Built of limestone and granite, in the style of the new building of the United States Supreme Court, Leche Hall constitutes the largest and most modern law school installation in the South. It occupies the area east of Highland Road. In the central portion facing on Highland Road are lecture halls, seminary rooms, an auditorium, court rooms, library administration, and the offices of the Dean and his staff. A wing extending toward the east contains the central reading room seating more than 150 persons, individual study and conference rooms, professors' offices, space for 120,000 volumes, and study cubicles to accommodate honor and graduate students engaged in special research.[93]

The law building was planned during Beutel's deanship, and one student said that if Beutel didn't actually design it, "he probably tried to tell them how to build it." Other sources report that President Smith claimed to have designed it, that Weiss claimed credit, and that Beutel also claimed credit. But according to Milton Harrison, "I don't know who gets the discredit." Harrison was referring to the fact that movement from the front to the back of the main floor of the building was possible only through the central courtroom/auditorium. The alternative was going down through the basement or up two flights of stairs to the top floor. The single elevator was inside the library stacks. The building had offices for a faculty of eight, plus the dean. Senior faculty members were each to have a corner office, and the junior faculty had the front offices along four galleries around the library stack core. The offices opened into the library stacks, as did smaller offices for secretaries and research assistants. By the time the Law School moved into another new building in 1970, it had grown so much that faculty members were occupying all of these offices, after sending research assistants and secretaries off to other spaces. The building was not air conditioned, but it did feature cork floors.[94]

The offices of the Graduate School occupied the first floor of the building, solidifying the connection between the Law School faculty and the Graduate School faculty. Behind the large courtroom were the quarters of the new School of Public Welfare Administration. The library's reading room had seating for 150 persons at large tables. When the Law School moved out of what is now Thomas Boyd Hall (then called the Administration Building), the *Reveille* and the School of Journalism took over that space.[95]

Architect Weiss conceived of the building on a monumental scale, including substantial art-deco touches to embellish the basic classical building. Marble, mahogany, and sculpture were featured, as in his State Capitol building. Highlighted on the front pediment, above the frieze, were three sculpted life-size figures. The central figure is that of a lawyer with a volume in his hands. On one side stands the figure of a soldier, indicating the part of those who have fought to safeguard rule by law; on the other is the figure of a laborer, representative of the role of the masses in support of law. Inside, above the entrance, was an inscription, "Laws Unsupported by the Morals of the People Are Ineffective." The main courtroom featured marble walls, and the two-level bench at the front featured mahogany panels. A large mahogany bas-relief plaque was set behind the judges' bench, a figure holding the scales of justice in one hand and a book in the other. It was the result of a $500 design competition won by Jules Struppeck, a graduate student in fine arts. When the courtroom was remodeled in 1970, the panel was removed and placed by the contractor in a trash heap, where it was discovered by Professor Robert A. Pascal, who salvaged it and obtained title to it from the contractor. It still hangs in his home.[96]

After climbing the one-story-high entrance steps and entering the two-story foyer, one sees in the floor a circular carved brass seal of the State of Louisiana and on the three walls three circular terra-cotta bas-relief plaques featuring historical figures. At the end of the right hall was the large first-year classroom just past the small practice courtroom. On the left, symmetry was maintained with the large second-year classroom at the end just past the symmetrically small senior classroom. The symbolism of the size of the senior classroom, even if not intentional, was not lost on the incoming freshmen.

The building was largely completed and occupied in December 1937. The formal dedication, a three-day affair held April 6–8, 1938, was in the tradition of the times. VIPs representing law schools throughout the country were present, along with leading judges and lawyers. The event included symposia on trends in legal education, procedural reform, and the position of civil law in America. The dedication corresponded with the formation of the *Louisiana Law Review;* former Harvard law dean Roscoe Pound's address at the dedication, "The Influence of the Civil Law in America," became the first leading article in Volume 1 of the review. Also participating in the dedication were Leon Green, dean at Northwestern, and Charles E. Clark, dean at Yale. Dean

Hebert presided. He would also preside at the dedication of the new law building in 1970.[97]

A full-page photo of the building dominated the *Reveille* issue reporting its dedication. "Leche Hall" was carved in stone along the frieze above the front columns, a second "Leche Hall" was carved over the entrance, and a circular metal medallion of the governor's profile was featured above that. Similar medallions were placed on fifteen other LSU buildings constructed during Leche's term as governor as part of the dedication of twenty-two major buildings constructed since Smith became president of the University.[98] The forty-first convention of the Louisiana Bar Association was also held in the new law building in April 1938.

Ironically, it was Hebert who became acting University president after the Louisiana Scandals broke and President Smith and Governor Leche resigned in June 1939. Leche was convicted in federal court of mail fraud based on sales of trucks to the state's highway department. Although Leche's wrongdoing was not connected with the University scandals, the building was unnamed at the time. The "Leche Hall" stones were reversed, and the Leche medallion was removed. The carved reference to "Leche Hall" on the cornerstone was plastered over, although Leche's identity as governor and member of the LSU Board of Supervisors remained. The structure has since been known simply as the Law Building.

Another of Hebert's clean-up duties as acting president was to announce the discharge of Weiss, Dreyfuss, and Seiferth as University architects. Payment of $25,000 was withheld. Payments to Caldwell Brothers for construction work amounting to $131,000 were also withheld. At issue were "extras" on buildings of more than $350,000, including three different claims of extras for Leche Hall amounting to $119,000, $84,000, and $18,000.[99]

Beutel returned to LSU to lecture in the 1960s. He had never seen the completed new building, although he had planned it. One of the rooms on the same level as the courtroom had been designed as a faculty lounge, with an accompanying washroom. It was not used as such, and Professor Joe Dainow took it over as his office, including the door into the washroom. To keep out traffic through his office, Dainow placed bookshelves in front of that door, so the only entrance to the washroom was through a window. Dakin remembered asking Beutel why he had designed the room with only a window for access.[100]

The *Reveille* in July 1938 ran an advertisement for Coca-Cola announcing the placement of ten new vending machines on campus and featuring an attractive coed inserting a nickel in a machine. The ad announced that one machine was located in Leche Hall. About the same time, the dormitory near Leche Hall that had housed graduate women was turned over to law students. It was believed that LSU was the only law school in the country with its own dorm.[101]

THE LAW LIBRARY

The library volume count at the beginning of the decade was up to 10,000. Beutel had stated that any good law school needed a library of 60,000 to 400,000 volumes, and he set about working toward that goal. He obtained the services of Alice Daspit (later Greenburg) to catalog the law library, which at that point had not been catalogued. Daspit had been an outstanding student at LSU who, as president of the Women's Graduate Club, held one of the highest honors that could come to a woman student. She was a graduate of LSU and of the library science school of Columbia University. Ever the public-relations dean, Beutel announced acquisition of all the civil codes and statutes of Quebec, as well as the reports of the Supreme Court of Canada, as part of a plan to build up the civil-law library. Daspit reported substantial additions to the collection, including old English yearbooks and reports from France, Puerto Rico, and the Philippines, as well as works by French commentators.[102]

Leavenworth Colby was hired in 1936 as assistant professor and was also given the title of librarian. (At the same time, E. Hugh Behymer was hired as assistant librarian and lecturer on legal bibliography. He had an A.B. from Indiana University and an A.B. in library science from Michigan.) The volume count doubled in 1936—on January 1, the library contained 14,000 volumes, and at the end of the year, 28,000 volumes. Many of the additions were gifts, including a full set of the *Harvard Law Review* donated by Isaac Heller, a prominent New Orleans attorney. Chief Justice O'Neill was instrumental in obtaining state government documents, and Congressman Overton Brooks in obtaining federal publications.[103]

The library contained 35,000 volumes in 1937 and was being enlarged at the rate of 10,000 volumes per year. The civil-law collection was the largest in the South and included the Lenel Collection, a private library purchased from Dr. Otto Lenel, privy counselor and professor at the University of Freiburg. He was a world-famous authority on Roman law, and his collection contained more than 6,500 titles on Roman and German law. When Colby came in, as Wex Malone described it, "he got big money from the administration, and the library was growing by leaps and bounds."[104]

After the library moved into its spacious quarters in Leche Hall, the *Reveille* ran a photograph of its "capacious dumbwaiter which runs up and down its shafts, serving the five floors of stacks from which the young lawyers draw their information."[105] The stacks were closed, so students generally had to request books from clerks in the top-floor reading room, and their requests were sent by air tubes to workers in the stacks who retrieved the books. However, law review students were allowed to use carrels in the stacks and to obtain their own books. They soon learned that the dumbwaiter was capacious enough to hold students and to allow them to surprise their friends when the drudgery of footnote-checking had to be overcome.

A letter to the *Reveille* editor from undergraduate student Oliver P. Schulingkamp complained about too much noise and too little fresh air in the main library, Hill Memorial. Seeking a better place to study, students walked across the Parade Ground to the new law library, but the "Law School boys" would "chase all non-law students out of their library because of crowded tables!"[106] Schulingkamp graduated from the LSU Law School in 1943 and later became a district-court judge in the Orleans Criminal Court. The "problem" of undergraduate students trying to study in the law library continued throughout the years, and the new law library still posts a sign that nonlaw students need special permission to enter.

TULLIS MOOT-COURT COMPETITION

Some types of moot-court activities were carried on from the beginning of the Law School. Mostly trial-level exercises, they often served as a form of campus entertainment as well as having an instructional function. Professors Tullis, Flory, Loret, and Bennett had all directed the moots during their tenure. The *Reveille* reported in 1934: "The glamor of a courtroom, where hidden dramas are reenacted, and secrets laid bare, will be brought to Louisiana State University campus, when the senior law students sponsor their annual moot court in April." The prosecutors were Theodore Cangelosi, Bert Bodenheimer, and Ben Dawkins; defense attorneys were Gordon Golson, Will Hall, and J. P. Jewell. Members of the pre-law club served as jurors. The trial involved a manslaughter case based on the movie *The House on 56th Street.* A moot court in conjunction with the journalism department, featuring a libel case, was also planned.[107]

In 1935, under Dean Beutel's modernization program, a more formal appellate moot-court program was instituted and the Student Moot Court Board was established. Beutel's announcement was typically boisterous—an "appellate moot court system, similar to those existing in all large universities, will be installed in the Louisiana State University Law School." It was to be run entirely by a board of honor students. Clyde W. Thurmon, a senior from Ruston, was elected chairman.[108]

The first moot court under the new system was less flashy than a murder plot; it involved the constitutionality of the Holding Company Act. Three judges heard the case: Judge Wayne G. Borah of the Federal District Court, Justice Archibald T. Higgins of the Louisiana Supreme Court, and Judge W. Carruth Jones of the State District Court. George J. Bailey of Abbeville and Clyde W. Thurmon were the finalists, and the winning team was composed of Knowles M. Tucker of Winnfield and Oliver L. Stone of Gretna.[109]

The four finalists in the 1938 competition appeared in front-page photographs in the *Reveille:* John Hickman and William Bronson on one team, and C. Paul Phelps and Horace Holder on the other. The topic again was serious, involving the constitutionality of legislation governing mineral rights. The finals were a matter of importance and prestige, being heard before the five members of the Louisiana Supreme Court—John B. Fournet, Archibald T. Higgins, Frederick M. Odom, Amos L. Ponder, and Wynne G. Rogers. Of course, wherever there's a student board, there is a banquet. Dean Emeritus Robert Lee Tullis was the speaker, along with Henry George McMahon and J. Denson Smith, who were the advisers to the board. Senior members of the board included Joe Sanders, who was then president of the LSU student body and who later became chief justice of the Louisiana Supreme Court. The banquet was the occasion to announce that the moot-court competition would henceforth be named after Dean Tullis. The competition that year was won by William H. Bronson and John A. Hickman.[110]

THE *LOUISIANA LAW REVIEW*

Dean Beutel, responsible for a revitalization of the *Tulane Law Review*, envisioned a law review for LSU, but it was not until the end of the decade that Dean Hebert was able to accomplish the task. President Smith, no doubt pleased with the result of his recommendation to found the *Southern Review* literary quarterly, recommended formation of a law review. The faculty adopted a proposal to do so, a proposal that was debated at length in its details and that included a faculty editor in addition to a student board of editors, but they did not approve a committee recommendation that book reviews be emphasized in the publication. Joseph Dainow was brought to LSU from Loyola specifically to be the faculty editor of the review as well as an assistant professor.[111]

The student editor-in-chief of the first volume of the *Louisiana Law Review* was B. B. Taylor Jr., who remembered that Professor Dainow "made me proof everything over and over again." He said that he personally proofread all 800 or 900 pages in that first law review issue. Taylor obtained his LL.B. from LSU and then a master's at Harvard. That contrasted with DeVan Daggett, Professor Daggett's son, who obtained an LL.B. at Harvard and then returned to LSU for the LL.M. Of Harvard, Taylor said, "their brightest boys weren't any brighter than our brightest boys." But they had many more boys.[112]

The first issue of the review was a *tour de force* showing the strengths of the Law School. Roscoe Pound's address at the dedication of the new law building, "The Influence of the Civil Law in America," was the lead article in Volume 1. Also featured were faculty articles by Harriet S. Daggett, Ira S. Flory and H. G. McMahon, Paul M. Hebert and Carlos Lazarus, Thomas Cowan, and a rare article (on Benjamin Cardozo) by Robert Lee Tullis. The publication of the first issue warranted a front-page *Reveille* photo of Guy Wimberly and F. Hodge O'Neal handing Joseph Dainow the first copy. Soon after, LSU was represented at the first national convention of law review editors by Professor Dainow. The second issue commenced what would become a mainstay of the review, an annual symposium by the faculty commenting on the work of the Louisiana Supreme Court for the previous term.[113]

The faculty chose the members of the law review. In Fall 1939, F. Hodge O'Neal was editor-in-chief and Claude O'Quinn comment editor. James

Bugea and Frank S. Craig Jr. were case-note editors. Six students with GPAs above 1.7 were named as members of the editorial board: Homer Belanger, Jean G. Craighead, Cyrus A. Greco, Lyndon B. Allen, Kenneth J. Bailey, and John M. Shuey. In addition, William Joel Blass, "whose average is only 1.53, but in the light of his Case Note which was published . . . we feel satisfied that he will make a good member of the Board." Work on the review was demanding and time-consuming. In October 1939, O'Neal resigned as chief justice of the Honor Court, and James A. Bugea and Claude O'Quinn, prosecutor and associate prosecutor for the court, also resigned. All three gave as reasons the "heavy work schedules in the Law school."[114]

Blass later became a member of the Mississippi legislature, a faculty member at the Ole Miss law school, and a justice of the Mississippi Supreme Court. O'Neal would obtain law doctorates from Yale (1949) and Harvard (1954) and then serve as law dean at Mercer University, Duke University, and Washington University in St. Louis. His dissertation on partnership law was published in the *Louisiana Law Review* in 1949.[115]

Wherever law reviews are, law review banquets cannot be far behind. The speaker for the first banquet was Dr. William L. Prosser, a friend of Wex Malone who would become a legend in torts law. He was then a professor of law at the University of Minnesota and editor of the *Minnesota Law Review*.[116]

A young secretary named Beverly Denbo became editorial assistant for the review in February 1940 (Volume 3), a position she occupied until her early death in 1972. In Summer 1941, Malone wrote to Acting President Hebert from the University of Texas where he was teaching for the summer, thanking Hebert for keeping up the law review funding but suggesting that funds be moved to give Denbo a $15-per-month raise. Denbo worked with more than thirty student editors-in-chief and numerous faculty editors. She married Charles Walker, who managed the Varsity Shop, and their gracious presence was a feature of generations of law review parties. It was common knowledge that she really ran the law review: "She was really an editor by the end." Several former editors noted that there were faculty editors in charge and there were student editors, but "it is my appreciation that Beverly was the technical editor and the contact between the student editors, the faculty supervisor, and the publishers."[117]

Five women, the largest number yet, enrolled in Fall 1930. The women formed a Co-ed Law Club, also referred to as "Queen's Counselors." The club was accepted into the national sorority Phi Delta Delta and was installed in March 1932 at a luncheon given by Professor Daggett. Charter members were Effie Moncure of Shreveport, Marguerite Abney of Abita Springs, Gwendolyn Webb of Farmerville, Frances Leggio of Baton Rouge, and two alumnae, Mary Bird Perkins of Baton Rouge and Mary Fulmer of Shreveport.[118]

Law students were allowed to attend University senior-class meetings and often dominated them. A *Reveille* headline proclaimed: "Filibustering of Seniors at Meeting Tuesday Is Silenced." The story reported that law students Charles E. Barham and Robert B. Jennings had argued for more than thirty minutes over whether the first candidate nominated was to be the first voted on. An editorial added, "There is no doubt that such meetings are excellent opportunities for lawyers-to-be to stand up in the name of law, order and the inalienable rights of the students. But to bellow forth in none too melodious tones at inopportune moments on what is right and what ought to be right without the slightest provocation is a miscarriage of diplomacy."[119]

Seniors in Fall 1930 started the tradition of sporting hats and black canes with curved handles and a silver band engraved with the student's name, year of graduation, and the words "The Louisiana State University Law School." As the *Reveille* put it, "walking canes will be carried, flourished and brandished" as a "badge to distinguish law seniors." That Class of 1931 announced that it hoped to lay the foundation for a Law School tradition, which indeed became the case. Under the leadership of Ward T. Jones, president of the law students for both the 1931–32 and 1932–33 terms, the seniors decided to wear derby hats and carry canes. In 1934, when the canes arrived, the *Reveille* reported that several seniors were seen swinging them, "but not menacingly as their older law brothers sometimes do when they become infuriated." The Class of 1935 continued the practice, which Frank Purvis, president of the law students, indicated had been in disuse in America but was an integral part of European law-school tradition. A photograph of seniors with the hats and canes continued to be *de rigueur* in the student newspaper; a November 1937 photograph featured Kenneth Banfield, G. M. Bodenheimer, and Maxwell Bordelon.[120]

Graduates of 1932 were the twenty-fifth graduating class of the Law School, and a reunion of graduates was held to celebrate the event. Dean Tullis wrote to the graduates, "You are ordered to show cause, if any you have or can, why you should not attend. Make your return in writing . . . within seven days." Some ninety guests attended the reunion.[121]

The first Edward Douglass White Lecture was held in February 1933, under an arrangement between Dean Charles Pipkin of the government department and Dean Tullis of the Law School whereby each institution chose the speaker in alternate years. The White Lecturer in 1937 was Thomas Reed Powell, Langdell Professor of Law at Harvard and then president of the American Political Science Association. Distinguished Louisiana lawyers also lectured during Spring 1938. Sidney L. Herold, a prominent Shreveport attorney, delivered a lecture titled "Some Problems Involved in Drafting a Mineral Code for Louisiana." Ironically, the top story in the *Reveille* on the day that Herold's lecture was announced featured photographs of a gushing oil well, Duplantier No. 1, located in the University Field south of the campus. The University had leased its 2,100 acres for mineral production in 1936, and it started earning substantial oil and gas revenues, adding to its prosperity. Other speakers in the series were Oliver P. Carriere, president of the law alumni, Archibald T. Higgins, justice of the state supreme court, and Benjamin B. Taylor of the Baton Rouge bar.[122]

LSU's chapter of Omicron Delta Kappa, the national leadership fraternity, was founded in 1933. Among the first fourteen students initiated were two law students, Henry Oscar LeStage Jr., second-ranking senior with a 2.56 average, and Melvin Evans, a junior with a 2.82 average who had served as a cadet major in 1930.[123]

Law students at the time had the opportunity for close relationships with students in the government department, which shared Leche Hall with the Law School. The department, under the leadership of Dean Pipkin of the Graduate School, attracted graduate students from across the country. Alvin Rubin recalled that Hubert H. Humphrey was one of those students, and there was "a lot of discussion at the time about social and economic issues. We were emerging from the depression, the country was in ferment, we were about to enter into a war. There was a lot of interest in social and political problems. I remember that we used to meet the government students in the coffee shop and that was a focus for debate about public issues." International relations and the proposed World Court were common topics of discussion. Professor Daggett lectured to Pipkin's international relations class on "The World Court and the Development of International Law Since 1920." Daggett and Pipkin were among twelve LSU faculty members who sent a telegram to President Franklin D. Roosevelt urging United States membership in the World Court. The society page of the student newspaper reported that Daggett had spoken to women students on the role that women should play in keeping the United States out of another war. Pipkin and Daggett also took part in the first annual session of the New Orleans Institute of International Affairs.[124]

Law students continued to participate in general campus activity. Bob Chinn was president of the student body, as were Russell Long and Vernon Woods. Many law students were on the debate team. In December 1935, law students Sam Wells and Aubrey Hirsch debated a visiting Oxford University debating team. The British debaters "both humorously and logically overwhelmed" the local debaters. Dressed in tweeds and speaking in their "splendidly modulated British diction," they presented a decided contrast to the LSU debaters' more formal styles of dress and oration. In 1939, the LSU debaters in a match against a British team were John Makar, a junior in the Law School, and Hubert H. Humphrey, then a teaching assistant in the Department of Government and Public Affairs. When he first arrived at the Law School, Makar was the subject of a feature article that included a photograph of him holding two decks of fanned-out playing cards. According to the article, he was a "professional magician, prestidigitator, sleight-of hand performer" who had appeared throughout the country.[125]

President Smith approved formation of a separate honor court for the Law School, foreshadowing things to come as law students began the slow process of separation from the main student body. Professor Flory, acting dean of the school, supported the move.[126]

Depression times were hard for most students. Sam D'Amico lived with a sister; otherwise, he recalled, "I would never have seen the inside of LSU." He added: "I used to sign a note every semester and pay it during the semester. That is the one thing that I give credit for to Dr. Smith who was then president of the University and . . . the bursar . . . for lending students money and helping them to get through school."[127]

Richard Gerard ('36) remembered that Huey Long came to the University periodically, gave talks in the Greek Theater, and then ordered the manager of the Field House to give students free candy and ice cream. Gerard went to football games on the trips that Huey sponsored.[128]

In the 1934 graduating class, Frances Leggio (later Landry) was the valedictorian, the first woman to win the honor, and her average was among the highest ever made. She did not recall being discriminated against; indeed, she said that her classmates "decided that I was taking pretty good notes; so that was one of the reasons they were so very nice to me." In her class, there was only one married man, "and we all felt sorry for him." DeLesseps S. Morrison, later mayor of New Orleans, was in the class; also Ben Dawkins Jr., later a federal district judge, and Theo Cangelosi, later a prominent lawyer and political leader in Baton Rouge. That class was also the first to have Paul M. Hebert as a teacher. Leggio was the only woman in her freshman class, but there were three women in the junior class and one woman in the senior class. When Leggio graduated, she was the only woman in the Law School. Few woman followed her, she thought, because of the financial difficulties at the time. Indeed, she worked afternoons as a secretary for two of her three years in law school. Many students had to keep two jobs to stay afloat.[129]

The *Reveille* reported in July 1933 that twenty-six students had earned straight-A averages for the previous term, three of them in the Law School: Frances Leggio, Melvin Evans, and William M. Hall. In the Fall 1935 semester, the overall student average for the University was 1.265 ($C = 1$; $B = 2$; $A = 3$). The Law School was more rigorous; its seniors averaged 1.224, juniors 1.139, and freshmen .876. The valedictorian in the Class of 1937, Albert T. Hughes, had a 2.507 average. B. B. Taylor Jr., valedictorian in 1939, had a 2.411 average.[130]

Richard Kilbourne ('35) remembered that LSU students were "more or less country boys like me." He said a "different class" of people went to Tulane, which "was always a pretty expensive school, too." During this time, graduates who took the bar exam were informed whether they had passed or failed "by coming down to the [supreme court] courtroom on the day of the swearing-in ceremony. If your name appeared on the list you went in, and you were sworn in. If your name was not on the list, you went home." LSU

Law School graduates continued to perform well on the exam. All six LSU graduates who took the winter bar exam in 1934 passed. Professor James Barclay Smith reported to the *Reveille* that the entire 1935 class had passed the exam.[131]

Few students married during law school, and they tended to hang around the school most of the day and evening. The "bull room" near the library reading-room entrance was the scene of many discussions, both on the law and on other topics. Law students often ate together, and the focus of social activity and jokes was the Law School. Law students in 1934 formed a basketball team to compete with agriculture students at the rodeo in November, the game played by bareback riders on horses and mules.[132]

The *Reveille* in October 1936 ran an interview with law freshman Claiborne Dameron of Port Allen. He was in his fifth year at LSU and entered the Law School after he received a B.A. "because I've always wanted to be a lawyer—with mixed motives of a desire to mete out justice, and a desire to earn a living." Law school required a change of study habits, he reported, requiring about three hours of concentrated study to get up two assignments. "Class attendance is not required, but we do have to keep up with the work." There was a strong spirit of camaraderie among law students, but Dameron said that finding jobs would be difficult: the law was a crowded field, with little opportunity for the women graduates.[133]

In 1938, Dameron ran for president of the student body against undergraduates Russell Long and J. M. Bennett. A letter to the *Baton Rouge Morning Advocate* written by Long's campaign manager referred to Dameron as "that rabble-rouser of the shyster factory." In response, Henry Lastrapes Jr., president of the Law School student body, demanded an apology on behalf of the school and decried the "degradation of any department of the University." At a later rally, Long's campaign manager, Dayton McCann, was continuously heckled by members of the audience who kept reminding him of his record—one year—in the Law School. Another speaker said that he was backing Long because "the Law seniors are trying to cram a candidate down your throat. All they are interested in is putting a man in office simply to have it to say that they were able to do so." Long received 1,892 votes, Dameron 1,203, and Bennett 796. In the runoff, Long received 2,100 votes and Dameron 1,650. Dameron was later selected as an Honor Court justice.[134]

Two French lawyers were exchange students at LSU in Fall 1937. Jean Antoine Blanchard, a graduate of the University of Bordeaux, planned to take a master's in government, and Suzanne Laclavere, who held a law degree from the University of Paris, planned to work on an LL.B. In 1938, Jean Meunier, a candidate for the *Docteur en Droit* from the University of Paris, was a student in the Law School. A member of the French Reserve, his arrival was delayed because of the war crisis. In exchange, Kenneth Banfield of Baton Rouge left for studies in France in August.[135]

Dr. Phoebe Morrison, one of three women professors of law in the country, lectured at LSU in September 1938. She also met with the Phi Delta Delta chapter and assisted the group in initiating Jean Craighead and Mrs. Charlie Holcomb Pitcher. Morrison, then an assistant professor at Yale Law School, had been a fellow student of Harriet Daggett's at Yale. (The third woman law professor was Barbara Nachtrieb Armstrong at the University of California in Berkeley.) A *Reveille* editorial boasted of the number of women students at LSU, referring to a movement in the late 1920s to keep women on the old campus and for the girls to have classes by themselves. "And this probably would have been the condition today if Dr. Smith hadn't exerted his influence to have the women students moved to this campus."[136]

On the eve of April Fool's Day, 1939, Frank Craig and B. B. Taylor climbed to the top of the Law School roof and then to the portico gable and placed a hat on the head of one of the carved figures featured there. "Frank Craig is sitting on my leg, my ankles, and I'm leaning over the front of the law building from my entire waist and arms and head. . . . I believe after we used the two canes and jammed the thing on his head. . . . It was great! We couldn't wait for the next day, April 1st. The next day there was nothing there." As it turned out, the night watchman they had bribed to let them into the stairway later went out and removed the hat.[137]

Alvin Rubin and Guy Wimberly were in a close contest for first and second rank in the class. "We made a great pretense of not studying. There used to be a dance, tea-dances and regular dances on Friday night. . . . Some were on Saturday night. I made it a point to appear at every one of these to which I was duly invited in order to give the appearance of being a wastrel of my time; so that he was thinking that I was not studying. He was there, too, and I'm sure he was doing exactly the same thing."[138]

A dormitory for women graduate students near Leche Hall became a law dormitory in the late 1930s, and "it apparently was a wild, wild situation. It was at the Law Dorm, I think that the infamous skunk stories started . . . with Guy Wimberly waking up one morning with a skunk on the foot of his bed and that skunk eventually ended up over in the Deke House, I believe." Actually, "Sparky Wade got the skunk from somebody over at the KA House, and he thought it would be great fun to take it to the Deke House, and somebody took it from the Deke House to Guy Wimberly's." Wimberly, for some reason, was called "Skunk" Wimberly, "so somebody decided to take it to his bed." The dormitory housed about sixty law students, and other students lived in fraternity houses and other places nearby, so that students were at the law building almost all day. Between classes, they were either in the library or in the "bull room," a lounge near the library entrance, until the library closed at 11 P.M. Only three students had cars, so there was nothing else to do, unless a student chose to go out of town for the weekend.[139]

Law School students as the decade was ending became "real tense about the whole world at the time." The student newspaper included more and more stories about the prospects of war. Dr. Leo J. Lassalle, dean of the College of Engineering, spoke to the YMCA on the European crisis, predicting a European conflict in which the U.S. would become involved. Interviews with European students centered on talk of war. A new faculty member was the famed sociologist Rudolph Heberle, who had fled Germany. Professor Pierre Crabites spoke to the Newman Club on the Czech crisis, predicting that a long war must involve America, and Kimbrough Owen, former *Reveille* editor and a student at European universities the previous year, spoke to students at the Methodist Student Center on the European situation. Fifteen LSU exchange students arrived in Le Havre to find Europe calmer but still seething with threats of war.[140]

FACULTY TIMELINE

1929–30	Tullis	Flory	Gore	Daggett	Smith, J. B.						
1930–31	Tullis	Flory	Gore	Daggett	Smith, J. B.						
1931–32	Tullis	Flory	Gore	Daggett	Smith, J. B.	Hebert					
1932–33	Tullis	Flory	Daggett	Smith, J. B.	Hebert						
1933–34	Tullis	Flory	Daggett	Smith, J. B.	Bennett						
1934–35	Flory	Daggett	Smith, J. B.	Bennett	Smith, J. D.						
1935–37	Flory	Daggett	Bennett	Smith, J. D.	Hebert	Beutel					
1936–37	Flory	Daggett	Smith, J. D.	Hebert	Beutel	Hall	Ireland	Colby	Cowan	Harper	Tain
1937–38	Flory	Daggett	Smith, J. D.	Hebert	Hall	Ireland	Crabites	Harper	Nilpert	McMahon	
1938–39	Flory	Daggett	Smith, J. D.	Hebert	Bennett	Hall	Cowan	Crabites	McMahon	Dainow	
1939–40	Flory	Daggett	Smith, J. D.	Hebert	Bennett	Cowan	Crabites	McMahon	Dainow	Malone	

5

THE FORTIES:
WORLD WAR II AND POSTWAR CHALLENGES

BEFORE THE WAR

The resignations of President James Monroe Smith and Governor Richard W. Leche and the subsequent scandals moderated the exuberance of the 1930s. The oncoming prospect of American involvement in World War II put students and faculty in a transitional limbo of uncertainty. Paul M. Hebert became acting LSU president in 1939, and Ira S. Flory became acting dean of the Law School.

Enrollment in the 1939–40 term was 134 students—57 first-year students, 31 second-year, 33 third-year, 9 in the last year of the four-year curriculum, and 1 graduate student. The majority of students were opting to take three years of pre-legal work before entering law school rather than choosing the four-year law program. Nearly half of the first-year students had obtained bachelor's degrees before entering law school. Flory remained acting dean during the 1940–41 term, until Paul M. Hebert's return that summer. With eleven members, the law faculty was still large for a declining student body. In addition to Flory and Paul M. Hebert, who taught part time, the continuing faculty included Professors Harriet S. Daggett and Henry G. McMahon, Associate Professor J. Denson Smith, Assistant Professors Dale E. Bennett, Joseph Dainow, and Wex S. Malone, and Lecturer/Librarian Alice Daspit. Joining the faculty that term were Professor Jefferson B. Fordham and Instructor Clyde W. Thurmon.[1]

Fordham, thirty-five years old, was an experienced professor who had been chief bond attorney for the federal Public Works Administration from 1939 to 1940. He replaced Thomas Cowan. An expert in local-government law, Fordham had the A.B., M.A., and J.D. from the University of North Carolina and a J.S.D. from Yale. He served at LSU until 1946, and later he became law dean at Ohio State University and then at the University of Pennsylvania. Fordham was paid $5,500 a year, the top professional salary in the Law School, and developed expertise in legislation and local-government law. He continued his interest in LSU over the years, visiting in Spring 1974 to assist in teaching a course on legislation. He had also been asked by delegate Walter I. Lanier ('61) to comment on the 1973 Constitutional Convention proposal on local government law. Fordham wrote that he was pleased that the proposal "reflects some of my notions" but predictably also stated that the proposal was too long and too detailed.[2]

Thurmon ('36) was an LSU law graduate from Ruston who was chairman of the first Student Moot Court Board and a finalist in the moot-court competition. He was a research assistant to Professor Daggett and a special lecturer in Spring 1940. He taught for one full term and was scheduled to teach again in 1941–42; however, the University Budget Committee cut personnel as the budget decreased, and as the youngest faculty member, Thurmon was notified that he would not be continued after that term. With that uncertain prospect, he resigned in August 1941 and joined the law firm of Blanchard, Goldstein, Walker, and O'Quin in Shreveport. He became a leading property and mineral-law expert.[3]

No curriculum committee was appointed in Fall 1941, and the entire law faculty acted on the extensive curriculum problems "on account of the decrease in enrollment and the national emergency." Enrollment declined to 104 students in Fall 1940. The 1941 *Bulletin* announced that the four-year curriculum in law had been discontinued, and enrollment in Fall 1941 was down to 71 students—25 first-year, 18 second-year, and 28 third-year. Tuition was still not charged to Louisiana residents, and the general fee for law students was $27.50. Freshmen and juniors were required to pay a $1.50 Senior Cane and Derby Fee to buy hats and canes to be given to the seniors. The library then consisted of about 42,000 volumes.[4]

Registration for the military draft was conducted on campus in Fall 1940. All males between twenty-one and thirty-five were required to register, and the *Reveille* featured a photograph of thirty-two-year-old Paul M. Hebert completing his form. He was one of the few university presidents young enough to be included in the draft. Hebert served as acting president from June 27, 1939, to June 30, 1941, when he returned to the Law School as dean.[5]

Major General Campbell Blackshear Hodges was selected by the Board of Supervisors as the new University president. Hodges, then sixty years old, was commander of the Fifth Corps Area of the U.S. Army and had been commandant at the U.S. Military Academy at West Point. He had been offered the presidency of LSU in 1926, but he did not accept it when he learned he could not retain his full military status if he accepted. In 1930 he was a candidate again, but because Hodges was known as an anti-Long, Huey intervened and named James Monroe Smith to the position. Paul Hebert, who was one of six finalists considered for the presidency, was commended by the Board for his service as acting president. He and sociologist Fred C. Frey were the two internal candidates. Student groups had recommended that Hebert be selected as permanent president and petitioned newly elected Governor Sam H. Jones to keep Hebert and Troy H. Middleton, vice-president and comptroller, in their positions.[6]

Speculation over the years has included the rumor that Hebert was not selected as president because of the anti-Catholic sentiments of some Board members, particularly Thomas Dutton. In his biography of Troy H. Middleton, Frank J. Price quotes the former president as saying, "I worked openly for Mac's appointment as president both before the Board of Supervisors chose Campbell Hodges and before it picked Harold Stoke. I am convinced that religious prejudice alone prevented Hebert's selection." It is of course true that Hebert was a leading Catholic layman, later to be a Knight of St. Gregory, but when asked by this writer in the early 1970s, he said that he did not think that religion played a part in the selection of the president. Also, Professor Melvin G. Dakin, in an oral-history interview, said, "I would be surprised if that [anti-Catholicism] would be carried to the point of excluding him from the presidency. I think there were other factors that worked there."[7]

Indeed, there were several other factors at work. Although Hebert's performance as acting president was outstanding, he was only thirty-three at the time, and the conservative Board of Supervisors would be expected to go with age and experience. Hebert did not come from the military-service tradition that many of the Board members were steeped in as undergraduates, the tradition of General Sherman and the Colonels Boyd. The Board was largely anti-Long by 1941, reflecting Governor Sam Jones's appointments, and members recalled what had occurred when a nonmilitary innovator like James Monroe Smith was named president. Also, the Longites in control of the Board in 1930 did not consider General Hodges when they selected Smith, to the disappointment of many Hodges supporters. The selection of a sixty-year-old retired army general from conservative north Louisiana seemed to meet the Board's goals and concerns. Also, the American Legion movement on campus was strong and urged similar goals and concerns. Many of the agriculture, engineering, and education faculty members were wary of the more liberal humanities and social-science faculty hired during the 1930s and feared that Hebert would be more tolerant of them than other candidates might be.[8]

When Hebert returned to the deanship, he had to deal with a distinguished faculty that was hardly shy and retiring. The law faculty was then engaged in committee discussions with the goal of drafting a statement of the objectives of legal education. "Mr. Malone, the chairman of this committee, reported that the three members of the committee had been unable to agree upon any single statement of such objectives and, consequently, he presented the three statements submitted by members of the committee." Typically, a long discussion ensued, but no decision was taken; they agreed to discuss the matters at a later meeting. The law faculty also had substantial discussions of curriculum changes, including the issue of whether to establish introductory courses to the common law and the civil law. The faculty minutes also record discussions of the quality of the law review. Dean Hebert "stated his impression of the caliber of student work in the last issue of the Review did not compare favorably with the quality of such work done at Tulane in past years and further pointed out that there was a complete absence of doctrinal civil law materials in any of the notes or comments of the last issue. Mr. Malone replied that he did not feel competent to express an opinion as to any work done in civil law fields but that he would challenge any criticism as to the case notes and comments within the realm of public law."[9]

The law faculty approved a petition to the Order of the Coif to establish a chapter at LSU, with Jefferson B. Fordham preparing the petition and Wex S. Malone assisting. Typically, the all-knowing faculty concerned itself with minutiae: "There was some discussion concerning whether the petition should be mimeographed or reproduced through a new process which involves the use of plates. The problem was referred to Fordham, and he was given full power to make the choice."[10]

Carlos Enrique Lazarus was a visiting professor during 1941–42 and also taught in the summer school.[11] He was a native of Honduras who earned a law degree at Loyola in New Orleans in 1937 after receiving a Bach. Comm. in 1931 from the Municipal School of Commerce in Manchester, England. Lazarus had been a researcher at LSU from 1937 until 1939, taught at Loyola from 1940 to 1941, then worked for the Louisiana State Law Institute on a number of its projects. He eventually became a full-time member of the law faculty in 1961, a position he held until his retirement in 1981.

Dale Bennett was actively working with the Louisiana State Law Institute on a criminal code for Louisiana. A consultant advising him was Newman F. Baker, then at Northwestern University Law School, who had taught at LSU in 1927–28. In September 1941, he and Bennett were involved in an accident driving to New Orleans for a meeting of the advisory committee. Baker was killed, and Bennett was seriously injured. A prominent visitor in Spring 1941 was Edward S. Corwin, then probably the most important constitutional-law scholar in the country. A professor at Princeton, he was visiting two of his students who were members of the government faculty. The Law Institute's February meeting was held at the Law School, and in addition to work on the criminal code, members heard an address by U.S. Solicitor General Francis Biddle. Work was also in progress on Harriet Daggett's compilation of statutes related to the civil code and John Minor Wisdom's report on a nonprofit corporation statute for Louisiana.[12]

New courses offered in 1940–41 included legislation and municipal corporations taught by Jefferson B. Fordham and trade regulation taught by Wex Malone. Courses not taught the previous year returned—insurance by J. Denson Smith, trusts by Harriet Daggett, and taxation by Fordham.[13]

F. Hodge O'Neal, who had been undergraduate valedictorian, was the valedictorian of the 1940 law class. He had an astounding 2.97 (out of 3.0) average and was awarded a Sterling Fellowship worth $1,500 for study at Yale. The valedictorian of the Class of 1941 was Kenneth J. Bailey of Abbeville. The *Reveille* continued to publicize the high bar-exam passage rate for LSU graduates. The Board of Supervisors was not so boastful. When a member announced the Law School graduates' outstanding performance on the bar exams, the Board decided to refrain from publishing such information "as it might be construed as a reflection upon the other law schools of the state."[14]

Harriet Daggett reported at a faculty meeting that the wife of a senior student was seriously ill after a miscarriage and that the couple was in serious financial difficulty. The faculty asked the dean to inquire how they could aid the student. "It was understood that after such inquiry, Dean Hebert would call upon each faculty member to make a contribution and that the total of such contributions would be applied by him as he thought best." The student newspaper reported Professor Daggett's talk to the YWCA on marriage. Among her comments were, "You can't always marry a sirloin steak, girls, more than likely you wind up with stew meat." In light of the military buildup, she warned the women to "beware of uniforms which are numerous now—they do something for every man." More seriously, she talked about the importance of the family and the decline of the American family—this was 1941. A sign of the times as the military draft was imposed was a *Reveille* article by lawyer-to-be Eddie Carmouche arguing that capital as well as labor should be conscripted.[15]

It was the custom during this period for moot-court trials to be based on acted-out incidents rather than cold records. The *Reveille* described one incident in March 1941, calling it the annual Law School hoax. It was a "kidnaping" in front of Evangeline Hall. A car stopped in front of the girls' dormitory, three couples came out of the dorm, and two men wearing overcoats walked up to the first couple, Kathleen Walker and Sidney Myers. Miss Walker was seized and dragged to the car. Myers, who was not in on the scheme, tried to stop the kidnaping and was knocked down long enough for the defendants to escape. Myers followed, attracting the attention of a night watchman, who simply walked away. Complaints were made to the police, who had been warned in advance and did nothing. Complaints to the *Reveille* were made, and ultimately Miss Walker was found by the student playing the sheriff. Walker and Myers later married and lived in Shreveport. The practice of acting out the crimes was also borrowed by the Pelican Boys State program for high-school students. In preparing for a kidnaping mock trial, a kidnaping occurred near Foster Hall and the victim was rushed away in a waiting car.[16]

Many Law School graduates were entering political life. As the Louisiana legislature met in 1940, the *Reveille* reported on graduates of LSU's Law School who were members. They included James J. Bailey, East Baton Rouge ('34); Theo Cangelosi, East Baton Rouge ('34); Francis Edwards, St. Landry ('37); A. K. Goff Jr., Ruston ('31); Walter Lanier, Thibodaux ('29); Ragan Madden, Lincoln ('33); Beverly Middleton, Iberville ('37); Turner B. Morgan, Caddo ('35); deLesseps Morrison, New Orleans ('34); and Joe Sanders, Sabine ('38).[17]

Russell B. Long was a first-year law student in 1940 when he stood in line to vote for the first time. As the *Reveille* headline put it, "Huey's Son Can't Vote." Though the previous year's student-body president presented a poll certificate, he discovered that he had failed to register to vote. "This is the most embarrassing moment of my life," he said. "Imagine a fellow studying law and not knowing how to vote."[18]

Politically active law students organized a Wendell Wilkie Club in Fall 1940. Organizers included Homer Lombard, Earl Morgan, Walter Peters, William Shaw, and Robert Williams. Counselors for the Honor Court were featured in a front-page *Reveille* photograph in October 1940. John Makar, chief justice, appointed Sargent Pitcher Jr. and Joseph G. Stulb Jr. as prosecutors, and J. Wilfred Landry Jr. and Alva Jones as defense counselors. Assistants were Alvin B. Rubin and Jack Burgess. Makar apparently had free time despite his law studies and Honor Court activities; he was featured in a *Reveille* feature story touting his skills as a magician. He had formerly toured with vaudeville summer shows and was booked as the "boy magician."[19]

AFTER PEARL HARBOR

Upon hearing news of the attack on Pearl Harbor, some 1,500 LSU students gathered for a spontaneous rally to denounce Japan. The students, some of them intoxicated, sang patriotic songs and yelled "Go to hell, Tokyo, go to hell." Professor Flory brought a radio to class, and the students listened to FDR's address to Congress and the nation. Flory then gave a patriotic speech and told the class that they should join the armed forces. On the other hand, in a speech to the student body, president and former general Campbell B. Hodges told the students to go back to class and study. They would serve their country best by finishing their studies instead of rushing off to war, he said.[20]

The Association of American Law Schools, meeting after war was declared, suspended some of its standards so that schools could accommodate students who wanted to enter military service and were unable to complete their schoolwork in a normal way. The LSU faculty allowed special examinations, "written or oral," for seniors about to be called into the military service. The Law School authorized a course in military law that would be offered to students throughout the University. A student who was about to be inducted had eighty-one hours of credit but was lacking three quality points required for a C average; he was allowed to graduate by a unanimous vote. The bar-exam committee recommended and the state supreme court adopted a proposal that restored the diploma privilege to graduates of approved Louisiana law schools who served in the military. A first-year student who reported that he would be called up within ten days was given special examinations in the courses he was taking. A senior about to be inducted into the navy, Aubrey Bacon, was granted an LL.B. degree with 68½ hours of credits. He was later killed in action.[21]

Another major impact on the Law School was the departure of Dean Hebert into the armed forces. He went on military leave on April 13, 1942, to serve as a captain, then major, then lieutenant colonel, in the army Judge Advocate General's office. He was chief of the Industrial Law Branch and influential in ensuring the cooperation of industry in the war effort. Henry George McMahon was named acting dean, but in July McMahon announced his impending entry into the armed services as a lieutenant, later lieutenant commander, in the navy. Dale E. Bennett succeeded him as acting dean. The faculty continued to dwindle as J. Denson Smith entered the army, serving as a captain in the Judge Advocate General's office, Jefferson B. Fordham joined the navy as a lieutenant, then lieutenant commander, and Joseph Dainow became a captain in the army Judge Advocate General's office. Wex Malone was on leave of absence for the 1942–43 academic year to become a senior attorney in the Defense Public Works Administration.[22]

The law faculty shared the wartime burden with the general LSU faculty. From July 1, 1941, to June 30, 1942, 57 faculty members gave up their positions to enter military service. From July 1, 1942, to October 15, 1942, 90 members left for the military. More than 150 LSU faculty members took leave to serve the war effort in military and civilian capacities. By Fall 1942, the regular law faculty consisted of Bennett, Daggett, and Flory. Daggett was appointed acting director of the Louisiana State Law Institute in Fall 1942 after Smith left for the military service. Bennett also served as an assistant to the president during the war years. At that point, midterm examinations were instituted to provide a means of giving credit to students called up before final examinations were given. The extra work of grading midterm exams was apparently too much for the diminished faculty; the exams were abolished in Fall 1943.[23]

As the faculty was reduced, courses were canceled and freshman students began taking upper-level courses—whatever was offered. Covering courses was a problem, and local attorneys were called on to assist. A. Leon Hebert, an honors graduate in 1937, served as a part-time lecturer teaching Louisiana practice. Richard O. Rush, valedictorian of the Class of 1943, was awarded "a year to year contract for the duration" as instructor. Frances Leggio Landry, Class of 1934 valedictorian, taught corporations, agency, and partnership. She said, "We were trying to keep the law school together, we were trying very hard to do it and in my class I had freshmen, juniors and seniors, and that was very hard to do."[24]

Since 1935, J. Denson Smith had been faculty secretary and signed the faculty minutes. During the war years, Florence H. Molaison took the minutes, identifying herself as "Secretary, Law School." Mrs. Molaison, with a B.A. from LSU in 1936, had been a legal secretary. She would remain as the dean's secretary and was associated with the Law School until her retirement in 1976. At a time when the top positions were not available to women, she was one of the many very competent women who served as middle managers at LSU and were a core of stability in the administration. Molaison's extraordinary competence was acknowledged by the students, to whom she was affectionately known as the "Gray Dean," reflecting both her powers and her silver hair.

In 1942, the Law School switched to a trimester schedule, extending the summer program and providing three terms of fifteen weeks each. On the main campus, the academic year was extended from nine months to twelve, so that students could graduate with a bachelor's degree in three calendar years.[25]

The program of the Law School was not suspended during the war years as was the case at some universities. Rather, the wartime program allowed students already enrolled to accelerate their progress before entering military service, allowed new students to proceed as far as possible before entering military service, and accelerated the training of students ineligible for military service to meet demands for personnel in government positions and private practice. Under the accelerated program, students could begin studies in any session, and it was possible to graduate during two academic years and two summer terms. Admission standards were relaxed to accept students with two years of college work.[26]

It was during this wartime period that LSU obtained a chapter of the Order of the Coif. Installation ceremonies were held on May 16, 1942, with

Dean Charles T. McCormick of the University of Texas Law School conducting the installation. The first honorary member chosen was Dean Emeritus Robert Lee Tullis, and the first president of the chapter was Professor Ira S. Flory. Three students were inducted: G. Dupre Litton, Russell B. Long, and Alvin B. Rubin. Rubin and Harvey Posner were law students who continued to be active in campuswide activities: Posner was president of Omicron Delta Kappa, and Rubin served as vice-president. Winners of the Tullis Moot Court Competition that year were Russell Long and Elmer Gordon West. Later, Senator Long would of course be instrumental in the naming of West and Rubin to the federal bench.[27]

Another illustrious member of the 1942 class was John J. McKeithen, who was elected Louisiana's governor in 1964. He recalled that he didn't have any difficulty in law school, but many of his friends did. That prompted him to be critical of the school, and he said that he was interested in "improving the method of teaching out there." Students "didn't know what the teacher wanted [them] to say in the [examination] paper." He cited his moot-court partner, who made an F in family law: "It shocked him so that he left school." McKeithen complimented Dean Hebert because, when a class was over, he would tell the class actually what the law was: "He was one of the few that would do that. The rest of them would just leave you out there." McKeithen cited Denson Smith, who "was the worst at that that I have ever seen in my life. . . . He would confuse you and leave you there." As with most students, McKeithen remembered his high grade. Wex Malone taught him criminal law, and McKeithen recalled, "I am proud to say that he told me that I had written the best paper in the class."[28]

McKeithen also recalled that Litton and Long were the envy of their classmates; both had state jobs while in school and owned automobiles. Alvin Rubin was far above his classmates in overall average, "but we had a group from the Shreveport area, and I won't call their names . . . who did not want Alvin to be valedictorian because he was a Jew." Rubin was, of course, selected as valedictorian. Litton recalled that about seventy-five students entered in 1939, and about a third of that number were graduated in 1942. Rubin was in the combined commerce and law course. The class had an unusual number of married students: Litton, Long, Mrs. Horace Lane, Mrs. Jean L. Percy, Mrs. Sargent Pitcher, and James T. Spence.[29]

Student enrollment continued to dwindle. In 1943, sixteen students were graduated; in 1944, five; in 1945, only three. One student remembered that when she entered in 1942, there were only about five people in her class: "There were just women and cripples." The law review continued in operation, as did the custom of a law review banquet. It was held at Mike and Tony's Restaurant "with the cost to be divided equally" among the faculty members. When Paul Hebert visited Baton Rouge on leave in 1943, he was a major and was the speaker at the banquet. Frank Purvis ('35) was an adjunct professor at LSU for two years, teaching insurance law when he returned from military service. He also taught insurance law at Tulane.[30]

The Louisiana Criminal Code came up for a vote in the legislature in 1942. Reporter Dale Bennett said that two law students who were also legislators, Wilbur T. "Brandy" McCain and W. O. "Bulldog" Noble, were taking his criminal-law course at the time. They played an important part in the adoption of the code. McCain, a senior law student, was appointed chief justice of the Honor Court in February 1943. Moot-court trials took on a change during the war as senior students in infantry studying military law conducted trials in the Law School courtroom. Cadet Colonel John Laborde, regimental commander and a law student, found a defendant accused of desertion in time of peace guilty. A Panamanian student, Roberto Aleman, was one of the 1943 graduates and editor of the law review. He was attached to Panama's embassy in Buenos Aires for two years after graduation and then began practicing law in Panama City. He visited the Law School in 1956 after he had represented his country at a meeting of American presidents called by President Eisenhower. He also returned in 1976 to accept an award of honorary membership in the Louisiana chapter of the Order of the Coif.[31]

The Class of 1945 had three graduates, Betty Ann Gremillion Ratcliff, editor-in-chief of the law review, Evelyn Cole, and Horace Pepper. But overall, there were more men than women in the whole law student body. Gremillion was Dean Hebert's research assistant when he left for military service, and she returned to the Law School to be his assistant after she passed the bar.[32]

THE POSTWAR ERA

By 1944, plans were underway to accommodate an influx of veterans attending law school. Acting Dean Bennett announced that an accelerated program would continue:

Under the accelerated war-time program, it is possible for a student to complete his law course in two full calendar years. This has helped the law school in seeking to meet the demands of law offices, state departments, and federal agencies for law-trained personnel. Discharged veterans are also beginning to return to the law school, and the accelerated plan will be continued as long as it is necessary in order to afford these men an opportunity to partially make up for the time spent in the service of their country. Refresher courses for soldier-lawyers, who completed their legal training before the war, will serve as a further aid to returning veterans.[33]

Wex Malone returned to the campus in June 1944, before the influx of veterans. He had a torts class of nine students, "and they were all practically handicapped in one way or another." Hebert returned from military leave effective September 17, 1945, followed by Smith, McMahon, Dainow, and Fordham. Fordham left LSU for a professorship at Vanderbilt University in Fall 1946, then went on to deanships at Ohio State and the University of Pennsylvania and a professorship at the University of Utah.[34]

After he completed his military service with the U.S. Coast Guard in 1945, Robert A. Pascal joined the LSU Law School faculty as a full-time assistant professor. In doing so, he passed up an opportunity to teach with Frederick Beutel, who was then dean of the law school at the University of Nebraska. Pascal had a law degree from Loyola, New Orleans, then obtained a master's in civil law at LSU in 1940 and an LL.M. from the University of Michigan in 1942. As a researcher, he assisted with the publication of the compiled civil codes of Louisiana prepared by the Law Institute. Pascal specialized in civil-law courses, jurisprudence, and conflict of laws, and he taught at LSU until his retirement in 1980.

In 1946, Milton M. Harrison became lecturer on legal bibliography while he worked with the Law Institute on the compilation of the Revised Statutes. He was a member of the LSU Class of 1941 and of the Order of the Coif and had been an editor of the law review. He served in the army Judge Advocate General's office and then in the Air Corps until 1946. Harrison became an assistant professor of law and assistant to the dean in 1948 and remained on the faculty until his retirement in 1983. In Harrison's letter of appointment, Dean McMahon referred to the concern with inbreeding and cited an understanding that Harrison would undertake graduate study within three or four years. His initial salary was $4,300 a year. But graduate school was not in the cards, as Harrison alternated his Law School teaching with service as assistant to the president of the University, vice-president and dean of academic affairs, dean of the Law School, and then associate dean.

The postwar housing shortage in Baton Rouge was a serious problem, and Harrison and his wife, Genie Taylor Harrison, lived in the basement in a dilapidated house near the Mississippi River. Their sharing one bathroom with two other couples led to the title of her 1981 cookbook, *Turnip Greens in the Bathtub*. The bathtub was often covered with grease, and it wasn't until they found some turnip greens in the tub that they realized that another couple was using it to dispose of the remains of their turnip greens.[35]

Summer 1946 saw Judge Alvin B. Rubin begin his service as an adjunct professor at LSU. Rubin had been released from the army that year, but there were no vacancies on the faculty at the time, so he began his law practice in Baton Rouge. He was scheduled to teach the summer-school course in security devices, but in July, Hebert called on him to teach the summer course in evidence because Professor Ira S. Flory had had an appendectomy and could not teach. Hebert called Rubin on Thursday or Friday, and the course began on Monday. "I have taught every regular semester since but one," said Rubin. He was proud of the fact that in 1980 he was the senior member of the faculty in terms of years of service. Not one to waste time, while serving on the federal district court in New Orleans, Rubin would ride the bus to and from Baton Rouge, reading briefs and advance sheets along the way. His students vied for the opportunity to pick him up and return him to the bus station and to get to talk with him during the drive.[36]

Another milestone occurred in January 1947, when Melvin G. Dakin was appointed to the law faculty, beginning as associate professor of law at a salary of $5,000 a year.[37] He had B.S. and J.D. degrees from the University of Iowa, where he belonged to the Order of the Coif and worked on the law review, and he had been on the faculty of the LSU College of Commerce from 1937 to 1941, teaching accounting and business law. During the war, Dakin worked with the U.S. Securities and Exchange Commission. He had been active in the American Association of University Professors and had worked with Acting President Hebert on several difficult tenure matters. He later obtained an LL.M. from Tulane during a sabbatical leave in 1956–57 and continued on the law faculty until his retirement in 1977.

Midyear 1947 was also the occasion for another change in Law School leadership. Hebert took leave to serve as a civilian judge at the Nuremberg Trials (U.S. Military Tribunal VI, I. G. Farbenindustrie personnel). When he completed that service, he returned to LSU as law dean for a year, then served as dean of the University, LSU's highest academic position, from 1949 to 1951. Henry George McMahon again became acting dean and then dean of the Law School from 1949 to 1952. Remaining on the faculty were Flory, Daggett, Bennett, Smith, Dainow, Malone, Pascal, Harrison, and Dakin. Harold W. Stoke had become president of the University in 1947, and Dakin was also tapped to be a special assistant to the president. His appointment would continue the tradition of having law faculty assist in the administration of the University, a tradition that several other faculty followed in subsequent years. Hebert was dean of the University under Stoke, a position he held until 1951, when Stoke resigned and Hebert entered private law practice with the Breazeale, Sachse, Wilson, and Hebert firm.[38]

With Mel Dakin remaining as an assistant to the president, the law faculty appointed Charles A. Reynard as a visiting professor for the 1948–49 session. Reynard had served as an attorney with the U.S. Department of Labor from 1939 to 1946 and came to LSU from the University of Utah. He held a B.S. in business administration and a law degree from Ohio State University and was a specialist in labor law and constitutional law. His visit became a permanent appointment, and he served on the faculty until his unexpected death in 1959. The correspondence at the time of his coming to LSU shows concern over the ever-present postwar housing shortage. Negotiations for housing in former military buildings on campus were unsuccessful, and few apartments and houses were available in the city. The Law School was eventually able to find a house for rent near the LSU Golf Club on Country Club Drive. Monthly rental was $85 per month, when Reynard was making $5,300 per academic year, plus $900 for summer teaching. Another concern was finding a school for Reynard's two young daughters. Dean Hebert sent applications for the LSU Laboratory School, indicating that the school gave preference to children of faculty. The girls were admitted.[39]

Another new faculty member who came in 1948, Albert H. Cotton, didn't stay long. Milton Harrison referred to him as a "little weasel that was sold to us by Yale." Cotton had a law degree from Duke University in addition to having been a Sterling Fellow at Yale. He had experience in government service, working with the general counsel of the Agricultural Adjustment Administration and then the U.S. Department of Agriculture, raising the possibility of developing an agricultural-law program at LSU. Cotton was also faculty editor of the law review. As it turned out, he had three wives, one in Europe, one in Kansas, and one in Washington. He couldn't decide which one he wanted to stay married to, according to Harrison. Also, "every now and then he would fail to show up on Mondays. You would find him ensconced in some jail in New Orleans, picked up for vagrancy. We had him for one year and then bid him goodbye."[40]

The legislative appropriation was reduced during the 1948–49 term, and Dean McMahon undertook to make budget cuts without adversely affecting the operations of the Law School. In February 1949, McMahon was granted leave to serve as city-parish attorney for Baton Rouge as the new form of combined local governments was being put into effect.[41]

Alice Daspit had served as librarian from 1938 to 1942 and guided the growth of the collection. Bessie Mitchell served as librarian in 1943, then Beverly Gordon Womack in 1944. A special appropriation in 1944 was the basis for acquiring valuable out-of-print materials that came on the market, and by May 1945 the collection had reached 60,000 volumes. Eilleen Murphy Kean, B.A., B.S. in library science from LSU, became librarian in 1945 and remained in the position until she was succeeded by Margaret Taylor Lane in June 1946. Mrs. Kean would not have been averse to continuing as librarian, but the University at the time did not allow pregnant women to work, and Mrs. Kean and her husband, attorney R. Gordon Kean ('48), were in the process of starting a family that eventually included six children.[42]

Peggy Harper was acting librarian from 1947 to 1949 while the search for a permanent librarian went on. Miss Harper was another of the Law School's mainstays. She had a B.A. and B.S. in library science from LSU and began working in the law library in 1944. She served as president of the Louisiana Library Association in 1968–69 and retired as librarian emeritus in 1980. Once again, Professor Flory was active in the growth of the collection; the dean asked him to serve as library advisor during this period. The school was then advertising that the library collection had grown to 74,000 volumes, making it the second-largest law library in the South.[43]

Kate Wallach became law librarian and a member of the faculty in September 1949, posts she held until her retirement in 1975. She was an extraordinary woman of great dignity and stature. She had earlier served as assistant librarian at the University of North Carolina and as a cataloger at the University of Michigan. Miss Wallach was a German refugee who had emigrated to the United States in 1935 along with her brother. She had received a J.D. from the University of Cologne in 1931. The Law School's student newspaper, reporting that Wallach had been admitted to practice in Berlin in 1933, said that was "a rare accomplishment at that time for a woman" and that she was a "model of excellence to the students she taught." After her emigration to the U.S., she earned an LL.B. from the University of Wisconsin. With her training in the civil law and in American law, she was exceptionally able to develop the library's collections. She, too, remained at LSU until her retirement. Letters written before her arrival in Baton Rouge also expressed concern over housing, and the Law School was able to find her an apartment on Lake Street adjoining the campus for $75 per month. Her beginning salary was $4,500 per year.[44]

Visiting civil-law scholars were returning. The distinguished comparative-law expert Max Rheinstein was a visiting professor in Fall 1949. He was a German refugee who became a law professor at the University of Chicago. He taught conflict of laws and a seminar in comparative law at LSU. Housing for Rheinstein was also a problem. The committee that allocated rooms in the Faculty Club was not disposed to accept "transients," and Dean Hebert had to ask President Stoke to intervene to obtain the "University's room" at the club. At the end of the decade, the leading speaker was Ernst Rabel, then a research associate at the University of Michigan and formerly a professor at the University of Berlin and director of the Kaiser Wilhelm Institute for Foreign and International Private Law. Professor Pascal had known him while he was studying at Michigan. Rabel lectured on the private laws of Western civilizations.[45]

Governor Edwin W. Edwards ('49) recalled that the postwar faculty was extraordinary—"the big names in modern Louisiana jurisprudence, Wex Malone, Denson Smith, McMahon, Mrs. Daggett, Joe Dainow, Dean Hebert, Pascal, you know, the people that wrote the textbooks and the books that have really, in my judgment, set the stage for subsequent faculty and subsequent law students to study law in Louisiana. . . . [T]hose of us who had the privilege of being at the LSU Law School at that time were touched by the most magnificent brains in special fields of law that I think this state has ever had."[46]

The desegregation issue, then called the "Negro problem," surfaced at the Law School in the late 1940s. A prophetic entry in the 1948 faculty minutes was the report of the denial, "in accordance with university policy," of the request of "Roscoe Turner, a negro" for admission. Turner argued that he would not be entitled to the veteran's exemption from taking the bar examination if he was to graduate from Southern University, which then was not an approved law school.[47] His claim invoked the U.S. Supreme Court's separate-but-equal doctrine, which focused on the factual issues of whether states were actually supplying equal educational facilities in professional schools for black students. To forestall integration of the LSU Law School, the State Board of Education, with the cooperation of the LSU Board of Supervisors, in 1946 authorized the establishment of a law school for black students at Southern University. The school opened in Fall 1947 with four faculty members and eight students.

Members of the LSU law faculty and library staff assisted with the establishment of the Southern University Law School. LSU faculty served as guest lecturers to assist the common law–trained Southern faculty by conducting the civil-code and civil-procedure courses that were audited by the Southern faculty in anticipation of teaching those courses. Professors Daggett, Dainow, and Smith taught under that program, and the LSU law library staff assisted in purchasing books for the Southern law library.[48]

The Law School was still small enough so that matters of academic probation and readmission were discussed by the whole faculty and were products of individual, case-by-case determinations. Those issues were the bulk of the matters discussed at many of the faculty meetings. Not adopted but discussed was Wex Malone's suggestion that the Law School begin aptitude testing of applicants. Tinkering with introductory courses continued; Fall 1946 saw a series of lectures to new students by Joseph Dainow, "by way of introduction to the study of law." Some signs of a return to normality were showing—effective Fall 1946, the Law School reverted to its prewar policy of admitting first-year students only in the fall semester.[49]

With a growing student body and the still-diminished faculty, a search was underway for new Law School faculty members. Indeed, in addition to regular faculty meetings to handle these matters, the members of the faculty held luncheon meetings on Tuesdays. Various changes in course sequencing and other such changes were also necessary to accommodate the increasing numbers of students. Enrollment rose to 267 in 1946: 132 first-year students, 92 second-year, 38 seniors, and 5 unclassified. Veterans of World War II constituted 87 percent of the total. In Fall 1947, total Law School enrollment was about 350, and some classes were so large they were held in the Law School auditorium.[50] That high enrollment, of course, was fueled by G.I. Bill benefits. Overall, LSU enrollment was less than 4,000 at war's end, and it exceeded 10,000 in 1946. Special concern for veterans was evidenced in the easing of admissions requirements, allowing military service to be substituted for one year of pre-legal study. Service in the merchant marine was given the same consideration. Placement of graduates was also becoming a problem, which Alvin B. Rubin was called upon to assist in solving. Minutiae continued to come before the faculty, such as a vote to accept the low bid for law-review printing even though it entailed a change in the type to be used. And, in response to a request from President Stoke, the Law School faculty replied that its opinion was that LSU should not renew the practice of granting honorary degrees.[51]

Another indication of an attempt to return to normality was the law review returning to four issues per year, after publishing two annual issues during the war emergency. The Southern Law Review Conference was held at LSU in 1948, and the details of preparations were the topic of a faculty meeting. It was decided to serve a buffet lunch "prepared by the wives of the faculty." It appears that Harriet Daggett voted in favor, along with the men. The faculty agreed to house one or more of the visiting faculty delegates as guests in their homes.[52]

When students returned to the campus in 1946, as Milton Harrison described them, "they were older. Many of them were married, some newly married. They were eager to get on with their lives, they had three to five years army experience. They worked hard; they played hard, and they wanted to get through with this business and get into the practice of law. There was none of the much more leisurely attitude of the students which prevailed among the students of the 30's. They had wives they had to support; they had to make a living; and more of them were working." When David I. Garrett ('48) turned in his exam to J. Denson Smith, he said it had been his hardest endeavor since D-Day. The students were not as competitive with each other as they would be later on; few of the students were "bucking" for Coif. Justice Fred A. Blanche ('48) recalled, "In my class was an assortment of majors, captains, colonels."[53]

In 1946, first-year courses were divided into sections to accommodate the large group. Classes were of course larger, the building facilities were taxed, and a full-day program with morning and afternoon classes was in place. No longer could faculty assign cases to be read from the reporters; there weren't enough copies, and secretaries started having to type out copies and run off mimeographs.[54]

Returning veterans who had been dropped from the rolls for academic reasons would be eligible for readmission on probation and on condition of forfeiting all D-graded credits. An indication of the impact of older law students and their separation from the younger students was the grant of a request to excuse law students from attendance at University convocations in the absence of special reasons for attendance. Another indicator was the tension caused when University administrators sought to apply the no-alcohol rules to the veterans in Law School. Men twenty-five to twenty-eight years old, who had been majors or colonels, would have a "minimum amount of liquor," as William M. Meyers ('48) put it. As a proctor in the law dorm, Meyers recalled an inspection by Arden O. French, dean of men, "and he was opening closet doors, of course, and inside most closet doors was sitting a big bottle of whiskey or something. I felt . . . that my days as 'house mother' were over. I never heard a word about it, however, and I thought that [he] was very discreet."[55]

The veterans did not have a close relationship with their professors. The faculty were treated with great respect and deference, but "we didn't knock on the commanding officer's door." Dean Emeritus and Mrs. Tullis attended ceremonies at the school, and they were treated most respectfully. The Class of 1948 was large—eighty-one graduates—and there were few job opportunities.[56]

Dale Bennett was considered by the students as the champion of their interests, in the way that Ira Flory had a special relationship with students. He received approval from the faculty to give students a trial examination. However, the faculty as a whole voted to recommend against granting the diploma privilege to veterans graduating from law school. It instructed the Law School representative to the Board of Governors to reaffirm the position that the privilege be extended only to students who had attended law school for two semesters before entering military service. The state supreme court was more generous to the veterans, however, continuing the diploma privilege to law school graduates who were veterans until 1959.[57]

Summer school was continuing as a regular part of LSU's law program. Dean Hebert announced that even though Tulane was opposed to having a summer session, he planned to notify Tulane casually that LSU was adopting an integrated program involving summer school. LSU, Tulane, and Loyola collaborated with the Veterans Administration in certifying textbooks to be purchased for veterans in law school. Another institution that was becoming entrenched was the rule limiting student cuts to 25 percent of the classes. Student (later supreme court justice) Mack E. Barham was allowed to take an examination even though he exceeded the cut limit because he had suffered an extended illness. However, the faculty defeated a proposal that the attendance rule be abolished. The faculty was still expected to continue writing for the law review, including a faculty symposium issue that discussed legislation adopted by the Louisiana legislature.[58]

The influx of veterans posed a housing shortage for students. There were few apartments available, and most people couldn't afford them anyway. There was some University housing provided for married students—the hutments—so-called temporary buildings constructed during the war which, however, stood until the 1960s. William Meyers lived first in the stadium dormitory and then in the law dorm. The move was an improvement, he said, not only because each room had a telephone and a lavatory, but because living in the law dorm provided an opportunity to get to know other students, to discuss law, and to study with groups. Eight students from the dorm were able to buy meal tickets and eat at Highland Cafeteria located in Highland Hall, a girls' dormitory near the Law School. A group of the younger girls at the cafeteria complained that the veterans were getting larger portions than they were. Some other students were able to join (or rejoin) fraternities and qualified for their meal plans.[59]

After he married during his senior year, Meyers rented an apartment on Highland Road near the Cotton Club for $22.50 per month, utilities included. Initially, single veterans received $50 a month on the G.I. Bill, plus fees, tuition, and books.[60] Married veterans received $90 a month. Clothing was still hard to get, and many students wore their military uniforms without insignia.

Albert C. Tate, a graduate of Yale Law School, came to LSU to take civil-code courses and was considered part of the Class of 1948. William Meyers recalled: "We were always kind of proud of the fact that here was a Yale man, and as brilliant as Al is, his grades were not necessarily better than some of the rest of the students. There was our Harvard man who was doing the same thing. I think he, Cleve Burton, was from Shreveport; so we had a Harvard man and a Yale man." Robert G. Pugh recalled that Tate would take no more than three lines of notes on a yellow pad in class and yet make high grades. Pugh was a veteran entitled to the diploma privilege, but his roommate, Edwin W. Edwards, had to take the bar examination. The hats-and-canes tradition continued, the Class of 1949 officers being featured in the *Gumbo* sporting theirs, including Treasurer Virginia L. Martin, President Clarence E. Romero, and Vice-President Edwin W. Edwards.[61]

Wex Malone continued to serve as law review faculty editor through Volume 8 (1947–48). His torts interests led him to a close friendship with William Prosser, and the two families toured Europe together for several years. Prosser would buy a new Mercedes in Germany, drive it in Europe, and then ship it to the U.S. Both men were superb raconteurs, and it was no doubt their interest in the bizarre that led faculty editor Malone to commission a book review of *The Famous Case of Myra Clark Gaines*. Prosser wrote, "She was the bonniest litigant this country has ever seen. She was sixty years in court, pressing a shaky, preposterous and altogether incredible claim against the owners of some of the most valuable property in New Orleans." Gaines finally obtained a judgment of more than $1,900,000 but died before collecting. Her heirs settled for $560,000. "It is to be hoped that they had the grace to give her a decent tombstone. I should like to see it." He also pointed out that Gaines's mother, Zulime, part gypsy and part Creole, a "fabulous creature straight from the Arabian Nights, lived with Clark without benefit of clergy for years, and then was or was not married to him, secretly and without a record." Moreover, he continued, "she had a husband living but he did or did not have a prior, undivorced wife," "Daniel Clark did or did not draw a new will, in which he acknowledged Myra"—a will "which was or was not destroyed after Clark's death by another stock character of melodrama, his wicked partner."[62]

Students were becoming more active and organized. The Student Faculty Relations Committee requested that trial examinations be given in first-year classes, and "it was the sense of the faculty that each would handle the indoctrination of the first-year class into the Law School type of examination in his own way by trial questions, explanation, etc."[63]

The peak of postwar Law School enrollment was 382 students in the 1947–48 term. The number of entering freshmen declined from 182 students in Fall 1947 to 140 in Fall 1948. Total enrollment in Fall 1948 was 347 students, 120 of them second-year and 86 third-year. The faculty consisted of eleven full-time members and three part-time lecturers—a student-to-full-time-faculty ratio of 31.5 to 1.[64]

Gillis W. Long, a student who entered in the late 1940s and graduated in 1951, described his Law School experience in a typical way, emphasizing the method of learning to think like a lawyer. He said he learned that "being a good law student and to some extent a good lawyer is a matter of instinct and a matter of thinking process rather than just intelligence alone." Long credited J. Denson Smith and Wex Malone with developing those skills, along with George Pugh, who was his advisor on his law review projects. He said, "I never looked upon law school as a learning of information, I looked upon law school as learning of processes. I think that's the way you have to look at it. I think those that look at it and find that they can get all the information in the world can't succeed."[65]

The 1949–50 academic year was Professor Ira S. Flory's last teaching year at LSU, ending thirty-six years of service to the institution. His teaching had run the gamut of the common-law curriculum, and students remembered his courses in federal procedure, evidence, bankruptcy, and negotiable instruments. He died soon thereafter, on September 3, 1950, at sixty-seven. Flory was paid $7,500 for the last term, and his pension benefit ($33\frac{1}{3}$ percent of his average salary for five years) was $2,270 per year. One student commented that Flory spoon-fed the law, "but he spoon-fed a whole lot of it that people digested real well."[66]

As the decade ended, the moot-court program was a noncredit exercise that was a requirement for graduation. "In moot court work the students draw the papers, argue cases, and learn complete trial procedures."[67] Students were required to write briefs and argue cases under the tutelage of upper-class students. The highest-ranking students were invited to participate in the Tullis

Moot Court Competition in their senior year, with supreme court justices normally hearing the final arguments and selecting the winning team.

The general University fee was then $22.50 per semester, plus a $15-per-semester law library fee and $5 student hospital fee. Law students were eligible for the University meal plan, which provided meals for $1.25 per day. Housing in the law dorm was $54 per semester. Although admission was not contingent on a minimum LSAT score, students were required to take the test, at a cost of $10. The catalog for 1949–50 detailed forty-one courses, fourteen of them listed as electives. Graduates were required to complete eighty-seven semester hours of credit.[68] The catalog contained the names, undergraduate institutions, and hometowns of all the students in the Law School. In that year, only fourteen students listed New Orleans as their hometown. Eight were out-of-state students, five from Mississippi, two from Texas, and one from Missouri.

The students who started law study in 1947—the graduating class of 1950—produced the largest class ever—97 graduates. That number would not be topped until the Class of 1969, with 144 graduates. In the 1950s, most graduating classes had fewer than 50 members. That class was unusually close, and its reunion tradition has continued into recent years. It established the Class of 1950 scholarships when the Law School had few scholarships available and, under the leadership of Louis D. Curet, it funded the Class of 1950 Professorship in 1997. Three of its graduates became members of the law faculty, George W. Pugh in 1952, Sidney A. Champagne in 1977, and Warren L. Mengis in 1982. Also in the class were Louisiana Supreme Court justice Luther F. Cole, Congressman Harold B. McSween, District Attorney Leander H. Perez Jr., and Jack C. Caldwell, president of the Law Institute and secretary of the Department of Conservation.

Ira Samuel Flory.
LSU Photograph Collection, RG # A5000, Louisiana State University Archives, LSU Libraries, Baton Rouge

Robert Lee Tullis.
LSU Photograph Collection, RG # A5000, Louisiana State University Archives, LSU Libraries, Baton Rouge

Harriet S. Daggett.
LSU Photograph Collection, RG # A5000, Louisiana State University Archives, LSU Libraries, Baton Rouge

Paul M. Hebert.
Courtesy, Mary H. McCowan

Wex S. Malone.
Courtesy, Charles N. Malone

George W. Pugh.
Courtesy, Jim Zeitz

Students, in cadet uniforms, and faculty, 1913.
Gumbo, 1913. Courtesy, LSU Special Collections

Class of 1941, and faculty.
First row, left to right: H.W. Bethard, L. A Fitch Jr., M. M. Harrison, John Makar, Ira S. Flory, C. A. Riddle, Jr., Charlie Pitcher, R. W. Harmanson, Sargent Pitcher. *Second row:* Benjamin Marlow, M. Shapiro, A. J. Spedale, Samuel E. Lee Jr., John M. Shuey, L. B. Allen, R. W. Williams Jr., Kenneth Bailey. *Third row:* J. A. Leithead, L. S. Thompson, J. G. Stulb Jr., John W. Landry Jr., A. J. Wyly, Hale M. Walker, Alva Jones, Joe T. Boston, W. R. Coenan.
Gumbo, 1941. Courtesy, LSU Special Collections

Senior class officers, 1949:
C. E. Romero, president; Edwin Edwards, vice-president; Virginia Martin, secretary-treasurer
Gumbo, 1949. Courtesy, LSU Special Collections

Law Faculty, 1953.
First row, left to right: Henry G. McMahon, Paul M. Hebert, Harriet S. Daggett.
Second row: J. Denson Smith, Joseph Dainow, Charles A Reynard. *Third row:* George W. Pugh, Kate Wallach, Melvin Dakin. *Fourth row:* Dale E Bennett, Robert Pascal.
Gumbo, 1953. Courtesy, LSU Special Collections

Phi Delta Phi, international legal fraternity, 1956.
First row, left to right: George Meadors, William Doran, Leonard Werner, Billy Hines, John Bivins, James Finley, Ed Blewer. *Second row:* Jerry Jones, Jack Watson, William Hollier, Charles Howard, Harry Sachse, James Pierson, John White Jr. *Third row:* Seth Lewis Jr., Thomas Hardeman, Patrick Caffery, Daniel Shea, Joe Lipsey, William Moss, J. Prewitt Nelson Jr., J. Bennett Johnston Jr.
Gumbo, 1956. Courtesy, LSU Special Collections

1962 Law Review.
First row, left to right: Frank Fontenot, Tilgham Whitley Jr., John Schwab, J.E. Davis, Anthony Correro, John Gresham. *Second row:* Grady Kitchens, Leila Cutshaw, David Bell, Wendell Lindsay, Shelby McKenzie.
Gumbo, 1962. Courtesy, LSU Special Collections

Class of 1967.
Courtesy, Carolyn H. Hargrave

1971 Law Review.
Left to right: Paul Spaht, Katherine Shaw (managing editor), Van Mayhall, Mike Page (editor-in-chief), Wood Sparks, Fred Sutherland, Ted Hodges.
Gumbo, 1975. Courtesy, LSU Special Collections

1975 Law Review.
Seated, left to right: Jim Walsh, Richard House, Reg Cassibry, Michael Rubin, Randy J. McClanahan, Marilyn Maloney. *Standing,* Steve Bullock, Martha Salvant.
Courtesy, Carolyn H. Hargrave

6

THE FIFTIES:
RETURN TO NORMALCY

The Class of 1950, with ninety-seven graduates, was the largest graduating class ever, but the postwar surge in enrollment quickly subsided. The Class of 1951 was down to sixty-eight graduates, and the Class of 1954 had thirty-two graduates. Total enrollment in Fall 1959 was 229 students, and the Class of 1959 had sixty-seven graduates. The students at the beginning of the decade were younger, and fewer of them were married. The faculty was stable and very productive. Eleven faculty members were on board, resulting in an extraordinary 11 to 1 student-faculty ratio in 1953. Students in the 1950s were impressed with their teachers, studying under "all of the people who wrote the books." The school remained rigorous, but with open admission, attrition was high. One student, not forgetting the stress of being cross-examined by J. Denson Smith, Wex S. Malone, and Robert A. Pascal, nonetheless said, "that was a privilege." Students at the time referred to the period of the fifties and sixties as the "golden age" of the Law School: "The school was smaller; the faculty, with little exception, was very strong."[1]

Henry A. Politz ('59), judge of the U.S. Court of Appeals for the Fifth Circuit, described his teachers in 1987:

> Dean Hebert as "The Tiger." And that he was. I never knew him to raise his voice. He didn't have to; when one sees a tiger come into the room it is not necessary for the tiger to roar to know it is there.
>
> Dean "Mac," Henry George McMahon, was a great, kindly man. That he would be known by the relaxed, personalized "Mac" was a tribute to the way the students returned his obvious concern for our welfare with a warm respect, indeed love.
>
> J. Denson Smith was "Big Red," despite his surprisingly diminutive physique, because of the power and force of his intellect. There was no

trifling with Big Red. Few tried the first time, none the second. He commanded the classroom.

Wex Malone kept us on our toes in class in a different way. He could be equally intimidating as Mr. Smith when he launched into the Aristotelian methodology with a student, but it was done with an air of expectant excitement. His moniker was "Sexy Wexy" because of his wry, face-grimacing comments about any sexually oriented reference or issue in a case.

Mel Dakin was affectionately known as "The Prince," not in any machiavellian sense but, rather, as the kindly and courtly person he was. He was a "prince" of a man. We struggled, trying to keep up with his awesome intellect, but I never heard a critical word about Mr. Dakin.

The venerable Harriet Daggett was "Ma" Daggett to us. She was something special. . . . she taught the six-hour course in successions-donations-community property. A grade in a six-hour course was big medicine and no one took Ma Daggett for granted, although her feared "senior-failing" years were behind her by the time she taught us. The portrait at the law school does a beautiful job of capturing our Ma Daggett, right down to the chain-smoking, nicotine stained fingers.

George W. Pugh was the youngest member of the faculty, but he was already striking fear in the hearts of both prepared and unprepared students. He taught me thirty years ago. This past summer . . . I heard his students saying the very same things members of my class said about him three decades ago.

Robert A. Pascal was a puzzlement. He obviously was a scholar but his idiosyncrasies interfered with his teaching. There was no member of the faculty with a greater desire for students to learn; unfortunately, we tended to focus on the form and not the substance. He was sometimes referred to as "Bouncing Bob" for the style of his lecture delivery.

Milton Harrison was another teacher without a nickname. Perhaps that was because he came over in 1957 as dean while Dean Hebert made one of his occasional forays into the practice of law. He was a gentle and thoughtful person. He had been the right-hand man to the then LSU president. . . . It appeared to be a smooth transition, a tribute to his political and personal skills.

Professor Reynard was nicknamed "The Fox" not because of any personality trait or characteristic, but simply because fox in French is reynard. He was well liked by both students and faculty, as well as by Governor Earl K. Long who asked him to serve as his legal counsel.

Finally we had Joseph Dainow, "The Word."[2] Although there were publications and trappings which would have suggested otherwise, the students viewed him as the least scholarly of the full-time faculty. There was considerable discomfort in his class, a pervasive disquietude that we might not be learning the "right" law.[3]

Judge Politz, a frequent Law School visitor in the 1980s and 1990s, noted that the 1950s faculty was a collegial group, partying and drinking together. He added, "I think they drank more than the faculty [does] now."[4]

FACULTY

Charles A. Reynard, visiting professor during 1949–50, became a regular faculty member for the 1950–51 term. His minimal seniority presumably also led to his succeeding J. Denson Smith as secretary of the faculty and recorder of the minutes of the meetings. Not that minute-keeping was of no consequence. At one point, the faculty voted to instruct him to cease his journalistic reports of debates and instead to report only actions taken and topics discussed "without reference to the personal views expressed by any individual."[5] This concern was apparently prompted by the fact that all faculty minutes were sent to the president of the University.

Ira S. Flory died on September 3, 1950, at age sixty-seven, soon after retiring in Spring 1950 with thirty-six years of service, including serving as acting dean from 1933 to 1935, when Tullis resigned, and from 1939 to 1941, when Hebert was acting president. LSU did not have a funded retirement system at the time, and there were few early retirements under an unfunded system that paid a maximum benefit of one-third of a retiree's salary, payable out of current state appropriations. Flory's salary during his last year was $7,500 ($51,800 in Year 2000 dollars), and his pension benefit was $2,270 per year ($15,845 in Year 2000 dollars). His obituary not only included the usual honors—Order of the Coif, Phi Kappa Phi, Phi Delta Phi—but also his membership in the First Methodist Church and the Masons. Warren Mengis, who took Flory's evidence course the last time he taught it, recalled the famous "forty-four questions." Flory had reduced his evidence course to those forty-four examination questions, which he used year after year without even changing the names—eight of them on each exam. Mengis memorized the answers to all forty-four questions and made an A after using up only one hour of the four hours allowed for the exam.[6]

Flory's illness precluded his teaching federal courts in Spring 1950, and that task was allocated to George W. Pugh, who had just graduated in February and taught the course to his former classmates. After this initial experience in law teaching, Pugh followed the path to Yale and, after two years in residence, was awarded a J.S.D. His thesis on the history of sovereign immunity was published in the *Louisiana Law Review*, of which he had been an editor. Pugh immediately returned to LSU to join the faculty in Fall 1952, starting as an assistant professor teaching evidence and workmen's compensation. He was also faculty editor of the law review. Pugh was on leave from 1954 to 1956 to work with the Louisiana Judicial Council and was the state's first judicial administrator. He returned to LSU for the Fall 1956 term with a promotion to associate professor. Pugh continued teaching at LSU, despite deteriorating eyesight, until his retirement in 1994.[7]

Jerome J. Shestack joined the faculty in Fall 1950. His hiring continued the LSU connection with Northwestern University, where he had been a teaching fellow. He had an LL.B. from Harvard, a B.A. from the University of Pennsylvania, and had studied at the University of Mexico. He also served as faculty editor of the law review. Shestack proposed a required readings program for students and circulated a tentative list of books, but no faculty vote was taken on his proposal and it was buried in the Curriculum Committee. Another attempt at innovation was his consultation with Professors Claude M. Wise and Waldo W. Braden of the speech department to offer a noncredit law course in public speaking. The faculty response was to place the item on the agenda for a subsequent meeting, but the item never reappeared. Shestack worked at the Covington and Burling law firm in Washington, D.C., in the summer of 1951, then took leave for the 1952–53 academic year to work as a deputy city solicitor for the City of Philadelphia. He did not return to teaching and instead entered private law practice. He became a prominent Philadelphia lawyer and, while serving as president of the American Bar Association in 1998, he addressed members of the Baton Rouge bar. Among the persons attending that lecture was Professor Melvin Dakin, who had served with Shestack on the faculty. Although he was at LSU for only a short time, Shestack had a large impact on some students. Congressman Gillis W. Long was one of his students and had a continuing friendship with him for years. Long was an attorney, then a congressman, in Washington, and Shestack practiced in Philadelphia. Long recalled, "I did exceptionally well in his class; he always thought I was a lot brighter than I was." Shestack was also active in Democratic Party politics. Another former student who worked with Shestack in civil-rights activities in the 1960s and 1970s was Ernest Morial, one of LSU's first black law graduates.[8]

Robert A. Pascal returned for the 1952–53 term after serving for a year as a visiting lecturer on American law at the University of Rome. His courses that term were diverse: family law, legal writing, common-law property, agency, and partnership. Henry G. McMahon reported in Fall 1953 on his efforts to revise Louisiana's civil procedure at the International Congress on Civil Procedure meeting in Vienna. Illness kept McMahon from the Law School in the spring semester of 1956, with Carlos E. Lazarus covering his course in security devices and Alvin B. Rubin in procedure. Professor Joseph Dainow was on sabbatical leave during the 1954 spring and summer semesters. He had a Fulbright award that provided for his teaching at the University of Paris and the University of Lyon. Professor Melvin G. Dakin accepted a visiting professorship in Spring 1955 to teach at Northwestern University Law School, and Joseph Dainow taught there in Spring 1956. Dakin recalled that the student body at Northwestern was well qualified, and that although the top students at LSU were equal to them, LSU's open-admissions policy produced a larger proportion of students who were not well qualified; hence the larger failure rate at LSU.[9]

Wex Malone began investigating the application of no-fault workmen's-compensation principles to automobile accidents. He lectured to a national group of compensation attorneys meeting in New Orleans in March 1952. He would be on leave for 1956–57. In 1957, Malone reviewed a three-volume torts treatise by Fowler V. Harper and Fleming James Jr. for the *Louisiana Law Review*. Harper was an LSU law faculty member during the Beutel deanship. Malone recommended the set, even at the steep price at the time of $60. The back cover of that issue of the law review advertised Charmatz and Daggett's *Comparative Studies in Community Property Law*, available for $6 from the LSU Press, and the *Proceedings of the Fourth Mineral Law Institute* for $7.50.

The LSU Press also released at that time Volumes 2 and 3 of *Order and History* by Eric Voegelin (*The World of the Polis; Plato and Aristotle*).[10]

A search was under way for what was referred to as the "foreign law professorship." Among the candidates was Jaro Mayda, who came to LSU for interviews and conferences in February 1956. An offer was made and accepted, but Mayda later wrote "resigning the position" accepted earlier in the year. A graduate of Masaryk University with a J.D. from the University of Chicago, he eventually settled as a professor at the University of Puerto Rico Faculty of Law. Mayda continued his relations with Louisiana law and with LSU, delivering the Bailey Lectures in 1969 on the subject of François Geny and modern jurisprudence. The lectures were the basis for a book on Geny published in 1978 by the LSU Press. The Louisiana State Law Institute published his English translation of Geny's *Méthode d'Interprétation des Sources en Droit Privé Positif* and his translations of civil-law treatises. He delivered the Bailey Lectures in 1973 on environmental control.[11]

In January 1957, a suitable scholar in foreign and comparative law was found, and Athanassios N. Yiannopoulos was hired as a research professor. He encountered visa problems and eventually had to apply for an exchange-visitor visa. By the end of the year, his immigration status was still unclear, and he did not arrive until February 1958. He was to undertake research assignments and would be given teaching responsibilities later. Yiannopoulos came with law degrees from the University of Thessaloniki in Greece (Diploma in Law), the University of Chicago (M.C.L.), the University of California in Berkeley (J.S.D.), and the University of Cologne (Dr.Jur.). He became the state's premier property-law scholar, but he began his research studies dealing with mandate and agency. His first study on Louisiana law was "Brokerage, Mandate and Agency in Louisiana: Civilian Tradition and Modern Practice." He remained at LSU for twenty years, moving down the Mississippi River to Tulane in 1979. By then, LSU offered a generous funded retirement system that allowed benefits to be paid after twenty years of service.[12]

The Law School expanded its efforts in law reform as well as scholarship. President Truman invited Harriet Daggett to act as a technical specialist at the Mid-Century White House Conference on Children and Youth, where she reported on developments in divorce laws and illegitimacy. Dale Bennett, one of the drafters of the Louisiana Criminal Code of 1942, was appointed as an advisor to the drafters of the American Law Institute's Model Penal Code, and he also began work in 1957 as coordinator and reporter of the Louisiana State Law Institute's Code of Criminal Procedure. Wex Malone was appointed as an advisor for the Restatement (2d) of the Law of Torts. Malone also published two books within the year, his casebook on workmen's compensation and a casebook on relational interests. He took leave for the 1952–53 academic year but returned in Fall 1953. Law librarian Kate Wallach's book *Research in Louisiana Law* was published by the LSU Press. Henry George McMahon was also working on a draft for a new Code of Civil Procedure for the Louisiana State Law Institute. Mel Dakin was a consultant to the Louisiana Tax Commission and the Louisiana Public Service Commission. Joseph Dainow served on several international and comparative-law commissions. With grants from the Ford Foundation, the American Society of International Law sponsored at LSU one of fifteen regional meetings designed to stimulate interest in international law.[13]

The law library collection was growing under the guidance of Kate Wallach; the library budget in 1954–55 was $20,000, and the collection reached 104,000 volumes. Wallach also received an unusual accolade: she was one of the few law librarians ever elected president of the Louisiana Library Association. Norma Mayo Duncan ('49) joined the library staff in Fall 1951. She would later head the Louisiana legislature's research staff and was director of research for the Constitutional Convention of 1973. Apparently the continuing use of the law library by noisy undergraduates prompted law students to continue to protest. Dr. Wallach reimposed the rule reserving the reading room for law students, members of the LSU faculty, and members of the bar. Undergraduate students had to obtain special permission and show a need for doing research in the library.[14]

Harriet Daggett was honored in Spring 1952 for having taught for twenty-five years at the Law School. A portent of things to come was her illness during part of the fall semester of 1955. Her courses were covered by LSU faculty and by Professors Leonard Oppenheim of Tulane and James Bugea of Loyola, who served as guest lecturers. Frank Craig Jr. ('40) taught mineral rights three times for Professor Daggett, first in 1958 when she was on sabbatical. She did not use teaching materials but taught from a list of cases, so Craig had to develop an outline himself. Daggett became ill again in 1959 and in 1960, and Craig finished the course for her. He also taught family law.[15]

Alvin B. Rubin was promoted from assistant professor (part-time) to associate professor (part-time), the recommendation noting that he was one of the ablest teachers on the faculty and that "we twice unsuccessfully offered him a full-time position." He taught tax law and estate planning in 1953, and special arrangements were made for practicing lawyers to enroll in the course when he taught the marital deductions and insurance aspects of estate taxation. He also taught an abbreviated course on the subject to members of the Shreveport bar in June. Another regular adjunct was Benjamin W. Yancey of the New Orleans bar, who started teaching the course in admiralty law in Spring 1956 and continued doing so until 1970. Theo Cangelosi taught municipal government and "found it very, very difficult." The students were smart and demanding, he said.[16]

The last faculty minutes signed by Charles A. Reynard were dated January 23, 1959. He died unexpectedly the following February 2 at age forty-five. The minutes of February 16 were signed by the new faculty secretary, George W. Pugh, and were primarily a memorial to Reynard. An Ohioan who came to Louisiana, Reynard came to be involved in practical politics and was executive counsel to Governor Earl Long during the 1956 legislative session. His eulogy was delivered by the long-time pastor of the University Methodist Church, Reverend William E. Trice, who began: "No one was better qualified to live than Charles Reynard; for the same reasons, no one was better qualified to die. He respected, studied, and taught the law of the land; but he lived, demonstrated, and practiced the way of the spirit. He discovered and harmonized the laws written in books with the law written in the heart. He understood and helped to establish the statutes on labor; but he knew equally well the unwritten code of love." He was also honored for his anonymous counseling of persons troubled with alcoholism, a problem he himself had overcome. The law review issue dedicated to him included his final work, "Governmental Regulation of Individual Employment Conditions in the United States."[17]

Donald H. Wollett, who came from New York University, was hired as a full professor with tenure in June 1959. He was an experienced law professor, having taught at Indiana University and Washington University and as a visiting professor at Harvard. He replaced Reynard, teaching in the public-law field, including labor law and constitutional law, and he left in 1961 to enter law practice in New York City.[18]

The law faculty was actively writing for the *Louisiana Law Review*, guiding the development of the state's legal doctrine. In addition to the annual faculty symposium commenting on Louisiana Supreme Court decisions, members of the faculty wrote six of twelve leading articles in Volume 13—Dainow on mortgages and privileges, McMahon on fact-pleading, Pascal on trusts, Pugh on sovereign immunity, and Rubin on taxes and arbitration. In addition, they produced six book reviews.[19]

Another difficult task for any law faculty is ensuring compliance with publication deadlines. On behalf of the law review, Professor Shestack moved that any faculty writer for the symposium who had not tendered his manuscript on time "be disqualified from all further perquisites that attach to faculty status." The motion met the same fate as most of his other motions—it died for lack of a second. It appears that faculty were not as concise as they might be in their symposium manuscripts, and it was recommended that they "attempt to reduce such material to approximately one half of that which was prepared last year." Another perennial problem was raised by Dr. Wallach. Faculty members whose offices in the law building opened directly into the library stacks "had been taking books from the shelves and retaining them in their offices without signing charge slips." More politic than Shestack, Wallach made no motion to deprive offenders of their perquisites but simply asked for cooperation. Faculty were also asked to make a special point of locking doors leading from their offices to the library stacks "to aid the security program." Professor Daggett complained about removal of pages from a *Tulane Law Review* article she had assigned to a class; "it was the consensus of the faculty that the Dean should be requested to publicize the event and ask that the guilty individual identify himself."[20]

Faculty approval was required for the selection of the editors of the *Louisiana Law Review* and for awards for the best articles. Although there was some concern that law review work interfered with class studies, freshmen with a B average or better were invited to participate in law review work after receiving their first-semester grades. Students with a lower average were not eligible to compete for membership until their third semester in the Law School. The faculty also retained authority over selection of student members of the Moot Court Board. Student articles required approval of a faculty advisor expert in the area as well as final approval by the faculty editor. That system would remain in effect until the early 1970s.[21]

The faculty remained closely knit, socializing with each other at a time when "we could all actually get into somebody's living room." Carlos Lazarus would remember, "we had little gatherings on week-ends, at Mrs. Daggett's house, for example, at Mr. Flory's house, at Dean Hebert's house." Lazarus and Malone were both good pianists and often performed. Dean Hebert was said to be proficient at playing the musical comb and paper.[22]

Signs of bureaucracy were appearing, and what could prompt those signs more than demands for secretarial services. The faculty minutes reflect a decision to appoint Mrs. Nell Vialet as coordinator of stenographic services. She was to be consulted when rush jobs were needed or when regularly assigned secretaries were not fully occupied with their duties. Mrs. Vialet remained a Law School secretary well into the 1970s, acquiring notoriety for her penchant for correcting bad grammar in faculty writings without telling the authors.[23]

Harriet Daggett was still the Law School's most visible figure on the main campus—she was the featured speaker at the November 1951 Leadership Day convocation at which outstanding students were honored. As the decade ended, members of the faculty were obtaining national stature. Wex Malone was elected to the American Law Institute in 1959, and Henry George McMahon was appointed to the fifteen-member advisory committee to the Commission on International Rules of Judicial Procedure. Attendance at the annual AALS meeting between Christmas and New Year in Chicago continued high; in 1953, each attendee received $80 in partial payment of expenses. Hotel rooms at the Edgewater Beach Hotel in Chicago were $6 for a single and $10 for a double.[24]

ADMINISTRATION

Paul M. Hebert left the Law School deanship in 1949 to become dean of the University, LSU's highest academic post, in the administration of President Harold W. Stoke. Stoke, unable to get support from a conservative Board of Supervisors for reforms that rankled LSU's athletic, engineering, and education constituencies, resigned as president in January 1951. Hebert then resigned as dean of the University and announced that he would enter private law practice in Baton Rouge with the firm of Breazeale, Sachse, Wilson, and Hebert. When he resigned effective February 1, 1951, the *Reveille* made it the top story. The professor/law dean/dean of the University/acting president/judge at Nuremberg was, at age forty-three, finally entering the private practice of law. He was quoted, "At the present time, I have an opportunity for professional association with a leading law firm which I cannot afford to refuse."[25]

Henry George McMahon served as dean from 1949 to 1952. A crisis arose in January 1951 when he announced that he would have to give up the deanship on the advice of his physicians. However, after surgery in the summer, McMahon continued as dean in August at the request of newly appointed president Troy H. Middleton. He remained as dean until February 1952, when Paul M. Hebert was again named dean. Hebert had practiced for about a year but returned as dean when McMahon, almost blind with eye trouble, requested relief. Hebert remained in the position until April 1957, when he again left to practice law with the Breazeale Sachse firm. That was twenty years after he was first named dean of the Law School and five years since he had been reappointed to the same position. Professor McMahon served as acting dean once more, from July 1 to the beginning of the fall 1957 semester, when Milton M. Harrison, who had served as assistant to the president for the previous seven years, was appointed as permanent dean.[26]

Another surprising change occurred two years later, on July 1, 1959, when Harrison left the deanship to accept a new position as vice-president and dean of academic affairs of the University. Even more surprising, Paul M. Hebert returned to the law faculty and was named dean of the Law School effective August 1. In the days before formal search committees, selection was not a public process, but it was thought among insiders that Alvin B. Rubin was the leading candidate for the deanship. Indeed, Hebert had asked Rubin to consider the deanship. But later, at lunch, Hebert told Rubin that Board member Theo Cangelosi had urged him to return because he was needed, and that he had decided to do so. Rubin said he would not consider being a candidate if Hebert decided to return. Hebert continued as dean and professor of law until his death in 1977. Later, Rubin reflected on Hebert: "He had the ability to lead a faculty in a way that's indispensable for a dean who is going to be effective. Essentially law schools are run by faculty, but faculty cannot in practical terms 'run' anything. There are too many views, too many people who have a solely academic frame of mind, and too many people whose vision is not practical and indeed perhaps should not be, so that the true leadership has to come from the molding of a faculty consensus with the dean as the chief executive." Rubin acknowledged that some persons thought

Hebert went too far in the executive role, that he was too dominant, but Rubin thought Hebert handled things just about right. Harrison returned to the Law School in 1961 after his final stint in central administration and served as professor and associate dean. He retired in 1983.[27]

VISITING PROFESSORS AND LECTURERS

Robert L. Henry Jr., the Law School's first professor specializing in common-law subjects, returned as a visiting professor in Spring 1950. He had served on the faculty from 1907 to 1911 and married Elaine Goodale Read, a Baton Rouge native, in 1908. Most of his career was spent as a judge of the Mixed Courts of Egypt, serving as a district-court judge until 1941 and on the court of appeals from 1941 to 1949. In the interim, he had taught at three other universities, served as dean of a college of law, and served in World War II. By 1949, Egyptian nationalism was rising, and the courts, which had been imposed by colonial powers, were abolished because they infringed on the country's sovereignty.[28] Henry substituted for Joseph Dainow, who was on leave to teach at the University of Puerto Rico, and he also worked with the Law Institute, assisting in the translation of the Planiol Treatise, work that had been begun by Pierre Crabites, who had also been a judge of the Mixed Courts. Henry was made an honorary member of the Order of the Coif during his visit. Faculty members recalled that life in Baton Rouge was something of a shock for the aging Henrys (he was sixty-seven), far removed from the life they had enjoyed as privileged expatriates in a third-world country. They did not remain in Baton Rouge, but they did present as gifts to friends some of the artwork and carpets they had acquired in Egypt.

Huey Blair Howerton Jr., visiting professor in 1950–51, came from the University of Mississippi, where he received his LL.B. in 1946. Howerton died in 1953 at a young age, and the faculty minutes recorded that he "was a source of great pleasure and intellectual stimulation for us all, and we had followed with interest the first unfolding of what promised to be a brilliant and highly useful career."[29]

Thomas A. Harrell ('51) was an attorney with the Louisiana Department of Revenue when he was named a special lecturer in the Law School in 1952.[30] He returned as a full-time faculty member in 1973 and retired in 1996.

Interest in the growing foreign-law collection led to the hiring of Jan Paul

Charmatz with the expectation of his doing research in foreign law. He was a graduate in law from the University of Prague, had been an associate prosecutor on the staff at the Nuremberg War Crimes Tribunal, earned a master's at the Yale Law School, and was subsequently a visiting lecturer there. He came as a visiting research associate professor to work in a nonteaching capacity, supervising the law review and founding a research program in foreign and comparative law. However, needs were such that he was called upon to teach the first-year course in civil-law property. It appeared that Charmatz's enthusiasm for civil law in Louisiana cooled after he read decisions of the Louisiana courts and decided they were not properly applying civilian principles. He stayed only two years and then moved on to teach at the University of Mississippi, Tulane, and Southern Methodist University. One of his admirers was Leah Lanier, a member of the dean's staff, who recalled that even though Charmatz was an expert on international law, he patiently listened to Joe Dainow's "lectures" on points of international law. A student who had close connections with Charmatz was John S. White Jr., who along with other law review students called him the "Black Prince." Charmatz lived in the Faculty Club and was known for drinking hot beer in great quantities.[31]

The Law School celebrated its fiftieth anniversary in elaborate ceremonies on November 16, 1956, including a morning session, a luncheon, an afternoon session, and an evening session. The focus was on developments in legal education and in comparative law. The president of the Association of American Law Schools, Maurice T. Van Hecke, delivered an address, as did John G. Gervey, advisor to the American Bar Association's Section on Legal Education and Admission to the Bar. Eugene V. Rostow, dean of the Yale Law School, and Hessel E. Yntema, professor at the University of Michigan, spoke on international legal issues. The evening ceremony was devoted to conferring honorary doctor of laws degrees on John B. Fournet ('20), chief justice of the Louisiana Supreme Court, and John H. Tucker Jr. ('20), president of the Louisiana State Law Institute. Paul Hebert's introduction to the program emphasized the fact that the Law School was designed from the beginning to emphasize a faculty of full-time professors and that it had continued to follow that ideal.[32]

Leon Lebowitz of the Baylor University law faculty also served as a visiting professor for Fall 1955, acting in addition as faculty editor of the law review. Upon his retirement from the Louisiana Supreme Court, Justice Sam LeBlanc taught a course in the spring semester of 1955.[33]

Richard Campbell of the University of Wisconsin was a visiting professor in 1956–57, teaching torts and relational interests while Wex Malone was on leave. Campbell, however, suffered continuing illnesses in Spring 1956 and could not complete his courses. Professor Bennett took over the torts course, and Robert L. (Buck) Kleinpeter ('50) of the Baton Rouge bar handled the course in relational interests.[34]

The continuing connection with European law professors was evidenced by the invitation to René David to deliver lectures at LSU while he was visiting the Louisiana State Law Institute in New Orleans.[35] He was then a comparative-law professor at the University of Paris and later at Aix-en-Provence. This was the beginning of a relationship with him and the University of Aix–Marseille that would continue for decades.

The Law School became a member of the American Society of Comparative Law in 1951, and Professor Joseph Dainow was chosen as LSU's representative to the society. LSU's connections with Professor Max Rheinstein of the University of Chicago Law School, who was a visiting professor in 1949–50, were continuing, and at Rheinstein's urging, the Law School invited scholars from Scandinavian countries to visit. The long-term connections with Northwestern University continued, and in 1952 Professor William Willard Wirtz of its law school was chosen as the Edward Douglass White Lecturer. An expert on constitutional law and labor law, Wirtz would later become secretary of labor in the administration of President John F. Kennedy. The White Lecturer in 1954 was Dean Jefferson B. Fordham of the University of Pennsylvania Law School, who spoke on "A Larger Concept of Community." Fordham had been a member of the LSU law faculty from 1940 to 1946, then moved to Vanderbilt University, after which he served as dean of the law school at Ohio State University.[36]

The White Lecturers were expected to deliver three lectures on a related theme, and the lectures were routinely published as books by the LSU Press. The 1956 White Lecturer was Walter Gellhorn, whose appearance was questioned by members of the local American Legion post. However, after some consultations, it appeared "that the Legion has decided against any open opposition to the lecturer." However, the Baton Rouge Citizens Council, a conservative anti-integration group, did seek to educate liberal law faculty members by inviting them to a meeting featuring a lecture by Walter J. Suthon Jr., a Tulane professor of civil law and former president of the Louisiana Bar Association, who was the author of an article in the *Tulane Law Review* titled "The Dubious Origin of the Fourteenth Amendment." Less controversial was the 1958 lecturer, Lon L. Fuller of the Harvard Law School, a philosopher and contract-law expert who lectured on freedom and the nature of man.[37]

Fall 1953 saw Professor Herbert F. Jalowicz of Oxford come to LSU to lecture on Roman law. Another visiting lecturer was André Tunc, then associated with the University of Grenoble. Visiting Professor Yvon Loussouarn of the Faculty of Law at the University of Rennes was in residence at LSU for the Fall 1955 semester. He published, for a Louisiana legal audience, "The Relative Importance of Legislation, Custom, Doctrine, and Precedent in French Law," suggesting that the supremacy of statutes was being weakened by the French judiciary, which was using innovative methods of interpretation. Two internationally known legal scholars lectured in Fall 1957, Jean Limpens, director of comparative law at the University of Ghent, and Abe Malmstrom, a professor of law at the University of Uppsala, Sweden. Law lectures focused on European integration as early as 1958, when Horst Ehmke of the University of Cologne lectured on "European Integration and Constitutional Law."[38]

The connection between the Law School and law reform was illustrated when some two hundred people attended the sixth annual meeting of the Legislative Services Conference at the Law School. The director of the California Legislative Council spoke on substantive law revision, as did LSU professor J. Denson Smith.[39]

CURRICULUM

A modest revision of the curriculum occurred at the end of World War II, under the Curriculum Committee chairmanship of Jefferson Fordham, but little had changed since then. The faculty did revisit the alternative curriculum (two years of undergraduate training and four years of law school) adopted with great fanfare during the Beutel deanship but which was discontinued during the war. This curriculum was studied again but not adopted.[40] The 1950–51 catalog listed a bare-bones curriculum with thirty-eight courses:

	Fall		Spring	
Course		Hours	Course	Hours
First Year				
100.	Introduction to Law	2	106. Torts II	2
101.	Contracts	3	107. Constitutional Law	4
102.	Criminal Law	3	108. Agency and Partnership	2
103.	Family Law	3	109. Obligations	4
104.	Legal Bibliography	1	110. Civil-Law Property	3
105.	Torts I	3		
Second Year				
116.	Sales	3	112. Common-Law Real Property	3
117.	Evidence	3	115. Criminal Procedure	3
118A.	Louisiana Practice I	3	118B. Louisiana Practice II	3
119.	Administrative Law	3	120. Corporations	4
123.	Workmen's Compensation	2	126. Commercial Paper	3
130.	Labor Law I	2	131. Labor Law II	2
136.	Insurance	2	143. Estate and Gift Taxation	2
140.	Legislation	3		
Third Year				
128.	Seminar: State and Local Tax	2	121. Mineral Rights	3
132.	Succession, Donations, Community Property	6	122. Federal Procedure	3
			125. Seminar: Contemporary Problems	2
133.	Conflict of Laws	3	127. Security Devices	2
134.	Local Government Law	3	129. Seminar: Law Office Practice	2
135.	Income Taxation	3		
142.	Seminar: Comparative Law	2	141. Adminstration of Insolvent Estates	3

Changes in the first-year curriculum proposed by Dean Hebert in 1953, when he returned to the Law School from private practice, were adopted by the faculty. A new course, Institutions of Law (3 semester hours), was added in the first semester to provide a general historical introduction to the study of law. The course in jurisprudence (3 semester hours) was moved into the second semester of the first year, making it a required course. Six hours of family law and of agency and partnership were reduced to 3 hours in one combination course offered in the second semester.

Hebert defended the need for the introductory and philosophical courses, rather than tossing students into case and statute studies without the guidance of a frame of reference:

> Our curriculum is, in my opinion, not sufficiently rich in historical consideration of: legal institutions, fundamental conceptions of law, divisions of law, Roman law, pre-codification of continental law, modern civil law, English "Common Law" and "Equity," Anglo-American Law, background of Louisiana law, comparison of Louisiana Civil Code with other modern civil codes. The general objective of such a course would be to develop a broad foundation on which to build the more advanced courses. The course would consider broad developments in the field of private law analytically and historically and from the viewpoint of broad comparisons. Dean Tullis' old course on Introduction to the Study of Civil Law performed such a function at one time.[41]

Torts continued to be allocated five semester hours, but the course was split into a Fall three-hour course and a Spring two-hour course so that first-year students would be exposed to five different faculty members in the Fall. Civil-law property and obligations were reduced from four to three hours in consideration of the introductory materials that would be covered in the institutions course.

Professor Eric Voegelin of LSU's government department faculty was tapped to teach jurisprudence, a course that was also open to advanced undergraduate students. Voegelin was one of the three men who became LSU's first Boyd Professors, the University's highest academic rank.[42] He no doubt brought great prestige to the law curriculum, but some of his more practical students were not impressed with his tedious lectures. One student seeking Voegelin's approval asked a question toward the end of the course. He asked which came first, Plato or Aristotle. Herr Voegelin simply responded "Dummkopf," and there were no more questions.

Procedure was not taught in the first year, but Henry George McMahon was urging a new two-hour course in judicial administration to be taught to freshmen. It was not adopted. At this time, eighty-five semester hours were required for graduation, and the grading system remained the traditional A-B-C-D-F used by the main campus. Professor Pascal proposed changes in Fall 1955, but no formal action was taken on the proposal. By 1956, Dale Bennett was also recommending a change to a numerical grading system. Many students recall the difficulties of having to make a B to counteract a D to avoid expulsion, and the faculty's standards were such that Bs were not easy to make. The system was not changed until the 1960s.[43]

Class size became a problem in the mid-1950s, and the faculty was split on a proposal to divide the freshman class into two sections. The advantages of smaller classes were weighed against the consequences of faculty teaching overloads and the lost time for research. Eventually the faculty took no formal action but left the matter to administrative disposition by Dean Hebert, who was in favor of the change. The sectionalization continued in subsequent years and was reaffirmed in a 1956 faculty meeting. The 1952–53 term also saw the reinstatement of the admission requirement of three years of undergraduate study, a requirement that had been suspended during the war and postwar period. Still, twenty-nine of the fifty-four entering students that year came with college degrees. Also, during these postwar years, students were allowed to enter the Law School during the spring and summer terms as well as in the fall semester. But financing the summer school was not easy. To accommodate new freshmen, eight courses were needed but only six had been budgeted; the faculty requested additional funds for the two additional courses in 1952.[44]

Some type of evaluation of faculty by students was underway, but "the instruction evaluation project is on a purely individual and voluntary basis, questionnaires being solely for the information of the instructor." Some faculty members, especially Joseph Dainow, wanted to provide the students with extra classes in their courses. In response to objections from a student-faculty relations committee, the faculty, led by Harriet Daggett, was opposed, except for make-up classes. She said it should be the obligation of each faculty member to teach the material in his assigned course within the hour limitations allotted in the curriculum. The faculty voted to allow no extra classes without the approval of the dean. Class attendance was a recurring concern often discussed at faculty meetings. At one point, the attendance rule had been deleted from the Law School bulletin, but the faculty concluded that the rule requiring that a student attend 75 percent of the classes should nonetheless remain in effect. Not all faculty were taking attendance, and they were reminded to do so. Although the custom had developed of allowing students to submit "unprepared slips" to avoid being called upon, the "use of unprepared slips by students was declared to be an individual matter for each faculty member's disposition."[45]

Academic standards remained high, and the small size of the Law School allowed decisions by the full faculty on petitions for readmission by students who failed to meet the C-average requirement. Faculty were also requested to identify students whose examination papers reflected "marked deficiency in English, spelling and grammar [sic]." Indeed, problems with poor student writing skills have been chronic, and the legal-writing issue is rehashed with regularity. An experimental legal-writing course in 1952–53 was found to require more resources than were available, and it was eliminated after only one year. A noncredit course in legal bibliography was moved to the second semester in 1953–54 to ascertain whether such instruction would be more effective after students had some knowledge of law. In 1954, all freshman law students were required to take a standardized test of English given by the College of Arts and Sciences. It was not clear what action would be taken if students did not pass the test, but it apparently was not a serious problem since only five students failed.[46]

When Saturday classes were canceled for the 1957 Homecoming celebrations, the *Reveille* pointed out that the cancellation did not apply to Law School and graduate classes.[47] The next year, when President Middleton suspended classes for a Mardi Gras holiday, the suspension did not apply to law students.

One of the first matters to come up under Dean Harrison's administration was student attendance at lectures given by visiting faculty and dignitaries. Students were required to attend two-thirds of those lectures, and those who failed to do so were required to submit some type of paper or book review. Melvin G. Dakin remembers one student who was assigned to do a review of *The Bramble Bush*. The student's report was not on Karl Llewellyn's classic introduction to law study but on a sexy novel with the same title. As was not unusual for situations in which mandatory rules are adopted, problems arose. Two law students indicated that their scheduled classes in advanced military science conflicted with some of the lectures in the series. The faculty then adopted an exception allowing the dean discretion in applying the lecture-attendance rule. Some form of the lectures requirement was retained into the mid-1960s, when it was abandoned. The first sign of an easing of regulations was a vote to impose no sanctions on students who failed to attend the lectures during the Spring 1969 series.[48]

The most important major curriculum changes came at the end of the decade, during the deanship of Milton M. Harrison. Charles Reynard was appointed chairman of the Curriculum Committee, to serve with Professors Malone, McMahon, and Smith. Malone described the time as one of experimentation: Harrison "was constantly eliciting suggestions," and "it was a time of discussion of ultimate objectives of the law school."[49] The curriculum, as changed by Hebert's proposals, had been based on a policy of theory first, then practice. But the faculty was more pragmatically disposed and decided to teach the practical first, then the philosophy and jurisprudence.

Another basic policy was the law faculty's unwillingness to adopt separate civil-law and common-law curricula. Background in both systems was required, and to accomplish that goal, the graduation requirement for the single unified curriculum was increased by twelve hours to the ninety-seven hours that remain today, probably the highest hours requirement in the country.[50]

The first urgent matter of the 1957 term was Professor Voegelin's departure from LSU to return to the University of Munich, making him unavailable to teach the first-year course in jurisprudence. The Curriculum Committee urged that the theoretical course be replaced in the first-year curriculum and be made an elective upper-class course. Professor Pascal objected to a permanent change, and it was decided to make the switch for the 1957–58 academic year.[51] As inertia progressed, the change became in effect a permanent one. In January 1958, the faculty also voted to make institutions of law an upper-class elective and replaced it in the first semester with family law. McMahon's desire for a first-year procedure course was accommodated with the creation of an introductory two-hour course in judicial procedure and administration. The new first-year curriculum looked like this:

Fall		Spring	
Course	Hours	Course	Hours
101. Contracts	3	105B. Torts II	2
102. Criminal Law	3	107. Constitutional Law	4
104. Legal Bibliography	1	108B. Agency and Partnership	3
105A. Torts I	3	109. Obligations	3
108A. Family Law	3	110. Civil-Law Property	3
111. Introduction to Procedure	2		

Another innovation was to require students to take three less practical, more theoretical courses in their second and third years in place of the courses that were removed from the first-year curriculum. The three courses had to be chosen from among institutions of law, international law, jurisprudence, common-law property, and a comparative-law seminar.[52] This "package course" requirement was perceived by students as a means of forcing them to fill classes that would not otherwise be taken and to take courses with professors in whom they had no interest. The package course requirement remained in force until the early 1970s, when the pressure of high enrollment made it difficult to offer the courses. It was ironic that Professor Dainow, who taught civil-law property, moved to make common-law property a required course and not just a package course. Professor Daggett, who taught primarily civil-code courses, seconded the motion, but it failed to pass.

Professor Pascal also moved that the Curriculum Committee report be rejected in its entirety, and again Professor Daggett seconded the motion. It failed to pass. Pascal sought to continue the institutions course in the first semester, but his motion died for lack of a second. Smith sought to offer the institutions course in the second semester, a motion seconded by Pascal, but it failed to pass.[53]

Under the existing 85-hour curriculum, a student could complete law school in six regular semesters or five semesters and two summer terms—three calendar years at most. Beginning in 1959, entering students would be allowed to commence the law program only in the fall semester and would be required to pass 97 semester hours to graduate with the LL.B. degree, requiring seven semesters or six semesters and two summer terms—three calendar years at least. The committee justification for the added hours was that "we are graduating students who have been forced to omit such basic courses as Federal Procedure, Income Taxation, Conflict of Laws, etc. . . . This is a matter which has recurrently suggested itself in the light of our efforts to teach something of two legal systems, plus the usual proportion of rapidly expanding areas of public law."[54] The report pointed out that the University of Minnesota law school had added a fourth year of legal training and that Iowa State had extended its resident requirement to seven semesters. Northwestern, Illinois, Southern Methodist, and Texas all required students to attend at least one summer term in addition to the traditional three years.

Explaining the curriculum changes to readers of the law review, Dean Harrison commented, "Although a study of law comparatively is desirable in any jurisdiction, in Louisiana it is essential." The new curriculum would ensure that graduates would be "well trained in the fundamentals of civil, criminal, procedural, commercial and public law. In addition, the graduates will be well prepared in legal history and legal philosophy, and they will possess the ability to evaluate continually our legal system against the needs of our society."[55] The rule also had the effect of requiring more summer-school courses—and incidentally more faculty slots to teach those courses. Under the new program, a total of forty-five courses were now available.

The Law School was not ready for experimentation with clinical programs. The Baton Rouge Legal Aid Clinic sought participation by law students in its program, and though the faculty stated that it supported the social policy of the clinic, "in the absence of facilities and resources to permit faculty supervision and under the present method of the clinic's operation, there is no substantial educational opportunity for law students in connection with this program." Students were permitted, however, to participate in the program on their own initiative. Flexibility was also not on the agenda when a local dentist sought to enroll as a special student in the Law School despite having failed to take the three years of pre-legal work normally required for admission. It was also not the time to switch to anonymous grading of exams, "and the general consensus was against the school's adopting any such policy."[56]

Another step into the national mainstream came when the faculty required, effective in Fall 1960, that applicants take the law-school admission test. It was a modest step, however. The minimum-index score (index = LSAT + [GPA × 100]) of 450 could be met by the minimum LSAT score of 300 and a 1.5 average (on a 3.0 system).[57] No limitation on the maximum number of students enrolling was imposed.

DESEGREGATION

A prophetic entry in the law faculty minutes in 1948 was the denial, "in accordance with university policy," of the request of "Roscoe Turner, a negro" for admission. Turner claimed that he was eligible to attend all-white LSU because he would not be entitled to the veteran's exemption from taking the bar examination if he were to graduate from the all-black Southern University School of Law.[58] That claim conformed to cases in the U.S. Supreme Court that focused on factual issues in determining whether states were actually supplying equal educational facilities in separate professional schools for black students. The denial of Turner's application was not brought to the courts.

It was the application in 1950 of Roy S. Wilson, an army veteran from Ruston, that made its way to a three-judge federal court. The judges were Wayne Borah of the Fifth Circuit Court of Appeals and district judges Herbert Christenberry and J. Skelly Wright. LSU president Harold W. Stoke and Law School dean Henry George McMahon testified in the case, as did Wilson, President Felton Clark of Southern University, and Dean A. A. Lenoir of the Southern University Law School. Testimony focused on comparison of facilities at the LSU and Southern law schools. The court ordered the admission of Wilson and also held that the lawsuit was properly brought as a class action. Judge Wright wrote the court's opinion. The LSU Board of Supervisors, staunch opponents of desegregation, voted to appeal the decision, but the United States Supreme Court affirmed the lower-court ruling without comment. Wilson's attorneys were stalwarts in developing NAACP civil-rights litigation—A. P. Tureaud of New Orleans, U. Simpson Tate of Dallas, and Thurgood Marshall of New York City.[59]

Wilson's enrollment on November 1, 1950, was the lead story in the *Reveille*. A photograph showed him accompanied by civil rights activist J. K. Haynes and Alex L. Pitcher, a Baton Rouge attorney. His tenure at LSU was short, however. Wilson resigned from the Law School on January 17, saying that "there was an investigation in progress on my background, and I knew what they would come up with. I knew I would be rejected." It appeared that Wilson had received a "blue discharge" or "Section 8" discharge from the army. The law faculty minutes stated that an investigation was under way by the dean of the University and the director of student life as to whether a "Section 8" discharge disqualified a student. No public action seems to have been taken on the matter, but when it was disclosed that Wilson had withdrawn from the Law School, the *Baton Rouge Morning Advocate* confirmed his withdrawal. His attorney, A. P. Tureaud, stated that the withdrawal was for financial reasons. The LSU Board's statement emphasized that Wilson had claimed to have an honorable discharge, when in fact his Section 8 discharge was neither honorable nor dishonorable.[60]

Decisions on desegregation and related matters were closely controlled by the Board of Supervisors, and the Law School had little control over the matter. When the federal district court ordered the admission, in June 1951, of Lutrill Amos Payne of Natchitoches as a graduate student in agriculture, Milton M. Harrison, then assistant to the president, was asked by the press whether LSU would appeal. His understated answer was simply that the question could only be answered by the Board. When desegregation of the undergraduate program was ordered, Board of Supervisors chairman J. Stewart Slack of Shreveport announced that eighteen attorneys, all LSU graduates, had volunteered to work on an appeal of the lower-court ruling. The omissions in this list are perhaps the most significant ones—no law faculty members or administrators, present or past, were listed. As the desegregation debate intensified during the decade, the gulf between University faculty and the Board widened. Some sixty-six LSU faculty signed a petition protesting legislation requiring the closing of integrated high schools.[61]

In Fall 1951, three black students applied for admission to the Law School and were accepted. Pierre S. Charles, Robert F. Collins, and Ernest N. Morial entered as the first black law students. By September, Ian Claiborne had been appointed proctor in the law dorm, and a committee of juniors and seniors was appointed "as added assurance that there would be no incidents as a result of assigning three Negro freshman students to live in the dormitory." Law School files indicate that more thorough investigations of the character references for the black students were made than in the normal case, but the three students were admitted without the need of a court order. In response to a letter from Dean McMahon requesting advice about how to proceed,

President Middleton sent a short hand-written note stating that if an applicant met the standards required of white students, "I see nothing that we can do but to accept him into the law school."[62]

A front-page *Reveille* photograph of a freshman moot-court argument featured Collins representing the state in a murder conviction appeal. He and Morial were moot-court partners, and they won the first round of the moot-court competition. Charles resigned after the first semester, but Collins and Morial continued at LSU and were graduated, Morial in February 1954 and Collins in May 1954. Morial would remember that "generally there was not a great deal of hostility, in my opinion. There were some who shunned myself and Collins, I guess. Some were cordial. They would speak to you when they were alone, but when they were with a group they might not say anything to you, because, I guess, they were fearful of being criticized by some of their white peers. Of course, we could not use . . . the facilities in Tiger Town. They were just off limits. The blacks could not go in there." Morial patronized Percy's Bar-B-Que, not far from campus, and he became friendly with the Franklins, who owned the place. It was a restaurant that served blacks in the front room and that had a back room for whites, with a back door.[63]

Paul M. Hebert praised Dean McMahon for his leadership as dean during this period: "The emotionally charged problem of racial integration was surmounted in his administration as he guided the Law School toward acceptance of court decrees. Thanks to Dean McMahon and his courageous faculty, there was no turmoil when the first Negro students were accepted and were graduated from the LSU Law School. The problems that erupted elsewhere did not disturb legal education at this University—a real achievement for any law school in the deep South."[64]

Morial and Collins were graduated in 1954, the year *Brown v. Board of Education* was decided.[65] Little was happening in law-school integration after their graduation, and the focus in the cases after *Brown* was on undergraduate and secondary-school desegregation. After Collins and Morial graduated, no black students were graduated until 1969, when Bernette Joshua and Gammiel B. Gray completed their studies. Morial became a state legislator, mayor of New Orleans, and a state appellate-court judge. Collins was appointed to a federal district judgeship in New Orleans.

The impact of *Brown* and the Louisiana legislature's attempts to circumvent it made their odd way into the 1957–58 Law School catalog. In 1956, a committee presented the legislature with thirteen acts designed to maintain segregation, which were adopted by both houses without dissenting votes. Act 15 required students to present a certificate of eligibility signed by a high-school principal or superintendent. A change to the teacher-tenure law also provided for the firing of any person who signed such a certificate. Although the attorney general advised that the act applied only to new students, district attorneys met and decided that continuing students were also covered. The catalog stated that the statute had been held unconstitutional by a federal district court, but that students should be aware that the requirement could be imposed later. The injunction against enforcement was heard before Chief Judge Herbert W. Christenberry and Judge J. Skelly Wright of the Eastern District of Louisiana. Ultimately, the Fifth Circuit upheld the lower-court ruling.[66]

The University community was reacting, in Fall 1956, against the legislature's opposition to desegregation. Dean Paul M. Hebert was one of five Louisiana lawyers who signed a statement deploring attacks on the U.S. Supreme Court. The statement, issued by George Wharton Pepper, a prominent Philadelphia lawyer, former U.S. senator, and former president of the American Law Institute, stated, "There are ways of bringing about changes in constitutional law, but resistance is not such a way. Changes may be wrought by seeking an overruling decision or by constitutional amendment. It is through the amending process and not by resistance, that the people and the states stand as the ultimate authority." An editorial in the *Reveille* castigated the legislature for adoption of the obstructionist statutes, and the State Baptist Student Union at its convention attended by a thousand students adopted a resolution urging the state to repeal the segregation measures.[67]

Meanwhile, state boards were more cooperative with the legislature. The LSU Board of Supervisors voted to enforce the law, and the State Board of Education did the same after a two-hour closed meeting with Senator Willie M. Rainach, chairman of the legislative committee on segregation, Representative John Garrett, vice-chairman, and William M. Shaw ('41), committee counsel. A student letter-writer responded, "I suggest that the State Legislature and the LSU Board of Supervisors require certificates from their members showing them to be advocates of academic freedom. It's my conviction that this would practically abolish both bodies."[68]

Resistance to desegregation at the undergraduate level reached a high point again in the summer of 1958 when the segregation committee looking for Communists investigated a number of LSU faculty members who had signed a petition against legislation calling for closing any school faced with integration. President Troy H. Middleton was summoned to appear before the committee, and he stated, "I have no evidence that anyone at the University has communist leanings."[69] The legislature's ire about the petition arose when two faculty members testified against the legislation, including Charles Reynard, still a member of the law faculty and former executive counsel to Governor Earl K. Long. The *Baton Rouge Morning Advocate* the next day featured front-page photographs of Reynard and English professor Waldo F. McNeir.

Less important than the admission of the black students at LSU, but instructive of how the law faculty operated and how tortuous their decision-making process was, is the discussion in Fall 1950 of a Yale Law School proposal to be submitted to the annual AALS December meeting. The proposal would have excluded from the association schools that excluded or segregated students because of race. The issue placed before the law faculty was that of instructing its delegates to the meeting on how to vote. Ultimately, the vote was to abstain, but only after a procedurally tortuous discussion that only law professors could tolerate. The events were: Professor Howerton moved that the Law School abstain from voting; seconded by Professor Reynard. Professor Bennett moved for an informal poll, which was ruled out of order. Professor Smith moved as a substitute that the school vote against the amendment; seconded by Bennett. The substitute motion failed by a vote of 4 to 6. Vote recurred on the main motion to abstain. That motion failed by 5 to 6. Bennett moved that the vote be cast against the Yale amendment; seconded by Smith. The motion failed by 5 to 7. Bennett then moved that the dean be authorized to vote according to his discretion; seconded by Smith. Professor Shestack moved as a substitute that LSU cast its vote in favor of the amendment. The motion was defeated by 5 to 6. Vote recurred on the main motion for dean discretion. The motion failed by 4 to 6. Shestack moved that the Law School's vote be cast for the Yale proposal; seconded by Professor Daggett. Motion carried by a vote of 7 to 5. Voting for were Daggett, Dainow, Dakin, Howerton, Malone, Reynard, and Shestack. Voting against were Bennett, Harrison, Hebert (by proxy), Pascal, and Smith.

Dean McMahon then asked that someone other than he be designated to cast the school's vote. Professor Malone was selected by unanimous vote. Smith moved that Malone be instructed to call attention to the division of faculty opinion and that the action was determined by a vote of 7 to 5; seconded by Malone. Motion carried. Smith moved that Malone be further instructed to state that those voting against the Yale amendment were of the firm conviction that such a resolution was beyond the purview of the AALS; seconded by Pascal. This motion carried unanimously. Howerton then moved for reconsideration of Shestack's motion to support the Yale amendment; seconded by Smith. The motion carried by a vote of 7 to 2. Howerton moved that the Law School abstain from voting on the Yale amendment at the meeting; seconded by Smith. This motion carried 9 to 1. It was also not unusual that the law faculty would not have a strong sense of abiding by the principles of *res judicata* with regard to faculty votes. At a meeting on December 8, Dean McMahon "stated that he was presenting no request, but was making one last effort to make the faculty see the seriousness of their decision to abstain." There was some discussion of the matter, but no action was taken.[70]

The AALS vote at the annual meeting was almost as procedurally confusing, the debate on the Yale proposal covering twenty-four pages of the proceedings, and the result was essentially the same. The AALS did not adopt the stringent Yale proposal and instead adopted a milder substitute without mandatory penalties for segregated law schools.[71] And, of course, a committee was appointed to study the issue.

The issue resurfaced in December 1951, when the AALS was to consider the moderate proposal of the Special Committee, the Yale report itself, and a Nebraska proposal. The LSU law faculty again displayed its split on the issue in typical convoluted procedures at its December 4 meeting. Dean McMahon stated that he opposed all three proposals and that if the faculty approved any of them, that a delegate be appointed to cast the school's vote at the meeting. Dainow moved and Shestack seconded to approve the special committee report. Reynard moved as a substitute to approve the Yale proposal; Dakin seconded. The substitute failed by a 4 to 5 vote, with McMahon breaking the tie. Dakin moved another substitute, the secondary Yale proposal; Malone seconded, and the motion to substitute carried. Voting for were Daggett, Dakin, Malone, Reynard, and Shestack. Voting against were Bennett, Dainow, and Smith. The vote then recurred on the now-substituted motion. It carried. Voting for were Daggett, Dakin, Malone, and Shestack. Voting against were Bennett, Dainow, and Smith. This time, Reynard abstained.

Malone then moved that if the choice were between the primary Yale proposal and the committee report, LSU would vote for the Yale proposal. The motion carried. Reynard then moved that if the Yale primary proposal were substituted for the committee report, LSU would vote for the primary proposal. The motion passed. After further discussion, Reynard moved that LSU vote to reject the special committee report. The motion carried.[72]

ASSOCIATIONS, INSTITUTES, AND PORTRAITS

The LSU Law Alumni Association was organized on Homecoming Day, November 3, 1951. Articles of incorporation were drafted by Solomon S. Goldman ('16) of New Orleans, general counsel of the Pan American Life Insurance Company, and attorneys Ben R. Miller ('27) of Baton Rouge, John C. Burden Jr. ('48) of Alexandria, Tom Stagg ('49) of Shreveport, and Oliver P. Stockwell ('32) of Lake Charles. Goldman was elected president, Miller vice-president, John M. Madison ('32) of Shreveport secretary, and Judge G. Caldwell Herget ('27) of Baton Rouge treasurer. Dean McMahon asked that faculty wives assist Mrs. McMahon in preparing sandwiches for the event. That was a formidable task, as some 350 Law School alumni and guests attended the session.[73]

One of the first tasks of the association was raising funds to commission portraits of distinguished law faculty. Ben R. Miller was able to commission Clark Hulings, the young son of one of his clients, to paint portraits of Robert Lee Tullis and Ira S. Flory. Later, Hulings did portraits of Harriet S. Daggett and Charles Reynard. These four portraits, of exceptional quality, still hang in the Law School, providing a glimpse of the early work of the artist, who became one of America's foremost western and landscape painters. Hulings received the coveted Prix de West from the National Academy of Western Art in 1973 and subsequently received three silver and two gold medals from NAWA competitions. Nina Nichols Pugh ('47), when sitting for a portrait by Hulings, asked that he make her look better than life—"ethereal"—as he had done for Harriet Daggett. Pugh recalled that Daggett's appearance could be somewhat sloppy, but that the portrait didn't focus on her yellowed hair and she was not smoking a cigarette.[74]

Hulings's father was Colonel Courtland Hulings, who came to Baton Rouge to open the Copolymer plant, which manufactured synthetic rubber for use in World War II.[75] One person who recalls the young Hulings is Robert (Rocky) Perkins, a Baton Rouge artist and grandnephew of architect A. Hays Town. Perkins recalls that Hulings did renderings for Town and that as a boy, he followed Town around to watch him painting. When I retired in 2000, it was Perkins who painted my retirement portrait, which hangs in the Law School with the Hulings portraits.

The Tullis and Flory paintings were presented to the Law School at a special ceremony on March 28, 1953, as gifts of the two professors' former students. They were accepted on behalf of the University by two members of the Board of Supervisors, Lewis Gottlieb ('16) and James E. Smitherman ('09). Gottlieb called Flory "the most modest person that I have ever met, and a lengthy, laudatory ceremony would have been absolutely painful to him." In presenting the portrait of Tullis, Victor A. Sachse ('25) stated, "All of Louisiana has benefitted from his courageous fight in the early nineteen twenties for American liberties and against bigotry and lawlessness. He showed us then, by his example, what a man of law should stand for in his community."[76]

The first session of lectures presented by the Mineral Law Institute organized by Professor Daggett was held in February 1953. Senior classes were canceled so that students could attend the lectures. The institute continued holding annual sessions for mineral lawyers, and its continuation was reaffirmed in 1959 even though Tulane Law School was then sponsoring a Mineral and Tidelands Law Institute.[77]

The School of Banking of the South, founded by the Southern Bankers Association, held its first classes at LSU in 1950. Paul M. Hebert was one of the first lecturers in the program, coordinating the banking-law course. One of his frequent guest lecturers was William D. Hawkland, who became chancellor of the Law School after Hebert's death. The law faculty was also commencing to plan continuing-education activities, and a proposal for a program in foreign, comparative, and international law was submitted to the Ford Foundation in solicitation of grant funds.[78]

A special committee of the Board of Supervisors was appointed to work with the Law School's planning and development. Board members Thomas W. Leigh ('24), Theo F. Cangelosi ('34), and James E. Smitherman ('09) were appointed. Additional lawyer members of the group included Ben R. Miller

THE FIFTIES: RETURN TO NORMALCY

('27), John H. Tucker Jr. ('20), and Jerome A. Broussard. Hebert was chairman and Henry George McMahon was the faculty representative. Among the proposals before the group was construction of a new law building, based on projections into the next twenty-five years, capable of accommodating 750 students. A new building was indeed completed in 1970, and a year later, the school had more than 750 students.[79]

The law auditorium was air-conditioned in 1953. Moot-court trials that year had to be held in the East Baton Rouge Parish Courthouse because of the remodeling work. Plans to air-condition the library and faculty offices were formulated in 1955 and reformulated in 1956. By this time, the law building was becoming crowded: it housed not only law students and faculty and the law library but also, in the front basement, the Graduate School of Public Welfare Administration and the Department of Government of the College of Arts and Sciences.[80]

Alluding to the ferment in legal education in the postwar period, Dean Hebert wrote about the extent of the changes that had occurred since Beutel's appointment as dean:

> Under Dean Beutel's leadership in 1935, the faculty was augmented, the course offerings were expanded and a broad conception of the possibilities of legal education of an enlarged scope found recognition and official support. The law faculty, in the intervening years, has been constant in its efforts to improve the processes of legal education, and the curriculum as it exists today is far different from the more limited course offerings of two decades ago. The impact of the developments in the public law field finds itself reflected in courses of labor law, federal, state and local taxation; international law, local government law, estate planning, government regulation of business, legislation and administrative law, all of which constitute separate subjects unknown to the law curriculum of a generation ago.[81]

STUDENT LIFE

Enrollment during the decade of the 1950s was stable, with an average of forty-eight graduates per year. The 1959–60 enrollment was 229 students—120 first-year, 65 second-year, and 40 third-year students (plus four unclassified). The attrition rate continued at a high level (only 38 of those 120 first-year students graduated in 1962), and plans were under way to impose admissions requirements. It appears that the Law School's graduation rate was a concern in other parts of the University, and Dean Hebert thought "it might be desirable for the Law School to reconsider the extent to which the Law School's policy should be correlated with that of the University. Accordingly, he appointed a committee consisting of Messrs. Reynard, Bennett, and Pugh to study the matter and report to the faculty within the next several weeks." It does not appear that the report prompted much action, and there was little change in the passage rate during the decade.[82]

A footnote on the times is that Dean Hebert thought it appropriate to mention in his annual report that the alumni had donated to the Law School its first photocopy machine, to be available to faculty and students, and to alumni as well, for reproduction of library materials.[83] This event was the beginning of the end of the traditional sales of mimeographed student notes, known as dope- or poopsheets. The informal franchise for those sheets, primarily consisting of mimeograph masters, was sold by graduating students to their successors. One rumor is that in 1965, about the height of the value of the franchise, the seller made enough on the sale to buy a new Mustang.

Student fees remained low—$80 per semester for Louisiana residents—with a $25 general fee, a $20 law library fee, and a $35 activity, infirmary, and Student Union fee. The Union fee, intended to finance bonds for the LSU Student Union Building, was imposed several years before the structure was built and then occupied in 1964. A semester in the law dorm cost $90, plus $10.80 for a telephone.[84]

Following the pattern of the World War II G.I. Bill–subsidized students, students in the 1950s were less aristocratic than the prewar student body. Congressman Gillis W. Long is typical of many law students when he said, in response to a question about why he chose LSU, "I really didn't have the money . . . and so I never really seriously considered going anywhere but to LSU Law School." He believed that the populist background of many LSU graduates resulted in LSU supplying the core of lawyers in the state for the medium and small towns and also for public service. Long also reflected the increasing professionalism of the Law School student body and its separation from the main campus. He had been president of the LSU student body before entering the Law School, but after graduation he "pretty well" stayed out of campus politics. Also typical, he was working while maintaining a full-time class schedule, and that was about all he could handle.[85]

Law students partied well, especially at football games, where the senior law students had a reserved section on the forty-yard line, behind the band and in front of the Medical School senior section. As one student recalled, "some of the guys would have an occasional drink to ward off the cold and things. It gets windy up there. Shelly [Beychok] was fighting off a cold and didn't want to get one. We were coming down the ramp, and the band is going along. Shelly decides that he needs to put on one of those big, fur hats that the band wears, and he reached over and he grabbed the french horn fellow's hat. That guy said something to Shelly, whereupon Shelly just throws the hat down the steps. The guy then grabs Shelly's homburg and throws it down. They get to going at each other." Eventually, Beychok had to pay for the French horn damaged by blows from his cane or he wouldn't be allowed to graduate.[86] That story was passed on in the Tiger Band for years, until the law students lost their special reserved section decades later.

That incident, and others, led to opposition by other students, especially the engineers, to the reserved-seating policy. A proposal before the Student Council to recommend that the athletic department discontinue the special section was voted down in 1958, but by a close 6 to 7 vote after a two-hour debate. Chairman Patrick A. Juneau Jr., then an undergraduate, was called on to break a tie. He would go on to enter the Law School, but he denied that his vote was influenced by that fact. He simply was in favor of maintaining tradition. Juneau would win the Tullis Competition in his senior year, and in 1973 he was a leading delegate in the Constitutional Convention. The reserved seats were especially valuable in 1958, the year LSU's football team won the national championship and the Sugar Bowl.[87]

The issue of reserved seating came up again in Spring 1959, but it consumed only twenty minutes and the reserved seats were preserved by a vote of 13 to 2. The two dissenters, Engineering Student Council president Marshall Clayton and engineering representative Richard Lowery, would not give up, however. They circulated petitions that were signed by some six hundred students and provoked an election on two constitutional amendments, one that would prohibit the Student Council from recommending (to the athletic department) reserving seats for law students and another to do the same with respect to medical students. That action provoked the political ire of law students and especially law student body president William F. Kline ('60). He proposed a third amendment that guaranteed the right of individuals or groups to petition the Student Council on any subject and the right of the council to express its opinions when requested. That petition garnered 1,100 signatures. Campaigning was vigorous, the *Reveille* reporting that "such terms as 'inherent rights' and 'unequal privileges' were frequently heard in small discussions." The student newspaper also suggested that the "true purpose" of the third amendment was to cloud the issue and nullify the two original amendments. Kline argued that the first two proposals would prohibit any group from ever petitioning the council for reinstating the practice in the future. Clayton called the law student amendment an "ill-disguised move to cloud the issue with innuendoes and confuse the student body at the polls."[88]

The election was held on October 7 and produced odd results. The second amendment aimed at Medical School seniors failed, allowing them to continue their special seating. The first amendment aimed at Law School seniors passed, by a vote of 1,442 to 1,409, but so did the third amendment proposed by Kline. Interpretation of the conflicting amendments was left to the Student Honor Court, which ruled that the third amendment prevailed, and the special section for the seniors was saved. Kline's success in campus politics mirrored his future; he was elected district judge in 1976 and served as chief judge of the Twentieth Judicial District Court in St. Francisville for twenty years.

Student parties were sometimes rowdy. The faculty minutes of November 30, 1953, stated, "There was a discussion of the report of the Dean of Men on the recent Barristers' Ball held by the legal fraternities of the Law School." The details of the discussion were not mentioned, but the item was included no doubt because the minutes were circulated to the president of the University. The dean also felt constrained to remind the faculty that he had posted a memorandum "calling attention to the matter of student dress," the casualness of which was another remnant of the World War II veterans.[89]

The wives of law students became more active as a social group as older, married men entered the Law School. Sixteen wives of midterm seniors received Ph.T. degrees (Putting Hubby Through) in January 1959 at a banquet held at Bob and Jake's Restaurant. President Troy H. Middleton and Dean Milton M. Harrison presented the certificates, and the *Reveille* featured a front-page photo of Harrison awarding the degree to Mrs. Marie Politz, mother of four children and wife of Henry A. Politz. By Fall 1962, more than one hundred married students were enrolled in the Law School, and seventy wives were part of the Law Wives organization. The "old wives" provided a skit of tales for the new wives that year at the home of Professor and Mrs. Henry George McMahon. Mrs. William D. Beck was president of the club that year.[90]

By the 1950s, it was well established that seniors would wear hats and canes to classes for the first week of the term and then to parties and special events. The hats and canes were also required dress for admission to the reserved section in the football stadium. Originally, students wore derbies (or bowlers as they were called in England), but they switched to black homburgs during World War II because of a scarcity of derbies. The traditional hat was reinstated in 1949. Curved canes were replaced in 1953 with white-topped swagger sticks. Women seniors sported the hats and canes as well as the men; a *Reveille* photograph showed Robert L. Curry III, Helen M. Simmer, and Robert K. Guillory with their gear.[91]

Faculty consideration of "psychological strain" among students led to Professor Dainow's suggestion to use trial examinations to prepare students for final exams. No vote was taken on his proposal, but several faculty members teaching freshman courses indicated that they intended to give such exams. Another initiative showing concern for student well-being came in 1952, when the fifty-four entering fall-semester freshmen were assigned to faculty members for counseling. The faculty also adopted a proposal from the Student-Faculty Relations Committee that exam grades not be posted until all examinations were concluded. When grades were posted on the bulletin board, names and grades of all students in each class were on display for all to see. That tradition continued until the Buckley Amendment (Federal Education Rights and Privacy Act) was adopted in 1974.[92]

At the beginning of the decade, the prospect of military action in Korea affected law students. The faculty voted to study what programs the Law School might undertake if shrinking enrollment "creates an excess manpower problem." University-wide enrollment at LSU was down to six thousand for Fall 1950, Dean of the University Paul Hebert tracing the downturn to the Korean Crisis. Few students would be expected to start their law studies in the summer, and the summer program was scaled back. The final examination in the agency class was moved from May 26 to May 28, 1951, to avoid a conflict with the "selective service tests." By 1952, an army directive granted no delays to commencement of service for ROTC students after four years in college, meaning that many students would be subject to call without delay at the end of their first year of law school.[93]

William E. Crawford ('55), for example, had completed his first year of law studies in 1949–50 and then was called up for service. He spent two years in the military and then returned to law school and graduated in February 1955. His former undergraduate debate partner, William G. Kelly Jr., graduated the year before in the Class of 1954, but then he had to enter the military and Crawford sold him his uniforms for $10. Some students left school before the end of the semester to enter active military service. A number of them—including Joe C. LeSage Jr., Jack J. Rogers, and Theodore C. Strickland of the Class of 1952—were nonetheless given course credit. The faculty declared that they had completed all work for the LL.B. and recommended that they be awarded degrees. Indeed, the Law School adopted a rule that permitted students called into military service during their final semester to be granted their degrees upon completing one-half the semester's work and certification of the instructor that the work was satisfactory. Strickland, chief justice of the Honor Court, had to be replaced when he was called to active duty. A front-page *Reveille* story featured a photograph of William T. Wise, Strickland's successor, and Elmo C. Lear, president of the Law School student body.[94]

In November 1950, the interfraternity moot court featured Gillis W. Long and Robert B. Shaw of Gamma Eta Gamma versus E. Drew McKinnis and William R. Veal of Phi Delta Phi. The *Reveille* gave the story top billing along with a photograph of the lawyers arguing before Judge Dale E. Bennett. That same issue of the student newspaper announced that Karl N. Llewellyn, then at Columbia, was scheduled to be the main speaker at the law review banquet. Of all Llewellyn's accomplishments as a philosopher and legal expert, the student writer focused on his work in Cheyenne Indian law.[95]

Two graduate students from Europe were welcomed in Spring 1956, Giuseppe Bisconti from Italy and Raymond Jeanclos from France. Bisconti had been a student of Professor Pascal's at the Facoltà di Giurisprudenza of the University of Rome in 1951–52. He was awarded the LL.M. degree in 1956 and became a successful international practitioner specializing in corporate matters. He also distinguished himself as president of the International Bar Association and, in that capacity, as a champion of civil rights, especially in

Africa. Jeanclos returned to LSU in Fall 1956 to take a position as a research associate working with Professor Malone in the field of comparative tort law. He was graduated in 1957 with the LL.M. and practiced law in Paris at 26 Avenue Kléber in the chic Sixteenth Arrondissement.[96]

The Law School faculty, given its academic and theoretical orientation, voted not to participate in the National Inter-Law School Moot Court Competition, partly because of the cost but also because successful participation would require the best students, thus interfering with law review work. In 1952, the faculty was asked again by Leon Hubert of the Tulane law faculty to consider participation in the program. The Law School did participate, and LSU hosted the regional moot court in November 1954. In Fall 1953, LSU was represented by Newton C. Dalton, William G. Kelly Jr., and Frank J. Peragine in the regional rounds of the National Inter-Law School Moot Court competition. However, the pendulum swung again in 1957, when the faculty reconsidered and recommended that LSU withdraw from the national competition. After student urging, delivered by judge-to-be Melvin A. Shortess as a representative of the Moot Court Board, the faculty reversed itself and continued the competition for another year.[97]

In any event, after 1959 the faculty voted unanimously to cease participation in the national competition and to focus instead on the internal Robert Lee Tullis Moot Court Competition. Members of the state supreme court regularly traveled to the Law School to hear the final arguments and select the winning team. Dean Tullis routinely attended the arguments named in his honor. He had retired as dean in 1934 and was ninety years old in 1954 when Dean Hebert reported that Tullis's health made it impossible for him to attend the program. Retirees at the time did not benefit from group health benefits, and Hebert led a fund-raising drive that raised $3,000 as the Tullis Appreciation Fund to help defray the costs of Tullis's treatment. He died on February 26, 1955.[98]

In 1957, three major Hollywood productions were filmed in the Baton Rouge area—*The Long Hot Summer*, with Orson Welles, Paul Newman, and former LSU student Joanne Woodward; *Band of Angels*, starring Clark Gable and based on the novel by Robert Penn Warren; and *Durango*, starring Jeff Chandler and Julie London. The author of the *Reveille* stories covering the filming was Rex Reed, who became a nationally known film critic. More to the point, the filming took place after Joanne Woodward had been nominated for an Academy Award for best actress for her performance in *The Three Faces of Eve*. After she won that Oscar, students in Annie Boyd Hall put up a sign, "Joanne Woodward Slept Here," and the *Reveille* ran a picture of a student in Woodward's old room offering tours in return for five cigarettes. Not to be outdone, the male students living in the law dorm put up their version of a sign stating that Joanne Woodward had slept there, too.[99]

The Southern Law Review Conference was held in April 1959 at LSU. George Stumberg, then a professor at the University of Texas, returned to LSU in 1959 to speak at the Coif initiation.[100]

The bar examination was in effect during the period, and the faculty voted to oppose its discontinuance. The movement to return to the diploma privilege was a response in part to the desires of Korean War veterans wanting to enter the job market quickly. Dean Hebert joined the other Louisiana law schools in filing a brief with the state supreme court opposing the adoption of the diploma privilege, but they did not prevail. The supreme court adopted the diploma privilege by a vote of 5 to 2. Some members of the law faculty, including Milton Harrison, worked with a committee to get the exam reinstated, but it was not until 1959 that this was accomplished by a rule to become effective in 1963. The *Reveille* in June 1957 featured a list of the twenty-five LSU law graduates—out of 101 total new lawyers—admitted at that time. A sign of the times was that two graduates were unable to attend: Lieutenant Harry R. Sachse was stationed at Fort Sill, and James L. Babin had been admitted to the bar earlier in the month before entering the military.[101]

As a low-tuition state law school, LSU offered few scholarships. In 1958, the Superior Oil Company commenced its funding of scholarships for freshman law students. The three-year scholarships provided $260 per year for fees and books and a subsistence allowance up to $40 per month. The first two recipients were David W. Robertson and Frank P. Simoneaux, and the 1959 recipients were Keith M. Whipple and Leon H. Whitten. The Law School also established the Continental Oil Senior Award of $250 per semester, which was first awarded to Charley Quienalty. The Law School Alumni Association also sought to provide more financial assistance to the school, and it raised its annual dues from $2 to $5 per year.[102]

An undated pamphlet attributed to Phi Delta Phi, titled *Civil Code Rally Songs*, appeared circa 1957–58.[103] The pamphlet featured a high-sounding quote from Napoleon on the cover—about his civil code being his greatest accomplishment—but it quickly switched to song parodies about the Law School and law professors. It featured the "Law School Alma Mater," to be sung to the tune of the "LSU Alma Mater" or "Ghost Riders in the Sky":

> Where pompous profs and fumbling students shade the tomes of law,
> There stands our dear old Alma Mater with its bloated maw,
> Crammed full of things that waken in our hearts a painful burn,
> And make us wonder why the hell the law we wished to learn.
>
> Regurgitate, O Alma Mater, all those frightful hours,
> Spent sweating Big Red while pretending intellectual powers,
> Our worth in life will be they worth, we fear to think it so,
> For when depravity attends, we'll have no place to go.

Some of the parodies were less than kind to certain members of the faculty, especially those referring to hung-over lecturers, and they prompted Dean Hebert on his return to the Law School deanship to urge at a convocation that the students halt distribution of the pamphlet. He was only moderately successful in that effort. Authorship of the song parodies is not conclusively established, but a confidential knowledgeable source suggests that some of the leading authors were Henry A. Politz, Frank L. Maraist, and B. Roy Liuzza of the Class of 1959.

7

THE SIXTIES:
STEADY GROWTH

"Tough!" That was the description Congressman W. Henson Moore III gave of the Law School he entered in 1961. "I'll never forget as long as I live looking at those grades to see if [I], in fact, made the cut, and what a feeling it was when I had." His class of 1965 had fifty-seven graduates out of a freshman class of about a hundred students. The students who made the cut were close knit: "We were not divided into sections or groups. So it was one class of Torts and one class of Contracts and one of Obligations and one of Family Law and each one of us got to have all the famous teachers of the day, and they were tremendous ones, people that I'll never forget. They certainly molded my life as much as anyone I can think of. People like 'Big Red' Denson Smith, and of course, Wex Malone, and many, many others . . . you were just privileged to study under them."[1]

Despite the difficult ninety-seven-hour curriculum, students kept coming in increasing numbers. The Class of 1960 had 45 graduates; the Class of 1969 more than tripled, to 144 graduates. A faculty of fifteen full-time members was on board for the 1960–61 term, and there were twenty-four teaching in the 1969–70 term. Total enrollment in 1960–61 was 219; in 1963–64, 299—an increase of 11 percent in the first-year classes during each of the previous four years.

The Vietnam-era student unrest at East and West Coast universities was slow in coming to the Law School at LSU. Students stated that it had little effect on them. A good number of the students worked between undergraduate school and commencing law study, and many were married or about to marry. "The idea was, if you were going to be a lawyer, the time for play was over." The most they did was to start a newspaper for law students called *Dicta*. Leon Gary was a good cartoonist who sometimes poked fun at the faculty, but "that's about as bold as we ever got."[2]

THE SIXTIES: STEADY GROWTH

Prosperity was contributing to budget increases for the Law School. The 1962–63 budget was $311,000, the 1963–64 budget was $383,000, and the budget for 1964–65 was $426,000. In the latter year, the law library book acquisitions budget was $49,000. A 1962 report by the American Association of University Professors stated that average faculty salaries at LSU were among the highest in the South. LSU and the University of Virginia were the only public institutions rated among the top three categories in salary ranges. Growing enrollment was, however, absorbing the increased funds. Two sections of each first-year class were now being offered, adding to the demands on personnel. Academic standards remained high. From 1960 to 1964, only 51 percent of entering Law School freshmen earned satisfactory scholastic records and were eligible to continue into the second year.[3]

CURRICULUM AND STANDARDS

The Law School adopted a major change in the grading system in 1960. It had used a numerical system until 1928, when it followed the rest of the University in using letter grades in a system under which an A was worth 3.0 points. A 1.0 or C average was required for graduation. Given the high standards of the Law School, few As and Bs were awarded, and a student who made a D or an F was hard pressed to make the 1.0 mark. To avoid the drastic effect of one or two poor grades, Professor Robert A. Pascal had proposed a numerical system in 1955, but it was not adopted. In the 1960 debate, he and Professor Donald H. Wollett argued "that numerical grading would provide a much more accurate, equitable, and precise method" of grading. Professor George W. Pugh feared that numerical grading would result in a lowering of standards, and Professor J. Denson Smith thought numerical grading would work in favor of the poorer students. The proposal to change the system passed, with Smith and Henry George McMahon asking that their abstentions be recorded in the minutes. The faculty adopted a 100-point system, with 85–100 designated as A; 75–84 B; 65–74 C; 55–64 D; and 54 and below F. However, a grade of less than 45 in any course would be treated as a 45 to prevent a low F from overly influencing a student's overall average. As adopted, there was no cap on high As. In 1966, the faculty decided that 89 would become the highest possible grade, to prevent a very high A from overbalancing several mediocre Cs, and the admonition was added that "the numerical grades 88 and 89 would be reserved for work of rare and unusual excellence."[4]

Law students often ask who graduated with the highest average. Once the numerical system was in effect, Karl W. Cavanaugh of the Class of 1965 had an overall average of 87.48.[5] Though it is difficult to compare grades over the years, with rules and faculty changing over time, it appears that he is the person with the highest average ever earned under the numerical grading system. But even that conclusion has to be qualified—he made four grades higher than 89 before the maximum grade was reduced to 89.

Complicating the system was the issue of the grade average required for graduation. Professor Pugh was concerned that allowing students to graduate with a 65.00 average, the lowest C, would result in lowered standards. The result was adoption of the rule that an overall 68.00 average was required to graduate. It was stated in the debate that this system was based on the grading scale in effect at the Northwestern University law school. The system remained in effect until 2000. The truncated numerical scale was not unanimously admired. Professor George W. Hardy suggested at a faculty meeting in 1969 that a letter-grade system be adopted, and reversion to a letter-grade system was regularly proposed in each subsequent decade. The faculty also reacted to some seniors who folded their arms and stopped working seriously; a new rule was adopted requiring that students make an average of 68.00 in two of the last three semesters, regardless of their overall average, in order to graduate. The rule was later tightened to require a 68.00 in each of the final two semesters.[6]

Students could still pursue a combined program of three years of study in the College of Arts and Sciences, then enter law school and, upon completion of the first year of law studies, qualify for a bachelor's degree. Two degrees, a B.A. or B.S. and an LL.B., could thus be earned in a six-year period. Professor William C. Havard of the government department objected to the combined degree, arguing that it did not provide enough coverage of social sciences and liberal arts to merit a degree from the College of Arts and Sciences. At the time, the Law School opposed the elimination of the combined degree, but it changed its position in 1974.[7]

The first-year curriculum was required, as were three "package courses," but no other courses were mandatory. Dean Paul M. Hebert was concerned that the Law School was graduating students who had not studied conflict of laws, common-law property, some civil-law courses, evidence, or federal jurisdiction. The consensus of the faculty, however, was not to adopt required upper-class courses. Typically, however, two committees were appointed to study curriculum development of the school, Committee A devoted to civil-law subjects and Committee B devoted to common law, public law, and commercial law.[8]

The implementation of the ninety-seven-hour graduation requirement resulted in an expanded summer program. Summer courses in 1961 increased from six to seven, providing summer compensation for an additional faculty member. In 1965, the summer-school program changed from a nine-week term, like the rest of the campus, to two six-week terms. Students could earn ten hours of credit in a summer, as opposed to six under the old system, allowing graduation in six semesters and one twelve-week summer program. The change also increased the number of teaching slots available for faculty, thus adding to faculty income over time. Though each faculty member who taught one course in a given summer received less income (14.7 percent of annual salary for a six-week term instead of 22.5 percent for the nine-week term), there would be more summer-school teaching slots available every summer. Enrollment in 1965 was 141 for the first summer-school session and 103 for the second.[9]

The Law School did not allow part-time students in the first year. On the application of the wife of a member of the English faculty, the law faculty refused to waive the rule that all first-year courses be completed in the first year. Indeed, part-time law study was always discouraged at LSU. The first-year curriculum was mandatory, and students were required to carry the full load. The Law School never provided a night program, again reflecting the academic roots of its founding as a University department rather than being a converted private law school. In the late 1960s, pressure mounted to adopt a night program—a problem that concerned LSU because the advocates were also trying to accomplish their ends by founding a new state-supported law school. Movements were afoot to open new schools in Monroe and in Lafayette, just as the faculty went on record to oppose a night division. The demand for new law schools was also often cited as the reason why LSU should continue with (nearly) open admissions, so that the demand for legal education would be met at the flagship state university. As LSU continued to admit large numbers of students, standards remained constant and the graduation rate remained relatively low. This was criticized as an inefficient process that wasted resources, but the political pressure to continue the open-door policy was strong.[10]

The decade of the 1960s began with an inspection by a reaccreditation evaluation team from the American Bar Association, composed of Dean Page Keeton of the University of Texas Law School and Professor Arthur S. Miller, then at Emory University Law School. It appeared to be a civilized visit, beginning with a reception at the dean's home, followed by a faculty supper at the Baton Rouge City Club. But it also appears that the report was not as favorable as hoped. The Law School faculty discussed the report "in detail," and they expressed "a number of objections, on the grounds that the report was erroneous and misleading." However, Dean Hebert reported that the final report stated that the Law School was in full compliance with ABA standards "and enumerated a number of points for consideration in the further development and improvement of the school." Those points would be debated again and again throughout the decade.[11]

Dean Hebert persuaded the faculty in 1962 to return to his concept of introductory historical courses in the first year. Courses in introduction to civil law and introduction to common law were added in the first semester. Civil-law property was moved to the first semester, family law was placed in the second semester, and agency and partnership were designated as an upper-class course. The first-year curriculum looked like this:

Fall		Spring	
Course	Hours	Course	Hours
Contracts	3	Obligations	3
Torts I	3	Torts II	2
Civil-Law Property	3	Constitutional Law	4
Introduction to Civil Procedure	2	Criminal Law	3
Introduction to Civil Law	2	Family Law	3
Introduction to Common Law	2		
Total Hours	15	Total Hours	15

In addition, one credit was given for legal bibliography, a year-long course. Writing later in the law review, Hebert acknowledged that law students traditionally reacted unfavorably to such introductory courses, but that he thought the foundations were important. His appreciation of student sentiment was accurate, and the introductory courses would remain unpopular with students. The growth in the number of upper-class courses was consistent—the catalog for 1965–66 listed fifty-two upper-class courses, and at the end of the decade, there were sixty-seven listed. A discussion in September 1966 indicated a faculty willingness to experiment in courses; possible offerings for the upcoming summer session included Roman law, government contracts, atomic-energy law, international transactions, international organizations, military law, and air law.[12]

Over the years, the entire faculty considered student petitions for readmission after exclusion for academic reasons. That painful and somewhat inconsistent process occupied an inordinate amount of faculty time. In 1963, prodded by new faculty members George W. Hardy and David W. Robertson, the faculty delegated that power to a committee, but to protect the members from pressure, "membership of the committee should be unpublished."[13]

The first quantitative admission requirements were imposed in Fall 1960; students had to have an index score of 450, the index combining the Law School Admissions Test score and the undergraduate grade-point average multiplied by 100. It was, to say the least, a minimal requirement, since the median LSAT score was about 500 at the time. The minimum score required for admission was raised later to 550, but even then, a student with a 1.0 (C) average could enter with an LSAT score of 450, about the twentieth percentile. For the first time, the Law School differentiated between in-state and out-of-state admission standards, the index for the latter being raised to 650. Some disquiet was raised, as it would be reraised dozens of times in the next decades, about using an objective LSAT-GPA formula for admissions standards. Associate Dean Milton M. Harrison urged allowing more discretion in admissions and using more indicators of ability, but the faculty in 1966 was not willing to do so, being motivated primarily by fears of political influence entering the admissions process. Also, as was not unusual, a committee was appointed to study the matter.[14]

The Law School did not seriously consider limiting enrollment to reduce overcrowded classes. The prevailing view was that the Law School "should continue to accept all qualified persons who apply for admission rather than adopt the policy of some other law schools which limit enrollment by means other than the satisfaction by applicants of certain minimum qualifications." LSU's strong populist ideal of education for everyone was still intact. However, the Law School also stated that the maximum size of any class should be seventy-five—some faculty believing that number should be fifty—and under such a plan, the Law School would need four new faculty members. Judge/Professor Albert C. Tate thought that selective admissions was poor policy, perhaps leaving rural areas without lawyers: "we may be preparing too elite a bar for what our people need. I mean Lake Arthur needs a lawyer, and the kind of lawyer that is good enough to get through LSU now can make more money somewhere else than by hanging out a shingle in Lake Arthur." Reflecting his basic populist values, Tate also thought a part-time night-school program was desirable.[15]

The increased ninety-seven-hour requirement for graduation was used to justify granting credit for what had been compulsory noncredit work—moot court and legal ethics. The 1964–65 Student Moot Court Board,[16] led by chairman Morris A. Lottinger Jr. and with the assistance of adjunct faculty advisor Ben R. Miller Jr., conducted studies to support expansion of the program and to award credit for the work involved. The faculty approved, and the credit program, still largely directed by the student board, was instituted in 1965–66 under the chairmanship of Paul R. Wimbish. Two hours of credit were provided in the junior year, and the course was required for all students except those participating in law review. Also still in existence was a course in law-office practice, originally taught by Alvin B. Rubin and then by several leading Baton Rouge attorneys. Visiting professor Harry Cohen, who taught the required noncredit course in legal ethics in Spring 1965, recommended that the course be granted credit. That proposal was adopted, but not until 1974.[17]

LSU students joined the national movement lobbying for a change in the name of the basic professional law degree from Bachelor of Laws to Juris Doctor. Although the arguments for the proposal might have been somewhat specious—that government civil-service jobs paid higher salaries to J.D. holders than to LL.B. holders—the faculty agreed to consider the request. Dale Bennett, chairman of the committee that studied the issue, was known as an advocate of student interests, so it was no surprise that the committee recommended the change. SBA student representatives Merritt B. Chastain, Kirby J. Guidry, and Donald L. Mayeux presented the student request to the faculty, stressing that the J.D. "would constitute better recognition of the professional nature of the law degree." The motion to approve the request was adopted unanimously. It was to be applied prospectively, but demands from alumni led to a program that allowed LL.B. graduates to replace their diploma with one indicating that a J.D. degree was awarded. It was indicative of LSU's position as a state-financed law school that it exchanged diplomas for a small fee that covered costs, rather than using the exchange as a means of soliciting substantial donations from alumni.[18]

Intense and concentrated discussions of the Law School's mission and curriculum were under way between 1966 and 1968. Dean Hebert started the process with Development Memoranda #1 and #2, containing forty-one pages of detailed observations and suggestions. Faculty responses were as detailed, expressing agreement and disagreement on virtually every point. By Fall 1967, the curriculum-study groups were reorganized. Faculty members were assigned to Committee A (common law, commercial law, public law) (Dakin chairman, Bennett, Currie, Klein, Malone, and Shieber); Committee B (civil law, comparative law, international law) (Dainow chairman, Lazarus, Litvinoff, Pascal, Smith, and Yiannopoulos); and Committee C (procedure, moot court, skills training) (Pugh chairman, Ellis, Hardy, Klein, and Sullivan). Not assigned to these committees were newcomers W. Lee Hargrave and Albert C. Tate, who met informally with research associate and assistant professor Claus Jurgen Drestler as the "Uncommittee." In a memorandum, Tate wrote that by failing to assign the three, Dean Hebert "had by implication created an Uncommittee of which they are members." With the presence of Judge Tate, the Uncommittee meetings were invariably more interesting and shorter than those of the other three committees.[19]

Committee B proposed in 1968 a drastic change in the organization of the law faculty and the freshman curriculum. It urged "that more emphasis on civil law courses as distinguished from common law courses was necessary." To that end, it urged that torts and contracts be removed from the first-year curriculum. It also proposed that the substance and content of the civil-law courses should be determined by tenured faculty teaching those subjects. Excluded from voting on those issues would be all untenured faculty and tenured faculty who did not teach those courses. Since 1935 at least, the entire faculty had participated in adopting all academic regulations. In addition, Committee B proposed to give control of the entire first-year curriculum to the faculty teaching civil law. Although it did not formally propose a division of the faculty into a civil-law department and a common-law department, the committee suggested that the matter be discussed.[20]

The proposal was debated at a contentious meeting held at the end of the academic year on May 28, 1968. Dean Hebert and Professors Dainow, Lazarus, Pascal, and Yiannopoulos spoke in favor of the proposal.[21] Hebert argued, somewhat surprisingly, that the "impact of the Torts and Contracts courses was so overpowering in the training of first-year students as to make it impossible for them to have a civilian orientation." Dainow also suggested that torts and contracts "were more gripping than the civil law courses and therefore threw the balance against a civil law orientation on the part of law school students."

Speaking against the proposal were Associate Dean Harrison and Professors Dakin, Ellis, Hardy, Hargrave, Klein, Pugh, Shieber, and Sullivan. They argued "that there was no antagonism between the civil law and the common law and that the goal of the Law School should be one of instructing students to take their places as Louisiana lawyers capable of using both the civil law method and the common law method in their work as lawyers." Hardy argued that support for and perpetuation of the civil-law system was an institutional goal of the Law School but not the purpose of the first-year program.

Interestingly, the dean was the only faculty member with an LL.B. from LSU who spoke in favor of the change. Crawford, Ellis, Hardy, Hargrave, Harrison, and Pugh, who were graduates of LSU's traditional LL.B. professional program, were not in favor. The vote on the proposal was 6 for and 10 against. In a memorandum to the dean, Judge Alvin B. Rubin, also holder of an LL.B. from LSU, stated that he favored emphasis on high quality and dynamic instruction in the civil law and that such instruction "can be as stimulating as torts and contracts." He argued against separate civil and common law faculties.[22]

One small change in the curriculum was made to accommodate Committee B. The introduction to common law course, which had few supporters, was eliminated. One credit hour was added to the introduction to civil law course and another hour added to civil-law property.

Perhaps the most dramatic part of the debate was the statement from

Dean Hebert that even if the faculty defeated the proposal, he would not feel bound *not* to present it to the Board of Supervisors, where he no doubt felt that the proposal might receive a warmer reception. In response, former AALS president Wex S. Malone suggested that he would be able to obtain support from the accreditation agencies to assure faculty control over the curriculum.[23] With that standoff, the proposal to split the faculty and to create separate departments of civil law and common law was forgotten.

Committee C's main proposal was designed to counteract the effect of large first-year classes and the resulting loss of rigorous training in analysis. It urged that one first-year class be subdivided into smaller sections of twenty-five students so that individual instruction could be emphasized. The faculty approved the proposal in principle, but it would be some time before it could be implemented.

The race issue was always in the background. The faculty minutes state that a black graduate of a Texas law school not approved by the AALS was denied admission, not because of race but because of failure to be transferring from an AALS-approved school. Newly arrived Professor Donald H. Wollett contributed a new section to the annual symposium on new legislation—Race Relations. He reported on the thirty-five acts and four proposed constitutional amendments adopted in 1960 to limit the application of *Brown v. Board of Education* and to counteract the sit-in demonstrations that were developing in the state. He stated, "the state's law in respect to public elementary and secondary education has, at the time of this writing, become so muddled that an intelligent appraisal of the legal situation is impossible." But he predicted, correctly, that most of the legislation would be held unconstitutional.[24]

On the horizon was a "head start" program for minority students planning to attend law school, sponsored by the Council on Legal Education Opportunity. Participation in such a program was considered in Summer 1969 but was postponed until 1970. Meanwhile, the movement to consider alternate admission standards was influenced by the prospect that some students who would not meet the objective minimum index requirement might complete the CLEO program and otherwise show ability to succeed in law school. After a sharp debate, the faculty voted to allow a maximum of two students to be admitted to the first year even if they did not meet the minimum index, provided that other evidence of capabilities was presented. Professor Smith asked the minutes to note that he voted against the motion because it was discriminatory in nature and favored a selected few. Dean Hebert and Professors Bennett, Lazarus, Pascal, Sullivan, and Yiannopoulos stated their agreement with Smith. Professor Pascal also submitted a four-page statement explaining his vote against the proposal.[25] Later, in the 1970s, the number of special-admission slots would increase substantially.

A boon to students was the elimination in 1967 of the attendance rule, which required attendance at three-fourths of the classes in a course to take the final examination. However, the Law School faculty decided to keep records of attendance and to monitor attendance. As one might expect, attendance dropped off, and "serious attendance deficiencies" were perceived. The attendance rule was reinstated in Fall 1968. A report disclosed that the champion class-cutters of the Class of 1968 were William G. Whatley, Rhett R. Ryland, and James R. Murrell III. The only dissenters on the vote to reimpose the rule were the two youngest faculty members, Hargrave and Klein. The rule remains in effect to this day. Professor Dainow, whose courses in security devices and international law reported the most absences, continued expressing his concerns over student attendance. When he complained that students were not attending his (inevitable) make-up classes, the faculty offered little sympathy. Instead, they decided that absences at a make-up class would not be considered in applying the attendance requirement.[26]

THE FACULTY: COMINGS AND GOINGS

Harriet S. Daggett's health deteriorated during Spring 1961, and she announced that she was retiring at the end of the academic year. She had served the Law School for thirty-six years, and her retirement dinner in September 1961 was a gathering of VIPs. LSU president Troy H. Middleton and Louisiana Supreme Court chief justice John B. Fournet ('20) joined Dean Hebert as speakers, and Thomas W. Leigh ('24), a former member of the Board of Supervisors, was master of ceremonies. Professor Daggett lived for five years after her retirement, dying from cancer on July 22, 1966. The memorial commemorating her service to the Law School would contain the oft-repeated statement that she was "the best 'man' on the Faculty."[27]

Professor Daggett had been instrumental in developing Louisiana mineral law, and an endowed chair in oil and gas law for her successor was in the offing. The Superior Oil Company committed to financing the chair for four years, providing annual support of $16,000 ($89,860 in Year 2000 dollars), a sum higher than any other law faculty salary in 1961. The company renewed the grant in 1965.[28]

The fifteen regular faculty members in Fall 1961 included new member George W. Hardy III, who was hired for the chair in mineral law and headed the Mineral Law Institute. A front-page *Reveille* photograph of Hardy and an accompanying story focused on the fact that he came from law practice in Alexandria with political figure and premier attorney Camille F. Gravel. Hardy had been the top graduate at Virginia Military Institute, a Rhodes Scholar at Oxford, and a law graduate from LSU in 1958. He was editor-in-chief of the law review and had two years' experience teaching law at the University of North Carolina and working as executive secretary of that state's constitutional revision commission. Later in the decade, he became a reporter for the Louisiana State Law Institute's proposal for a mineral code, which was adopted in 1974.[29]

Hardy established cooperative programs with the Petroleum Engineering Department at LSU and participated in interdisciplinary courses with members of that faculty. He was active in the American Association of University Professors, participating in an investigation of LSU's refusal to make facilities available to the Young Democrats for a speech by pacifist Wade Mackie concerning world disarmament.[30] Typically, it was a long report. He remained at LSU until June 1973, when he became dean of the college of law at the University of Kentucky. He later became dean of the law school at the University of Houston, then moved into law practice in Lafayette. He died there on November 26, 1996.

After several intermittent teaching assignments while working with the Law Institute for ten years, Carlos Lazarus was appointed a regular associate professor of law beginning in Fall 1961. He came with a degree from the Municipal School of Commerce in Manchester, England, and a law degree from Loyola University Law School. He began teaching diverse courses—legislation, donations and community property, corporations, and negotiable instruments. He was indeed a generalist teaching so many courses, and he referred to himself as a "utility man." In January 1962, Milton M. Harrison completed his service as vice-president of the University and returned to the law faculty with the newly established title of associate dean. He would remain until his retirement in 1983.[31]

In 1961, Donald H. Wollett announced that he was leaving after two years at LSU to practice law with a New York law firm specializing in labor law and industrial relations. Thomas S. Currier came to LSU in Fall 1962 in his place and remained for two years. Currier was a native of Shreveport and had studied at Princeton, Stanford, and Centenary before receiving his LL.B. from Tulane. He was also a former research assistant at Yale Law School, practiced with the Stone, Pigman, and Benjamin law firm in New Orleans, and was an assistant professor at Tulane. He was a promising writer, co-authoring with his Yale teacher James W. Moore an article titled "Mutuality and Conclusiveness of Judgments." While at Tulane, he collaborated with Dean William Ray Forrester on a casebook on federal procedure. Currier taught labor law and constitutional law at LSU and was faculty editor of the law review. He left for the University of Virginia Law School in 1964, where he became one of the school's strongest professors in constitutional law and procedure, then moved into law practice in New York City with the Mudge Rose law firm.[32]

David W. Robertson ('61) had been awarded the Greater Washington, D.C., Alumni Fellowship, which provided a summer internship with Senator Russell B. Long; after graduation, he returned to Washington to work as a legislative assistant for Long during 1961–62. Deciding to try a teaching career, he came to LSU on a one-year appointment as instructor in 1962–63, anticipating working on a graduate degree at Yale the following year. To accommodate the Law School when Professors Pascal and Smith were scheduled for sabbatical leaves, he agreed to serve another year and was an assistant professor for 1963–64. Robertson was an honors graduate of the Law School and served as managing editor of the law review. While teaching at LSU, he was a consultant to the Louisiana State Bar Association's Law Reform Committee preparing a revision of the Louisiana corporations law and was faculty advisor to the moot court program, inaugurating a program of written critiques of preliminary briefs submitted by students. He then followed in George W. Pugh's footsteps to become a Sterling Fellow at the Yale Law School, earning the LL.M. and J.S.D. Robertson would eventually become one of the most distinguished professors at the University of Texas Law School while retaining an ongoing interest in Louisiana tort law and procedure that resulted in several publications in the *Louisiana Law Review*. He returned to LSU as a visiting professor for the 1974–75 term.[33]

J. Hector Currie came to LSU in Fall 1963 as a visiting professor to teach the introduction to common law and bankruptcy. He accepted an offer for a regular faculty appointment in January 1964 and, after a year in Europe during 1964–65, returned to LSU. He was soon a beloved fixture at the school. A new course in copyright law was established for him. He was a distinguished gentleman as well as an extraordinarily knowledgeable person who had been a Rhodes Scholar and held the B.A. and M.A. from Oxford. He received his law degree in 1942 from the Yale Law School, and he served on the University of Mississippi law faculty from 1948 to 1963. Currie resigned from the Ole Miss law faculty at the same time Dean Robert J. Farley was forced to resign by political pressure because he was supporting the court-ordered integration of the university. James Meredith had been admitted as a student for the 1962–63 term, followed by riots protesting his admission and determined resistance by Mississippi political figures. Currie was a member of the American Association of University Professors at Ole Miss and signed a statement adopted by the local AAUP on October 3, 1962, "which defended the federal marshals and called for law and order on the campus."[34]

Currie's teaching style was somewhat different from the typical LSU pattern. He was primarily a lecturer, rather than focusing on problems and hypothetical-fact scenarios. He had the ability to cover substantial amounts of information, as indicated when he wrote to Dean Hebert agreeing to teach bankruptcy, saying, "I have given the course for four hours, but I can cover the material in three."[35] He was an extraordinarily talented lecturer, often quoting from the textbook, and it was difficult to distinguish between his speaking style and the polished style of the quoted matter. Students were also awed by the fact that he had invested in Delta Airlines stock when it was still flying crop-dusters and then held on to it as it increased in value. Nonetheless, he did not own an automobile and walked to the Law School from a modest apartment close to campus on East State Street. Currie retired in December 1980 and moved to Vicksburg, Mississippi. For several years, he commuted to Jackson to teach at the Mississippi College School of Law. He died on December 14, 1994.

Benjamin M. Shieber began his service at LSU in Summer 1964, teaching federal procedure. He would add labor law, civil procedure, and constitutional law to his teaching arsenal. Shieber was an honors graduate of Columbia University Law School in 1953 and an editor of the *Columbia Law Review*. He clerked for Judge Edmund L. Palmieri of the Southern District of New York, then practiced law for ten years in New York City, specializing in labor law. He had a long-term interest in the law of Brazil and was part of a three-man lecture team that went to Brazil during August 1965. Shieber continued his service at LSU until his retirement in July 1988, and since then, he has regularly been present in the Law School, doing research and remaining active in arbitration matters.[36]

A law graduate from the University of Leiden, Anton G. Pos, was in residence 1964–65 auditing courses and serving as a research assistant to Dainow. Also at LSU at the time was Claus Jurgen Drestler from the University of Hamburg. His dissertation was a comparative study of tort law, but his assignment at LSU was as a researcher working with A. N. Yiannopoulos in the field of property law.[37] Drestler returned for the 1967–68 term as an assistant professor and research associate, but ultimately he decided to pursue a law practice in Germany rather than remaining at LSU to specialize in research in civil law.

Saul Litvinoff joined the law faculty as a visiting professor in the 1965–66 term. Along with Yiannopoulos, he was expected to form a core of eminent civil-law scholars who would prepare the treatises that would also be the basis for civil code revision.[38] Litvinoff was an Argentinian scholar who held B.A., LL.B., S.J.D., and S.C.D. degrees from the University of Buenos Aires and an LL.M. from Yale Law School. He had taught at the University of Puerto Rico's law school. He would become a regular faculty member the following term and remained at LSU for the rest of his career.

Donald J. Tate ('55) of the Evangeline Parish bar and editor-in-chief of the law review came to the Law School as a visiting professor in 1965–66. He was a former judicial administrator for the Louisiana Judicial Council. Tate was designated an associate professor for the 1966–67 term and headed the moot court program. From 1967 to 1969 he was a special lecturer and also participated in the legal bibliography course. In 1969, he served as chief-of-party for the Law School's Vietnam legal-administration project.[39]

William E. Crawford ('55) came to the Law School as assistant dean and associate professor starting in December 1965. He was editor-in-chief of the law review and had practiced law in New Orleans with the Chaffe, McCall, Philips, Burke, Toler, and Hopkins firm.[40] He began teaching in the torts field and assumed administrative duties in the dean's office. He was an experienced lawyer, thirty-seven years old at the time, and he followed in the footsteps of Professors Hebert, Dakin, and Harrison in taking an administrative position on the main campus. He served as assistant to Chancellor Cecil G. Taylor during Spring 1969.

While George W. Pugh served as a visiting professor at the University of Virginia Law School for the 1966–67 academic year, Francis C. Sullivan of Loyola (Chicago), head of the comparative study of criminal justice, was a visitor at LSU.[41] His connections with LSU would grow over the term of the project, and he remained at LSU as a regular faculty member and then as acting associate dean and dean. Sullivan had a J.D. from Loyola (Chicago) and an LL.M. from New York University and had experience working in the U.S. Government Defense Agency. He retired effective July 1, 1986, and became professor, then dean, at the Memphis State Law School. He died on January 9, 1992.

Accepting offers for Fall 1967 were W. Lee Hargrave and Michael R. Klein. Their personnel records, along with those of David Robertson and William T. Tete, indicate a new reality in hiring young faculty—draft boards. As the Vietnam War heated up, Dean Hebert often wrote letters to draft boards to seek occupational deferments for the new young faculty. Hargrave was hired on a one-year contract that was renewed the following year. He had graduated as valedictorian of his class in Summer 1967 and started teaching civil-law property and legal bibliography the following Fall. He had been editor-in-chief of the law review and valedictorian of his undergraduate LSU class in 1964, when he earned a B.A. in journalism. Klein received a J.D. from the University of Miami in 1966 and an LL.M. from Harvard in 1967 and had served as editor of the *Miami Law Review*. He had a special interest in zoning and land-use planning, and a new course in that field was established, along with a seminar in urban planning. He came to LSU in part to help Melvin G. Dakin prepare a treatise on Louisiana expropriation law under a grant from the Bureau of Roads and the Department of Highways. Klein was a strong supporter of Hubert H. Humphrey for president and publicly called persons opposed to him "pigs" and "creeps." In response, 106 law students signed an ad in the *Reveille* saying that they "do not feel it is necessary to resort to the undignified practice of name calling to support Richard M. Nixon for president." Klein taught through the Spring 1969 semester and then headed to Washington, D.C., to practice with the Wilmer, Cutler, and Pickering firm.[42]

Judge Albert C. Tate Jr., then on the Third Circuit Court of Appeals, took a leave of absence and taught at the Law School for the 1967–68 term. Tate's memory of his experience reflects both his extraordinary credentials and the flexibility of Dean Hebert:

> Dean Hebert called after Dean McMahon died. I was presiding judge in the court in Lake Charles. He called to ask if I would accept the McMahon appointment. I thought it over, and I was tempted. I went to see him and I said, "Would you be interested if I took it for just a year, and make up my mind during that?" After all I had thirteen years in the judiciary. He said, "No, that would be fine, but we are going to give you tenure; so that you can be sure that it is set. You don't have to wait for another vote, or anything like that." So I came as a tenured professor.

Tate was a native of Ville Platte but was reared in New York, attended prep school there, and graduated from George Washington University and Yale Law School.[43] He attended LSU in 1947–48 to study Louisiana law and received a certificate in civil-law studies. These were academic credentials that the politically active (and proudly pro-Long) Tate seldom bragged about, and he purported to be a simple Cajun. His quirky speech and inability to speak in complete sentences reinforced that rural image, but he was without doubt one of the top jurists in the state and his opinions are models of clarity and precision. His concern for his students was overwhelming and cemented his relationship with them even after he fell off the small podium in the front of his classroom and later walked into a sliding glass door at a student party.

Ever perceptive, Tate said, "One of the frustrating things about faculty meetings as compared to judicial conferences is nothing was ever decided. You had these brilliant talks, brilliant minds running around, and then nothing was ever decided." Hebert ran the Law School, Tate said, along with Florence Molaison, but not in the faculty meetings. He also said that the civil-law faculty and common-law faculty were "complaining to me about Mac Hebert taking the [other] side. . . . That was . . . a great balancing act."[44] Tate returned to the Third Circuit, teaching part-time for one year, before moving on to the Louisiana Supreme Court and then the federal Court of Appeals for the Fifth Circuit.

Klein took leave for the 1969–70 academic year. In his place, Frederick W. Ellis ('59) would be at the Law School full time during the academic year. Ellis provided assistance on the litigation team headed by Dean Hebert that was asserting Louisiana's interests in offshore oil and gas revenues in the U.S. Supreme Court and would also contribute to the Law School program as a member of the teaching faculty. Ellis was editor-in-chief of the law review, had practiced in Lake Charles with the Hall, Raggio, and Farrar law firm and in the oil industry before becoming a special assistant attorney general in 1966. He remained on the faculty, specializing in mineral law and environmental law, until he returned to private practice in Baton Rouge in 1982. He died on February 5, 1994.[45]

When a federal program established sea-grant colleges along the lines of existing land-grant colleges, LSU qualified and the Law School agreed to participate in the program. As the program developed, the Law School hired H. Gary Knight, then a practicing attorney in California, to teach half time and research half time. Knight had an A.B. from Stanford and a J.D. from Southern Methodist University and had practiced in Los Angeles. After several years of activity in marine-resources law, including being designated Campanile Charities Professor of Marine Resources Law in 1971, his attention switched to the developing field of artificial intelligence. He resigned in 1985 and entered a Ph.D. program in psychology at the University of Texas.[46]

William T. Tete ('67) joined the faculty in 1968. He was an editor of the law review and followed the traditional path of graduate studies at Yale, earning an LL.M. He taught the introduction to civil law, obligations, and modern social legislation. Tete also participated in the work of the Tidelands litigation project during 1971–72. He moved to New Orleans, where he was a visiting professor at the Tulane Law School before entering law practice in the city.

Also joining the faculty at the end of the decade was Howard W. L'Enfant Jr. ('66), who started in the 1969–70 term.[47] He had taught at Loyola Law School for two years and was an LSU honors graduate and editor-in-chief of the law review. He remains on the faculty today.

The staff of adjunct faculty continued to include Benjamin W. Yancey of the New Orleans bar teaching admiralty and R. Gordon Kean ('48) of Baton Rouge teaching a course in state and local taxation. A. Leon Hebert ('34) taught evidence in Fall 1964. The three of them continued their teaching in subsequent years. Elven E. Ponder ('52) taught torts, Ben R. Miller Jr. ('61) was faculty moderator of the Moot Court Board, and Alvin B. Rubin ('42) continued teaching law-office practice. Baton Rouge practitioner Bailey E. Chaney ('50) also taught the course in law-office practice as an adjunct for several years. He had declined an offer to become a regular faculty member and preferred to continue his law practice. Robert L. Roland ('49) was an adjunct professor teaching taxation. He explained, "The lectures and the discussions with students are enjoyable. That's what I like about teaching. The exams are a pain in the butt." W. Shelby McKenzie ('64) began his career as an adjunct, teaching primarily the insurance course, in the 1969–1970 term.[48]

Rubin had been teaching as an adjunct professor since 1946 and was interested in teaching one course every semester. The faculty concurred and voted to invite him to attend all faculty meetings. The 1966 Homecoming activities recognized his service as special lecturer in law on the occasion of his appointment as a district judge for the Eastern District of Louisiana.[49] Rubin continued as an adjunct faculty member after his appointment, usually traveling from New Orleans by bus so he could work during the trip. One of his students would be designated to pick him up at the Greyhound bus station.

THE FACULTY: GROWING ACCOMPLISHMENTS

One of Dean Hebert's early assignments upon his return was a definition of duties for Professor A. N. Yiannopoulos's Research Chair in Comparative Law. Yiannopoulos did not desire a permanent full-time research position, and they agreed that he would teach two courses for 1960–61, jurisprudence and a seminar in foreign and comparative law. Hebert also took advantage of the situation to accommodate his own interests in promoting civil-law history—Yiannopoulos was to deliver five noncredit lectures to the first-year class on the background of the civil-law system. Faculty discussion of the lectures was the occasion for a general discussion of the future of the Law School and the extent of its emphasis on civil law and common law. As always, no consensus was reached, and the report of the faculty views took four pages of single-spaced text in the minutes. The next meeting even featured a discussion of how much detail the minutes should contain. Some faculty sought to instruct the new secretary, George W. Pugh, to report only actions taken, as his predecessor was charged to do. This time, however, the faculty voted to allow the secretary to report the meetings in his journalistic style. By the mid-1960s, another junior faculty member became the faculty secretary and keeper of the minutes—Benjamin M. Shieber. His minutes tended to be concise and brief, and when Professors Pugh and Pascal moved that he include more detailed information about personnel matters, that motion failed to pass.[50]

The Law School was honored with its first Boyd Professorship, awarded to Henry George McMahon in 1963. He was the twelfth member of the LSU faculty to receive the highest academic rank in the University. McMahon was cited as the author of seven books and fifty articles, and especially for his work in drafting the 1960 Louisiana Code of Civil Procedure. His co-reporters on that project, Leon Sarpy of Loyola and Leon D. Hubert of Tulane, credited him with the most significant contribution to civil procedure since 1825, when Edward Livingston "skillfully blended Continental procedural principles with judicial administrative provisions of Anglo-American origin." The law review also reported his accomplishments with a student symposium on the new code. McMahon had been actively engaged in the professional placement of law students, having practiced in New Orleans and maintaining connections with many law firms. By the 1960s, the Law School was beginning to take a more active role in assisting the increasing numbers of its graduates to find jobs. In 1961, the Student Bar Association published its first placement brochure containing the photographs and résumés of all the law graduates.[51]

The December 1961 issue of the law review featured articles on assumption of the risk in tort law in a symposium organized by Wex Malone and his friends. They comprised a who's-who of torts scholars in the country: Leon Green, professor at Texas; Page Keeton, dean at Texas; Robert E. Keeton, professor at Harvard; John H. Mansfield, professor at Harvard; Willard H. Pedrick, professor at Northwestern; and John W. Wade, dean at Vanderbilt. Malone's work at the national level led to his appointment to the executive committee of the AALS in 1961. That same year, he was named national president of the Order of the Coif at its triennial convention. He was also on leave during the Spring 1962 session to teach at the University of Southern California and during the summer to teach at the University of North Carolina. Malone received one of two Distinguished Faculty Fellowships in 1964, the first year of the awards established by the LSU Foundation. Malone's influence on Louisiana tort law and on the national education community resulted in his being designated a Boyd Professor in 1966. LSU attendance at the AALS end-of-the-year meeting in 1966 featured a special occasion: Wex Malone acceded to the presidency of the association. His presidential address was an early call to law schools to train "legal technicians who would be able to offer inexpensive legal services to a wider scope of persons and to a wider variety of problems than the fully trained lawyer does."[52]

Malone's influence on Louisiana tort law especially was growing as a generation of his students became leaders of the bench and bar. He had long argued against the imprecision and confusion in the concept of "proximate cause," a doctrine that confused fact-finders in torts cases. He advocated a more direct and transparent "duty-risk" policy analysis in which judges would determine the scope of a defendant's duty as a matter of law. The Louisiana Supreme Court in 1962, in the case of *Dixie Drive It Yourself System v. American Beverage Company*, basically adopted Malone's approach, and a tort revolution was launched under the skilled hands of Justices Albert C. Tate and Mack Barham. Writing in 1970, Malone reported with some satisfaction that "the course of decisions subsequent to Dixie presents an interesting pattern indicating that generally the courts of appeal have received the opinion with understanding and have applied it with considerable ingenuity and common sense." He would report later, however, that the tort revolution had gone beyond the point he could accept—the revolution had gone beyond the aging revolutionary.[53]

It was also ironic that the alleged champion of common-law legal realism would see his influence in this tort-law development as an example of the renaissance of the civil-law tradition in Louisiana. Justice Mack Barham described the willingness of the courts to reexamine precedent, saying, "The application of other concepts involved in delictual responsibility such as last clear chance and res ipsa loquitur, the jurisprudence determining the validity of testaments are just a few of the areas in which the court has shown its willingness to find new language and new rationale in applying the statutory and codal law."[54]

Joseph Dainow won a Fulbright grant for the 1962–63 academic year to lecture at the University of Ghent. He had received an earlier Fulbright grant to lecture in Paris and Lyon and was a Guggenheim Fellow in 1954. The *Reveille* reported that the University of Ghent had awarded Dainow an honorary doctorate in recognition of his services.[55]

Robert A. Pascal returned to Rome in 1963–64 on a second Fulbright grant and participated in seminars sponsored by the University of Rome's Institute for Comparative Law. Seven professors—three Italians, two Americans, one Englishman, and one South African—participated in the seminars.[56]

By mid-decade, A. N. Yiannopoulos had published a volume of materials for the introduction to civil law course and had completed his translation of Aubry and Rau's *Cours de droit civil français* (6th ed., 1946). His monumental articles on usufruct, precursor to his *Louisiana Civil Law* treatise on the subject, were published in 1967. His treatise on *Property* was published in 1967 and *Personal Servitudes* in 1968. Professor Litvinoff started his research on the law of contracts and obligations, publishing his opening work, *Offer and Acceptance,* in 1967. The first volume of Litvinoff's treatise on the law of obligations was published by the West Publishing Company in 1969.[57]

Professor George W. Pugh was selected as one of six U.S. law professors to make special studies of judicial administration in twenty different countries throughout the world. Under this four-year program—the Comparative Study of the Administration of Justice, financed by the Ford Foundation—Pugh did field research in France, the Union of South Africa, and the Philippines. The Ford Foundation was attempting to assist in the broadening of the comparative approach to law in American law schools, and Pugh produced a criminal-procedure casebook reflecting that approach. As a result of his studies, Pugh also published a number of articles on comparative criminal justice.[58] The University of Virginia sought to hire Pugh, but his Louisiana roots were too deep and he returned to LSU.

Librarian Kate Wallach's enviable reputation in her field was reflected in her election to the presidency of the American Association of Law Librarians for 1966–67. She was granted faculty status in recognition of her "scholarship in law and her professional attainments, as well as a recognition of her many contributions to the Law School's teaching program through the years." The law library's holdings in 1961 had increased to 110,000 volumes, strengthening both the Continental and the Anglo collections. A $1,600 grant from the LSU Foundation in 1963 went toward buying the *Statutes of the Realm,* a set of early English statutes. Jules and Frances Landry donated a complete set of *Louisiana Acts* to the LSU Foundation for the law library. By 1964, the volume count had grown to 119,000 volumes, twenty-first in size among law-school libraries in the United States. The 1966 volume count was 132,000. Wallach, a member of the executive board of the American Association of Law Libraries in 1964, addressed the American Library Association conference that year, speaking to general librarians about the role of law libraries.[59]

Professor Dale Bennett participated in a national conference on bail and criminal justice held in Washington, D.C., and sponsored by the Department of Justice.[60]

Dean Hebert suffered a mild heart attack on July 12, 1962, and he was hospitalized. He was able to return to the dean's office part time on October 1, 1962, and to continue as dean. His summer activities in 1964 included participation, along with the Tulane and Loyola Law School representatives, in a mission to Central America sponsored by the International House of New Orleans. His activities included meetings with the dean of the University of Costa Rica Law School about possible exchanges of professors and students. In February 1965, Dean Regelio Sotela of the University of Costa Rica Law School was a visiting professor at LSU, participating in several civil-law courses.[61]

As the decade ended in 1969, Professor J. Denson Smith was appointed an Alumni Professor, a new distinguished rank at LSU granted to faculty exhibiting the highest levels of teaching accomplishment.

INSTITUTES AND GRANTS

The Mineral Law Institute, founded in 1953, continued its activities under the leadership of George W. Hardy III after the retirement of Harriet Daggett. The institute presented annual programs for lawyers and landmen and published papers on oil and gas topics.

The Louisiana State Law Institute, a state agency that was housed at the Law School, continued its close relationship with members of the law faculty. J. Denson Smith continued to serve as its director, and a number of faculty members were responsible for its accomplishments in the 1960s. The Code of Civil Procedure, adopted in 1960, was drafted primarily by Henry George McMahon, along with Leon Sarpy of Loyola and Leon D. Hubert Jr. of Tulane. The Code of Criminal Procedure, with Dale E. Bennett as the principal draftsman, was adopted in 1966. Co-reporters were Leon D. Hubert Jr., representing Tulane, and Adrian G. Duplantier, representing Loyola. A. N. Yiannopoulos translated the *Obligations* volume of the Aubry and Rau treatise, which became Volume 1 of the West Publishing Company's series, *Civil Law Translations.*

The Institute of Advanced Civil Law Studies was proposed in 1965 and commenced operations with Joseph Dainow as its head. Its objectives were to establish relations with other civil-law countries and to promote the study of civil law and comparative law. Little funding was provided, and its growth was slow.[62] Its mission was expanded in 1976 and the name changed to the Center of Civil Law Studies.

In Summer 1966, the Law School received a modest $7,500 grant from the Ford Foundation under an AALS program financing field studies in the social sciences. In connection with a summer course in modern social legislation, students were given a total of five hours credit and a stipend. In addition to the course, students observed social agencies in the area—legal aid, juvenile court, social-welfare services, nursing homes, etc. Among the students paired for the field trips were Lee Hargrave and Henry Sanders, not coincidentally the top-ranking and lowest-ranking students in the senior class. The decision to make the application for a grant pursuing such nontraditional credits caused some qualms—J. Denson Smith announced that he would abstain from voting on it—but it was adopted. The course was taught by Walter Wadlington III, a Tulane law graduate and faculty member at the University of Virginia, assisted by Leila Obier Cutshaw, a 1965 graduate of the LSU Law School who also had a degree in social welfare. Cutshaw would later continue teaching the course in social legislation as an adjunct, then would become a full-time member of the College of Business faculty teaching business law.[63]

Melvin G. Dakin was asked by the Louisiana Department of Highways to undertake a study of expropriation law in Louisiana under a grant from the U.S. Bureau of Roads. He was the principal researcher, and Assistant Professor Michael R. Klein also worked on the project. They produced a treatise on eminent-domain law that undertook a functional analysis of damage awards in the case law. The contract was a major supplier of jobs for recent graduates and students. Margaret A. O'Meara (Correro) ('66) worked as a research assistant during most of the project. Thomas R. Blum ('68) and Robert W. Collings ('68) worked as student researchers then as full-time research assistants. Other members of the class of 1968 who worked on the project were Howard R. Fussell, John L. Goldsmith, Donald L. Mayeux, and Darrel V. Willet Jr.[64]

George W. Hardy III and H. Gary Knight were planning and then implemented in 1970 a graduate program in marine resources law that combined twelve hours of marine-sciences work in addition to twenty hours of law courses.[65] This interdisciplinary curriculum was part of LSU's sea-grant program. However, the program failed to attract many students, and the emphasis of the sea-grant program was more on research than on teaching.

Student opposition to the war in Vietnam was growing, but it never became intense at LSU. Indeed, when the New York University's law school chose not to administer a legal-reform program in Vietnam because of student unrest, the U.S. State Department turned to LSU to conduct the project. Louisiana's legacy of French law, which also had influenced the legal system of Vietnam, was important in this request. The project called for providing assistance in establishing an independent judicial system for South Vietnam and to assist in the drafting of basic codes.[66]

The faculty's discussion of the project pitted the pro-international-programs wing of the faculty against some faculty members who were opposed to the war in Vietnam. Professors Francis C. Sullivan and George W. Pugh, who had participated in the Ford Foundation comparative study of criminal justice, were in favor. Pugh emphasized that the Law School was not being asked to participate in a war but to help a government improve the institutions that administered justice. Benjamin M. Shieber argued that the faculty's disapproval of the project would demonstrate its opposition to the war and might thereby help to bring about a change in U.S. policy and prevent involvement in future Vietnams. He saw the State Department project as an attempt to co-opt University support for the war. Dale E. Bennett opposed the project on the more practical ground that the school's principal responsibility was to the state of Louisiana. The vote on the motion to proceed with a proposal was 9 yeas and 2 nays, with several abstentions.[67]

Francis C. Sullivan administrated the project in Baton Rouge. Donald J. Tate was the chief-of-party in Saigon, and Lee Hargrave was assistant chief-of-party. Hargrave has perhaps the distinction of being a person who went to Vietnam to avoid the draft. When he was first hired in 1967, he obtained a one-year occupational deferment for teaching, but it appeared in 1968 that his draft board was reluctant to renew it.

Four justices of the Vietnamese supreme court visited the Law School in September 1969 to confer about the project and to meet with University administrators. Four appellate and trial judges came to LSU in May 1970 for seminars on American law and procedure. Assisting Frank Sullivan in conducting the seminars were A. N. Yiannopoulos, Jean-Louis Baudoin, Saul Litvinoff, and Judges Albert Tate Jr. and Jerome E. Domengeaux. University president John A. Hunter visited the Saigon office in October as part of a tour of Southeast Asia and the Philippines.[68]

Disappointed at the lack of progress in the project and reacting to personal and family concerns, Tate returned to the United States on September 11, 1969, and recommended an early termination of the project.[69] After consultations with USAID officials, the University decided to continue the contract with the twenty-six-year-old Hargrave acting as chief-of-party in Saigon. He remained in Saigon for nine additional months, and he and Sullivan produced the final recommendations and report. Hargrave returned to the United States in the summer of 1970 and returned to teaching in the fall. Among the services provided under the contract were critiques of drafts of five basic codes that would replace legislation enacted during the French domination of Vietnam. Those codes were adopted by a decree law promulgated on December 20, 1972, and Vietnam's chief justice at that time wrote his appreciation for the assistance provided by LSU. The impact of those codes, of course, was negligible in light of the surrender of the South Vietnamese government to the Viet Cong on April 20, 1975.

Chief Justice Tran Van Linh was able to escape from Saigon by boat as the city was overrun and reached the Philippines safely. He spent some time as a refugee in Chicago and Oklahoma and then moved to Baton Rouge in 1976, where he earned a master's degree in library science at LSU. He worked at Tulane's law library and then completed his career as comparative-law librarian at the LSU law library. The affection and appreciation that the Law School had for Judge Linh was shown when he was chosen as an honorary member of the Order of the Coif in 1984.

Donald Tate practiced law in his hometown of Ville Platte for several years and then returned to law teaching, this time at the Southern University School of Law.

VISITORS AND LECTURERS

The flow of professors visiting for a semester or two as well as short-term lecturers continued—lawyers, government officials, faculty from U.S. law schools, and faculty from foreign law schools. Students benefited from the exposure to this diverse group, whether they wanted to or not, because they were required to attend four of the five scheduled lectures each semester.[70]

Former dean Frederick K. Beutel, then a law professor at the University of Nebraska, lectured in 1961. It was his first visit to LSU since he had abruptly resigned as dean in 1937 and his first look at the "new" law building he was instrumental in designing. An LSU faculty member during the Beutel years, Jerome Hall, returned to give the 1962 White Lectures. He spoke on the philosophy of comparative law, and the LSU Press published a book based on his lectures, *Comparative Law and Social Theory*.[71]

Wex S. Malone took a sabbatical leave for the 1964-65 academic year, and Harry Cohen of the University of Alabama was a visiting professor for the spring semester covering Malone's first-year torts course. Also visiting that term was Clive M. Schmitthoff of the City of London College, who offered an intensive seminar in international trade. The seminar was designated a "package" course to encourage students to register for it. Also emphasizing international trade was Hans G. Bagner, a member of the faculty of the University of Stockholm Law School and a practitioner in the field. Giovanni Pugliese from the University of Rome team-taught the introduction to civil law with Professor Yiannopoulos. In an interview with the *Reveille*, Pugliese said that his U.S. students "respect the teacher more. They seem calmer and more in earnest about their studies than are Italian students, and pay stricter attention to lectures."[72]

One of the most dedicated and popular visitors was Jean-Louis Baudoin from the University of Montreal, Quebec. He taught the freshman course in obligations. The faculty sought to keep Baudoin and offered him a tenured position. He returned home, however, eventually to became a judge of the Quebec court of appeals.[73]

Another innovation was the hiring of a faculty member primarily to serve as an instructor in legal bibliography. Priscilla F. R. Apperson, a law graduate of the University of Virginia, as she would often remind her unimpressed students, was hired for that position under a one-year contract and also to serve as a reference librarian. This was another of the experiments in teaching legal research and writing, an ongoing problem at the LSU Law School as at most law schools. Apperson left after one year.[74]

Also appointed in 1963 as a part-time lecturer in family law and research associate was C. Jerre Lloyd ('59), former judicial administrator for Louisiana. He assisted Dean Hebert in writing his historical sketch of the LSU Law School and taught family law in Spring 1964 while Robert A. Pascal was on leave in Italy. Lloyd left to become judicial administrator for the Orleans Juvenile Court and eventually practiced law in his native Lake Charles.[75]

Douglas Johnston of the University of Western Ontario visited in 1964–65, teaching civil-law courses. He held several degrees, M.A., LL.B., M.C.L., LL.M., and J.S.D., and after his year at LSU he won a special fellowship at Yale preparatory to further work in international law.[76]

The most famous speaker at LSU in the decade was LSU graduate Hubert H. Humphrey (who had received a master's degree from the University), then vice-president of the United States. He received an honorary doctor of laws degree in April 1965 and delivered a University-wide lecture in the Parker Agricultural Center. Willard Wirtz, secretary of labor, spoke at the Law School.[77]

Obtaining lecturers was aided by the establishment of the Bailey Lectures. The lectureship honored James J. Bailey ('34), who died in 1961. The inaugural lectures in 1965 focused on the Uniform Commercial Code, reflecting Dean Hebert's interests in banking and commercial law and the prospect of Louisiana studying the adoption of the UCC. The lecturers were the nation's leading UCC experts—Robert Braucher of Harvard; William D. Hawkland, dean of SUNY and later to be the LSU Law Center chancellor; Norman Penney of Cornell; and Grant Gilmore, University of Chicago.[78]

Another visitor, giving lectures in the class on corporations, was F. Hodge O'Neal ('40), then a professor at the Duke Law School. Even space law received attention. Myres S. McDougal, Sterling Professor at Yale, discussed "Customary Law of Outer Space" in his Law School lecture.[79]

ANOTHER "NEW" BUILDING

The 1938 law building was crowded. Not only was the Law School growing in its quarters on the main and top floors of the building, the government and social welfare departments, which occupied the basement, were also expanding. With sectionalization of the first-year class and the addition of more upper-class courses, finding classroom space was a problem. Smaller offices designed for research assistants and secretaries were assigned instead to the growing numbers of junior faculty. The dean's suite had been moved from the top floor (with its majestic view of the Parade Ground and the Memorial Tower) to the north end of the basement off the library stacks.

Dean Hebert had sought support for a new building with a planning committee appointed in the 1950s, but progress was slow. In the early 1960s, law students were mobilized to help win support for and to plan a new building. Cyrus J. Greco ('63) recalled serving on a committee composed of students living in the law dorm, who suggested improvements for the dormitory. By 1964, Hebert reported that the Board of Liquidation of State Debt had not acted favorably on a request for funds for architectural planning. Instead, the Law School would have to proceed with requests to the State Bond and Building Commission. Unstated at that point was the fact of life in Louisiana politics that the governor's support would have to be sought. It would also remain unstated that governors often sought various services from the Law School, as when Charles Reynard had served as executive counsel for Earl Long. Such demands continue to this day. But in the mid-1960s, Governor John J. McKeithen ('42) was searching for someone to head the litigation team representing Louisiana in its demands against the federal government for oil and gas revenues from offshore production. It is thus not surprising that the report of an informal summer faculty meeting in 1965 contains the following two paragraphs:

> Dean Hebert advised the Faculty that Governor John McKeithen had requested him to take charge of the litigation involving the tidelands on behalf of the State, and that he had accepted the appointment.
>
> Dean Hebert also informed the Faculty that the Governor had announced, at a luncheon held that day, that top priority would be given to a program of basic improvements and additions to the Law School's physical facilities. This program will involve an outlay of approximately $4,000,000.[80]

Governor McKeithen announced his intention to finance improvements to the law building at a luncheon with LSU president John A. Hunter and members of the Board of Supervisors. The new law building would be occupied in 1970. In an oral-history interview, McKeithen remembered that Hunter and Hebert met with him and said they needed a new building. Why, he asked? Because the old building was not large enough and they wanted a new location on the north end of the campus or on the Burden property away from the main campus.[81]

McKeithen, a graduate of the Law School, rejected the idea of abandoning the old law building. "That's too beautiful of a building. It's in the right location, and too many people have memories. I'm not going to support moving it." Hebert acquiesced, "We can put a big addition on the back." McKeithen added, "I was just a student, but I respected him greatly then, and Paul Hebert and I became close friends from then on. I've never known a man I've respected more or who in my opinion was more honorable."[82]

Although Hebert seldom took public positions endorsing candidates for office, he did participate in a TV program in 1966 supporting a constitutional amendment allowing the governor to serve two consecutive terms, an appearance that prompted Gillis W. Long ('51) to charge that LSU was slipping back into politics and the president of the Young Men of Louisiana to wire his objections to President Hunter. McKeithen also called on Hebert in 1968 to serve as a member of the state's Labor Management Commission of Inquiry, which was charged with investigating corruption involving unions and businesses in the Baton Rouge area.[83]

In a sense, the governor's desire for an addition rather than a new law building was met. The old and new buildings were connected, but in such a way that only the most persistent persons could find the hallways connecting the two structures. The new building was almost self-sufficient, and indeed, the Law School released most of the old building to other departments, keeping only the library stacks, the auditorium, and the top floor for the Law Institute. Plans for a new law dormitory were also drafted, but it was never built.[84] Meanwhile, the termite-infested old law dorm, formerly a girls' dormitory, was torn down during the construction project. Later, as the Law School grew, efforts were made to recapture some of the lost space in the old building, but that was long in coming.

Dean Hebert's involvement with the Tidelands litigation would be time consuming, so an additional faculty member, William E. Crawford, was hired to teach and serve as assistant dean. Associate Dean Milton M. Harrison became heavily occupied with the planning of the new structure. He chaired the advisory committee to the architect, serving with Professors Dakin, Pugh, Shieber, and Smith. They consulted with Dean Russell Sullivan of the University of Illinois Law School and visited several other new law buildings during this period—Illinois, NYU, University of Chicago, Northwestern, and Columbia. Harrison was involved with the minutiae of obtaining approvals from the University bureaucracy, bargaining off a faculty library, for example, in favor of larger faculty offices. He recalled a number of offices he had occupied that offered only a view of a tar-covered roof, "and this is not a good way to spend your life, to look up from your desk in an office and all you can see is the dirty top of a building. Whatever you do, have the building and all the openings in the offices on the outside of that building. If that requires a doughnut, OK." Perry M. Segura was the architect for the project. The general contractor was Milton J. Womack, Inc.[85]

The new building was financed by an allocation of $3 million in state funds and $1.3 million in federal grants. Construction began in November 1967, and the building was formally accepted in October 1969. Segura designed a four-story rectangular structure with a glass-and-limestone exterior. Inside was a three-story light well and an open courtyard on the second floor. Fluted columns on the exterior gave a hint of the traditional LSU quadrangle arches and the white limestone matched the exterior of the old building, but it was nonetheless a contemporary structure departing from the style of the quadrangle buildings and the old law building. According to a brochure announcing the completion of the addition, an "ingenious abutment of a modern structure to a traditional one achieves compatibility because only one building is visible from either direction, and it provides maximum use of space." It is true that the new building is not seen from the Parade Ground perspective and that the old building is not seen from the front entrance to the new structure, but the side views from the parking lots are somewhat jarring.[86]

The addition contained 133,705 square feet of space and was ready for occupancy in February 1970. It contained six large classrooms on the first and second floors with 150-, 100-, and 75-person capacities, and four seminar rooms on the third floor. Curved tiers of desks and seats around a podium allowed students to be close to the faculty. A new courtroom was included, and the courtroom in the old building was renovated as an auditorium seating 350 persons. The art-deco touches of the old courtroom were covered over with modern acoustic panels, as were the ornate mahogany woodwork and marble panels. Ironically, renovations of the old building in 2001–2002 would attempt to recapture the flavor of the old courtroom. Administrative suites were located on the first and second floors, and some thirty-five faculty and staff offices with window walls were on the third and fourth floors. A library reading room on the ground floor led to open stacks on the second, third, and fourth floors in the interior of the building with views into the courtyard. Enough space for 300,000 volumes was anticipated.[87] The new stacks were connected with the interior stacks in the old library, and the top-floor reading room of the old library became the home of the Civil Law Collection donated by Colonel John H. Tucker Jr. of Shreveport.

A fountain was installed in the courtyard in October 1971, in memory of Harriet S. Daggett. It was done in cast stone and mosaic and featured ten great names in legal history. Often, students had to be told that Alfonso X was the Spanish king who commissioned the *Siete Partidas* and not a colleague of Malcolm X in the Black Muslims. The fountain in memory of LSU's famous woman professor was donated by Paul Dorsay Perkins in memory of his wife, Mary Herron Bird, and his daughter Mary Bird Perkins, both LSU law graduates.[88] The fountain, with a single jet of water, became known to law students as the Daggett Memorial Bidet, a nickname that her surviving colleagues said Professor Daggett would have enjoyed.

Students in Summer 1969 were asked to move out of the old library and into the new one so that renovation of the old reading room could begin. A big problem, however, arose when the air-conditioning demands of the new library were beyond the capacity of the incoming lines. The result was that the air conditioning could not be turned on and the students had a hot summer.[89] Another "mistake" was the small beige tiles that covered the hallways in the upper floors, giving them the feeling of a bathroom. Over the years, they tended to fall off. One of Vice-Chancellor Sidney A. Champagne's proudest accomplishments in the 1990s was the removal of the tiles and the plastering of those hallways.

STUDENT ACTIVITIES

The Louisiana Supreme Court in 1959 reimposed a bar-examination requirement for graduates of the state's ABA-approved law schools. The law faculty had long objected to the diploma privilege, and Dean Hebert said, "The reestablishment of the bar examination for graduates of the state's four law schools is an important and desirable development. Almost continuously since Pearl Harbor Louisiana has had a diploma privilege which was first adopted as the means of meeting the problems of students entering the military service. This was followed by a progressive liberalization of the privilege until it finally embraced admission without examination for all graduates of the Louisiana law schools." The effective date of the new rule was postponed to allow students in the pipeline to avoid the exam. The 1963 graduates were the first to be subject to the new requirement.[90]

Students recalled that the Law School was still a small operation, with the students and the faculty all knowing each other: "We were small, and we were blessed with that faculty that was a very close-knit faculty. . . . I mean they were personal friends with one another." The legal fraternities were popular, and one student estimated that 90 percent of the students were members. They were not exclusive societies, and they provided a good means for students to meet with faculty members in a social setting.[91]

The faculty was nonetheless considered rather formal. One student remembered that when the air conditioning went out in the auditorium, Dean Hebert came in for his ethics class and kept his coat on. "We were about to pass out, yet he gave the lecture with his coat and tie on. It was quite an experience to watch him. He was drenched in perspiration but never gave any indication that he was aware of the heat." Whether the rule was written or not, students even in the late 1960s wore dress shirts and ties, and many wore coats as well. No one wore blue jeans. One of the students who started in 1964 stated, "I think my class may have been one of the last to wear ties to class." He continued, "My classmates adhered to the tie policy during our first year, but thereafter most of us stopped wearing them." And some who wore them did so only as a formality—like the student who wore the same red tie every day. That 1964 entering class also brought some whiffs, albeit small ones, of the student unrest of the 1960s. Marijuana was not unknown at the time, nor were sandals and long hair.[92]

Tuition and fees for resident students were still low at $130 per semester.[93] They were increased in Fall 1968 to $180 per semester.

In May 1966, thirty-six students were awarded degrees. That was still a small class, but students began coming to the Law School in greater numbers. The 1965–66 freshman enrollment was 161, increasing by 35 percent to 218 freshmen in 1966–67. Total enrollment in those two terms was 330, then 439, increasing by 33 percent. The Law School was about to experience immense changes. In Fall 1966, the law faculty minutes reported that "faculty members are teaching classes of more than 100 students in first-year courses in which the analysis and discussion method of instruction is used, and classes of almost 100 in second and third-year courses." Similarly, seminars were overcrowded. At the time, all graduates had to be approved by a faculty vote, and even as late as 1966 Joseph Dainow wanted a separate vote on each graduate, considering matters in addition to scholastic record.[94]

Upper-class students oriented the incoming freshmen in an informal program held in the auditorium, followed by the sale of poopsheets to the captive audience at $5 per course. G. Bradford "Bumpy" Ware ('65) was the student who entertained the freshman students with anecdotes about the faculty in Fall 1964, transferring the collective lore and myths of the school. Among the stories spread was that students in the front row of Professor Pascal's class would be those called on, so the students fought for seats in a tight square in the center of the room. The first class day, Pascal picked out the people in the center of the square and interrogated them. Cary deBessonet remembered the polished approach of the professors in the first-year courses, building on small amounts of material and discussing it thoroughly: "Professor Malone spent two or three weeks on the first few little ole blurbs in the book." DeBessonet said that upon pursuing a graduate degree at Illinois he realized the strength of legal education at LSU: "I was amazed by how much legal theory I knew compared to the other graduate students who were there."[95] Also beginning law study in 1964 were two students who would enter the U.S. Congress at a young age, John B. Breaux (who became a senator) and Wilbert J. Tauzin II (who became a congressman).

Parking space was an increasing problem. A target of law-student ire was nonstudents parking in the law lot near the corner of Highland Road and Dalrymple Drive. Persons attending services at the nearby Catholic and Episcopal student centers often used the lot. Student Bar Association president John R. (Bob) Fitzgerald ('64), who coincidentally was active in the Catholic Student Center, was quoted in the *Reveille* complaining about the inconvenience to faculty and students, but he also emphasized the lawyerly argument about potential danger in case of fire. In 1965, it was SBA president Rogers M. Prestridge ('66) who presented the parking complaints to James Reddoch, dean of student services. Catholics were still the problem when on Sundays and Holy Days of Obligation they parked on curbs and double-parked, preventing cars from leaving the lot. Of course, Prestridge too focused on the dangers in case of fire.[96]

The mid-1960s law students were concerned about military service and the impending demands of the draft as the conflict in Vietnam grew more intense. Many students opted for the JAG Corps, the National Guard alternative, or other forms of military service. Students who completed undergraduate school normally obtained deferments for the period of their law study, followed by military service upon graduation. Others who had completed only basic ROTC before entering law school were allowed to enroll in ROTC as law students and postpone their induction until after graduation. Some needed extra courses to graduate in time, and Dean Hebert recommended that their petitions be granted "because of hardship to the student caused by Selective Service requirements." Indeed, many law students were still participating in the ROTC program as late as the middle 1960s. Kenneth E. Gordon Jr., a Law School freshman in 1963, was also a cadet colonel in command of the Army Brigade. The deputy corps commander that year was Robert L. Cole, then a senior in business administration, who would enter the Law School as a freshman the following year. The connection with the military extended to the air science faculty. Captain Gilbert L. Dozier ('66) was a member of the cadre and taught air science while he was a student in the Law School.[97]

A number of law graduates were in Vietnam during the war, including Joseph J. Baiamonte ('68), Thomas R. Blum ('68), Paul Marks Jr. ('69), and John F. Pugh Jr. ('67). They and other lawyer friends would gather as the "Saigon Bar Association," meeting at the Continental Palace Hotel near the old opera house that was the seat of the South Vietnamese National Assembly. Some students like M. Hampton Carver ('70), H. Alston Johnson ('70), and Paul H. Spaht ('71) finished law school expecting to serve two years as required by their ROTC commissions. As it turned out, however, they graduated as the war was winding down and were required to serve only three months.[98]

The draft law and regulations were obviously well studied by many law students, who were often assisted and counseled by Professors Benjamin M. Shieber and William T. Tete. That was not unexpected for Shieber, known for his antiwar views, but Tete was a hawk on the issue of the Vietnam War as well as a libertarian, and "it's ironic that he knew so much about the draft laws and he ended up performing this role." Shieber gave a lecture on dissent to an undergraduate class, Law as a Humanity, in Fall 1971. He told the students that dissenters were not only to be tolerated under the Constitution but that "the dissenter is an asset by disagreeing with flaws in the system." Shieber later estimated that he had handled about 250 cases involving wrong classifications, erroneous medical classifications, and general questions concerning the draft itself. He was also active in the Vietnam Moratorium Committee protests and served as chairman of the American Association of University Professors.[99]

The old law dorm, long-term termites included, was torn down when construction started on the new building. But it did have a last hurrah, in addition to the sign "Joanne Woodward Slept Here" mentioned in the last chapter. During the time when Dwight D. "Ike" Eisenhower was campaigning for president and Adolph Eichmann was on trial in Israel, a sign appeared saying, "We Like Eich." The sign was accepted humorously by most, but not by Professor Joseph Dainow, who called on his friend Alvin B. Rubin to assist in combating anti-Semitism at the Law School. The Louisiana-reared Rubin was eventually able to convince the foreign-born Dainow not to worry.

The last of the hutments, World War II–vintage temporary buildings located on Nicholson Drive near the LSU Gates and used for housing many married law students, was demolished in 1963 to make room for concrete-block apartments.[100]

Although the impact of desegregation was slight in the Law School environment, it was an ever-present campus topic. University administrators closed the swimming pool during the summer of 1964, allegedly because of opposition to integrated swimming. Students started a petition objecting to the closure, a petition that garnered substantial *Reveille* publicity in the form of stories and letters. The official explanation was that a recent Alaska earthquake had caused damage to the pool. The petition was presented to the Board of Supervisors, which "gently" rejected it. A *Reveille* editorial protested:

> This University is integrated, but not totally integrated. Means will be used in the future to bring about integration of the swimming pool, the football team, fraternities and sororities, the entire life of the LSU student, like it or not. Unfortunately, since the Board has shown it is not

interested in recognizing peaceful protest, much less giving consideration to it, the effort may not be peaceful. It may not have the Reveille and the SGA as a control. It may be done by demonstrations which may lead to rioting, the very thing this petition has sought to prevent. For the effort, the Reveille, SGA and 1400 members of this University received a slap in the face.

The pool, closed on June 15, 1964, was not opened for general recreational swimming until the Board ordered it reopened in April 1965 after a noisy spring of student petitions, debates, and threatened demonstrations. A petition in favor of opening the pool had more than four thousand signatures; the petition in opposition had some five hundred names.[101]

The Union and Hatcher Hall barber shops were temporarily closed when seven barbers resigned after Union officials instructed them that the civil-rights acts required them to cut the hair of black students. Four African American students had requested haircuts on September 10, 1964, and were refused. Carl Maddox, director of the Union, stated that LSU intended to abide by court orders and provide equal treatment to African American students. A later *Reveille* editorial cartoon by Mike Randall showed Mike the Tiger (holding a *Playboy* magazine) appearing at the barber shop for a haircut, only to be told, "I'm sorry sir, but we don't cut Tigers' hair here."[102]

Fewer students were in the Arts and Sciences/Law joint-degree program, and virtually no law students were cross-registering in undergraduate and graduate courses. The Law School, with its older students, was less involved in SGA and sports activities, and it was becoming a more self-contained professional program. To an unfortunate extent, too, the law faculty was less involved in discussions, committees, and joint activities with campus faculty and was addressing with greater tenacity the internal problems of teaching increasing numbers of students.

A related development occurred in 1969 when the law students requested a commencement ceremony separate from the general LSU ceremonies. Traditionally, law graduates were recognized en masse at the large ceremony, as were undergraduates and masters, and only Ph.D. students walked across the stage and were individually hooded. Student Bar Association president James J. Brady and John F. Robichaux, chairman of the student-faculty relations committee, appeared before the faculty and urged support of a separate commencement ceremony. Such a graduation ceremony "would be more meaningful to [graduates] and their families as a way of marking the accomplishment of their professional training as lawyers." The faculty approved the student initiative. University officials rejected the proposal at first, reconsidered upon Dean Hebert's urging, then approved it. The first separate commencement was held on Saturday, May 31, 1969, in the Union Theater, rather than in the Parker Agricultural Coliseum. Law graduates were thus freed of being herded through the cow chutes before entering the arena. The seniors then began a tradition of electing their commencement speaker, choosing for the first event Professor J. Denson Smith.[103] The two student marshals at this first graduation ceremony were members of the junior class, both later to become Law School faculty members—Winston Day and Alston Johnson.

About the same time, the University was considering the elimination of Saturday classes, and the Law School would eventually follow suit—but slowly. The matter was still under discussion in October 1970, and it was defeated in November 1970.[104]

The law faculty continued its close supervision of and participation in the law review. It spent considerable time debating the coverage of the faculty symposium on recent cases in light of the establishment of intermediate courts of appeal. As usual, there was a debate but no vote on the matter. A vote to continue doing what was done before was finally taken, with reconsideration coming the following year. When the matter was broached again in 1962, the mushy decision was to cover court of appeals decisions that were final, "reserving, however, to faculty members the right to write separate articles on pending decisions." The approval of Graydon K. Kitchens Jr. as associate editor of the review was conditioned on his not simultaneously holding the office of president of the Student Bar Association. Rules preventing law review students from participating in the Tullis Moot Court Competition came and went as views changed about equalizing honors in the Law School. In the 1966–67 competition, law review student Raleigh C. Newman was also a winner of the competition, along with teammate Bobby D. Sutton.[105]

The increasing number of students in the Law School relieved pressure on the faculty for early selection of students for the law review. In 1966, Professor Currier, faculty editor of the review, proposed that selection of candidates be postponed until the end of the first year, and the motion carried. But implementation was slow. Students with a grade of 80 after the first semester were invited for the 1967–68 term, but the general rule of admission after the first year was also reaffirmed—affirmed in principle only, however, because as late as Spring 1970, second-semester students with averages of 80 and above were still being invited to participate in the law review.[106]

The *Reveille* announced in 1964 the twenty-fifth anniversary of the law review, stating, "All over Europe and Latin America, in Japan and Korea—even the Kyuku Islands, the Law Review is distributed, read and regarded as one of this nation's leading legal journals." The editor that year was Karl Cavanaugh; managing editor was Kenneth D. McCoy Jr.; associate editors were Anthony J. Correro, Wendell G. Lindsay, and George A. Kimball. At the end of the semester, Correro and Lindsay were graduated, and the remaining editors were joined by James S. Holliday Jr., Paul H. Dué, Howard W. L'Enfant, and Gordon E. Roundtree.[107]

The choice of law review editors for the 1969–70 term produced a strong board that would change the law review substantially (and exhibit an affectation for first initials): as editor-in-chief, P. Michael Hebert; managing editor, James R. Pettway; senior associate editor, H. Alston Johnson; associate editors, P. Raymond Lamonica, Harry R. Zimmerman, and Lawrence R. Anderson. Their volume, Volume 30, became the first in which a faculty editor was replaced with a faculty advisor. The change indicated substantially greater student autonomy in publishing the review and terminated the practice of requiring the faculty editor to "sign off" or approve all articles before publication. For the several years when the courtly Hector Currie was faculty editor and exercised a deft editorial pencil, there were few difficulties. His successor, Fred Ellis, was somewhat more heavy handed, and the board was successful in changing the system. William T. Tete was the first faculty advisor under the new system.

James F. Abadie ('67) was the editor of the intermittent student newspaper *Dicta*. The most memorable issue featured a bikini-clad goddess of justice with an effigy of football coach Charles McClendon being hanged on the scales of justice. That issue congratulated Sutton and Newman on their moot-court win, adding the inside scoop that Newman was going to offer a moot-court poopsheet for sale. That same issue contained the famous Law School faculty football team:

Head Coach: Pepsodent Paul Hebert was fit for the job because he spent so much time away from the team with his recruiting activities;
Left end: Don Tate, best known for his razzle-dazzle pass routes that no one can follow;
Left guard: Ben Shieber, as he will guard anything that even tends in this direction.
Center: Yiannopoulos. When try-outs were held he immediately tried out at the center position because he thought it meant that the whole game centered on him.
Right guard: Pascal, who has always excelled at guarding what is right.[108]

Substantial scholarships were being established. The November 1, 1961, issue of the *Reveille* announced the winners of the first Superior Oil Company Scholarships—James M. Johnson and Wendell G. Lindsay of Lake Charles and James L. Dennis of Monroe.[109] Another scholarship that law students were eligible for was the Greater Washington, D.C., Alumni Scholarship, which provided for a summer internship in the Senate office of Russell B. Long. The winner in 1960 was David W. Robertson.

A cold spell hit Baton Rouge in January 1962, and frozen pipes and flooded dorms were the occasion for a brief holiday when the freeze paralyzed the campus. Classes were dismissed on Friday, Saturday, and Monday, and students went ice-skating on University Lake.[110]

Edward C. Abell Jr. ('63), who was a mimeograph operator for the Law Institute making $1 an hour, had the opportunity to assist some law students in making posters for a purported new organization. At the time, talk abounded about radioactive fallout from nuclear testing that would allegedly cause genetic mutations. The law students formed the Society for the Transmission of Unmutated Descendants (STUD) and offered their immediate services to women so they could have babies that would not be affected by the fallout. Their posters called for immediate action to preserve the human race and specified a phone number to call, the number of the Law School's student lounge. Everybody involved thought it was great fun, until several weeks later Abell was called into the dean of men's office and confronted by police investigators. An investigator had gone undercover at the Starmist Lounge on Nicholson Drive and, after talking to various law students there, he came up with the names of about fifteen STUD participants. The police thought the group was part of a pacifist movement, and it took Dean Hebert's intervention to calm the incident down. Abell stated, "Well, he was very understanding. He's an old Deke you know. He wasn't too disturbed about that. He didn't laugh a lot with us, but it was obvious that he didn't think it was too bad a deal." More difficult was confessing to J. Denson Smith about the improper use of the mimeograph machine. Abell showed Smith a copy of the poster, and Smith, "taking off his glasses like he did," said, "Well, Ed, you really can't expect to issue this sort of an invitation to the ladies and not have some repercussions."[111]

The lions of the Law School had become somewhat predictable. Dale Bennett had his courses outlined in a stack of index cards that he kept in the same order as the poopsheets used by the students. Joseph Dainow, too, had his course standardized, particularly his example of a locomotive followed by boxcars to illustrate that a pledge was valid only if pulled by a valid debt; when that issue was covered, one student was prepared with a train whistle that he tooted as Dainow drew the train on the blackboard. In response to an anonymous message left on the blackboard, Robert A. Pascal lectured that a person leaving such messages was a moral coward. Several times in the following classes there appeared more messages, now signed by "Moral Coward." During that time, the students referred to McMahon as the white dean and Hebert as the black dean, ostensibly based on hair color, but perhaps also reflecting the feelings of some students. Some students also variously referred to Mrs. Leah Lanier and Mrs. Florence Molaison as the real deans of the Law School: "We had two deans at the law school in those days, who didn't have dean status. One was Dean Lanier who was a secretary in the Dean's office, and the other was Dean Molaison. So we called them deans also. Mrs. Molaison in those days was Dean Hebert's secretary, and she ran the entire office, and that is who ran it. Now Mrs. Lanier did other things, also, in connection with admissions, but that was it."[112]

"Don't Tread on Me," proclaimed the *Reveille* in a cutline under a photograph of "George," a square of concrete sunk (no one knows why) in the sidewalk in front of the law building. The newspaper repeated the myth that students who wished to make passing grades must refrain from stepping on "George." According to legend, the unwary student who treads on "George" will fail the next test. Later, on another slow news day, a front-page closeup showed "George" decorated with a skull-and-bones drawing; the concrete square was now referred to as "Deadly George." In 1963, the *Reveille* asked "Who painted 'George'?" in a lead story reporting another repainting of "George" right before exam time. "George" made the *Reveille* again in July 1965 after being repainted with white daisies on a field of blue—four coeds had objected to the previous color scheme of chartreuse and red-orange. The *Reveille* emphasized that this act represented the feminization of "George," which was usually subject to night paintings by fraternity members rather than sorority girls.[113]

The feminization of the Law School was slow in coming. Graduates in the teens included three women; 1920s, three; 1930s, ten; 1940s, eighteen; 1950s, fourteen; 1960s, seventeen. But of the women graduating in the 1960s, eight were in the Class of 1969. The trend upward would explode in the 1970s. The 1969 women graduates included the second and third black graduates of the Law School, Gammiel B. Gray (Poindexter) and Bernette Joshua (Johnson). Gray became a prosecuting attorney in Virginia and then a member of the bench there. She serves as circuit judge of the Sixth Judicial District in Prince George County. Joshua was a law clerk for Ernest N. Morial, former mayor of New Orleans, then a law clerk for the managing attorney for the New Orleans Legal Assistance Corporation (NOLAC). She became a district judge in the Orleans Civil District Court and then a justice of the state supreme court, where she still serves.

Answering questions about hats and canes in a *Reveille* interview, Henry G. McMahon said, "Traditions are rather loose things, you know." Before World War II, hats were customary wear for men and derbies were traditional with young lawyers. Lawyers-to-be were too impatient to wait for the bar exam to "wear—or shall I say affect—the cloth of the attorney," he said. But there were hazards associated with wearing the hats to football games: "It was hazardous to adhere to the custom until the University abolished coke bottles at football games."[114] The story in the *Reveille* was accompanied by a photo of three students in their hats and canes—Gordon Hackman, B. Dexter Ryland, and Richard D. Chappuis Jr.

A newly formed chapter of the Phi Alpha Delta legal fraternity was installed at LSU in May 1963. Justice was Rogers M. Prestridge; vice-justice was Floyd A. Roddy; clerk, William Henson Moore; treasurer, John W. Wilson; marshal-elect, Hardy Spence. Melvin G. Dakin was faculty advisor.[115]

Refreshments served at a freshman smoker for new students in 1961 included "cakes, punch, cookies, coffee and cigars." No liquor, but cigars! There were other indications, however, that many law students were moving in faster lanes. A *Reveille* advertisement for the Cohn-Turner men's store urged students to consult Pat Shows, Law School campus representative for Cohn-Turner. A later ad featured a photo of Shows, stating he's "the fellow who'll lay down the law on winning fabrics. Introduce yourself soon if you care how you look to girls." Then again, "Shows, struggling law student, is C-T's campus rep., and can put you into the hottest, newest fabrics that ever had a girl say: 'yes.'" As exams were approaching, the Cohn-Turner ad read that Shows, "when he's not cramming his skull full of law theories at L.S.U., makes it his business to help Big Men On The Campus select good clothes."[116]

Professor George W. Hardy spoke to the pre-law club, telling the group that a student would most likely succeed in law school if he had "stretched his mind" as an undergraduate. He urged them to take courses that would teach logic, self-expression, and an understanding of all cultures. At that meeting, Andre C. Broussard ('71) was elected president and Joseph W. Rausch ('73) was chosen freshman representative.[117]

The *Reveille* covered the Spring 1965 moot-court semifinals with a full-page spread featuring six photographs. A former city policeman was convicted of rape by a jury of coeds. The winning lawyers were Frank Trosclair Jr. and Daniel Scott Brown on one team and Donald E. Bradford and John Robert Harrison on the other. Judge Thomas B. Pugh was presiding judge, and witnesses included law freshmen Edwin K. Hunter and James F. Abadie.[118]

Moot-court lecturers were a diverse group: federal district judge E. Gordon West and George Mathews, president of the Baton Rouge Bar Association, started the series, followed by Professors George W. Pugh and Henry G. McMahon and Adjunct Professor Alvin Rubin, and then attorneys Tom Phillips, Robert L. Kleinpeter, and Alva Brumfield, and state district judge C. A. Barnett. West's lecture emphasized the "new" discovery rules that were being put into place, and the student newspaper's continued fascination with events in the Law School was shown by its running a front-page photo of West lecturing in the courtroom. The Flory Trials and Tullis Moot Court Trials were routinely covered. The *Reveille* reported, for example, that the defendants accused of attempted robbery and murder were found not guilty by "jury members from Alpha Xi Delta sorority." Defense counsels were James D. Davis and Buck Sadler, and prosecutors were Elton Dry and Pat

Juneau. The judge was Baton Rouge attorney Luther F. Cole. A photograph of five members of the supreme court hearing the Tullis Finals was also featured. The winning team that year was Leon Gary Jr. and Eldon T. Harvey II. Their opponents were Richard E. Lee and W. Henson Moore.[119]

State politics in the 1960s mirrored LSU Law School events of previous years. The leading candidates for governor in the fall 1963 race were all LSU law graduates: Robert F. Kennon ('25), Gillis W. Long ('51), John J. McKeithen ('42), and deLesseps S. Morrison ('34). Professor William C. Havard, government professor and political expert, reflected conventional wisdom when he predicted in a lecture that it would be a three-man contest between Kennon, Long, and Morrison. He was wrong—McKeithen won the Democratic primary and then defeated Republican Charlton Lyons.[120]

8

1970–1977:
RUNNING HARD TO STAY IN PLACE

The Class of 1970 had 134 graduates. The Class of 1977 more than doubled that number, with 293 students graduating.[1] It remains the largest in the history of the Law School. The increasing enrollment in the 1970s posed serious problems in itself, but coupled with static budgets and midyear budget cuts, it made implementation of new programs difficult. Indeed, keeping the basic core of the institution intact was a demanding challenge. Limitation of enrollment was inevitable, bringing about a substantial change in the Law School's mission and a turning point in its history. The year 1977 also saw the unexpected death of Dean Paul M. Hebert and a major change in the Law School's administration.

ADMISSIONS AND BUDGETS

The Fall 1971 total enrollment was more than 900 students and the entering class, under virtually open admissions, numbered 498. Even with four sections of first-year classes, each section included about 125 students. The 1,000 enrollment mark was exceeded in Fall 1975. The demand for legal training at LSU was fueled both by its reputation for a strong program and by its low fees, which at that time were $510 per year for full-time resident students. Nonresidents paid $1,060 per year. Comparable tuition fees at Tulane were $2,275 and at Loyola $1,700. More students from the New Orleans area were making the trip upriver to attend LSU. Class size strained the effectiveness of the traditional methods of instruction and made grading four-hour essay exams an overwhelming chore for the faculty. Faculty members were expected to grade all exams themselves, and a faculty member teaching two freshman sections faced the daunting task of grading 250 exams. The prospect of additional funds to hire more faculty was bleak, and budget cuts were imposed.

In January 1970, Dean Hebert and Student Bar Association president Winston R. Day reported that because of financial problems three research assistants had been dismissed, one faculty slot had not been filled, and only two faculty members had received pay raises. In July 1971, a 3-percent midyear budget cut was imposed on the University.[2]

In response to the crisis, the faculty adopted a statement that "the present condition of a burgeoning student body with no increase in faculty is severely endangering the quality of legal education." More important, it recommended that the first-year class entering in Fall 1972 be limited to three hundred students, four sections of seventy-five students each. To meet the concerns of the Board of Supervisors and state political officers, 90 percent of those students would have to be Louisiana residents. Minimum entrance standards were not to be altered, but the three hundred applicants with the highest index scores would be admitted. The quota of special-admission students, to accommodate minority-student recruitment, was fixed at ten. Campus administrators requested that the law faculty reconsider its recommended departure from traditional open admissions, but the faculty did not budge and the dean supported the limitation. The Board of Supervisors approved, at least if the legislature did not increase the Law School's appropriation, which it did not do, and a drastic change for LSU was in place. The Fall 1972 total Law School enrollment was down to 856: 315 freshmen, 300 juniors, and 241 seniors.[3]

Dean Hebert meanwhile was pursuing a strategy for increasing the Law School's funding as well as decreasing the control over those funds exercised by the Baton Rouge campus administration. Some small success occurred in the appropriations bill for 1971–72 operations, which allocated $737,484 to the Law School, "at the discretion of the Board of Supervisors." The Board and the campus administration, of course, would be reluctant to decrease that sum in light of the legislative preference. That budget figure compared with a total budget of $181,941 for fiscal 1959 and $300,625 for fiscal 1964.[4]

Hebert and Judge Minos D. Miller Jr. ('47), a leader of the Law Alumni Association, met in 1973 with Governor Edwin W. Edwards ('49), asking for increased funding and a line-item appropriation for the Law School free of campus control. The governor acceded to the requests; the main priority for additional funds was faculty salary increases. The lobbying efforts met with success during the summer legislative session, and the appropriations bill included an additional appropriation of $450,000 for the 1973–74 term. The faculty went "on record as offering its sincere thanks and congratulations to Judge Miller and all others who participated in the splendidly successful effort to obtain the additional appropriation."[5] Although the additional appropriation was not technically conditional on the acceptance of more students, Hebert reported strong legislative sentiment for such action and proposed that an additional 75 students be accepted in Fall 1973, for a total of 375 students in five 75-person sections in the first year. The additional section of 75 students was continued for several years, but the approval of the larger freshman class was accompanied by a warning that the faculty was unable to support such a large class without additional members and additional financial support. Enrollment of first-year students for 1974–75 was 377; 1975–76, 407; 1976–77, 385; 1977–78, 371.[6]

A regression and correlation analysis of the effectiveness of the law-school index as a predictor of success in law school was the subject of a major study headed by Benjamin M. Shieber, completed in 1970. Examining the records of 747 students in five entering classes from 1961 to 1965, the study concluded that the index was an adequate predictor of success; a student meeting minimum standards had a 75-percent chance of receiving an average of 66 or better.[7] Nonetheless, some faculty had argued that the minimum index should be raised to improve the legal profession. The debate on that issue would continue for several years, with the populists, including Dean Hebert, wanting to give opportunities to as many students as possible. Among the leaders of the group advancing higher standards were Milton M. Harrison, along with George W. Hardy, the latter also urging return to a system of letter grades. Also in the background was a reaction of some faculty members who did not want to "sentence to death" students who failed to pass and thus would be liable to be drafted and sent to Vietnam. The debate over admission and retention standards was never clearly decided. Rather, it morphed into the problems of increasing numbers of students and was eventually subsumed by the adoption of limits on the number of entering students.

One change in admissions requirements passed with little controversy in 1974—the elimination of the joint B.A.-J.D. program that allowed students to earn an undergraduate degree and a law degree in six years. In the future, applicants would need an undergraduate degree to be admitted. Indeed, few students were pursuing joint degrees, and the change produced little opposition. Still, entry into the legal profession would now be a longer process, normally seven years after graduation from high school. In addition, the Law School took advantage of the opportunity to raise the minimum admissions index slightly. Over a four-year period, the minimum-index score was raised from 650 to 700. That latter score required a 2.5 (on a 4.0 system) undergraduate GPA and a 450 on the LSAT—still not a demanding requirement, since the median LSAT score was about 500.[8]

The middle of the decade saw an accreditation report from the American Bar Association and the Association of American Law Schools that reaffirmed the school's accreditation but also focused on budgetary matters and problems in handling the large numbers of students. Among the recommendations: improve the student-faculty ratio; improve faculty salaries and support; add library staff and funds; let the faculty determine the optimum size of the student body within funding limits; and increase the availability of clinical programs.[9]

FACULTY RECRUITMENT

Finding staff to teach the courses needed by the growing student body was difficult, and recruiting new faculty was an ever-present and demanding task. Thirty-five tenure-track, full-time faculty were hired between 1970 and 1977, including seven in 1972, six in 1976, and seven in 1977. During that period, twenty-one law faculty members left LSU, by transfers to other schools, returning to private practice, retirement, or death. The net gain was fourteen faculty, and the total number teaching in the 1976–77 term was thirty-eight. In addition, twenty-eight visiting professors, along with the local adjunct professors, were called on to assist in instruction during the 1970 to 1977 period.

LSU's task of covering the standard American law curriculum plus the Louisiana civil-law curriculum always required unique recruitment strategies, which were intensified by the heavy demand for new faculty. To cover the civil-law curriculum, LSU had to recruit from civil-law countries as well as from its own top graduates in order to accomplish its goals. The long-term service of Professors Dainow (Canada), Lazarus (Honduras), Yiannopoulos (Greece), and Litvinoff (Argentina) was an important component of the mix. Over the years, faculty members with LSU LL.B. degrees were also an important stabilizing component—Daggett, Hebert, Smith, McMahon, Harrison, Pugh, and Hardy. (Pascal held a master's degree from LSU and one from Michigan, but his LL.B. was from Loyola.) Stability at a time of increasing mobility in the U.S. teaching market was also provided by the American law component—Flory, Bennett, Malone, Dakin, Reynard, and Currie. To foster an adequate diversity of views, an effort was made to maintain a balance among the foreign-trained faculty, the LSU degree holders, and the Americans trained in other states. An additional strategy had been to encourage LSU graduates to pursue graduate studies at other law schools, particularly Yale, for a broadening experience before beginning to teach. Indeed, if one looks at all degrees held by the faculty in the early 1970s, there were almost as many Yale as LSU degrees. An informal "inbreeding index" based on the percentage of faculty with LL.B. or J.D. degrees from LSU hovered around 30 to 40 percent during most of the school's history. But from 1970 to 1972, it reached 48 percent as the need for new faculty continued to mushroom. By 1977, however, it was down to 42 percent.

Among the new personnel were Marc Hershman, who came as a research associate in the Sea Grant Legal Program in 1970. A graduate of Temple University Law School, he was a frequent campus speaker on environmental issues, lecturing on "Phase II of the Environmental Movement" in November 1971, in which he was one of the first to describe the movement to open levees in the Mississippi Delta to rebuild the delta and form new estuaries. Hershman joined the faculty as an assistant professor in 1974, teaching one course per semester, then left in 1976 to accept an offer from the University of Washington in its Institute of Marine Studies. He was director of the School of Marine Affairs at Washington when, in 2001, President George W. Bush appointed him to the Commission on Ocean Policy, charged with considering the impact of offshore oil-drilling activities.[10]

Cheney C. Joseph Jr. ('70), an assistant district attorney in Baton Rouge, began his association with the law faculty as an adjunct professor teaching criminal law in Fall 1971. His undergraduate degree was from Princeton, and he had returned to his hometown for law study. A member of the Order of the Coif and the law review, Joseph accepted a full-time position in February 1972 and has remained on the law faculty ever since. He served as assistant director of the Criminal Justice Program and on several Law Institute criminal-law projects. Over the years, Joseph took several leaves, to serve as district attorney of East Baton Rouge Parish and as United States attorney for the

Middle District of Louisiana, as well as state district court judge *pro tempore* on two occasions and as executive counsel to Governor Murphy J. Foster. He would also serve as vice-chancellor of the Law School.[11]

N. Gerald LeVan ('62) joined the faculty in 1971 as an associate professor after practicing law in Shreveport and serving as a visiting professor in 1969. He specialized in estate and gift taxation and successions and remained at LSU until 1983, when he returned to private practice. LeVan had a bachelor's degree from Southern Methodist University and was editor-in-chief of the *Louisiana Law Review*.[12]

Gerard A. Rault Jr. ('68) joined the faculty as an assistant professor in the summer of 1971 to direct the newly established clinical education program. He had taught at Southern University School of Law in 1970–71 and, after a year at LSU, moved back to his native New Orleans to join the Loyola Law School faculty, where he continues to teach.

Bernard J. Zimmerman spent a year and a half teaching at LSU as he was working his way west. He was born in Munich, reared in New Jersey, graduated from the University of Rochester and the University of Chicago Law School, and then became a law clerk for Judge Frederick J. R. Heebe of the U.S. District Court, Eastern District of Louisiana. He was at LSU during the 1971–72 term teaching torts, civil procedure, constitutional law, and administrative law.[13] He went on to San Francisco and joined the law firm of Pillsbury, Madison, and Sutro, where he practiced until 1994. Zimmerman became a magistrate judge with the U.S. District Court, Northern California District, after serving as an advisor to the constitution-drafting commission for the Commonwealth of the Northern Mariana Islands.

The next year, 1972, was a banner recruiting year, with seven new faculty members hired—Paul R. Baier, Ronald L. Hersbergen, H. Alston Johnson III, P. Raymond Lamonica, Katherine Shaw Spaht, Roger A. Stetter, and William H. Theis. Baier had a law degree from Harvard and had taught at the University of Michigan and University of Tennessee law schools. Hersbergen had a law degree from Iowa, Stetter from Virginia, and Theis from Northwestern. Johnson ('70), Lamonica ('70), and Spaht ('71) were graduates of LSU. Johnson had been awarded a scholarship from the government of France to do a year of postgraduate study at the University of Grenoble.[14] The period of study in France was a mixed blessing. It was a time of widespread student strikes, and classes were canceled more often than not. Grenoble was a good skiing area, however. Lamonica also had a master's degree in government, had clerked for Judge Ben C. Dawkins of the U.S. District Court in Shreveport, and had practiced law in Baton Rouge with A. Leon Hebert. The recruitment of Professor Spaht added a second woman to the faculty, joining librarian Kate Wallach. She had worked for the Louisiana Legislative Council before joining the faculty.

Stetter took a year off in 1975–76 to visit at the University of Tennessee and then left in 1977 to practice law in New York with the Mudge, Rose, Guthrie, and Alexander firm. He later moved to New Orleans to practice there. Theis had an interest in criminal law as a result of his service in the U.S. Navy Judge Advocate General's office. He took leave in 1976–77 to earn an LL.M. at Columbia, taught for the 1977–78 term, and then returned to Chicago to practice and teach. Johnson was a stalwart on the faculty, teaching until 1984, when he entered private practice in Baton Rouge with the law firm of Phelps Dunbar. He continued teaching at the Law School as an adjunct professor. Hersbergen left in 1975, returned in 1976, and continued at LSU until his retirement in 1993.[15] He was one of the early experts in the field of consumer protection. Baier, Lamonica, and Spaht remain on the LSU faculty.

The 1973 recruiting class brought four new faculty members: James A. Gray II, Thomas A. Harrell, P. Michael Hebert, and David E. Soileau.[16] Gray was LSU's first black faculty member. A native of Baton Rouge, he had degrees from Morehouse College and Harvard Law School and taught from 1973 until 1977, when he moved to New Orleans to enter into law practice with the Jefferson, Bryan, and Gray firm. Harrell ('51) was a specialist in mineral law who had practiced in Shreveport with Blanchard, Walker, O'Quin, and Roberts from 1953 until 1970. He was also vice-president of the Cenard Oil and Gas Company in Dallas. Harrell had been an adjunct faculty member in 1952–53 when he was acting chief counsel to the Louisiana Department of Revenue. He remained on the faculty until his retirement in 1996. Hebert ('70) was an editor of the *Louisiana Law Review* and practiced with the Vinson and Elkins firm in Houston from 1970 to 1973. He taught at LSU from 1973 to 1975, when he took leave to serve as legislative assistant in Washington for Senator Lloyd Bentsen of Texas. He then entered law practice in Austin with McGinnis Lockridge and Kilgore in 1976. Soileau ('67) was a law review editor who also had the distinction of clerking for both Judges Albert C. Tate and Alvin B. Rubin. He taught from 1973 to 1977 and then entered law practice in New Orleans.

The need for new faculty never ended. In 1974, Professor Frank L. Maraist ('58) was recruited and came on as a full professor. Maraist, an honors graduate of the Law School and winner of the Tullis Moot Court Competition, had practiced law in Baton Rouge with Sanders, Miller, Downing, Rubin, and Kean and then in his native Vermilion Parish with Deshotels and Maraist. He made the obligatory trip to Yale for an LL.M. (1969) before beginning a teaching career at the University of Mississippi. After a visit at the University of North Carolina for the 1973–74 term, he came to LSU to teach and research in the torts, procedure, and admiralty fields.[17]

The 1975 additions included John S. Baker Jr., Julio C. Cueto-Rua, and Walter H. Mizell. Baker was a graduate of the University of Dallas and the University of Michigan Law School. He had clerked for Judge Herbert W. Christenberry of the U.S. District Court, Eastern District of Louisiana, and served as an assistant district attorney in Orleans Parish. He is a specialist in criminal law, and he continues to serve at LSU. Mizell was a graduate of the University of Texas, and he served at LSU until 1977, when he returned to private practice. Cueto-Rua, a civil-law specialist from Argentina, had a unique appointment. He originally came as a visiting professor, but he became a regular faculty member who was in residence at LSU only during the spring semester of each academic year. He could thus escape the cold Argentine winters but spend the rest of the year at his law practice in Buenos Aires. He continued that arrangement until his retirement in 1991. Cueto-Rua was a graduate of the La Plata Law School with an LL.M. from Southern Methodist University. He had also taught at SMU for five years, leaving to become president of a political party in Argentina when conditions changed there. He had also served as minister of commerce for the national government in Argentina.[18]

The 1976 recruiting class included Hirschel T. Abbott Jr., Joseph T. Bockrath, Martha Chamallas ('75), David S. Clark, and Winston R. Day ('70), as well as the return of Ronald L. Hersbergen and Howard W. L'Enfant.[19] Abbott was a graduate of the University of Virginia Law School, where he was a member of the law review and the Order of the Coif. He was a partner with the Stone, Pigman, Walther, Wittmann, and Hutchinson firm in New Orleans from 1971 until 1976. He remained at LSU for one year and then returned to the firm in New Orleans. Bockrath brought a California perspective to the law faculty. His A.B. was from California State University and his 1971 J.D. was from the University of California's Hastings School of Law. He had been a professor of marine sciences at the University of Delaware. Bockrath became a Law School stalwart, still serving as this is written. Chamallas was a graduate of Tufts University and the LSU Law School, where she was editor-in-chief of the law review and a member of the Order of the Coif. She clerked for Judge Charles Clark of the Fifth Circuit Court of Appeals and then returned to LSU to teach the following year. She remained on the faculty until 1981, when she joined the faculty at the University of Iowa and then later at the University of Pittsburgh. Clark also brought a California perspective; his J.D. and his J.S.M. were from Stanford Law School. He taught at LSU for two years and then moved on to Tulsa. Day was a member of the *Louisiana Law Review* and a member of the Order of the Coif who had practiced with the Jones Walker law firm in New Orleans. He also taught at the University of Mississippi and Tulane. He would continue at the Law School, with some leaves to work in state government as deputy secretary of the Louisiana Department of Natural Resources and as the first secretary of the Louisiana Department of Environmental Quality. He would also serve as acting dean and later as chancellor of the Law Center. Hersbergen returned to LSU after taking a year off to teach in Iowa, and L'Enfant returned from his detour to Kentucky and remains at LSU.

The 1977 new faculty included Bruce N. Bagni, Christopher L. Blakesley, Sidney A. Champagne ('50), Alain A. Levasseur, Patrick H. Martin, Charles R. McManis, and Kenneth M. Murchison.[20] Bagni received his law degree from Indiana in 1974, where he had served as an editor of the law review. He remained at LSU until 1980, when he left to work for the U.S. Department of Justice. Blakesley had a J.D. from the University of Utah and a J.S.D. from Columbia, as well as an M.A. from the Fletcher School of Law and Diplomacy at Tufts University. He had an interest in foreign and comparative law, had spent several years in Europe, and was an attorney in the Office of the Legal Advisor of the U.S. Department of State. He left in 1981 to teach at the McGeorge School of Law of the University of the Pacific, but he returned in 1988 and retired from LSU in 2002. Champagne was an honors graduate and law review member who became a leading CPA in the state and a well-known estate planner. He had taught as an adjunct in the College of Business before leaving his practice and coming to the Law School full time. Levasseur held law degrees from the University of Paris and an M.C.L. from Tulane, as well as a certificate from the City of London College. He had also taught at Tulane, practiced in Paris, and worked for the World Bank. He remains on the faculty at this writing and is associate director of the Civil Law Center. Martin came with a law degree from Duke and a Ph.D. in history from LSU and also remains on the faculty, where he specializes in oil and gas law. He was an attorney with the Gulf Oil Corporation and taught at the University of Tulsa College of Law. McManis was a student of Hodge O'Neal and had a law degree and an M.A. from Duke. He taught at LSU for a year and then rejoined O'Neal at Washington University in St. Louis. Murchison, a native of Alexandria, Louisiana, held a B.A. from Louisiana Tech University as well as a law degree and a master's degree from the University of Virginia. He subsequently obtained an S.J.D. from Harvard Law School. Murchison clerked for Judge John D. Butzner Jr. of the U.S. Court of Appeals, Fourth Circuit, and was a judge advocate in the U.S. Air Force from 1973 to 1977. He continues to serve on the faculty.

FACULTY AND STAFF ACTIVITIES

Students over the years developed a special affection for three long-term staff members who earned a reputation for being exceptionally helpful and solicitous: Peggy Harper, Leah D. Lanier, and Florence H. Molaison.

Peggy Harper first came to the Law School as an acting junior cataloguer in the main library in July 1943 after she completed her library-science degree at LSU. She moved to the law library in 1944 and remained with the library until her retirement in July 1980, rising through the ranks to become a full librarian and retiring as librarian emerita. Along the way, she was acting librarian in 1948–49 and again in 1974–75, and was head of technical services.[21] Indeed, she and Kate Wallach *were* the library for several decades, and it was Miss Harper who dealt with the student workers and who was de facto reference librarian for law students.

Leah Devall Lanier transferred from the Registrar's Office, where she had worked with the legendary Ordell Griffith, to the Law School on August 15, 1947. (Miss Griffith, who served LSU for more than forty years in the Registrar's Office, trained several generations of LSU staff until retiring in 1986 as director of admissions.) Mrs. Lanier occupied the first office that students encountered when they walked into the administrative suite in the basement of the law building, and she was the point of contact for the students' myriad problems and concerns. Once students learned that her name was English (La-neer) rather than French (Lon-yay), all was in good order. In 1972, she retired as admissions counselor, a position in which she worked closely with Associate Dean Milton M. Harrison, and was succeeded by Mrs. Mary Mattox, another long-time Law School staff member.[22]

Florence H. Molaison was Dean Hebert's secretary. Bearing various titles from the beginning of her employment at the Law School in 1936 to her retirement as administrative assistant in 1976, she was Dean Hebert's doorkeeper and confidante. Students wanting to see Dean Hebert, and junior faculty as well, relied on Mrs. Molaison's advice on when and how to present various requests and petitions to the dean. She had followed Hebert to central administration when he was dean of the University from 1949 to 1951, but she did not follow him into his last foray into private practice, correctly predicting that he would return to the Law School before long. Seeking permission for her to remain in her job beyond the normal retirement age, Dean Hebert's request to Chancellor Paul W. Murrill stated, "In a real sense she has been the Dean's 'alter ego' and is entitled to a generous share of the credit for Law School accomplishments during many, many years."[23]

Associate Dean Milton M. Harrison had supervised the construction of the new building, and once it was completed and occupied, he resigned as associate dean and in February 1971 returned to full-time teaching. Francis C. Sullivan then became associate dean. Dean Hebert took his only sabbatical leave from September 1972 to February 1973, during which time he visited several universities and law schools. His sabbatical report contained observations about Canadian law schools and how they approached teaching both common-law and civil-law courses.[24]

Professor Hargrave was on loan to the Constitutional Convention of 1973 for the calendar year to serve as coordinator of legal research. The convention delegates met in Independence Hall, a large auditorium in downtown Baton Rouge that featured wrestling matches once a week, thus assuring an early adjournment on at least one day of the week. The research staff of CC/73, however, was accommodated in the fourth floor of the Law School building, using temporary partitions in space that had been reserved for library-stack growth. Ironically, the person in charge of arranging the space was Delegate Perry M. Segura, who was the architect of the 1970 law building.

H. Gary Knight was appointed to the Advisory Committee on the Law of the Sea by the legal advisor to the U.S. State Department, and he assisted the U.S. delegation to the U.N. Law of the Sea Conference in 1973.[25]

William T. Tete completed his initial one-year contract, and in 1970 he was offered a standard three-year contract as an assistant professor. Tete's libertarian views were featured in a speech on law and freedom that he gave to the Young Americans for Freedom. He asserted that European judges were less free to act capriciously than were judges in the United States.[26]

Paul R. Baier was a Judicial Fellow at the U.S. Supreme Court from 1975 to 1976, producing among other things a film on the history of the Supreme Court. He was also executive director of the Louisiana Commission on the Bicentennial of the U.S. Constitution.

Frank L. Maraist visited at Tulane University in 1978 and served as judge *pro tempore* of the Louisiana Nineteenth Judicial District Court (East Baton Rouge Parish) during 1979.

Katherine S. Spaht performed an important public service from 1977 until 1979 when she served as chair of the Advisory Committee to the Joint Legislative Subcommittee, which was drafting legislation revising Louisiana's community-property system. The proposal introduced equal management into the system and was adopted effective January 1, 1980.

George W. Pugh continued writing his comparative study of criminal justice, ruminating on reforms of American criminal justice in light of a study of the French system. He also published in 1974 his treatise, *Louisiana Evidence Law*. Carlos Lazarus in 1971 completed his two-volume English translation of the Aubry and Rau treatise, *Successions and Donations*. William E. Crawford was the coauthor in 1978, with Françoise Grivart der Kerstrat, of an English translation of the French Code of Civil Procedure.[27]

A hot topic during the period involved the possible development of geothermal resources in Louisiana, and Law School faculty addressed some of the legal problems associated with development of this resource. Lee Hargrave addressed the initial constitutional problems at the 21st Mineral Law Institute, and Thomas A. Harrell discussed those and other issues at several oil and gas conferences.[28]

During this period, the French government subsidized the IDEF (l'Institut International de Droit d'Expression Française), an organization of lawyers from countries influenced by French law, and French speakers H. Alston Johnson III and Lee Hargrave, neither of whom was opposed to *tourisme juridique*, participated in IDEF conferences. Johnson attended a conference in Mauritius in 1973 and spoke on *respondeat superior* in the Louisiana Civil Code. Hargrave attended a 1974 conference in Tunis and spoke on the rights of women in Louisiana.[29] Hector Currie, meanwhile, continued his interest in the English legal system. He was on sabbatical leave in Fall 1972, traveling to England to study its legal history.

Cheney C. Joseph Jr. and P. Raymond Lamonica worked with an advisory committee of judges to produce the *Louisiana Judge's Benchbook*. They also published the *Louisiana Law Enforcement Handbook* for the Louisiana District Attorneys' Association.[30]

Saul Litvinoff published the second volume of his treatise on *Obligations* in 1975 and was active with the Central American Banking School, which was patterned after the School of Banking of the South to provide training programs for Central American bankers. He participated in classes in Baton Rouge and in Honduras. Litvinoff became director of the Center of Civil Law Studies in 1977, and Alain A. Levasseur became associate director. A. N. Yiannopoulos continued work on his series of property treatises, publishing the second edition of *Personal Servitudes* in 1978.[31] Yiannopoulos's extensive research in property law was also resulting in legislation revising the Louisiana Civil Code. He was reporter for the Law Institute's revision of Book II of the Civil Code covering the basic rules of civil-law property, which was adopted by Acts 1978, No. 728.

By the 1970s, the retirement system for LSU faculty members was substantially improved. First, there was a move from an unfunded, noncontributory system with a maximum benefit of one-third of a retiree's maximum salary to a more generous funded contributory system for LSU employees established in 1971. Then, in 1978, LSU faculty were folded into the State Teacher's Retirement System, which provided a regular retirement benefit equal to 2.5 percent of an individual's salary for each year of service.[32] A rash of retirements followed the changes, some faculty having sufficient years in service to receive a pension benefit that approached 100 percent of their salaries. The emeritus faculty members were encouraged to remain in residence at the Law School, with staff support and offices in the "pasture"—small offices around the old library reading room on the top floor of the old building.

Retirements were announced in 1973 for Joseph Dainow, at the end of the spring semester, and for J. Denson Smith, at the end of the summer term. Smith had served on the faculty since 1934, and he would continue to act as director of the Law Institute for several years. Dainow had served at LSU since 1938, and he remained active in civil-law research. Smith's letter to Dean Hebert announcing his retirement was revealing: "I am firm in my desire not to have any kind of ceremony in connection with my retirement. There is nothing beneath this except that the very thought gives me the cold shivers."[33]

Another major retirement came in 1974 when Wex Malone announced that he would take early retirement. Malone was at the height of his powers and vowed to end his teaching career while he was still in top form. He remained a constant visitor at the Law School, encamped in his office in the pasture, where he continued his research and writing. He was a source of continuing help to the growing corps of young faculty members learning their way through the initial law-teaching experience. One of his former students, David Robertson ('61) of the University of Texas Law School, came as a visitor for 1974–75 to cover Malone's torts courses. Two years after he retired, Malone was awarded the 1976 William L. Prosser Award, given by the AALS to a person who has contributed greatly to the development of tort law.[34]

Dale E. Bennett retired in 1976 after more than forty-one years of service. His many accomplishments, already spread forth among these pages, included what students remembered most—he was a "constant champion of the student's cause."[35] He was dean when he founded the Student Faculty Relations Committee and had continued as a member ever since.

Melvin G. Dakin retired in 1977 after thirty years of teaching on the law faculty, in addition to his earlier tenure in LSU's College of Commerce. He took the office next to Malone in the pasture and continued with his consulting, research, and writing. Dakin and his wife, Ande, continued to live in their home on Newcomb Drive until 2001, when, in their nineties, they moved into St. James Place, a retirement center. He died in November 2002.

George W. Hardy III became dean at the University of Kentucky Law School in 1973, the newspaper article announcing the administrative appointment carefully adding that the new administrator was a past president of the

American Association of University Professors. Howard W. L'Enfant Jr. followed Hardy to Kentucky in 1974.[36]

Another development as the faculty increased and became more active was the establishment of an Executive Committee composed of five elected faculty members, plus the dean and associate dean.[37] The committee served primarily to advise the dean, but it could also act on behalf of the faculty on matters not involving hiring and promotions. The committee never became an important governing mechanism, however, for most of its actions were subject to faculty review, and indeed its recommendations and actions were often reversed by the full faculty.

One of the first items of business for the Executive Committee was to determine faculty sentiment about a plan to reduce the number of hours required for graduation. A straw vote on reducing the requirement from 97 to 90 hours, proposed by Professor Bennett and seconded by Professor Shieber, indicated that a majority of the faculty would support the plan.[38] But no formal action was ever taken.

A 1975 faculty meeting also indicated some of the silliness that goes on in academia. The University invited President Gerald Ford to attend LSU's Bicentennial celebration and requested that the Law School authorize awarding him an honorary degree. The Law School acquiesced in the request, "but only upon his visit to the University for the activities" associated with the Bicentennial.[39] President Ford in fact did not accept the invitation, and the conditional degree expired by its own resolutory condition.

VISITORS

The need to staff courses produced a large number of visiting professors, from Europe as well as the United States, teaching in regular semesters as well as in summer school. They added an extraordinary range of viewpoints to present to the students and to younger faculty members. The impressive list included: Jean-Louis Baudoin, University of Montreal, 1970; Julian C. Juergensmeyer, University of Florida, 1970, 1972; Frederick K. Spies, University of Arkansas, 1971; Jerome F. Leavell, College of William and Mary, 1972; Michael T. Johnson, University of Houston, 1972; Charles W. Quick, University of Illinois, 1973; John T. Hood Jr., Louisiana Court of Appeals, Third Circuit, 1973; Marcus L. Plant, University of Michigan, 1974, 1976, 1980, 1984;

Peter G. Stein, Cambridge University, 1974, 1977, 1979, 1983, 1985; Marcel Garsaud Jr., Loyola University, 1974, 1975; K. D. Kerameus, University of Athens, 1974, 1986; Warner Lawson Jr., Ohio State University, 1975, 1977; Richard N. Pearson, Boston University, 1975–76; Bernard C. Audit, University of Paris, 1975, 1977; William L. Crowe, Loyola University, 1975; Donald F. Clifford Jr., University of North Carolina, 1975; Karl P. Warden, Vanderbilt University, 1975; George L. Bilbe, Loyola University, 1976, 1978; John B. Neibel, University of Houston, 1976; Françoise Grivart de Kerstrat, University of Aix—Marseille, 1976–77, 1988; F. Hodge O'Neal, Washington University, 1976, 1977; R. Dale Vliet, University of Oklahoma, 1976, 1977, 1978; Frank J. Trelease, University of Wyoming, 1976; Samuel D. Thurman, University of Utah, 1977; Christopher Osakwe, Tulane University, 1977, 1978; Henry A. Politz, U.S. Court of Appeals, Fifth Circuit, 1977, 1986, 1987; Thomas H. Sponsler, Loyola University, 1977; and Daniel G. Gibbens, University of Oklahoma, 1977.

The Edward Douglass White Lecture in April 1970 was given by A. Leo Levin, vice-president of academic affairs and professor of law at Yeshiva University. He argued that legal processes can be improved with help from the field of psychology. Continuing the Canadian connection, Paul A. Crepeau of McGill University and director of the Civil Code Revision Commission of Quebec gave the Tucker Lecture in Spring 1974. A highlight of the 1975 lecture series was Professor T. B. Smith's Tucker Lecture, "Civil Law Reform in a Mixed Jurisdiction." A professor at the University of Edinburgh, he lectured wearing traditional kilts, and his lecture is remembered more for its style than its substance.[40]

An old stand-by, Professor Jefferson Fordham, who had been a member of the LSU faculty, returned for a month in 1974 to participate in the courses on local-government law and legislation. While here, he gave an open lecture on the impeachment process during the gathering demands to impeach President Nixon.[41]

CURRICULUM AND REGULATIONS

A faculty committee studied the grading system again in 1972 and recommended keeping numerical grades. An informal poll of the faculty indicated that twelve of them supported the numerical system and nine wanted a letter-grade system. When another committee again proposed a change to a letter-grade system in 1973, Professor Bennett moved to table the entire grading issue. The motion passed.[42]

P. Michael Hebert made a comprehensive study of the Law School curriculum as part of his summer 1974 activities. He submitted a twenty-two-page report that proposed several changes, but that in its introduction reflected the reality of curriculum revision as a slow process: "Apparently, it occurs primarily as a result of individual initiative and only when it does not drastically alter the affairs of those who are not in full accord with the revision. As a result, any change is effectuated only by 'tinkering' with the existing curriculum rather than a radical revision of the whole program."[43]

In 1975, more than one hundred course offerings were listed in the catalog. Not all were offered regularly, but over the years, the addition of new courses was substantial. Included were trendy offerings in corporate finance, consumer protection, law and medicine, social legislation, law and poverty, environmental legal problems, land-use planning, water rights, marine-resources law, and maritime personal injuries. Another curriculum change was to beef up instruction in legal ethics. The noncredit one-hour course was abolished, and a required two-credit-hour course called Legal Profession was instituted. Employment discrimination was installed as a new course, as well as a course in labor arbitration and collective bargaining.[44]

A seemingly minor issue arose in 1970, one that would continue to be debated up to the present—whether class periods should be fifty or sixty minutes long. For years, classes were fifty minutes long, with a ten-minute break between. But then the fall semester was compressed to complete the semester before Christmas, and the spring semester was shortened to make room for the longer twelve-week summer term. To do this while maintaining the same total hours of instruction in a semester, classes in Spring 1970 were lengthened to sixty minutes. The change was supposed to be a one-year experiment. Inertia won out again, however, and the change persisted. Student and faculty discontent with shorter regular semesters surfaced, and the Law School returned to longer semesters in 1974. But the sixty-minute classes remained despite some demand to return to the fifty-minute class periods.[45]

The Law Alumni Association sought to become more active in the internal operations of the Law School, recommending that the best answers to examination questions or the faculty members' model answers be placed on reserve in the library. The proposal was not accepted, the faculty view being that "availability of 'model' answers would stultify individual analysis by these students, who, instead of engaging in their own analysis of possible and actual examination questions during their review and when writing their answers, would use the 'model' answers as their own answers to questions on the same general areas of the law." The faculty also did not approve a bar-review course, thinking that such a course was not within the Law School's role and was not necessary.[46]

Another bureaucratic mechanism evolved to ensure the same coverage in all five freshman sections in each course. The teachers of each course were organized into committees with the obligation of meeting regularly to ensure coverage of the materials contained in the course descriptions adopted by the faculty.[47] As one might expect with independent-minded law faculty members, execution of the charge was not always even.

Indeed, the Law School's deliberative process was never very efficient or very pretty. A prime example involved the fifteen-hour rule, a longstanding attempt to encourage depth over breadth by limiting upper-class students to fifteen credit hours per semester. In Fall 1970, three students requested waivers to schedule sixteen hours of credit, and the faculty responded with a general rule that allowed any student with an average of 75 or better to take sixteen hours in both semesters of the senior year. Not stated but understood at that time was the fact that the usual residency requirement would apply, and that students taking the extra courses could not use that device to accelerate their graduation. But that understanding did not hold up when a difficult case arose. In November 1970, a student petitioned to graduate without complying with the requirement of six regular semesters, citing personal-hardship reasons that were not disclosed to the faculty. In a jumble of motions, substitute motions, and motions to reconsider, the petition was granted, reconsidered, defeated, and then made a general rule applicable to all seniors then in Law School. In light of this mixed-up decision-making, the faculty was then reluctant to allow any student to take overloads.[48]

The Law School began a clinical program in the 1970s. In October 1970, student leaders R. Bradley Lewis and J. Arthur Smith spoke before the faculty urging the educational advantages of a clinical program proposed by the faculty's clinical education subcommittee. The faculty vote on the proposal ended in a tie, and Dean Hebert announced that he wanted to consider the matter further before casting the deciding vote. He eventually decided to adopt the program, and LSU was awarded grant funds from the Council on Legal Education for Professional Responsibility financed by the Ford Foundation. The grant financed a faculty position for a clinical professor, and Gerard A. Rault ('68) was hired as assistant professor and director of clinical education. He began service in the summer of 1971 and conducted the clinic for one year. P. Raymond Lamonica ('70) joined the faculty in 1972 and took over the clinical program. The program gave litigation and client-contact experience in civil cases to twenty students. The class was divided into small groups or firms, and each student was given responsibility for one case and served as associate counsel on several others. Cases were selected from the Public Defender's Office and the Legal Aid Society.[49]

Tinkering with the curriculum was inevitable. In 1971, criminal law was shifted to the first semester and family law was moved into the upper-class curriculum. Civil-law property was shifted into the second semester as a four-hour course. The package course requirement succumbed to the large numbers of students and the difficulties of scheduling the courses, but not without a fight. Again, there was a barrage of motions and substitute motions proposing abolition, retention, or just suspension. Professors Dainow, Pugh, and Ellis were especially vocal about retaining the requirements, but the motion to terminate the rule was approved. Another casualty in the numbers war was a program of small sections for at least one freshman course. The trial of the program in 1970–71 was abandoned for the 1971–72 term.[50]

The experimentation in teaching legal bibliography and legal writing continued. The school was unable to supply adequate instruction in legal writing to so many students, so the legal bibliography course was trimmed to lectures and a final examination. In Fall 1973, recent graduate John S. Odom Jr. ('73) was named instructor in legal bibliography, and he supervised senior law students working with the first-year students.[51]

An attempt to ameliorate the demands of the first-year program was proposed by Professors Hardy and Harrison. They proposed to reduce the course load to twelve semester hours each semester of the first year, moving criminal law and constitutional law into the second year. In addition, their proposal reduced the total hours required for graduation to 91. After the usual parliamentary maneuvering—motion to table; substitute motion; second motion to table—the proposal was tabled.[52]

Technology was not the faculty's forte. When the question of students using tape recorders in classes arose, "it was moved by Mr. Hardy that it be announced that it is the sense of the faculty that reproduction of lectures for commercial purposes is an actionable wrong and that it is the policy of the faculty that class lectures cannot be recorded by any means without the prior permission of the faculty member concerned. The motion was seconded by Mr. Pugh, and passed."[53]

A student recommendation to use anonymous grading was ignored. The *Reveille* had reported a discussion of the issue by the Student-Faculty Relations Committee in which some students reported distrust of certain faculty members who might favor one student over another. Professor Bennett was quoted as saying that when it came time to make job recommendations, associating a name with a paper was a great advantage. As usual, the faculty adopted no rule but allowed each faculty member the discretion to use anonymous grading. Another attempt to cease enforcement of the attendance rule was voted down, and Associate Dean Sullivan reminded recalcitrant faculty of their obligation to report violations of the rule. A student request to allow students to attend faculty meetings was denied, even though the students probably had a right to attend under the state's open-meetings law. They never did bring a lawsuit, however. Faculty action was equivocal on the issue of students serving on Law School committees. Professor George W. Pugh moved to appoint two students to each committee. Professor Shieber made a substitute motion to allow each committee to decide on student membership and whether they would vote. The substitute motion passed.[54]

The Law School lecture series was wounded but had not yet died. Committee chairman George Hardy reported that interest had decreased and that it was a problem to obtain lecturers. He asked that he be removed as chairman and also moved that the committee be abolished. The motion failed, but it appears that no further lectures were scheduled.[55]

PROGRAMS AND INSTITUTES

Professor A. N. Yiannopoulos was the driving force behind establishment of the LSU summer program in Greece in 1971, a program that emphasized international and comparative law. It featured European faculty, LSU faculty, and other American law teachers. Students from LSU as well as other U.S.

law students were invited to attend, and classes were conducted in English. The program continued, with classes at the University of Thessaloniki and other locations in the Greek Islands, until Yiannopoulos's retirement from LSU in 1979. A successor foreign program was developed in Aix-en-Provence in France at the behest of Professor Alain Levasseur, where it continues. Professor LeVan proposed a summer session in Montreal, which was approved by the faculty, but it did not develop.[56]

A major initiative developed in continuing legal education. A grant from the federal Department of Health, Education, and Welfare financed a director's salary without cost to the Law School.[57] A program in continuing education was founded in 1970 with Associate Dean Sullivan as the driving force. Gary Lee Boland became director of the program and was primarily responsible for its initial development. It sponsored a conference for lawyers in Rome in July 1971. Professors Pascal, Pugh, and Yiannopoulos prepared materials for the program, "Continental and American Law: Insights and Contrasts" (LCLE 1971).

The four Louisiana law schools sponsored a CLEO program in the summer of 1971. The program, designed to prepare minority law-school students for law study, was held in New Orleans at Tulane's law school, with each law school providing a teacher. Lee Hargrave was appointed from LSU. Earlier, in 1969, Professor Benjamin M. Shieber taught in the CLEO program held at Southern University. In 1973 and again in 1975, he taught in the program at the University of Houston.[58] James A. Gray II also taught in the Houston program in 1975.

The ABA's Standards for the Administration of Criminal Justice were presented to about three hundred appellate-court judges from throughout the United States at the Law School in February 1972. Organized by Associate Dean Sullivan, head of the criminal-justice program at LSU, the five-day conference featured former Supreme Court justice Tom Clark and Leon Jaworski, then president of the ABA and later to be Watergate special prosecutor. The criminal-justice program, begun in March 1971 with initial funding from the Louisiana Commission on Law Enforcement, also presented a program on recent developments and proposed legislation to the Louisiana judges' spring conference. The program joined with the Sigma Delta Chi professional journalism fraternity to present a program on the law and the press. Francis C. Sullivan gave the keynote address, Cheney C. Joseph Jr. moderated a panel on covering criminal proceedings, and Lee Hargrave moderated a panel on the newsman and his sources. Joseph J. Baiamonte ('68) returned to LSU after completion of military service with the army in Vietnam. He came initially for a short appointment to assist Frank Sullivan in conducting the criminal-justice program, but he remained at the Law School as director of the Alumni Association and started a placement office before moving on to become a researcher with the Louisiana State Law Institute.[59]

The twentieth annual meeting of the membership of the Louisiana State Law Institute was held at the Law School in March 1970, with Justice Mack E. Barham as the lead speaker. George Hardy passed an important milestone as the decade began with the completion of his draft of a mineral code for the Law Institute and its subsequent passage.[60]

A joint J.D.-Master's of Public Administration degree program in cooperation with the College of Business was adopted in 1976.[61]

LIBRARY

In 1972, Kate Wallach published her *Louisiana Legal Research Manual,* updating and enlarging two more historically oriented books on sources of Louisiana law. Dr. Wallach had relinquished the heavier administrative duties as librarian in 1970, but she had continued as comparative-law librarian. She retired from that position on July 1, 1975. When she came to LSU in 1949, the law library collection had 75,000 volumes and the annual book budget was $15,000. In 1975, the collection contained more than 205,000 volumes, and the book budget was $156,000.[62]

Dr. Wallach was succeeded for a short time by John S. Marsh, who was named administrative director of the library in June 1969. Though this was an administrative appointment by the dean and not subject to faculty vote, he was well paid at a rate of $15,000 per year ($71,700 in Year 2000 dollars). His tenure was short, though, and he resigned after six months amidst complaints that he was not given adequate authority. He returned to New York to work as librarian for a large law firm.

Earl A. Morgan ('47) was hired as director of the library by Dean Hebert in February 1970. Morgan was a retired air force colonel in the Judge Advocate branch. His, too, was initially an administrative rather than a faculty position, but later in 1970 the faculty authorized offering Morgan a position as associate professor. Soon after he began work, he faced a 10-percent midyear budget cut and a moratorium on book purchases. He remained until 1974, when he entered private practice in Baton Rouge.[63]

Upon Dr. Wallach's retirement in 1975, the Law School contracted with Roy Mersky, librarian at the University of Texas, to consult and advise on the future of the library. Mersky's contribution to the Law School was more than his report—it was his recommendation to hire Lance E. Dickson as librarian. A law graduate from the University of Cape Town in South Africa, Dickson earned a master's degree in library science at the University of Texas after he emigrated to the United States. He was an associate librarian to Mersky at Texas and came to LSU in 1975. He then began an illustrious career at the law library, emphasizing a level of service that was extraordinary, and he substantially enlarged the collection. Dickson remained at LSU until 1987, when he became librarian at the Stanford University Law School.[64]

LAW REVIEW

The *Louisiana Law Review* matured and prospered under its new regime of increased student autonomy, averaging about 1,300 pages per volume during the 1970s. A larger student body was producing a larger group of student writers, and the review during the period was strong in student work. Circulation was about 2,100 copies per issue. When the proposed editorial staff for the law review was presented to the faculty in 1973, Professor Pascal urged that the student staff of the law review be abolished. He recommended that a professional editor be employed who would proceed with faculty advice to publish items deemed publishable. His motion died for lack of a second. The next year, however, the law review seminar, in which credit was awarded to law review students for presenting and critiquing works in progress, was abolished. (It would be reestablished several years later.)[65]

Volume 32 of the law review was dedicated to Beverly Denbo Walker, editorial assistant since Volume 3, who died suddenly on June 21, 1972.[66] She was de facto copy editor, grammarian, and *doyenne* of the law review. She had worked with thirty student editors-in-chief during her tenure and was the institutional memory of the review. She was succeeded by Susan Kane and then by Gladys Dreher in 1976, who remained as editorial assistant until 1986.

Emphasis on development of the civil law was demonstrated by a special fifth issue of Volume 34, which was devoted to articles by a number of renowned international scholars. It was edited by Professor Emeritus Joseph Dainow, who kept active in the field after his retirement. Volumes 35 and 37 also featured additional special fifth issues devoted to civil-law topics. The pattern of the law review was to publish a wide variety of topics, loosely clustered around three themes: general American law topics, civil and comparative law, and Louisiana legislation and jurisprudence. For example, Volume 33 included the following topics, in addition to the faculty symposium on recent Louisiana cases: Section 8g of the NLRA: A Rationale; *Fuentes v. Shevin*, procedural due process, and Louisiana creditors' remedies; harmless error in criminal cases; agreements not to compete; master's vicarious liability for torts; declaratory judgments in Louisiana; the renaissance of the civil-law tradition in Louisiana; spendthrift trusts in Louisiana; medical malpractice; duty-risk alternative to proximate cause; mental commitments; collateral mortgages; symposium on the ABA minimum standards for criminal justice; admissibility of other crimes evidence; and *Argersinger v. Hamlin:* the Gideon of misdemeanors.

The law review continued publishing the annual faculty symposium on the work of the Louisiana appellate courts. Student editors often complained about running the symposium, pointing to some faculty contributions that were less "analytical" and more "reportorial" than desirable. Also, the faculty writers, with whom the editors had little leverage, invariably missed their deadlines. However, a survey of readers indicated that the symposium was the most popular feature of the review, and *Shepherd's Citations* normally indicated that it was the most-cited part of each volume.

DESEGREGATION

By the end of 1977, twenty-two black students had graduated from the Law School. As mentioned earlier, the first black student was admitted in 1950 as a result of a court order, but he resigned shortly afterward. Black students were admitted without court action during the 1970s, though a statewide consent decree in the 1980s calling for affirmative action to desegregate higher education did include LSU and Southern's law schools. Robert F. Collins and Ernest N. Morial were the first black graduates, graduating in 1954 and returning to their native New Orleans. But it was not until fifteen years later, in 1969, that the third and fourth black students were graduated. They were Gammiel B. Gray (Poindexter) and Bernette Joshua (Johnson). A law-student newsletter published in April 1970, the *Livingston Press,* contained an article by black law student Lloyd Givens, generally approving of a plan to recruit black students, but he pointedly observed that the plan "sounded its own death knell when it announced that it had no financial aid to offer."[67] An article by Robert W. Fenet ('72) in that issue pointed out there was only one black among 461 law students.

The LSU Council on Campus Minorities, chaired by Professor Cecil L. Eubanks of the government department, turned its attention to black student enrollment in the Law School in Spring 1973, a time after the limitation of enrollment. At that time, five blacks were enrolled in the Law School, one of them a first-year student. The committee recommended (1) that the Law School take greater advantage of the exception to the admissions standards that had been approved by the Board of Supervisors and use the full complement of ten special admissions; (2) that special-admissions students be allowed to take half of the normal first-year load; and (3) that the Law School institute a tutoring program. In response, the Law School agreed on the need for a larger number of minority students but disagreed with the lighter-load recommendation, keeping to its long-held position against part-time law study. It also agreed to set up a tutorial program for minority students. As mentioned earlier, the Law School participated in CLEO programs and committed itself to admitting successful graduates. Still, the numbers were slow to increase, and the feared flunk-out rate at LSU led many highly qualified applicants to choose to attend a law school where graduation was not as much in doubt.[68]

Four years after Gray and Joshua graduated, Ralph E. Tyson was graduated in 1973. He practiced in Baton Rouge, then became a district-court judge, and more recently was appointed district judge for the U.S. District Court, Middle District of Louisiana.

Minority enrollment started to increase slowly. Four black students graduated in 1974 (Raymond L. Cannon, Dennis J. Dannel, William M. Dauphin Jr., and Charles L. Patin Jr.), four in 1975 (David M. Chretien, Winston Decuir, Wilbur C. Fuller, and Joe L. Smith), two in 1976 (Sylvia R. Cooks and Ernestine S. Gray), and seven in 1977 (Juanita P. Baranco, Michael J. Bonnette,

Paul H. Colomb, Leo C. Hamilton, Melvin L. Hawkins, Donald R. Minor, and Gail E. H. Ray).

The Law School's first regular black faculty member, James A. Gray II, came on board in Fall 1973.[69] Earlier, in Spring 1973, a prominent black professor from the University of Illinois, Charles W. Quick, was a visiting professor. Gray was a native of Baton Rouge, with honors degrees from Morehouse College (B.S. in mathematics) and Harvard Law School. He had also served in the U.S. Marine Corps from 1967 to 1970. Gray taught full time from 1973 to 1975 and conducted the CLEO program in Houston in Summer 1975. He continued to teach part time until 1977, while he practiced law in Baton Rouge. He then moved to New Orleans to enter law practice with the Jefferson, Bryan, and Gray firm. He had been strongly recommended to the Law School by William J. Jefferson, then a legislative assistant to Senator J. Bennett Johnston, and it was Jefferson's firm that Gray joined in New Orleans. Jefferson was later elected to the U.S. House of Representatives. Gray was married to Ernestine F. Gray ('76), who later became a juvenile-court judge in Orleans Parish. Gammiel Gray, who was graduated from the Law School in 1969, was his sister.

STUDENTS

Not only did the size of the student body increase dramatically during the early 1970s, but the proportion of women students also increased. Six women had graduated between 1908 and 1930; 10 women graduated in the 1930s; 18 in the 1940s; 14 in the 1950s; and 17 in the 1960s. In 1969 alone, 8 women were graduated, a prelude to the explosion that came in the 1970s: 134 women were graduated from the LSU Law School between 1970 and 1977, 7 percent of the total number of 1,832 graduates in that time. The figure for 1976 was 33 women, and the number in 1977 was 41 women graduates.

On the mundane level was the practical problem of a lack of bathrooms for the women, even in the new building, leading to the conversion of some male restrooms for the females. The women as well as the men, according to Mary Terrell (Joseph), "all dressed professionally as we were expected to do." Jean Talley Drew ('71) recalled, "I didn't find any disadvantages to being a woman," and "if anything . . . we were probably treated extremely well. Many of the older professors were extremely courtly and courteous in their dealings with us and just quite kind."[70]

A 1971 *Reveille* story proclaimed that Phi Alpha Delta was the only legal fraternity that accepted both male and female members, and the accompanying photograph included Diane A. Jenkins ('72) as vice-justice, along with A. J. Lord, chief justice; James C. Dixon, marshal; Jacque D. Derr, clerk; and John S. Odom, treasurer. The Moot Court Board for 1972-73 was headed by Nora K. Duncan ('73), serving with vice-chairman Byron D. Magbee and secretary Christopher L. Zaunbrecher.[71]

Katherine L. Shaw ('71) was featured in a *Reveille* profile when she was the highest-ranking junior and won a $2,000 scholarship from the American Association of University Women.[72] Both her parents were LSU law graduates (Jean G. Craighead, '40, and William M. Shaw, '41), and she had attended undergraduate school at the University of Mississippi. She reported studying four hours a night in preparation for the next day of classes and commented that law school was not the place to seek a husband. Nonetheless, she married classmate and fellow law review editor Paul H. Spaht after they were graduated from the Law School.

Jerusha (Judy) Stewart (Ernst) ('77) estimated that at least a third of her class members were married. With more women and more married students attending the Law School, the inevitable would occur: the editor-in-chief of Volume 36 of the law review, Susan R. Kelly ('76), was married to associate editor David S. Kelly. The editorial staff of Volume 37 included a married couple serving as associate editors, Jeanette G. Garrett ('77) and J. David Garrett. Diane A. Jenkins ('72), who was married to Louis E. Jenkins ('72), spoke to a Women in Law audience in Fall 1976, telling them that developing competence was the key to their success in a male-dominated profession. Jenkins, chief counsel in the East Baton Rouge District Attorney's Family Service Division, also advised the thirty-five students attending the meeting, "You're going to get attention from male members of the bar and judges, but you can run afoul if your relationships aren't properly set with other females."[73]

Law students became more active in campuswide student government as Vietnam War protests grew and a student-rights movement was developing. A Law School senior, twenty-six-year-old Art Ensminger, was elected president of the Student Government Association for the main campus for the 1969-70 term when antiwar activities were heating up and attempts to reduce regulations on women students were in motion. A Vietnam War protest on the Parade Ground in October 1969 drew some two thousand people. Ensminger established a Department of Student Rights and the Ombudsman Committee before he died, an apparent suicide victim, on February 5 or 6, 1970. A program he advocated, phone counseling for troubled students, was put into effect largely as a result of his death. Members of Ensminger's law class made a donation of books to the library in his memory.[74]

The Ombudsman Office became an important group staffed largely by law students. It started operations in Fall 1969 chaired by Richard G. Crane ('71), with a budget of $4,000 from the SGA. Its task was to "give legal aid to legitimate student complaints." But the student staff had to walk a thin line between giving general advice about the law and the unauthorized practice of law. Among the active law student members were Albert T. Berry, Lawrence J. Centola Jr., David C. Kimmell, Michael Patterson, Gordon M. Propst, Darrell D. White, and Ralph J. Zatzkis, all of the Class of 1971. One of the office's first requests was to place two law-student observers in the Campus Security office each night during Ole Miss week, a week of pep rallies and/or riots before the Ole Miss football game, to observe proceedings and discourage student harassment by police. Not surprisingly, the request was denied by Campus Police Chief Charles Anderson.[75]

Law student Ben Hanchey ('70) appeared before the Traffic Appeals Board to urge the board to abide by a statute, La. R.S. 17:1803, that limited student parking fines to $1. The provision from Act 297 of 1958 had been introduced in the legislature by Speedy O. Long ('59) when Long was a senior in the Law School and had a special interest in the legislation. The Traffic Board agreed to comply with the statute, but Dean of Student Affairs James W. Reddoch overruled the board and imposed a $5 fine in a test case involving a law student. The next step was a "friendly" lawsuit filed by the SGA to test the validity of the statute. Law students John F. LaVern ('70), Richard G. Crane ('71), and Gordon M. Propst ('71) were the main proponents. The litigation, finally decided by a state supreme court decision in 1972, produced a judgment in favor of the University. Judge Albert C. Tate Jr. wrote for the court that the statute was invalid because it interfered with LSU's constitutional grant of power to manage the University.[76]

Darrell D. White and Lawrence J. Centola Jr. (both '71) represented two women students penalized by their standards board for refusing to sign in and out of their housing units as required. They argued that the rules were "unfair," but they were rebuffed by the Associated Women Students Judicial Board. The University Court, however, reversed and found the regulations inequitable. The chief justice of the court happened to be a law student, Ben R. Hanchey ('70), and John E. Seago ('70) was also a member. The opinion concluded that the coed regulations were "contra clearly enunciated University policy providing equal treatment for its students in matters governing student conduct." Dean James W. Reddoch reacted to the decision by questioning the authority of the student court to rule on the validity of University rules and regulations. Richard Crane's response was, "As far as I'm concerned University Court is dead as a body by which students can obtain reasonable changes of rules and regulations of the University." Some 1,200 students gathered on the Parade Ground on March 6 to protest the discriminatory treatment of women students. Another rally at the Catholic Student Center on March 11 drew 350 students. But it would be several years before the rules were changed.[77]

In Fall 1971, a controversy arose over the action of the dean of women to "lock up" the women students in their dorms during Hurricane Edith. Mark G. Murov ('73) defended the power of the dean to restrict the students to their dorms, saying that "telling college age men or women when to come in out of the rain is absurd but citing it as a violation of the criminal code is just as absurd." Steven M. Irving ('74) warned in April 1972 that statements by a freshman law student at Free Speech Alley that the public had a right to use the levees was wrong. He strongly urged that students not use the levee if a landowner objected. In Fall 1973, Alan J. Robert ('74) served in the position and warned students in a *Reveille* interview that standard apartment leases in the area required waiving virtually all rights under the civil code. But students seemed to prefer off-campus housing. Another ombudsman (or is it ombudswoman?) in that term was Martha Chamallas ('75), who reported that students requesting permission to live off campus were usually allowed to do so.[78]

An Ombudsman study group headed by Lila M. Tritico ('75), then a junior in the Law School, criticized the University's plan that was supposed to equalize the rules applicable to men and women living in campus housing. It urged a plan to allow students "more control of their own lifestyles." While an undergraduate, Tritico had been president of the Associated Women Students and protested the unequal sign-in/sign-out cards required in the women's dorms by failing to sign her cards. She was then convicted of rules violations by the Committee on Student Conduct. In Fall 1976, Bernard F. Duhon ('77) was ombudsman, and his assistant was Frederick J. Plaeger II ('77). In *Reveille* interviews, they said that most of the office's activities involved problems that students were having with their landlords and assisting them with University disciplinary proceedings. The office also distributed a pamphlet, *To Sue or Stew: That Is the Question*, explaining the procedure for instituting small-claims suits in the Baton Rouge City Court.[79]

A prominent first-year law student in Fall 1971 was John Bentley Alexander, who was also serving as president of the campuswide Student Government Association. He had been an activist in undergraduate school and a columnist for the *Reveille*, pursuing policies of eliminating *in loco parentis* regulations on students. His term was a continuing barrage of proposals, hearings, and speeches. He also sponsored a program on Bach and appointed an SGA poet laureate, Richard H. Kilbourne Jr. ('76). So active was he, in fact, that he resigned as president after the fall semester grades were released. Facing scholastic probation, Alexander referred to his "excruciatingly modest performance in the Law School this past semester." He said that he planned to become a serious law student and start writing his memoirs. "I have already written the chapter titles and will probably reveal some of them in my farewell address," he said. He later said that his farewell speech "will cover the future of student politics, the importance of music and God, man, history and the universe." His more immediate objective, however, was to become a candidate for the Baton Rouge City Council. He desired to raise the level of political activity, saying that politics can be an honorable profession: "It is as important as plumbing." It was during that campaign that he developed his famous line that the apathetic people in Louisiana got better government than they deserved.[80]

Campus politics lapped into the Law School again in Spring 1974. Law School senior August H. Tabony ('74) was a vice-president of the Student Government Association when a front-page *Reveille* story disclosed that he had been an undercover police officer for the Baton Rouge City Police for five years. His employment was discovered when his name was found listed in city-parish budget documents as an employee of the Intelligence Division. He was quoted as saying that there was no conflict between his receiving a full-time salary from the city and a monthly check for $100 from the SGA.[81]

Tabony had also announced his candidacy for SGA president just before the exposé. Also running for SGA president at the time were two other law students, both freshmen, Gary Elkins ('76) and John Porterfield ('76).

Tabony's campaign was put on hold because he had to concentrate on defending himself during impeachment proceedings. He had been at one time a member of the Students for a Democratic Society and later a member and president of the Progressive Students Alliance. Assistant Ombudsman Oliver Schrumpf ('75) defended Tabony, arguing that his duties consisted mainly of preventing violence and that it was a "misunderstanding and presumption that he has been 'spying' on and 'busting' activist students." Prosecuting Tabony was Stephen M. Irving ('74), who alleged conflicts of interest and malfeasance in office. Tabony's impeachment trial, scheduled for Wednesday, March 21, was postponed for lack of a quorum. Ironically, that was the same day as the run-off election for SGA president, which saw Elkins defeating Porterfield. When the trial was finally held, Charles Yeager ('74) became co-defense counsel. The Student Assembly voted not to remove Tabony by a vote of 21 to 19.[82]

An unusual student disciplinary matter was decided by the law faculty when first-year student Ralph Long made an unauthorized entry into Professor J. Denson's Smith home with the intent of annotating his obligations class examination paper located therein. The incident occurred on a Saturday morning when Smith, director of the Louisiana State Law Institute, and his wife were in New Orleans attending an institute meeting. However, their maid entered their home a block from the University on May Street at 6:30 A.M. and surprised Long. He ran out but was eventually caught because he had left his car keys on a table in the house. The maid called the police, who found Long standing by his nearby parked car. Though the Ethics and Grievances Committee had recommended indefinite suspension of Long, the faculty voted to expel him from the Law School and to recommend expulsion from the University. He also pleaded guilty in city court to the crime of criminal trespass. Presumably the guilty plea to a minor offense was satisfactory to Professor Smith, who was a close friend and long-time golfing partner of Sargent Pitcher Jr. ('41), the East Baton Rouge Parish district attorney.[83]

From the time of its founding, the Law School and its students were featured in the *Gumbo*, the LSU yearbook that included all colleges and students. The publication was financed by a mandatory student-activity fee. Law students, however, sought to have their own annual in the 1970s. Once the LSU administration agreed to assign to the Student Bar Association part of the activity fee paid by law students, the SBA began publication of its own annual, *L'Avocat*.

The first volume of *L'Avocat* was published in 1976, with Sera H. Russell III ('78) as editor, Durelle L. Allen Jr. ('77) as publisher, and Ned D. Wright ('77) as business manager. That initial publication was dedicated to retiring professor Dale E. Bennett "for leadership, dedication, and service" and to Marguerite Hebert "for courage and determination." Hebert was a law student who continued her studies while she battled cancer and the effects of its debilitating treatment. She died on May 14, 1976, just before graduation, after having taken one of her final exams in a hospital while under an oxygen mask. She was awarded her J.D. degree posthumously after receiving credit for an independent research project under the direction of Professor Katherine S. Spaht.[84]

Perhaps the most distinctive aspect of the male students pictured in that first *L'Avocat*—and the faculty photos as well—was their hair, long and longer, and not especially well combed. The musical *Hair* had opened on Broadway in 1968, and its influence was still in effect at LSU. (When the traveling company of *Hair* performed at LSU in 1972, local archconservative groups tried to force LSU to cancel the contract.[85])

Some new student organizations, and a fading one, were also evident. The new groups included Women in Law, and its group photograph featured Juanita P. Baranco, Agna Caire, Sarah J. Campbell, Abigail Lazarus, Peggy LeBlanc, Lourdes Naranjo, Joanna W. Nicholson, Judy Pierce, Karen Lee Price, Midge Slaughter, Diane Sorola, and Chris Stickman. The other new group was BALSA, the Black American Law Students Association. Its photograph featured fourteen members—Willie Armstrong, Juanita P. Baranco, Sylvia R. Cooks, Cindy Courville, Bonnie Foster, Ernestine S. Gray, Melvin L. Hawkins, Anthony J. Johnson, Alvin Jones, Don Minor, Frederick Prejean, Gail E. Ray, Leo Wiggins, and Rudy York. A once-prominent, and soon to be anachronistic, group was the Law Wives Club, a group that in the 1976 photograph featured twice the number of members as Women in Law, but which later disbanded.

The highlighted events selected by the *L'Avocat* editors included the Tullis Moot Court and the Flory Trial Competition, the fall picnic (which featured a beer truck rather than just kegs of beer), football games, the Barristers' Ball, and the spring crawfish boil. Also featured was the perennial parking problem at the Law School, the "horrible parking problem. You had to get there at 7:30 in the morning to be sure you got a place."[86]

Student publications also included the *Civilian*, the law-student newspaper. It was an outgrowth of *Section Fo' Stuff*, which was begun by Oliver G. "Rick" Richard ('77) and Helen "Ginger" Roberts ('77) for their section during their freshman year. They remained on the *Civilian* staff, joined by Bill Lowery and Clay Latimer. The *Reveille* continued its fascination with the Flory Trials, one issue featuring a front-page photograph of Michael Roy Fugler ('72) questioning Miss Lotta Assa, who admitted she enjoyed the pleasures of the flesh with just about anyone.[87]

L'Avocat survived the first-year jinx and continues to be published. The 1977 volume featured another student innovation, the Assault and Flattery Show, in which the students satirized the faculty and each other. Director Oliver G. "Rick" Richard, along with writers Steve Brainis, Judy "Tukey" Pierce, and Helen "Ginger" Roberts, produced a satire based on *The Devil and Daniel Webster*. Titled "The Devil and Tom Harrell (A Morality Play); or, The Devil Made Me Do It," it featured Professor Harrell (played by Ted Hoyt) granting an option on his soul to the Devil, Saul Litvinoff (played by Kyle Schonekas), in return for the gift of good teaching. When the obligation came due, Harrell resisted payment and was represented at trial by Robert A. Pascal, the Priest of Good Order or POGO (played by Thomas M. Hayes III). As the trial unfolded, POGO saved Tom Harrell, albeit with a *deus ex machina* ending. The angel Cheney Joseph (played by A. Edward Hardin) descended from the heavens (seated on a chair), appeared to POGO, and gave him a poopsheet. Consulting the poop, POGO realized that the court lacked proper diversity jurisdiction because the citizenship of the Devil had not been proved. The case was dismissed.[88] The Assault and Flattery Show also survived the first-year jinx and remains a staple student activity at the Law School, sometimes better and sometimes worse.

Poopsheets or student outlines were passed on by former students (some in onerous transactions, others gratuitous). According to a *Reveille* story of the time, freshman law students had to learn to collect poop, "any information that can be gathered from outside sources, especially upperclassmen. This poop has proven to be extremely valuable in passing finals. In fact the average freshman may spend as much time collecting as studying."[89] The "Black Beauty" poopsheet for civil-law property was especially popular. It was the one that was designed for Professor Dainow's property course, Dainow being known for insisting that students respond with "the word." The Black Beauty ended with the statement, "Beware when the word is a semi colon." But the traditional mimeographed poopsheets that were routinely sold were now an anachronism, killed by the Xerox machine.

The passing rate on the Louisiana bar examination during the 1970s remained quite high despite the increasing numbers of graduates. The passing rate was 90 percent or better for eight of the ten July bar exams in the decade, and 87 percent for the other two years. Associate Dean Sullivan addressed pre-law students at LSU, telling them, "We know of no one graduate of LSU Law School who passed the bar exam and wants to practice law, that isn't doing something in the field."[90]

Spring 1974 was the time for streaking on campus. On Thursday, March 7, campus streaking started about 7:15 P.M. when five nude men ran out of the Law School onto the Parade Ground as a crowd of three thousand spectators cheered. The streakers ran around the Parade Ground then back behind the Law School, gathering new adherents. It was not disclosed how many, if any, of the streakers were law students, but the crowd grew to some thousand streakers going around the fraternity and sorority houses. Campus Police Chief A. L. "Luke" McCoy's comment was understated: "It has gotten away from the streaking point. It appears to be a case of public nudity."[91]

ORGANIZATION AND ADMINISTRATION

Governance of LSU generally, and of the Law School in particular, changed in the 1960s and 1970s. The slow movement in Law School changes was accelerated upon Dean Hebert's death in 1977.

While Hebert was acting president of the University, he served on a committee that proposed a constitutional amendment adopted in 1940 to insulate the University from political influence. With fourteen-year overlapping terms, the members of the Board of Supervisors, though appointed by the governor and confirmed by the senate, had substantial independence. The Constitutional Convention of 1973 continued the Board as a constitutional entity, but with shortened ten-year terms, which would allow for more gubernatorial control. Nonetheless, Dean Hebert endorsed the proposed constitution. He acknowledged that it could have been much better, but that it was a major improvement over the previous document.[92] He also supported Alternative A, which was adopted and which preserved a separate LSU board, over Alternative B, which provided a single board for all public higher-education institutions.

In 1965, LSU's central administration was further bureaucratized with an additional level at the top. Referred to as the LSU System, this entity was established by statute, and John A. Hunter, then president of the University, became president of the System. He was assisted by several vice-presidents. The head of the Baton Rouge campus became a chancellor assisted by vice-chancellors. The first chancellor was Cecil G. Taylor, long-term dean of the College of Arts and Sciences.

At the same time, the Medical School, located in New Orleans, became a separate campus of the System administered by its own chancellor instead of by a dean. It also obtained a separate budget line item. The change, with respect to the Medical School, was more formal than substantive, reflecting the reality of substantial independence for the strong medical school located in New Orleans away from Baton Rouge administrators. Other campuses outside of Baton Rouge—LSU in New Orleans and LSU in Alexandria—also became headed by chancellors. LSU-Eunice and LSU-Shreveport also became separate campuses headed by chancellors when they were founded in 1967. The colleges and departments in Baton Rouge remained under the governance of the chancellor of the Baton Rouge campus.

One of the divisions of the University with a strong statewide constituency was the College of Agriculture, with its experiment stations and extension-service offices located throughout the state. Its long-term dean, J. Norman Efferson, succeeded in obtaining designation as a "campus" in 1972, and he became chancellor of the LSU Center for Agricultural Sciences and Rural Development. A problem was that, although the Agriculture Center's experiment stations and extension program were located throughout the state, its teaching function was performed primarily on the Baton Rouge campus, and it was through the Baton Rouge campus that degrees had to be conferred. A complex system of split appointments for faculty who engaged in teaching as well as research was instituted, and the precedent of two "campuses" on one parcel of territory was established.

The independence of the Agriculture Center encouraged the Law School to push for a similar status, and the faculty supported the dean's efforts to have the Law School "assume the status of an autonomous unit" as well as having a line-item in the state budget. The fact that the Law School was receiving increased funding and had secured special appropriations for two years, as discussed earlier, tempered the demands for separation on that point, but tensions between the Law School and the central administration also came in the form of control over promotions and tenure in Spring 1974. The law faculty and Dean Hebert recommended promotion of five law faculty members to the rank of professor—Ellis, Hargrave, L'Enfant, LeVan, and Knight. In accordance with University custom, the dean was asked to rank the candidates for promotion, a ranking that would be available to other reviewing committees and authorities. But Dean Hebert urged promotion of all five and was reluctant to risk having some of them not promoted. Eventually, all five were promoted, but the prospect of similar future problems was another spur to independence.[93]

Independence did not come in Dean Hebert's lifetime, the dean suffering a fatal heart attack on February 3, 1977, while appearing before the Finance Committee of the Board of Regents to present the Law School's proposed budget. He was sixty-nine. A funeral mass was held at his parish church, Sacred Heart, with services conducted by his good friend, the retired bishop of Baton Rouge, Robert E. Tracy.[94]

Hebert's friend Oliver P. Stockwell ('32) was chairman of the LSU Board of Supervisors during the selection of Hebert's successor, and Stockwell was instrumental in getting the Law School established as a separate campus headed by a chancellor who reported to the System president. Stockwell recalled, "Finally we brought it about right after Dean Hebert died, but it was the same principle that he worked on." In terms of selecting the chancellor, "we had some good men in the law school, who I'm sure could have done an excellent job as Chancellor," but the Board wanted to get an outstanding person to carry on where Hebert left off. A Board resolution adopted on the anniversary of Hebert's death celebrated his accomplishments and gave him the posthumous designation of Chancellor Emeritus. The new campus was named the Paul M. Hebert Law Center.[95]

9

RUMINATIONS AND CONCLUSIONS

TEACHING, PUBLIC SERVICE, AND SCHOLARSHIP

Traditional dogma assigns three basic functions to state university law schools—teaching, public service, and scholarship. A simple and reasonably accurate conclusion would be that LSU's Law School, from 1906 to 1977, did a very good job in its educational mission of training lawyers. Since the late 1930s, it also did well in service to Louisiana law reform. It did a decent job in scholarship, but it could have done much more.[1] However, it is hard to fit LSU into this simple analysis. One should probably categorize LSU's Law School, to use current terminology, as a "boutique" law school with missions different from most state law schools. What makes LSU unique is the Romanist-law influence in Louisiana private law and the corresponding emphasis on statutory law in all aspects of the state's legal system.

Consider the teaching mission, generally regarded as LSU's forte. Courses in federal-law subjects, evidence, procedure, and even torts can be taught using national casebooks. However, covering the core of the state's private law—obligations, family law, property, community property, successions, sales, security rights, to name a few—requires more effort on the part of the teacher. Comparison with decisions in other states is often of little help. Instead, comparison with European civil-law countries is called for. Absent canned materials, professors have to develop their casebooks and treatises that emphasize Louisiana statutes and Louisiana cases in light of civil-law history. Being forced to innovate, however, has had distinct advantages. It forces a focus on all the aspects of one system, a deeper analytical and critical process, without the luxury of simply listing the position of the majority of states and the minority of states on each legal point. Beginning with Dean Tullis, this approach instilled an analytical rigor that impressed, if not amazed, students and produced generations of outstanding lawyers. The early faculty was demanding, and that tradition was maintained by successors over the years. Once that tradition was ensconced, the approach to federal-law courses was much the same, since the federal courses were normally statutory. Ira S. Flory in his heyday was respected for his exposition of the law of evidence and federal jurisdiction. Even constitutional law, as Charles Black would point out, was an exercise of expansive construction of basic principles, much like civil-code construction.[2]

Perhaps the best example of this fusion in the curriculum is the freshman course in criminal law. The basic rules of criminal law in Louisiana were derived from the common law of crimes, under the Crimes Act of 1805, and not from European models. Quite early, these offenses were made into specific, albeit disorganized statutes, for judges had no power to establish crimes. Edward Livingston's *Criminal Code* draft, though admired in many countries, was never adopted. It was in 1942, under the leadership of Professor Dale E. Bennett, that the Law Institute drafted a simple, coherent, well-organized criminal code that was simple to read and easy to apply. The course in criminal law, at Bennett's hand, became a typical statutory course. Comparison to other states was possible, and a national casebook was used. But the student, long before the adoption of the Model Penal Code, had a simple, straightforward statute to apply. This code, drafted by a common-law-trained professor, was the perfect vehicle, surprisingly, to teach statutory construction (and, dare I say, civil-law method?). With the text to read, the history of the provisions readily available, the comments of the drafters at hand, and the leading cases available, the student could come to class with a good knowledge of the basics. Class could then be devoted to problems at the edge and to the policies to be applied in solving the next level of problems to reach the courts. Even in the first semester, the course was not a "survey" course; it was an exercise in "doing" law and not just talking about it.

Christopher L. Blakesley, with a legal education from Utah and Columbia plus substantial foreign experience, has remarked that the LSU student is better prepared to deal with statutes than students he has seen at other law schools. He wrote:

> Louisiana is the only state of the Union that has a *Civil Code of the European style*. Because of the *Civil Code*, and because we also have a com-

mon law foundation in other legal arenas, we are able to teach students *all of the basics* of both. We teach them how to resolve legal problems as would common law, as well as European or Latin American jurists. If they do what they should, they develop the capacity to understand how their colleagues from both of these systems think about the law and solve legal problems. The *"Civilian" or Civil Code* aspect of Louisiana provides not only a fascinating and rich legal history, it provides the educator the wherewithal to allow our students to become adept in both the common law and the civilian traditions and the legal analysis required in each.[3]

Symeon C. Symeonides, educated in Thessaloniki and at Harvard, also found merit in the mixed-jurisdiction approach: "Is there anything wrong with Louisiana being a mixed jurisdiction? Not particularly. As [a] comparatist, I cannot complain. This is a comparative-law paradise. As a civilian, I am less sure but I can think of many instances where Louisiana has improved on the original civil law model."[4]

This is not to say that all of LSU's law faculty were outstanding teachers. Far from it, and a quick glance through oral-history transcripts will give a recurring list of the boring ones. Most of those, even scholars of the greatness of Jerome Hall or Eric Voegelin, did not enjoy good reputations among students. But there was a critical mass of very good, very gifted classroom performers who inspired others and who maintained the school's reputation in this area during the period under study.

Judging how good the teaching is at a school is difficult, but the students who consume the product are no doubt an important resource in that inquiry. As many of the quotations throughout this book indicate, law students at LSU thought they were being well taught. Many of those who went on to graduate school were surprised at how much better prepared for advanced legal studies they were than most of their classmates. Those who went to practice with top out-of-state law firms would report that their education was as good as or better than that of graduates of prestigious law schools in other states. Bar-exam results in Louisiana and Texas have confirmed that LSU's students were well prepared for the practice of law.

Public service at LSU was primarily in drafting legislation for the state, within and without the Law Institute. One Assault and Flattery Show highlight was a student portraying the less-than-humble A. N. Yiannopoulos singing "I Write the Laws," a parody of the hit, "I Write the Songs." But in fact he *did* write the laws—his revision of Book II of the Civil Code during the 1970s and 1980s. So did Dale Bennett, drafting the Criminal Code in 1942, and later the Code of Criminal Procedure. Henry G. McMahon had drafted the Code of Civil Procedure of 1960. Bennett, Lazarus, and Harrison had led the compilation of the Revised Statutes of 1950. Litvinoff drafted revisions of the Law of Obligations. Spaht drafted the revision of Matrimonial Regimes Laws. McGough was principal drafter of the Children's Code. Hargrave was coordinator of legal research for the Constitutional Convention of 1973. Hardy drafted the Mineral Code. Pugh drafted revisions of the Law of Evidence. This exceptional body of legislative work was no accident.

It was designed by Dean Hebert and several of the law faculty, along with leading lawyers of the state, beginning in the 1930s, to revitalize and reform the state's laws and reassert the primacy of statutory law in the state. In response to Gordon Ireland's claim that Louisiana was a common-law state, Daggett, Dainow, Hebert, and McMahon responded not only with a dissenting view but with a promise to develop more teaching and doctrinal materials to teach Louisiana law. They were instrumental in hiring faculty to write Louisiana treatises and in founding the Louisiana State Law Institute with the goal of fostering translations of European civil-law materials and the drafting of new legislation to modernize Louisiana's law.[5] These activities were encouraged and subsidized by the Law School. Indeed, the intensity demanded of these public-service projects was one of the reasons that many faculty were doing so little other research and writing so few books and journal articles. The public-service component went beyond Louisiana projects. Dale Bennett was on an advisory committee for the ALI's Model Penal Code, and Wex S. Malone was on the committee to write the Restatement of Torts. Harriet Daggett served on several commissions to reform family laws.

Before the 1930s, little scholarship came from Dean Tullis and Ira S. Flory; their teaching and administrative duties were too heavy. Harriet S. Daggett began her writings in the 1930s, and with James Barclay Smith, she participated in the LSU research renaissance, writing two of the first six titles published by the LSU Press.[6] Hebert and J. Denson Smith published their theses and other articles in the *Tulane Law Review*. With the founding of the *Louisiana Law Review*, some start was made to further foster faculty as well as student scholarship. The systematic treatises were yet to come. For a brief time, the scholars hired in the 1930s, like Jerome Hall, were productive, but after the Louisiana Scandals and World War II occupied the school's energies, the rate of publications was low. Among those who became more active in the 1950s was Wex Malone, with several casebooks in the torts field and speculative writings in major law reviews. Yiannopoulos's treatises on property were first published in 1966 and 1968, and Litvinoff's obligations treatises were published in 1969 and 1975. There was greater encouragement for publications in the 1980s and 1990s, resulting in an outpouring of books and articles that earned some praise for the institution. But this took time in coming, and the demands in the 1960s and 1970s as enrollment increased and teaching loads grew heavier slowed the development of a culture of research and publication.

THE CIVIL LAW AND COMMON LAW NON-DEBATE

Some students and some faculty at LSU have addressed, usually on too high a level of generality to be useful, the so-called clash between the civil law and the common law in the state's law and in the Law School's curriculum. More specific inquiry has led me to believe, from my days as a student at LSU, that there is no real conflict. To put it simply, there is "law" to be drafted and adopted, to be construed and applied, to be taught and learned. To pursue the metaphor I used earlier, once the substance of the criminal law was adopted as a matter of legislative policy and put in the form of a code, the task of the attorney, the judge, the law professor, and the law student was to analyze the text, its history, the purposes of the drafters, the basic policies involved, and so on, and to decide cases. If the substance came from the principles developed in England and known as the common law, that history had to be studied. If the form was a code, basic principles required fidelity to the document, as was basic in the civil law. If there were gaps to be filled and conflicts in the code to be resolved, they were to be done in a rational and logical manner, considering basic policies and basic values. The same analysis applies if one looks to substantive principles that came from the civil law—community property, for example. The sources of the concepts are French and Spanish, as developed in early Louisiana practice. The form is in the generalities provided in the civil code. When conditions changed and equal management was adopted by the legislature, the latest substance and the latest form of the rules came to the forefront. Fidelity to the law requires knowledge of the history and the current purposes of the legislature. It isn't a war; it isn't a battle—it's a simple matter of fidelity to the product of the lawgiver as demanded by democratic principles. The process was described as early as 1928 by Pierre Crabites, Tulane graduate, New Orleans elitist, judge of the Mixed Courts of Egypt, and later professor at LSU. He wrote: "We have been caught in the American maelstrom. The only salvage that remains is a Louisiana incrustation which has in it something of the Civil Law, and something of the Common Law, but which after all is an uncatalogued creation, but a viable institution because it typifies the composite genius of the soul of the true Louisianian."[7] Frederick Beutel, writing in 1929, stated he was not anti–civil law, but wrote of convergence. The common-law states were depending more on statutes and uniform laws, and civil-law countries were developing a mass of jurisprudence in cases. He advocated teaching comparative law and also codification of laws.[8]

My fellow students between 1964 and 1967 did not seem to perceive the institution as schizophrenic and involved in a civil war. My impression of the students since is the same. We were able to assimilate the various aspects of the two systems and to deal with them. It is no different from speaking two different languages and being able to think in both.

Part of the debate arises in definitions, which tend to be at least a century behind reality, characterizing what the civil and common law *were* as opposed to what they *are* today in Europe, England, and the United States. The more the students and professors see of current practices in foreign countries, the less they are willing to spend time on the debate. Indeed, to refer to common law as something in effect in other states of the United States ignores the role of the statutes and uniform laws that have covered almost the entire field of human endeavor. Another problem is that many of those who wanted to participate in a civil law/common law debate were partisans on one side who largely were educated in only one tradition. They didn't know enough about the other tradition to appreciate the reality.

In any event, with the exception of the 1968 curriculum proposals discussed earlier that were rejected and thankfully forgotten, it is inaccurate and unhelpful to analyze the civil/common law debate as something important in the Law School. That is not to say that the civil law was not important and that its background makes LSU different from other law schools. As I said earlier, the traditional focus on statutes and codes at LSU makes the LSU graduate different and better able to handle the multitude of statutes that one encounters regularly in federal law.

In an oral-history interview, my philosophically oriented classmate and colleague William T. Tete described the situation accurately. The faculty did not have a civil-law versus common-law division. The division was more philosophical. While most civilians advocated law in some sense as reason, so did some of the teachers of common-law subjects. Hector Currie, who taught the much-maligned introduction to common law, didn't have any fight with the civilians, and he himself was the ultimate in advocating reason in the law. The legal realists were the more active opponents, stressing the role of judges and eschewing the possibility of elaborating overall theories of law. The tensions were between advocates of natural law and advocates of legal realism. Some civilians, like Joseph Dainow, were more advocates of realism than of natural law. J. Denson Smith illustrates the straddle. He was a graduate of LSU and of Yale, and he taught both common-law contracts and civil-law obligations. Indeed, the adoption of those two courses in the freshman curriculum came after Dean Tullis retired and during the early faculty meetings under Beutel that expressed concretely his approach to covering both systems.

Wex S. Malone's evaluation corresponded to Tete's and reflected his legal-realism roots: "There were those who felt Louisiana should become lined up with the general approach to law in the rest of the country. Not that it took the form necessarily of common law, because a great deal of the most creative stuff we have now is statutory. The movement from judge to administrator, the breakaway from a single principle, broad principle approach, down to the breaking of law into labor law and breaking into all of these, it seems to me, represents a division much broader than the comparison to common law." He continued, "A better description of this would be monism vs. pluralism; monism being the thought that everything is to be moved back to one something basic in the way of principle. Pluralism is that we have many, many origins of our needs."[9]

Dean Hebert, supported by Robert A. Pascal, was a traditionalist in these curriculum matters. It was he who advocated introductory courses that would cover the history of legal systems and who wanted to teach legal philosophy in the first year. He convinced the faculty for a while, but those courses were banished to the upper-class curriculum during one of his leaves from the Law

School. He was able to revive the introductory courses in civil and common law upon his return, but eventually he had to give up on the common-law introductory course. What remains is the course in introduction to civil law, with various names and coverage over the years, but including a comparative element. It remains a controversial orphan in the curriculum, with supporters and detractors. But the debate is not so much about civil versus common law; it is a debate about the value of *any* introductory courses.

Some have speculated that the philosophical divisions in the faculty were related to the large number of Catholics who taught at LSU, at least since the 1930s, and who reflected a natural-law view. But that argument assumes that the Catholic faculty was a bloc. They never were, and there was a division among conservative Catholics, liberal Catholics, and apostate Catholics, and they landed on all sides of the curriculum issues.

But, and most important, despite some differences, the Law School was always a civil and civilized place.

THE FLUNK-OUT RATE

Some 3,900 students were graduated from the Law School between 1906 and 1977. During that time, although the figures are not precise, at least an equal number of students who enrolled in the Law School did not graduate. A passage rate of 50 percent or less during the early years was not unusual. By 1977, it was about 75 percent. In any event, a prospective student would necessarily consider the feared LSU flunk-out rate in deciding whether to attend the Law School. Actually, the term "flunk-out rate" is inaccurate. Many students who did not graduate dropped out voluntarily rather than being excluded because of low grades. Granted, many dropped out in part because of marginal grades, but others did so for various personal reasons or because they simply did not like law school. One aspect of LSU's open-admissions policy, coupled with low tuition, was that it gave students an opportunity to try law study without having to go through a strict admissions process and without incurring great expense.

In the early days, the LSU Law School's passage rate was not substantially different from those of other LSU departments and other law schools and was simply not an issue. As other law schools became more selective and achieved higher passage rates, LSU kept its traditional assumptions about enrollment and standards.

My experience as a student (1964–1967) and as a faculty member (1967–2000) was that the havoc wreaked on the students was not as severe as often portrayed and that the opposing values of the system were important. One important concern was always maintenance of high standards to assure that LSU graduates would be the best lawyers, and graduates took pride in that fact. Lessening the standards was not an option. Raising admission standards was a possible means of increasing the passage rate, but the social cost of that approach would have involved denying an opportunity for many students to study law at all. The historic role of the state university in a populist (Longite, if you wish) state was to provide opportunity to the poor and to the unsophisticated rural student. It was a value that was of special importance to me, the first generation in my family to graduate from college as well as from law school.

My freshman classmates who did not graduate, as far as I can tell, were not permanently ruined by their experience. I note that they include bank presidents and corporate leaders. Over the years, I've met, in various social settings, former students who did not graduate, and seldom have I sensed animosity. Some will even recall their grade in my course and mention that it was higher than their average. Unfortunately, there is little hard data available about the attitudes of those students, and the impact of noncompletion is hard to discern.

Two specific examples stand out, however. Camille F. Gravel, one of Louisiana's best lawyers and a prominent political leader, was excluded in 1937 in his second year for failing to meet academic requirements. In 1937, Dean Hebert wrote to the dean at Catholic University to recommend admission of the "young Gravel" who had shown ability at LSU even though he had not yet developed strong study habits. Gravel did not graduate from Catholic University, but he did pass the bar examination. He eventually became a member of the LSU Board of Supervisors and was also selected as an honorary member of the Louisiana Chapter of the Order of the Coif in 1985 for his service to LSU and the Law School.

John A. Dixon was a freshman at LSU in 1939, where he was a moot-court partner of John McKeithen. Dixon made 4 Cs and an F in family law under Professor Daggett. Disappointed, he voluntarily resigned and became a high-school teacher and coach. He then entered the military service, was captured in Sicily, and was a prisoner of war for twenty-one months. After the war, he entered Tulane Law School and was graduated in 1947. He became a distinguished lawyer in Shreveport, a court of appeals judge, and a member of the Louisiana Supreme Court. He retired as chief justice in 1990.[10]

As this book goes to press, there is considerable pressure to raise fees and raise admission requirements. The prospect is that the Law School will become more elitist in economic terms and in LSAT scores—but at the loss of opportunity and service to the non-elite applicants.

THE PEOPLE WHO PASSED THROUGH

Any educational institution benefits from the stability that results from good teachers remaining at the school for a long time. As this study shows, LSU enjoyed the benefit of many such faculty. Of those who served between 1906 and 1977 and who subsequently retired, twenty-one served for twenty years or more. Of the faculty serving as this is written in 2002, fourteen have twenty or more years of service.

At the same time, there are benefits to be derived from the diversity of views and new approaches that come from the teaching of a national corps of faculty working their way through the nation's legal-education system. Indeed, the fact that faculty leave an institution is not necessarily a bad sign. If they leave for a more prestigious institution with a good feeling for the schools that helped them along, it makes those schools look good and gives them participation in the national network of scholars. LSU benefited from such faculty. A few examples from the years between 1906 and 1977:

Name	Service	Years	Went to
Frederick K. Beutel	1935–37	2	William and Mary; Nebraska
Thomas A. Cowan	1936–40	4	Nebraska; Wayne State; Rutgers
Pierre Crabites	1936–41	5	Came from Mixed Courts of Egypt
Thomas S. Currier	1962–64	2	Virginia; Mudge Rose law firm
Lance E. Dickson	1975–87	12	Stanford Law Library

Name	Service	Years	Went to
Jefferson B. Fordham	1940–46	6	Vanderbilt; Pennsylvania
Jerome Hall	1935–39	4	Indiana
Fowler V. Harper	1936–37	1	Indiana; Yale
Robert L. Henry	1907–11	4	Mixed Courts of Egypt
Marc Hershman	1970–76	6	University of Washington
Thomas W. Hughes	1911–12	1	Dean, University of Florida
Charles R. McManis	1977–78	1	Washington University, St. Louis
David W. Robertson	1962–64	2	University of Texas
Jerome J. Shestack	1950–52	2	Philadelphia lawyer; ABA president
James Barclay Smith	1928–35	7	University of Kansas
George W. Stumberg	1919–23	4	University of Texas
Clarence M. Updegraff	1917–19	2	University of Iowa
Eric H. W. Voegelin	1953–58	5	University of Munich; Stanford

HARD GRADERS VERSUS SOFT GRADERS

When the law faculty was small, maintaining consistent grading standards was apparently not a serious problem. Some student oral-history comments suggest, however, that Harriet Daggett's grading was idiosyncratic, with a tendency to level the grade-point averages of law review editors. Former students often cited the case of a student to whom she awarded an A in the senior successions course so that he would be able to graduate—if he promised never to practice law. He graduated, kept his promise, and became a successful automobile dealer. During these early days, it is probably also fair to say that the Law School had few easy graders. Another story was that when exam papers were turned in to Professor Flory, he piled them into two stacks. The law review students whose papers were in the right-hand pile he referred to as the sheep; the other pile was for the goats.

As the faculty grew in size and multiple sections of the same course were offered by different instructors, consistency in grading standards was difficult to achieve. And as the rest of the academic world became more concerned about the "flunk-out" rate, some law professors tended toward "easier" grading. Indeed, as older faculty members retired and the institution started to lose its collective memory about standards, a split developed between the hard graders and the easy graders. This difference in point of view expanded into other issues about retention standards, waivers, readmissions, and other academic regulations. First George Pugh and then Lee Hargrave started collecting statistics about the grade distributions of the faculty members. Although it was never a stated policy, it was clear that the administrators were dividing the faculty among the sections with an eye toward balancing grades in the sections. As computers became more common, I used my Apple II to develop an index (the HHA or Hargrave Hard Ass Index) that graded the degree of difficulty of each faculty member.

Some of the most serious disputes and the most intense disagreements among faculty members related to grading standards and the quality of Law School graduates. That area was much more contentious than the civil law versus common law issues. As admissions became more selective, the retention rate increased, but it was not until the 1980s and 1990s that the retention rate increased substantially.

THE STUDENTS

The contrast between the students entering in 1906 and in 1976 is startling. The "boys" who first came needed a high-school diploma and two years of college study to be admitted and could earn an LL.B. in two years of study—a total of four years. The older men and women who entered in the 1970s needed a college degree to be admitted to a course of study that covered seven semesters or six semesters plus summer school, a total of seven or often eight years.

Though the fees at LSU were always low, the law students before the 1930s were typically children of the rural elite. Room and board in Baton Rouge was beyond the reach of the state's poor majority. The character of the student body started changing in the 1930s as the influence of populism and Longism was felt. But it was after World War II and the financing provided by the G.I. Bill of Rights that the dam broke and poor and middle-class students came to the Law School in large numbers. That movement continued into the 1970s, with LSU's low fees drawing more students from New Orleans and its suburbs. Interviewed in the 1980s, Dean Cecil Morgan of Tulane stated,

> I'll tell you what we have thought at Tulane, and I think there's some observation that you could make about it. LSU draws from the rural part of the whole state, and its graduates go back to their own home localities. Lots of them go further in different places, but I mean that, as a rule, LSU has been the training ground for the majority of lawyers in the areas of the state outside New Orleans. Loyola has served a special purpose here in New Orleans and has given the opportunity for the working people to go to school and get a legal education. . . . Tulane has had the opportunity in New Orleans to draw on some of the more well-to-do people and some of the leaders of New Orleans itself, and has fed the large firms in New Orleans. As we have pointed out, this is changing now. . . . Nowadays, they [large firms] are recruiting from LSU, and some from Loyola; but the greater number of the big law firms that are recruiting locally are going back to LSU. Tulane went through a period, not so long ago, of losing its reputation as a place for civil law training in New Orleans, and LSU took it over. Tulane was struggling for national recognition and gained it.[11]

Indeed, in a wider-angle view of Louisiana's legal profession, the growth of the LSU, Loyola, and then Southern law schools transformed children of the lower and middle classes into the majority of the profession. It became a more democratic and, some critics would say, more business-oriented profession, rather than a genteel vocation of noblesse oblige.

LSU graduates tended to become community leaders and political leaders. Local politicians became state politicians, and students at LSU would meet peers from all over the state and develop wider circles of friendships. As Edwin Edwards put it, "I thought it was a great help to me, especially in 1971 when I was running for governor, to have a contact in practically every area of the state with someone that I had had an association with in law school. Almost without exception all of them were very, very helpful to me in the campaign in areas where I was virtually unknown."[12]

In 1952, forty-four years after the founding of the Law School, Robert F. Kennon ('25) was the first graduate to be elected governor. John J. McKeithen ('42) served as governor from 1964 to 1972, and Edwin W. Edwards ('49) was governor from 1972 to 1980, 1984 to 1988, and 1992 to 1996, after having been a member of the U.S. House of Representatives from 1965 to 1972.

On the federal level, Russell B. Long ('42) was elected to the U.S. Senate in 1948 and served until 1987. J. Bennett Johnston Jr. ('56), after serving in the Louisiana House and Senate, was elected to the U.S. Senate in 1972 and served until 1997. John B. Breaux ('67) served in the U.S. House of Representatives from 1972 to 1987 and then was elected to the U.S. Senate to succeed Russell Long.

Graduates who served in the U.S. House of Representatives include: Overton Brooks ('23), served 1937–1961; Patrick Thomson Caffery ('56), served 1969–1973; Anthony Claude Leach Jr. ('63), served 1979–1981; Gillis William Long ('51), served 1963–1965 and 1973–1985; Speedy O. Long ('59), served 1965–1973; James O. McCrery III ('75), elected in 1988; Harold Barnett McSween ('50), served 1959–1963; William Henson Moore III ('65), served 1975–1987; Wilbert Joseph (Billy) Tauzin ('67), elected in 1980.

Hundreds of graduates have served as state and federal district-court judges and on the state courts of appeal. Graduates serving on the Supreme Court of Louisiana have included: Mack Barham ('46), Fred A. Blanche Jr. ('48), Luther F. Cole ('50), James L. Dennis ('62), John B. Fournet ('20), Pike Hall Jr. ('53), Joe B. Hamiter ('23), Frank W. Hawthorne ('24), Bernette J. Johnson ('69), Catherine D. Kimball ('70), Amos L. Ponder Jr. ('12), Joe W. Sanders ('38), Albert C. Tate Jr. ('48), and John J. Weimar ('70). William J. Blass ('40) served on the Supreme Court of Mississippi.

Serving on the federal Fifth Circuit have been six LSU graduates: Elmo P. Lee ('11), Wayne G. Borah ('15), Alvin B. Rubin ('42), and Henry A. Politz ('59), in addition to James L. Dennis and Albert Tate Jr., who moved from the state supreme court to the federal appeals court.

Of seventy-seven federal district judges who have sat in Louisiana, twenty-four were graduates of the LSU Law School: James J. Brady ('69), Helen G. Berrigan ('77), Wayne G. Borah ('15), Robert F. Collins ('54), Benjamin C. Dawkins Jr. ('34), Rebecca F. Doherty ('81), Stanwood R. Duval Jr. ('66), Jack M. Gordon ('54), Robert G. James ('71), Henry A. Mentz ('43), Lansing I. Mitchell ('37), John V. Parker ('52), Frank J. Polozola ('65), G. Thomas Porteous Jr. ('71), Gaston L. Porterie ('16), Alvin B. Rubin ('42), John M. Shaw ('56), Thomas E. Stagg Jr. ('49), James T. Trimble Jr. ('56), Ralph

E. Tyson ('73), Earl E. Veron ('59), Donald E. Walter ('64), E. Gordon West ('42), and Jay C. Zainey ('75).

The previous chapters have listed the twenty-nine LSU graduates who served on the LSU law faculty between 1906 and 1977. LSU graduates have served as faculty at other law schools as well. Best known was F. Hodge O'Neal ('40), who also was awarded doctorates from Yale and Harvard. He taught at Ole Miss, Mercer, Vanderbilt, Duke, Minnesota, and Washington University in St. Louis, and served as dean at Mercer, Duke, and Washington University.[13]

David W. Robertson ('61) joined the University of Texas law faculty in 1966 after teaching at LSU and Leeds University and remains there holding the W. Page Keeton Chair in Tort Law. Gregory B. Adams ('73) is at the University of South Carolina; James E. Bailey ('85) is at Lewis and Clark Northwestern School of Law; Martha E. Chamallas ('75) taught at Iowa and Pittsburgh and then moved to Ohio State University; Alejandro M. Garro ('79) is at Columbia; Phillip L. McIntosh ('78) is at Mississippi College; and Steven J. Willis ('77) is at the University of Florida.

Six graduates teach at Loyola in New Orleans: Dian T. Arruebarrena ('80), George L. Bilbe ('70), Catherine L. LaFleur ('76), Gerard A. Rault Jr. ('68), Bernard K. Vetter ('64), and James E. Viator ('85).

Eight LSU graduates teach at Southern University's Law Center in Baton Rouge: Cary deBessonet ('68), Alfreda Sellers Diamond ('86), Ernest S. Easterly III ('77), Michelle Ward Ghetti ('83), Cynthia Picou ('70), Thomas E. Richard ('75), Winston W. Riddick ('74), and Evelyn L. Wilson ('83).

The work of Kate Wallach and Lance Dickson is continued as several LSU graduates have been active in law libraries. Kent McKeever ('80) is the director of the law library at Columbia University, and Claire M. Germain ('75) is also in New York, heading the law library at Cornell University. Juan F. Aguilar ('66) was library director at New Brunswick and then at Drake University before retiring in 1984. Mary Brandt Jensen ('84) is library director at the University of Mississippi.

THE TRANSITION

A composite of faculty photographs was made in the early 1970s, picturing what some believe was a high point of the Law School. The lions who had staffed the school since the 1930s were still on board, and a new generation of dedicated younger faculty was finding its way under their guidance. The 1972–73 lineup included Dean Hebert and Associate Dean Sullivan, and the faculty, in order of seniority, were: Smith, Hebert, Bennett, Dainow, Malone, Pascal, Harrison, Dakin, Wallach, Pugh, Yiannopoulos, Lazarus, Hardy, Currie, Shieber, Litvinoff, Crawford, Ellis, Sullivan, Hargrave, Knight, Tete, L'Enfant, Hershman, Morgan, Joseph, LeVan, Baier, Hersbergen, Johnson, Lamonica, Spaht, Stetter, and Theis.

As T. Harry Williams described LSU, it was a small, sleepy, southern school until the 1930s. That is also a fair characterization of the Law School. The explosion of the Beutel expansion transformed LSU into a major player among state law schools, and the steady hand of Paul M. Hebert preserved the gains despite the difficulties of World War II and the influx of the G.I. Bill veterans. The Law School was preparing to make a quantum jump in the late 1960s and 1970s—a new building; new grant-funded programs, largely under the leadership of Frank Sullivan; foreign programs; a clinical program; CLEO programs; continuing legal education; judicial education programs; and others—and the faculty research impetus was increasing. This development was postponed by the enrollment crisis and budget crises of the early 1970s and the difficulties of keeping the core of the institution intact. By 1977, however, enrollment was declining after the imposition of limitations on admissions. Frank Sullivan was generally considered to be Hebert's heir apparent, and few doubted that Hebert had the personal respect and prestige to be able to name his successor when he retired.

But it was not to be. Dean Hebert died unexpectedly from a heart attack suffered while he was presenting the Law School's budget request to the Finance Committee of the Board of Regents on February 3, 1977. The subsequent transition was not an easy one, and the status of the school in 1977 marks a watershed in the history of the Law School and an appropriate place to end this study. Things would change substantially.

It wasn't until April 1979 that William D. Hawkland came on board as Hebert's successor. An inconclusive dean's search was followed by the establishment of the Law Center as a separate LSU campus and then by a search for a chancellor. The establishment of the separate campus led to more separation of the academic life of law students and law faculty from the rest of the University. Private fund-raising efforts to supplement state appropriations would follow. Replacing the now-retired "lions" would be a long process. Tuition increases would be necessary. Women students would increase to the point of reaching 50 percent of the student body. The average age of the students would increase. Married students with different social lives would change the character of student life. In all of this, however, the Law School sought to maintain its tradition of quality and the expectation that LSU lawyers would be the *best* lawyers. The emphasis, to use the cliché, was on *throughput*. LSU students may not have had the median LSAT scores of students at peer institutions, but guided by a faculty with rigorous standards and putting in the required hard work, LSU graduates would be equal to or better than their counterparts.

NOTES

1. LAWYERS IN EARLY LOUISIANA

1. Francis Parkman, *LaSalle and the Discovery of the Great West* (Boston: Little, Brown, 1905), 307.

2. Henry S. Foote, *The Bench and Bar of the South and Southwest* (1876; rprt., Buffalo: William S. Hein, 1994), 193; Hans W. Baade, "Marriage Contracts in French and Spanish Louisiana: A Study in 'Notarial' Jurisprudence," *Tulane Law Review* 53 (1978): 1, 9, 12. See also Elizabeth Gaspard, "The Rise of the Louisiana Bar: The Early Period, 1813–1839," *Louisiana History* 28 (1987): 183–97.

3. William B. Hatcher, *Edward Livingston: Jeffersonian Republican and Jacksonian Democrat* (Baton Rouge: Louisiana State University Press, 1940), 100; Edward F. Haas, "Louisiana's Legal Heritage: An Introduction," in *Louisiana's Legal Heritage*, edited by Edward F. Haas (Pensacola, Fla.: Perdido Bay Press, 1983), 1–6; Gaspard, "The Rise of the Louisiana Bar."

4. John Henry Wigmore, "Louisiana: The Story of Its Jurisprudence," *American Law Review* 22 (1888): 890, 897.

5. Cecil Morgan, *The First Constitution of the State of Louisiana* (Baton Rouge: Louisiana State University Press, 1975), 20; Alain A. Levasseur, *Louis Casimir Elisabeth Moreau-Lislet: Foster Father of Louisiana Civil Law* (Baton Rouge: Louisiana State University Law Center Publications Institute, 1996), 99–101; Gaspard, "The Rise of the Louisiana Bar," 183–97; George Dargo, *Jefferson's Louisiana: Politics and the Clash of Legal Traditions* (Cambridge: Harvard University Press, 1975); Henry Plauché Dart, "The History of the Supreme Court of Louisiana," *Louisiana Law Reports* 133 (1914): xxx, xxxi.

6. C. W. Ellis, "The Louisiana Bar, 1813–1913," *Louisiana Law Reports* 133 (1914): xxvi; *Biographic and Historical Memoirs of Louisiana*, edited by Allen Johnson (1892; rprt., Baton Rouge: Claitor's, 1975), I, 83; Wigmore, "Louisiana: The Story of Its Jurisprudence," 890, 897.

7. Morgan, *The First Constitution of the State of Louisiana*, 15, 17; Lee Hargrave, *The Louisiana State Constitution: A Reference Guide* (Westport, Conn.: Greenwood Press, 1991), 2.

8. John T. Hood Jr., "The Louisiana Lawyer," *Louisiana Law Review* 18 (1958): 661, 663.

9. Samuel B. Groner, "Louisiana Law: Its Development in the First Quarter-Century of American Rule," *Louisiana Law Review* 8 (1948): 350, 376, 379; Foote, *The Bench and Bar of the South and Southwest*, 193; *Biographic and Historical Memoirs of Louisiana*, I, 80, 81.

10. Wigmore, "Louisiana: The Story of Its Jurisprudence," 890, 898.

11. Henry W. Scott, *Distinguished American Lawyers* (New York: Charles L. Webster, 1891), 44 (Benjamin is the only Louisiana lawyer listed in this publication, which contains short biographies of sixty-two prominent lawyers); *Biographic and Historical Memoirs of Louisiana*, I, 87.

12. *Biographic and Historical Memoirs of Louisiana*, I, 81; *Dictionary of American Biography* (New York: Scribner's, 1957), VIII, 582; Thomas J. Semmes, *The Civil Law as Transplanted in Louisiana: A Paper Read Before the American Bar Association at Saratoga Springs, N.Y., August 10th, 1882* (Philadelphia: G. S. Harris and Sons, 1883), 243.

13. Semmes, *The Civil Law as Transplanted in Louisiana*, 43.

14. A. Oakey Hall, *The Manhattaner in New Orleans; or, Phases of "Crescent City" Life*, edited by Henry A. Kmen (1851; rprt., Baton Rouge: Louisiana State University Press, 1976). See especially 74–90, describing a visit to the courts. Ibid., xiv.

15. Robert Stevens, *Law School: Legal Education in America from the 1850s to the 1980s* (Chapel Hill: University of North Carolina Press, 1983), 5.

16. Schmidt was also the editor of and principal author of the *Louisiana Law Journal*, published in New Orleans in 1841 and 1842 by E. Johns. It was reprinted by Dennis & Co. of Buffalo, N.Y., in 1964. He self-published a book, *The Civil Law of Spain and Mexico* (New Orleans: T. Rea, 1851), which he dedicated to "Christian Roselius, Esq., professor of civil law in the University of Louisiana." See Paul Brosman, "The First Hundred Years," *Tulane Law Review* 22 (1948): 543, who states, in note 3: "As early as 1837 Randall Hunt had given law lectures in the city, and in 1844 the Louisiana Law School, directed by a Mr. Schmidt and including Christian Roselius among its lecturers, began legal instruction with a small class. However, these and other efforts at the formal training of law students appear to have yielded scant success, although the Schmidt venture survived until the Law Department came into being." Robert Stevens, former provost and law professor at Tulane, states in his study of legal education: "When Tulane wanted to establish a law school in 1847, it absorbed the Louisiana Law School, run by the Swedish scholar, Gustavus Smith." Stevens, *Law School*, 5 (citing unpublished research papers). Adrian G. Duplantier, "The Law Schools," *Louisiana Law Reports* 245 (1963): 43; John P. Dyer, *Tulane: The Biography of a University 1834–1965* (New York: Harper & Row, 1966), 67, 68.

17. Stevens, *Law School*, 36, 76.

18. Ibid., 139; Duplantier, "The Law Schools," 43; Hood, "The Louisiana Lawyer," 661, 662.

19. 163 U.S. 537 (1896); 339 U.S. 629 (1950) (which required admission of blacks to the University of Texas Law School because of the lack of equal education offered at the newly founded law school at Texas State University of Negroes in Austin); A. A. Lenoir, "Historical Sketch of the Southern University Law School," *Louisiana Law Reports* 245 (1963): 157.

20. "Historical Sketch of the Committee on Bar Admissions of the Supreme Court of Louisiana," *Louisiana Law Reports* 245 (1963): 72.

21. William Ivy Hair, *The Kingfish and His Realm: The Life and Times of Huey P. Long* (Baton Rouge: Louisiana State University Press, 1991), 52; Sue Eakin, ed., *Little Hu: The Boy Who Planned to Be Governor* (Winnfield, La.: Louisiana Political Museum and Hall of Fame, 1997), 130; T. Harry Williams, *Huey Long* (New York: Alfred A. Knopf, 1969), 78.

22. Williams, *Huey Long*, 74.

2. THE BEGINNINGS: 1904–1920

1. Louisiana Constitution (1845), Art. 137 (the provision continued as Art. 143 in the Constitution of 1864); Louisiana Acts (1884), No. 43; Dyer, *Tulane*, 25.

2. Louisiana Constitution (1879), Art. 30; Marcus M. Wilkerson, *Thomas Duckett Boyd: The Story of a Southern Educator* (Baton Rouge: Louisiana State University Press, 1935), 225–39.

3. Wilkerson, *Thomas Duckett Boyd*, 158, 164, 166, 273.

4. Quotation ibid., 209; Dan R. Frost, *The LSU College of Engineering* (Baton Rouge: Louisiana State University College of Engineering, 2000), II, 1; Wilkerson, *Thomas Duckett Boyd*, 212.

5. Wilkerson, *Thomas Duckett Boyd*, 214; quote from *Reveille*, 8 March 1906, p. 2.

6. *Bulletin* (1906), 76; Wilkerson, *Thomas Duckett Boyd*, 214–15; *Reveille*, 17 May 1906, p. 2.

7. Wilkerson, *Thomas Duckett Boyd*, 215, states that twenty-six students were enrolled. Paul M. Hebert, "Historical Sketch of the LSU Law School," *Louisiana Law Reports* 245 (1963): 137, 138, states that nineteen students were enrolled. The *Reveille* reported that twenty-five students initially took the first-year course and twenty-nine others took one or more subjects (8 November 1906, p. 2). *Reveille*, 27 September 1906, p. 1, 8 November 1906, p. 2.

8. *Bulletin* (1906), 77, 83. The *Louisiana Acts* (1908), No. 227, provided "that no fee for tuition shall be charged to any student or cadet who is a bona fide resident of the State of Louisiana unless said student or cadet be pursuing a special, graduate, or professional course of study." *Bulletin* (1908), 133; Hood, "The Louisiana Lawyer," 661, 662.

9. *Bulletin* (1906), 83; Moyse, Hermann, Sr., interview by Nina Pugh, audiotape recording 4700.1472, 24 May 1982, p. 7, LSU Law School Oral History Series, T. Harry Williams Center for Oral History Collection, LSU Libraries, Baton Rouge [hereafter cited as OHP]; Stockwell, Oliver P., II, interview by Nina Pugh, audiotape recording 4700.1462, 12 December 1983, p. 2, OHP; *Reveille*, 17 October 1910, p. 6.

10. Wilkerson, *Thomas Duckett Boyd*, 216, 203. The 1906 *Bulletin* (p. 78) stated that the Law School occupied the "first floor." The 1909 *Bulletin* (p. 21) described the area as the basement, as did Dean Hebert in his historical sketch of the Law School. Hebert, "Historical Sketch," 137, 140; *Reveille*, 5 February 1912, p. 4; Tucker, John H., Jr., interview by Nina Pugh, audiotape recording 4700.1467, 24 May 1983, p. 1, OHP; *Profile of a Law Center: Louisiana State University, Baton Rouge* (Baton Rouge: LSU Office of Publications, 1970), 2.

11. *Bulletin* (1906), 78–79; Moyse, p. 13, OHP.

12. Hebert, "Historical Sketch," 137, 138; *Bulletin* (1906), 77, 82; Minutes of the LSU Law School Faculty, Chancellor's Office, Paul M. Hebert Law Center, Louisiana State University, Baton Rouge [hereafter cited as Minutes], 27 March 1974.

13. *Bulletin* (1906), 82 (the bar examination at the time was an oral one); Moyse, p. 1, OHP.

14. *Reveille*, 22 April 1912, p. 4; *Louisiana Acts* (1924), No. 113; "Historical Sketch of the Committee on Bar Admissions of the Supreme Court of Louisiana," *Louisiana Law Reports* 245 (1963): 72; *Reveille*, 3 October 1918, p. 1.

15. Another ongoing battle with Tulane at the same time involved attempts by the now-private school to obtain state appropriations. Thomas Boyd was successful in opposing that proposal in the state legislature. See Wilkerson, *Thomas Duckett Boyd*, chs. 12 and 13; Dyer, *Tulane*, 119–23.

16. Dyer, *Tulane*, 138: "In 1902, Monte M. Lemann and Ralph J. Schwartz received the Bachelor of Arts degree at Tulane. That fall both of them went East for their law degrees, Lemann to Harvard and Schwartz to Columbia. When they returned home to New Orleans in 1906 they were added to the faculty. . . . Hardly had they received their appointments before they were in conference with Dean Saunders over an agenda containing a list of reforms which the two young men felt would bring the law department up to the level of Eastern law schools."

17. *Bulletin* (1906), 76; Prescott quote in Hebert, "Historical Sketch," 137, 139.

18. *Bulletin* (1906), 83.

19. Ibid., 80; *Reveille*, 5 February 1907, p. 2, 15 March 1907, p. 2, 27 March 1908, p. 1 (one lecture was titled "Edouard Livingston, the Greatest Lawyer of Louisiana"); *Bulletin* (1908), 132; Alfred J. Bonomo, *Lectures on the Civil Code of Louisiana by Hon. Eug. D. Saunders* (New Orleans: E. S. Upton Printing, 1925); W. O. Hart, *Fragments of Louisiana Jurisprudence: Twelve Lectures Delivered to the Students in the Law Department of the Louisiana State University* (Baton Rouge: Daily State Publishing, State Printers, 1908), 150 ff.

20. *Bulletin* (1906), 80.

21. *Reveille*, 12 February 1909, p. 1, 11 January 1913, p. 4, editorial (rejoicing over the practical aspects of moot court and how more than any institution in the South, LSU emphasizes the moot court idea: Students did a criminal moot court under Prof. Williams in the first year and a civil case under Prof. Tullis in the second year.), 1 November 1913, p. 1, 15 November 1913, p. 1, 22 November 1913, p. 6, 3 October 1914, p. 1, 19 December 1914, p. 7, 25 November 1915, p. 2, 16 November 1916, p. 3. Blanchard was a former congressman, U.S. senator, justice of the state supreme court, and governor. He was a founder of the Blanchard Walker law firm in Shreveport. See Mark T. Carleton, "Newton Crain Blanchard," in *The Louisiana Governors: From Iberville to Edwards*, ed. Joseph G. Dawson III (Baton Rouge: Louisiana State University Press, 1990), 198.

22. Hebert, "Historical Sketch," 139; Moyse, p. 5, OHP; "Proceedings of the Golden Anniversary Celebration of the Louisiana State University Law School," *Louisiana Law Review* 17 (1957): 505–508.

23. *Gumbo* (1908), 15; William W. Smithers, preface to *Criminal Sociology* by Enrico Ferri (1917; rprt., New York: Agathon Press, 1967), xxiv.

24. Smithers, preface to *Criminal Sociology* by Enrico Ferri, xxiv; Joseph I. Kelly, "The Gaian Fragment," 6 Ill. L. Rev. 561 (1911), and "The *Titanic* Death Liability," 7 Ill. L. Rev. 137 (1912).

25. Hebert, "Historical Sketch," 140. The surmise is supportable by Wigmore's interest in Louisiana law, as shown in his essay "Louisiana: The Story of Its Jurisprudence," *American Law Review* 22 (1888). In that article, at p. 890, Wigmore stated: "Few subjects so well reward attention as the unique position in American jurisprudence occupied by the law of Louisiana, and the singularly interesting course of events which out of such varied material has given us the system of law now so much in contrast with the other systems of the Union." (The article, with some revisions, was reprinted in vol. 1 of the *Southern Law Quarterly*, later renamed the *Tulane Law Review*, in 1916.) Early in his career, Wigmore was a professor of American law at Keio University in Japan (William R. Roalfe, *John Henry Wigmore: Scholar and Reformer* [Evanston: Northwestern University Press, 1977], 20–31). He also was the author of *A Panorama of the World's Legal Systems* (Washington, D.C.: Washington Law Book, 1936). Wigmore was also active in the

Association of American Law Schools and the Legal Education Section of the American Bar Association (Roalfe, *Wigmore*, 105–12).

26. *Alumnus* (1909), ads after p. 126; Hebert, "Historical Sketch," 140.

27. *Bulletin* (1909), 11; *Reveille*, 7 November 1907, p. 3; Robert Llewellyn Henry Jr., Personnel File. The Mixed Courts of Egypt were imposed by colonial powers and "had exclusive jurisdiction over civil and commercial litigation between natives and foreigners, and between foreigners of different nationalities." The judges were chosen by ability, from Egypt and abroad. Mark S. Hoyle, *Mixed Courts of Egypt* (London: Graham and Trotman, 1991), 13, 21. See also Jasper Yeates Brinton, *The Mixed Courts of Egypt*, rev. ed. (New Haven: Yale University Press, 1968), 229. Another judge of the district court, Pierre Crabites from Louisiana, served from 1911 until 1936, after which he was appointed to the LSU law faculty.

28. *Alumnus* (1909), 44.

29. *Bulletin* (1909), 17; *Alumnus* (1909), 84, 85, 86.

30. *Reveille*, 12 November 1910, p. 1.

31. Hebert, "Historical Sketch," 140, 141; Association of American Law Schools, *Directory of Teachers in Member Schools: Teachers' Directory* (St. Paul: West, 1925), 74. This directory has been published annually under various titles since 1923. Henceforth, all references will be cited as *AALS Directory of Law Teachers*.

32. *The Formal Presentation to the Law School of Oil Portraits of Dean Emeritus Robert Lee Tullis and the Late Professor Ira S. Flory on Saturday, March 28, 1953, at 2 O'Clock P.M.* (Baton Rouge: Louisiana State University Law School Alumni Association, 1953), 16; Miller, Ben R., Sr., interview by Nina Pugh, audiotape recording 4700.1438, 17 May 1983, p. 8, OHP; Moyse, p. 11, OHP. The reference is to Tullis's second wife, Octavia Gayden Perkins. Hawthorne, Justice, interview by Nina Pugh, audiotape recording 4700.1413, 15 August 1984, p. 3, OHP; Gold, Leo, interview by Nina Pugh, audiotape recording 4700.1406, 8 August 1984, p. 4, OHP. Tullis's first wife was Maggie Josephine Texada of Rapides Parish (*Reveille*, 23 January 1919, p. 3). Moyse, p. 4, OHP; *Reveille*, 23 January 1919, p. 3.

33. *Reveille*, 22 April 1912, pp. 4, 13 December 1917, p. 6; Tucker, p. 2, OHP.

34. Gaharan, Phillip S., interview by Nina Pugh, audiotape recording 4700.1407, 15 November 1983, pp. 2, 3, OHP; Hawthorne, p. 3, OHP.

35. Jennings, Robert B., Sr., interview by Nina Pugh, audiotape recording 4700.0425, 1 June 1983, p. 10, OHP; *Whangdoodle*, 1 June 1930, 1.

36. *Bulletin* (1909), 17.

37. *Louisiana State University Law Register 1977* (Baton Rouge: Louisiana State University Law Center, 1977), 64.

38. *Bulletin* (1909), 184, 185–90 (1908), 134; Moyse, p. 13, OHP.

39. *Bulletin* (1911), 211.

40. Ibid., 212, 217; *Reveille*, 11 February 1911, p. 1.

41. *Reveille*, 25 March 1911, p. 1, 1 April 1911, p. 1.

42. *Bulletin* (1916), 119.

43. Ibid. (1919), 121.

44. Ibid. (1916), 260.

45. *Reveille*, 30 March 1916, pp. 1, 8, 9 November 1916, p. 4; Wilkerson, *Thomas Duckett Boyd*, 293.

46. Edwin Corwin McKeag's surname is so spelled in the LSU *Bulletin* (1910–11), 217; in his book, *Mistake in Contract: A Study in Comparative Jurisprudence* (1905; rprt., New York: AMS Press, 1968); and in the case reports. However, the "Hall of Fame" plaque in the Law Building spells the name "McKeagh."

47. McKeag, *Mistake in Contract*. The author's biographical data is found at p. 133. McKeag appears as counsel in *Campbell v. Weber*, 80 N.J. Eq. 533, 85 A. 225 (1912) and 79 N.J. Eq. 519, 81 A. 732 (1911); *Watson v. Mayor*, 79 N.J. L. 216, 74 A. 301 (1909); and *United New Jersey R. & Canal Co. v. Parker*, 75 N.J. L. 771, 69 A. 239.

48. *Bulletin* (1911), 210; Thomas Welburn Hughes, *An Illustrated Treatise on the Law of Evidence* (Chicago: Callahan, 1907), iv; *Reveille*, 1 October 1910, p. 2; *Alumnus* (1909?), 185–86, reprinted in *Reveille*, 17 December 1910, p. 7.

49. *Louisiana State University Quarterly* 6 (1911); *Reveille*, 13 May 1911, p. 3, 5 October 1912, pp. 1, 3.

50. *Reveille*, 27 September 1913, p. 3, 14 October 1911, p. 5.

51. *LSU Quarterly* 4 (1911): 109–10; *Reveille*, 8 March 1913, p. 6, 27 September 1913, p. 3.

52. *Bulletin* (1909), 230, lists him as a 1901 LSU graduate then residing in New Orleans and practicing law. *Reveille*, 4 October 1913, pp. 2, 3. Ira S. Flory to U.S. Attorney General John G. Sargent, 6 January 1928, in LSU Law School Archives [hereafter cited as LSU Law Archives], Box 58.

53. The *Louisiana Reports* contain two of Blackshear's early cases: *Town of Minden v. Crichton*, 118 La. 747, 43 So. 395 (1907), contesting the constitutionality of a road tax; and *State v. Robertson*, 133 La. 806, 63 So. 363 (1913), an appeal of a manslaughter conviction. Marshall Shaw, a retired lawyer in Homer/Shreveport, reports that a search of the Claiborne Parish public records indicated that Blackshear practiced law in Homer and recorded numerous oil and gas transactions. Shaw, phone conversation with author.

54. Flory to Sargent, 6 January 1928. A search of Westlaw's ALLFEDS-OLD database did not reveal any cases decided by a judge named Blackshear; presumably he did not get the judgeship. Carver, Marshall Hampton, IV, interview by Nina Pugh, audiotape recording 4700.1393, 4 November 1983, OHP, reports having visited Blackshear in New Orleans as a child in the early 1950s with his father, who had been associated with Blackshear in oil and gas ventures in the Natchitoches area. Tucker, p. 2, OHP. Also, "Incidentally, he was a brother-in-law of B. B. Taylor."; Morgan, *The First Constitution*, 5; *Reveille*, 27 October 1942, p. 3. A small (3½-by-6-inch) six-page pamphlet contained in the Rare Book Collection of the LSU Law Library is "Biographical Sketch of Judah P. Benjamin," with David Blackshear listed as the author. No publisher is listed, and the only additional identification is "1314 Massachusetts Ave., N.W., July 17, 1942." The material presented in the pamphlet has a heavy emphasis on the fact that Benjamin was Jewish.

55. *Reveille*, 5 October 1912, pp. 1, 3; John R. Pleasant, "Remarks by Mr. John R. Pleasant, Law Class of '28," in *The Formal Presentation to the Law School of Oil Portraits of Dean Emeritus Robert Lee Tullis and the Late Professor Ira S. Flory on Saturday, March 28, 1953, at 2 o'Clock P.M.* (Baton

Rouge: Louisiana State University Law School Alumni Association, 1953), 6; *AALS Directory of Law Teachers* (1925), 25.

56. Hebert, "Historical Sketch," 141. Pleasant ("Remarks," 6) stated, "Most of us here will recall his method of explaining and analyzing the most complicated cases by drawing two or three lines on the blackboard and using a few letters of the alphabet." Ben R. Miller, p. 8, OHP; Kitchens, Graydon, interview by Nina Pugh, audiotape recording 4700.1424, 14 August 1984, p. 3, OHP.

57. *Reveille*, 27 February 1919, p. 1; *AALS Directory of Law Teachers* (1930), 114; Carl C. Wheaton, *Cases on Federal Procedure* (Chicago: Callaghan, 1921).

58. See Clarence M. Updegraff, *Arbitration and Labor Relations*, 3rd ed. (Washington, D.C.: Bureau of National Affairs, 1970). The over-the-hill-to-Hastings pattern included the well-known William Prosser and Rollin Perkins. *Familytreemaker.com,* Social Security Death Index.

59. *Reveille*, 2 October 1919, p. 1, 27 February 1919, p. 1.

60. Stumberg, Jo, interview by Susie Crews, audiotape recording 4700.0061, 13 July 1978, pp. 1, 25, OHP; Ben R. Miller, p. 9, OHP; George W. Stumberg, "Government in Louisiana during the French and Spanish Regimes" (senior thesis, Louisiana State University, 1909), in Hill Memorial Library, Louisiana State University, Baton Rouge; *Gumbo* (1909), 35; *Reveille*, 14 December 1912, p. 7; *AALS Directory of Law Teachers* (1930), 103 (1961), 325; *Documents and Minutes of the General Faculty of the University of Texas: Report of the Special George W. Stumberg Memorial Resolution Committee Filed Jan. 14, 1965* (Austin: University of Texas, n.d.), 8475.

61. George W. Stumberg, *Principles of Conflict of Laws* (1937; rprt., Brooklyn: Foundation Press, 1963); George W. Stumberg, *Cases on Conflict of Laws* (St. Paul: West, 1956); George W. Stumberg, *Guide to the Law and Legal Literature of France* (Washington, D.C.: U.S. Government Printing Office, 1931), iv; *AALS Directory of Law Teachers* (1961), 325; *Reveille*, 2 October 1919, p. 1.

62. *Gumbo* (1908), 58; Moyse, p. 8, OHP. The caption under Lyles's football photograph in the *Gumbo* stated that he played in eight out of ten games and played against the University of Havana in Cuba on 25 December 1907. LSU won 56–0. *Gumbo* (1908), 122, 5; *Reveille*, 2 October 1907, p. 1.

63. *Gumbo* (1908), 130–31, 158–59.

64. Ibid., 65.

65. Ibid. (1909), 61, 62, 66, 67, 70.

66. Moyse, p. 1, OHP; *Reveille*, 13 May 1920, p. 1; Moyse, pp. 6, 2, 8, OHP.

67. Moyse, p. 9, OHP.

68. *Reveille*, 8 October 1910, p. 5, 14 January 1911, p. 1.

69. Ibid., 29 April 1911, p. 3, 6 May 1911, p. 9.

70. *Gumbo* (1912), 4; *Reveille*, 7 October 1911, 3.

71. *Gumbo* (1913), 68, 74. Presumably the diploma privilege was still in effect for LSU students.

72. *Reveille*, 17 October 1914, p. 5, 19 December 1914, p. 1, 6 March 1915, p. 4, 8 December 1915, p. 1.

73. Ibid., 6 October 1915, p. 4, 15 October 1916, p. 7.

74. Ibid., 27 September 1913, p. 4.

75. Ibid., 13 March 1915, p. 7, 20 April 1916, Alumni Supp., p. 4, 30 March 1916, pp. 1, 8.

76. Tucker, p. 3, OHP; Peter A. Soderbergh, *Tower, Tablet, and Tree: LSU and the American Legion* (Baton Rouge: Boyd-Ewing Post 58, American Legion, 1983), 3, 5; *Reveille*, 3 May 1917, p. 1, 10 May 1917, p. 4, 3 October 1918, pp. 1, 5, 17 November 1918, p. 1, 19 September 1917, p. 1, 13 December 1917, p. 1.

77. *Reveille*, 4 April 1918, p. 3; Soderbergh, *Tower, Tablet and Tree*, 11; *Reveille*, 13 March 1919, p. 5, 10 April 1919, p. 1, 26 September 1918, p. 1.

78. *Reveille*, 21 November 1918, p. 2.

79. Ibid., 10 April 1919, p. 5.

80. Ibid., 16 January 1919, p. 8.

81. *Gumbo* (1918), 233, 234.

3. THE SEMI-ROARING TWENTIES

1. *Reveille*, 29 September 1922, p. 2; Roberts, Robert, Jr., interview by Nina Pugh, audiotape recording 4700.1456, 14 November 1983, p. 1, OHP; *Profile of a Law Center: Louisiana State University, Baton Rouge* (Baton Rouge: Louisiana State University Office of Publications, 1970), 3; *Bulletin* (1925), 37; Hebert, "Historical Sketch," 137, 142.

2. Matthew J. Schott, "John M. Parker," in *The Louisiana Governors*, ed. Dawson, 215; Williams, *Huey Long*, 140–43; *Reveille*, 15 October 1920, p. 1, 14 January 1921, p. 1, 7 April 1922, p. 1, 24 September 1920, p. 1.

3. *Bulletin* (1923), 38.

4. Jennings, Robert B., Sr., interview by Nina Pugh, audiotape recording 4700.0425, 1 June 1983, p. 1, OHP. That room later became the meeting room for the LSU Board of Supervisors. *Bulletin* (1926), 42. A copy of the *Bulletin* in the law library is annotated in pen, indicating 5,830 square feet on the first floor and 5,200 square feet on the second floor, for a total of 11,033 square feet. The description of the new campus in the *Bulletin* was quite detailed, referring, for example, to four miles of sewer pipes operated by automatic pumps whereby "the sewage is forced over the levee into the Mississippi River." Ibid., 49.

5. Ibid. (1922), 124. A slight loophole remained in that a student who "was conditioned" in three hours of course work could be admitted, but was required to make up the deficiency. This provision was terminated in 1927 (*Reveille*, 25 June 1927, p. 1). Candidates for admission had to complete two full years of college work or have a credit of thirty-six college hours. The change was made in response to a change in AALS requirements. *Reveille*, 1 November 1929, p. 1.

6. La. Acts. 1924, No. 113; "Historical Sketch of the Committee on Bar Admissions of the Supreme Court of Louisiana," *Louisiana Law Reports* 245 (1963): 72.

7. *Reveille*, 2 July 1927, p. 1, 9 July 1927, p. 2, 20 July 1928, p. 1.

8. *AALS Directory of Law Teachers* (1961), 363–64; *Reveille*, 3 October 1924, p. 1; *LSU Alumni News* 4 (1926): 2, 3; Pleasant, John R., interview by Nina Pugh, audiotape recording 4700.1445, 10 June 1983, p. 7, OHP.

9. *Reveille*, 12 December 1924, pp. 1, 3, 3 January 1925, p. 1, 6 February 1925, p. 2.

10. Editorial, "The Association of American Law Schools and the Standards of Legal Education in the South," *Tulane Law Review* 4 (1930): 236; *Bulletin* (1926), 154; *Reveille*, 2 December 1927, p. 7.

11. *Bulletin* (1926), 156; Stewart, Ashton, interview by Nina Pugh, audiotape recording 4700.1469, 20 May 1983, p. 2, OHP; *Bulletin* (1927), 158.

12. Miller, Ben R., Sr., interview by Nina Pugh, audiotape recording 4700.1438, 17 May 1983, pp. 20, 21, OHP.

13. *Reveille*, 27 January 1928, p. 1; *Bulletin* (1930), 126.

14. *Bulletin* (1924), 8; *AALS Directory of Law Teachers* (1953–54), 334; *Reveille*, 28 September 1923, pp. 1, 2; 6 February 1925, p. 1.

15. *Bulletin* (1924), 15–16.

16. Rabun, Armand, interview by Nina Pugh, audiotape recording 4700.1453, 14 August 1984, p. 8, OHP, states that he was from Tennessee. *AALS Directory of Law Teachers* (1925), 29 (1930), 45; Cotton, W. D., interview by Nina Pugh, audiotape recording 4700.1394, 15 August 1984, p. 10, OHP; Jennings, p. 2, OHP; Gold, Leo, interview by Nina Pugh, audiotape recording 4700.1406, 8 August 1984, p. 18, OHP.

17. *Reveille*, 20 October 1925, p. 4; *AALS Directory of Law Teachers* (1930), 18; *Reveille*, 25 June 1927, p. 1.

18. Cotton, p. 3, OHP; Gaharan, Phillip S., interview by Nina Pugh, audiotape recording 4700.1407, 15 November 1983, p. 4, OHP.

19. "In Memoriam: Harriet Spiller Daggett," *Louisiana Law Review* 27 (1966): 1; Campbell, John T., interview by Jean Talley Drew, audiotape recording 4700.1390, 1 March 1987, p. 3, OHP; *Bulletin* (1926), 59–60, 365.

20. *Bulletin* (1927), 237–44; "In Memoriam: Harriet Spiller Daggett," 1, 2; Herma Hill Kay, "The Future of Women Law Professors," *Iowa Law Review* 77 (1991): 5, 6.

21. *Reveille*, 20 February 1925, p. 8, 13 December 1929, p. 1; *AALS Directory of Law Teachers* (1926), 50; *Bulletin* (1927), 237–44; *AALS Directory of Law Teachers* (1925), 46 (1926) 50 (1927) 55 (1928) 57 (1929) 61 (1930) 68; Jennings, pp. 8, 9, OHP; Kilbourne, Richard, Sr., interview by Nina Pugh, audiotape recording 4700.1423, 24 August 1983, p. 21, OHP; Landry, Paul B., Jr., interview by Nina Pugh, audiotape recording 4700.1426, 27 October 1983, p. 19, OHP; Law School Hall of Fame plaque.

22. *AALS Directory of Law Teachers* (1961), 9; Newman Freece Baker, *Legal Aspects of Zoning* (Chicago: University of Chicago Press, 1927). W. B. Munro of Harvard reviewed the book favorably in the *Political Science Quarterly* (*Reveille*, 6 January 1928). Baker, *Legal Aspects of Zoning*, ix; Baker, "Some Legal Aspects of Impeachment in Louisiana," *Southwestern Political and Social Science Quarterly* 10 (1930): 359–87, quotation 387 (emphasis in the original). In the latter publication Baker was identified as affiliated with Tulane University.

23. *AALS Directory of Law Teachers* (1961), 339. The 1983 edition of Verrall's casebook identifies him as a professor emeritus, Hastings College of the Law. The earlier 1960, 1966, and 1977 editions culminated in Harold E. Verrall and Gail Boreman Bird, *Cases and Materials on California Community Property* (St. Paul: West, 1983).

24. *AALS Directory of Law Teachers* (1961), 313.

25. James Barclay Smith, *Some Phases of Fair Value and Interstate Rates* (Baton Rouge: Louisiana State University Press, 1931). The first number in the series was also written by a law faculty member, Harriet Spiller Daggett, *The Community Property System of Louisiana with Comparative Studies* (Baton Rouge: Louisiana State University Press, 1931). James Barclay Smith, *Studies in the Adequacy of the Constitution* (Los Angeles: Parker and Baird, 1939), xi; Tucker, p. 15, OHP.

26. Gold, p. 20, OHP; Stewart, pp. 16–7, OHP; Jennings, pp. 4, 9, OHP.

27. Walsh, Scallan, interview by Nina Pugh, audiotape recording 4700.1468, 24 June 1983, p. 2, OHP; Purvis, Frank, Jr., interview by Nina Pugh, audiotape recording 4700.1453, 4 November 1983, p. 5, OHP; Paul Landry, p. 9, OHP; Landry, Jules, interview by Nina Pugh, audiotape recording 4700.1428, 21 April 1983, p. 5.

28. *Reveille*, 20 May 1921, p. 2; Roberts, pp. 7, 8–9, 15, OHP.

29. *Reveille*, 20 May 1921, p. 6, 17 October 1921, p. 1, 25 November 1921, p. 1; Campbell, p. 3, OHP; *Reveille*, 21 April 1922, p. 1, 9 July 1927, p. 1.

30. LSU Law Archives, Box 46. Flory's personnel file shows an increase from $1,800 to $2,100 per academic year. His letter requested an increase from $1,900 to $2,200. The figure in Year 2000 dollars was computed at *http://www.westegg.com/inflation/infl.cgi*, 28 January 2002.

31. William Minor Lile to Ira S. Flory, 25 February 1925, Lee Hargrave Personal Papers.

32. Ronald L. Davis to Mr. Ira S. Flory, 9 February 1925, LSU Law Archives, Hargrave Papers, Box 1, Folder 1; W. M. Phillips to Ira S. Flory, 25 February 1925, Office of the President Records, RG A0001, University Archives, LSU Libraries, Box 39, Folder 567.

33. Rabun, pp. 17, 19, OHP; Gold, p. 18, OHP.

34. *Reveille*, 10 March 1922, p. 2. Information on Winsome Ware supplied by Edwin O. Ware III (Class of 1951), who reported that he has possession of her notary seal. *Reveille*, 13 April 1928, p. 2.

35. *Reveille*, 3 February 1926, p. 1.

36. Ibid., 8 October 1920, p. 1. East Baton Rouge Parish delegates were Eugene Cazedessus, Charles A. Holcombe, and W. Carruth Jones. *The Louisiana Constitution of 1921* (Baton Rouge: Thos. J. Moran's Sons, 1955), xi; *Reveille*, 8 April 1921, p. 3, 17 December 1920, pp. 1, 2.

37. Hamiter, Joe B., interview by Nina Pugh, audiotape recording 4700.1411, 10 June 1983, p. 3, OHP; Ben Miller, p. 2, OHP; *Reveille*, 25 May 1923, p. 1.

38. Darsey, Glenn, interview by Nina Pugh, audiotape recording 4700.1399, 27 May 1983, p. 1, OHP; Roberts, pp. 19, 21, OHP; Darsey, pp. 11, 15, OHP; *Reveille*, 20 February 1925, p. 1; Darsey, pp. 15, 16, OHP.

39. Darsey, p. 3, OHP.

40. *Reveille*, 15 December 1925, pp. 1, 2, 8 January 1925, p. 1.

41. Cotton, p. 23, OHP; Stockwell, Oliver P., II, interview by Nina Pugh, audiotape recording 4700.1462, 12 December 1983, p. 2, OHP.

42. *Reveille*, 22 January 1927, p. 1; Ben R. Miller, p. 10, OHP.

43. *Reveille*, 13 December 1929, p. 1, 21 March 1930.

44. Ibid., 1 February 1927, p. 1, 26 March 1927, p. 1.

4. THE EXTRAVAGANT THIRTIES

1. Hair, *The Kingfish and His Realm*, 102, 107, 128; Williams, *Huey Long*, 494.
2. Williams, *Huey Long*, 494, 495, 500; *Reveille*, 14 November 1930, p. 1.
3. Williams, *Huey Long*, 502; Hair, *The Kingfish and His Realm*, 211, 229.
4. Williams, *Huey Long*, 775–79.
5. Hair, *The Kingfish and His Realm*, 229; Carolyn H. Hargrave and W. Lee Hargrave, *A History of Graduate Education at Louisiana State University* (Baton Rouge: Louisiana State University Graduate School, 1976) 7; *Reveille*, 20 March 1931, p. 5.
6. *Reveille*, 14 November 1930, p. 1, 6 February 1931, p. 1; Frost, *The LSU College of Engineering*, II, 63, 75.
7. Litton, Dupre, interview by Nina Pugh, audiotape recording 4700.1431, 26 October 1983, p. 14, OHP; Thomas E. Ruffin, *Under Stately Oaks: A Pictorial History of LSU* (Baton Rouge: Louisiana State University Press, 2002), 74; *Reveille*, 16 April 1935, p. 1 (the *Southern Review* was an outgrowth of the *Southwest Review*, a joint publication by LSU and Southern Methodist University); Soderbergh, *Tower, Tablet, and Tree*, 61.
8. Daggett's book, *The Community Property System of Louisiana with Comparative Studies* (1931), was the first of a handful of books that bore the imprint of LSU Press before its formal establishment in 1935. James Barclay Smith, *Some Phases of Fair Value and Interstate Rates* (Baton Rouge: Louisiana State University Press, 1931). Daggett's study on community property with comparative notes received favorable comment in the *Mississippi Valley Historical Review*, and her article on the nature of the wife's interest in community property was being published in the *California Law Review*. *Reveille*, 2 October 1931, p. 1, 23 October 1931, p. 5; Landry, Paul B., Jr., interview by Nina Pugh, audiotape recording 4700.1426, 27 October 1983, p. 19, OHP.
9. *Bulletin* (1931), 51.
10. Bennett, Dale, interview by Nina Pugh, audiotape recording 4700.1386, 19 April 1983, p. 8, OHP.
11. *Reveille*, 18 October 1929, p. 1, 25 October 1929, p. 1, 22 November 1929, p. 5.
12. Stewart, Ashton, interview by Nina Pugh, audiotape recording 4700.1469, 20 May 1983, p. 7, OHP; Paul Landry, p. 6, OHP; Edwards, Earl, interview by Nina Pugh, audiotape recording 4700.1403, 8 August 1984, p. 21, OHP; Stewart, p. 14, OHP; Walsh, Scallan, interview by Nina Pugh, audiotape recording 4700.1468, 24 June 1983, p. 14, OHP.
13. Stewart, p. 7, OHP.
14. Some twenty-three law students wrote to President Atkinson deploring the conditions leading up to the proposed removal of Tullis, contending that many of them had attended the conference "believing that it was for an entirely different purpose." Kennedy countered that he had told "each one that the discussion would concern Dean Tullis and Professor J. B. Smith, and to let their consciences be their guides as to whether they wanted to be present" (*Reveille*, 13 December 1929, p. 1); *Baton Rouge Morning Advocate*, 10 December 1929; *Shreveport Journal*, 11 December 1929; Williams, *Huey Long*, 496.
15. *Whangdoodle*, 1 June 1930, 1; Jennings, Robert B., Sr., interview by Nina Pugh, audiotape recording 4700.0425, 1 June 1983, p. 5, OHP.

16. Williams, *Huey Long*, 497; Tate, Albert, Jr., interview by Nina Pugh, audiotape recording 4700.1464, 9 November 1983, p. 6., OHP; Walsh, p. 6, OHP; Official Transcript 10743 (in Student Records, Paul M. Hebert Law Center).

17. Williams, *Huey Long*, 497; Frost, *The LSU College of Engineering*, II, 61.

18. That the *Whangdoodle* was the work of TNE, a secret fraternity on campus, was brought out at the trial. *Reveille*, 14 November 1930, p. 1, 21 November 1930, p. 1.

19. Williams, *Huey Long*, 780 (an account less favorable to Long appeared in the *Reveille*, 6 May 1958, p. 5); *Reveille*, 20 July 1934, p. 1.

20. *Reveille*, 8 March 1935.

21. *Kennedy v. Item Co.*, 3 So. 2d 175 (La. 1941). The major allegation was the erroneous statement that Kennedy was sentenced to a term in the penitentiary, as for a felony, rather than in the parish jail, the usual punishment for the misdemeanors of which he was convicted. A similar error was made by the *Reveille*, and its editor published a retraction after a complaining letter from Kennedy was published in the student newspaper. In that letter, Kennedy stated that he never admitted to editing the pink sheet and that he simply "took the rap." *Reveille*, 28 October 1932, p. 3.

22. Rabun, p. 6, OHP; Cangelosi, Theo F., interview by Nina Pugh, audiotape recording 4700.1391, 19 January 1984, p. 7, OHP.

23. Tate, p. 7, OHP; Edwards, Earl, p. 23, OHP; Jennings, p. 3, OHP; Jewell, Tom, interview by Nina Pugh, audiotape recording 4700.1416, 20 June 1984, p. 2, OHP.

24. The cane, presented by J. C. Hood and Armand Rabun, was engraved, "To Dean Robt. L. Tullis—presented by the L.S.U. law class of 1933." *Reveille*, 21 July 1933, p. 3; Jennings, p. 2, OHP; *Reveille*, 28 September 1934, p. 1, 2 October 1934, p. 1.

25. *Baton Rouge Morning Advocate*, 18 July 1935, p. 1: "LSU Law School put on probation by AALS because of conditions under which KKK was given a degree. Continued the probation." Jennings, p. 26, OHP; Williams, *Huey Long*, 780; Purvis, Frank, Jr., interview by Nina Pugh, audiotape recording 4700.1453, 4 November 1983, p. 4, OHP; Bennett, pp. 5, 8, OHP.

26. Henry C. Dethloff, "Huey P. Long," in *The Louisiana Governors*, ed. Dawson, 228; Gerard, Richard, Sr., interview by Nina Pugh, audiotape recording 4700.1408, 13 August 1984, p. 16., OHP; Dakin, Melvin G., interview by Nina Pugh, audiotape recording 4700.1397, 18 February 1986, pp. 19–20, OHP.

27. James Monroe Smith to Dean F. K. Beutel, 24 May 1937, in LSU Law Archives, Hargrave Papers, Box 1, Folder 1.

28. *Reveille*, 14 June 1935, p. 1; *AALS Directory of Law Teachers* (1930), 11; Harriet S. Daggett, "A Comparison of the German Community Property System with That of Louisiana," *Tulane Law Review* 4 (1929): 27.

29. Paul Macarius Hebert, "The Origin and Nature of Maritime Liens," *Tulane Law Review* 4 (1930): 38; Dyer, *Tulane*, 242, 275; Paul Brosman, "The Statutory Presumption," *Tulane Law Review* 4 (1930): 16, 5 (1931): 178; Harriet S. Daggett, "The Wife's Action for a Separation of Property," *Tulane Law Review* 5 (1930): 55. Professor Daggett was adept at multiple publications; the two articles in the law review would appear as chapters in her book on community property. See also Harriet S. Daggett, "Trends in Louisiana Law of the Family," *Tulane Law Review* 9

(1934): 89; Harriet S. Daggett, "Is Joint Control of Community Property Possible?" *Tulane Law Review* 10 (1935): 589. Pierre Crabites, "The Capitulations Are in Harmony with the Present State of Egypt," *Tulane Law Review* 5 (1931): 245; Henry George McMahon, "The Exception of No Cause of Action in Louisiana," *Tulane Law Review* 9 (1934): 17; Henry George McMahon, "Parties Litigant in Louisiana," *Tulane Law Review* 10 (1935): 489; Joseph Dainow, "Unrestricted Testation in Quebec," *Tulane Law Review* 10 (1936): 401.

30. *New Orleans Times-Picayune*, 6 June 1935, editorial; Frederick K. Beutel, "The Necessity of a New Technique of Interpreting the N.I.L.: The Civil Law Analogy," *Tulane Law Review* 6 (1931): 1; Frederick K. Beutel, "Common Law Judicial Technique and the Law of Negotiable Instruments: Two Unfortunate Decisions," *Tulane Law Review* 9 (1934): 64, 22; Frederick K. Beutel, "The Pressure of Organized Interests as a Factor in Shaping Legislation," *Southern California Law Review* 3 (1929): 10; Frederick K. Beutel, *Experimental Jurisprudence and the Scienstate* (Bielefeld: Gieskeking, 1975), 10. Correspondence in Beutel's LSU personnel file indicates that attempts were made to have the LSU Press consider publication of his book. Tactful letters from Charles East and Les Phillabaum suggested that the Press did not have the resources to consider the book while it was still being reviewed by other presses.

31. Louisiana State Bar Association, *Report of the Louisiana State Bar Association* 1 (1935): 80, 84; ibid. (1935–41): 125.

32. Sanders, Joe, interview by Nina Pugh, audiotape recording 4700.1458, 26 January 1984, p. 4, OHP; Gerard, p. 4, OHP; Pugh, John F., Sr., interview by Nina Pugh, audiotape recording 4700.1450, 24 May 1983, pp. 1, 4, OHP.

33. John F. Pugh Sr., p. 3, OHP; Paul Landry, pp. 2, 7, OHP; D'Amico, Sam, interview by Nina Pugh, audiotape recording 4700.1398, 23 May 1983, p. 3, 8, OHP.

34. Bennett, pp. 8, 9, OHP; Gerard, p. 3, OHP; Dale Bennett to Paul M. Hebert, 19 June 1937, in Personnel Files, LSU Law Archives.

35. Harrison, Milton, interview by Nina Pugh, audiotape recording 4700.1412, 22 March 1983, p. 41, OHP; Malone, Wex, interview by Nina Pugh, audiotape recording 4700.1433, 28 March 1983, p. 5, OHP.

36. Paul Landry, p. 6, OHP; Harrison, p. 42, OHP; Tate, p. 4, OHP. Gerard, p. 4, OHP, said of Beutel and the bar examination that, "as I understand it, after he took maybe the first two days of the three-day examination, he was told he couldn't possibly pass; so he didn't show up the last day." Gerard added, "I think it might have been Alex Andrus who was a poet of sorts."

37. Paul Landry, p. 7, OHP; Dakin, p. 21, OHP; Craig, Frank S., Jr., interview by Nina Pugh, audiotape recording 4700.1395, 28 June 1984, pp. 2, 3, OHP.

38. Louisiana State University, *Biennial Report of the President (1935–37)* (Baton Rouge: Louisiana State University, 1937), 119; James Monroe Smith to Dean F. K. Beutel, 24 May 1937, in LSU Law Archives; Undated Memorandum filed with Smith to Beutel, 24 May 1937.

39. Hebert, "Historical Sketch," 137, 143; *Reveille*, 11 June 1937, p. 6, 14 September 1937, p. 1.

40. Francis C. Sullivan, "Highlights of the Professional and Academic Careers of Paul Macarius Hebert," *Louisiana Law Review* 37 (1977): iv (Supplement); *Reveille*, 18 September 1936, p. 1 (Hebert replaced James F. Broussard as dean of administration); Hebert, Mrs. Paul M., interview by Nina Pugh, audiotape recording 4700.1414, 23 June 1983, p. 2, OHP; *Bulletin* (1938), 8.

41. "Dean Hebert and the LSU Law School," *L'Avocat* (1977): 4.; Bennett, pp. 10, 17, OHP.

42. *Reveille*, 27 June 1939, p. 1, 27 June 1939 (Extra Edition), p. 1; *Bulletin* (1941), 169.

43. Louisiana State University and Agricultural and Mechanical College, *A Survey Report by a Commission of the American Council on Education* (Washington, D.C.: American Council on Education, 1940), 25.

44. Minutes, 9 September 1935, p. 1.

45. Ibid., 24 September 1935. (The degree was actually instituted in 1939; Minutes, 27 September 1939.) Conversation of author with Robert A. Pascal, retired professor, LSU Law School, n.d; Minutes, 14 September 1935, 2 October 1935, 7 October 1935, 5 November 1935; *Bulletin* (1936), 217.

46. *Bulletin* (1936), 212; *Reveille*, 1 May 1936, p. 1; Minutes, 10 February 1936; *Reveille*, 27 April 1937, p. 2.

47. Stevens, *Law School*, 159, 167 n. 33; *Reveille*, 18 September 1936, p. 1.

48. Minutes, 7 January 1937, appendix, 3; *Reveille*, 4 February 1938, p. 1; Minutes, 19 October 1937, 29 November 1939.

49. *Reveille*, 18 September 1936, p. 1.

50. Ibid., 4 May 1937, p. 5, 14 May 1937, p. 8.

51. Ibid., 12 November 1935, p. 1, 7 February 1936, p. 10.

52. Williams, *Huey Long*, 779.

53. *Reveille*, 6 December 1935, p. 1.

54. *Report of the American Bar Association* 60 (1935): 124; Williams, *Huey Long*, 780, citing *New Orleans Times-Picayune*, 5 and 10 May 1935; *Reveille*, 7 January 1936, p. 6, 10 January 1936, p. 1; *Report of the American Bar Association* 61 (1936): 922; *Reveille*, 13 May 1936, p. 1.

55. Hair, *The Kingfish and His Realm*, 282 ff.; Williams, *Huey Long*, ch. 22; *AALS Proceedings*, 1934, pp. 9, 14.

56. *AALS Proceedings*, 1935, pp. 9, 10. That teacher was reputed to be Wayne Morse of Oregon, later to become a U.S. senator.

57. Ibid., 19.

58. Ibid., 23. The speaker was James Angell McLaughlin of Harvard Law School.

59. *Reveille*, 8 April 1938, p. 1; 9 April 1938, p. 1.

60. Paul M. Hebert, "Professor Dale E. Bennett: A Dedication," *Louisiana Law Review* 36 (1976): vii; Bennett, pp. 1, 3, OHP; Cangelosi, p. 4, OHP.

61. Smith came as an instructor and was promoted to assistant professor in Fall 1937. *Reveille*, 11 June 1937, p. 2, 3 March 1936, p. 7; J. Denson Smith, "Impossibility of Performance as an Excuse in French Law: The Doctrine of Force Majeure," *Yale Law Journal* 45 (1936): 452.

62. As reported by Gerard, p. 17, OHP. Sanders, p. 5, OHP; Bennett, p. 15, OHP; Paul M. Hebert, "Dedication," *Louisiana Law Review* 33 (1973): iii–vi.

63. D'Amico, p. 6, OHP; Paul Landry, p. 3, OHP; Craig, p. 9, OHP; Sanders, p. 4, OHP; *Reveille*, 12 October 1937, p. 5, 22 September 1938, p. 2; *AALS Directory of Law Teachers* (1953–54), 158. Hall's two books are *Theft, Law and Society* (Boston: Little, Brown, 1935) and *Readings in Jurisprudence* (Indianapolis: Bobbs-Merrill, 1938).

64. See Walter Hug and Gordon Ireland, "The Progress of Comparative Law," *Tulane Law*

Review 6 (1931): 68; Gordon Ireland, "Constitutional Amendments: Power of Conventions," *Tulane Law Review* 6 (1931): 7; Editorials, *Tulane Law Review* 6 (1931): 99; Gordon Ireland, "The Use of Decisions by United States Students of Civil Law," *Tulane Law Review* 8 (1934): 358.

65. Gordon Ireland, *Boundaries, Possessions, and Conflicts in Central and North America and the Caribbean* (Cambridge: Harvard University Press, 1941); Gordon Ireland and Jesús Galindez, *Divorce in the Americas* (Buffalo: Dennis, 1947).

66. Paul Landry, p. 3, OHP; Sanders, p. 6, OHP.

67. Gordon Ireland, "Louisiana's Legal System Reappraised," *Tulane Law Review* 11 (1937): 585; Kenneth M. Murchison, "The Judicial Revival of Louisiana's Civilian Tradition: A Surprising Triumph for the American Experience," *Louisiana Law Review* 49 (1988): 1; Mack E. Barham, "A Renaissance of the Civilian Tradition in Louisiana," *Louisiana Law Review* 33 (1973): 357; Pierre Crabites, "Louisiana Not a Civil Law State," *Loyola Law Journal* 9 (1928): 51; Leonard Greenburg, "Must Louisiana Resign to the Common Law?" *Tulane Law Review* 11 (1937): 598; Harriet Spiller Daggett, Joseph Dainow, Paul M. Hebert, and Henry George McMahon, "A Reappraisal Appraised: A Brief for the Civil Law of Louisiana," *Tulane Law Review* 12 (1937): 12; Robert Lee Tullis, "Louisiana's Legal System Reappraised," *Tulane Law Review* 12 (1937): 113.

68. Paul M. Hebert to Colby, 21 August 1937, in Personnel Files.

69. Frederick K. Beutel, *Toward an Experimental Definition of the Criminal Mind* (Philadelphia: University of Pennsylvania Press, 1942); Thomas A. Cowan, *The American Jurisprudence Reader* (Dobbs Ferry, N.Y.: Oceana, 1956); Thomas A. Cowan, *Essays in the Law of Torts* (New Brunswick, N.J.: Rutgers University Press, 1961); *Reveille*, 19 March 1937, p. 9 (citing the *Illinois Law Review*).

70. Raggio, Thomas, interview by Nina Pugh, audiotape recording 4700.1454, 13 August 1984, p. 3, OHP; Craig, p. 4, OHP; Rubin, Alvin, interview by Nina Pugh, audiotape recording 4700.1457, 15 December 1983, p. 17, OHP; Pascal, conversation with author; Litton, p. 12, OHP.

71. Harrison, p. 3, OHP; Malone, pp. 11, 13, OHP.

72. Craig, pp. 20, 21, OHP; Crabites memo, 25 May 1939, in Personnel Files.

73. Reveille, 13 October 1936, p. 7, 23 October 1936, p. 5, 24 November 1936, p. 6A, 9 March 1937, p. 1, 16 March 1937, p. 5, 30 October 1936, p. 6B; Pierre Crabites, *Unhappy Spain* (Baton Rouge: Louisiana State University Press, 1937); Pierre Crabites, *Americans in the Egyptian Army* (London: G. Routledge and Sons, 1938); *Reveille*, 16 March 1937, p. 6.

74. Personnel Files, Paul M. Hebert Law Center, Louisiana State University, Baton Rouge; Fowler V. Harper, Review of *Hugo L. Black: A Study in the Judicial Process* by Charlotte Williams, *Louisiana Law Review* 11 (1951): 498; Taylor, B. B., interview by Nina Pugh, audiotape recording 4700.1465, 20 January 1984, p. 7, OHP; Personnel Files.

75. Personnel Files; Beutel to Montana Law School, 7 April 1937, in LSU Law Archives; *AALS Directory of Law Teachers* (1947–48), 246.

76. Purvis, p. 7, OHP; Percy, J. Hereford, interview by Nina Pugh, audiotape recording 4700.1444, 27 October 1983, p. 21, OHP; Kilbourne, p. 21, OHP.

77. *Reveille*, 20 November 1936, p. 2; 4 May 1937, p. 1, 21 September 1937, p. 8.

78. Ibid., 2 February 1938, p. 2.

79. Minutes, 2 March 1937, 12 November 1936.

80. *Biennial Report of the President (1935–37)*, 119.
81. *Reveille*, 11 June 1937, p. 2; Beutel to McMahon, 12 April 1937, in LSU Law Archives; Paul M. Hebert, "In Memoriam: Henry George McMahon," *Louisiana Law Review* 27 (1967): 162.
82. *Reveille*, 11 June 1937, pp. 2, 6; Personnel Files; *Reveille*, 12 July 1938, p. 1.
83. Personnel Files.
84. *Reveille*, 21 April 1938, p. 2; Paul M. Hebert, "Editorial: The Law Review and the Law School," *Louisiana Law Review* 1 (1938): 157; *Bulletin* (1942), 20; Minutes, 29 January 1941.
85. Malone, p. 9, OHP; Ira S. Flory, "Editorial: The Law School," *Louisiana Law Review* 2 (1939): 155; *Reveille*, 16 September 1939, p. 11; Personnel Files; Malone, p. 10, OHP; Paul M. Hebert, "Dedication," *Louisiana Law Review* 34 (1974): v–x. Flory to Hebert, 30 December 1940, in LSU Law Archives.
86. Gerard, pp. 14, 15, OHP.
87. Minutes, 29 January 1941.
88. Taylor, p. 7, OHP.
89. Harrison, pp. 2, 3, OHP.
90. *Reveille*, 13 April 1939, p. 1.
91. *State Bar of Louisiana Reports* 1 (1935): 80; *Reveille*, 28 April 1936, p. 1.
92. *Reveille*, 6 October 1936, p. 1, 16 October 1936, p. 1.
93. *Bulletin* (1939), 155 (1937), 220.
94. D'Amico, p. 14, OHP; Harrison, pp. 9, 40, 41, OHP; Odom, Huntington, interview by Nina Pugh, audiotape recording 4700.1442, 5 June 1984, p. 2, OHP.
95. *Reveille*, 5 April 1938, pp. 1, 12B.
96. Ibid., 12 September 1957, p. 7E; Robert A. Pascal to Vice-Chancellor Glenn G. Morris, 26 June 2001, in LSU Law Archives.
97. Hebert, "Editorial: The Law Review and the Law School," 157; *Bulletin* (1938), 155; *Reveille*, 12 March 1938, p. 1; Dainow, "Dean Hebert and the LSU Law School," 4.
98. *Reveille*, 13 January 1970, p. 6; Ruffin, *Under Stately Oaks*, 75.
99. Mark T. Carleton, "Richard Webster Leche," in *The Louisiana Governors*, ed. Dawson, 247; *Reveille*, 27 June 1939, p. 1, 13 January 1970, p. 6, 3 October 1939, p. 1.
100. Dakin, pp. 21, 22, OHP.
101. *Reveille*, 19 July 1938, p. 3, 20 August 1938.
102. *State Bar of Louisiana Reports* 1 (1935): 80; Gerard, p. 5, OHP; *Reveille*, 8 December 1933, p. 2, 8 October 1935, p. 1, 3 March 1936, p. 2.
103. *Biennial Report of the President (1935–37)*, 117; *Reveille*, 19 January 1937, p. 2.
104. *Bulletin* (1937), 221; *Reveille*, 10 November 1936, p. 5; Malone, p. 6, OHP.
105. *Reveille*, 26 March 1938, p. 3.
106. Ibid., 7 January 1939, p. 6.
107. Ibid., 23 March 1934, p. 1, 6 April 1934; 13 April 1934, p. 1.
108. Minutes, 5 November 1935; *Reveille*, 22 October 1935, p. 1.
109. *Reveille*, 17 April 1936, p. 8.
110. Ibid., 21 April 1938, p. 1, 27 April 1938, p. 1.
111. Minutes, 12 November 1936, 13 January 1937 (the faculty did not adopt a recommendation

that specified in detail the types of articles to be published, including a heavy proportion of book reviews); *Reveille,* 21 April 1938, p. 2.

112. Taylor, pp. 6, 13, 14, 21, OHP.

113. *Reveille,* 1 December 1938, p. 1, 9 December 1938, p. 1.

114. Minutes, 12 September 1939; *Reveille,* 27 October 1939, p. 1.

115. *Mississippi College Law Review* 18 (1998), 115, 175; Frank L. Maraist, "In Memoriam: F. Hodge O'Neal," *Louisiana Law Review* 51 (1991): 939; F. Hodge O'Neal, "An Appraisal of the Louisiana Law of Partnership," *Louisiana Law Review* 9 (1949): 307, 450.

116. *Reveille,* 3 May 1939, p. 2.

117. Tate, p. 2, OHP; "In Memoriam: Beverly Denbo Walker," *Louisiana Law Review* 32 (1972): 495; Malone to Hebert, 14 June 1941, in LSU Law Archives; Meyers, William, interview by Nina Pugh, audiotape recording 4700.1437, 1 March 1984, p. 14, OHP; Malone, p. 21, OHP; Tate, p. 3, OHP; Stoker, Jimmy, interview by Nina Pugh, audiotape recording 4700.1463, 1 February 1984, p. 16, OHP.

118. *Reveille,* 26 September 1930, p. 1, 4 December 1931, p. 1.

119. Ibid., 17 October 1930, pp. 1, 2.

120. Ibid., 21 November 1930, p. 1, 14 October 1932, p. 1, 16 February 1934, p. 1, 2 October 1934, p. 2, 9 November 1937, p. 5.

121. Ibid., 13 May 1932, p. 1; 27 May 1932, p. 1.

122. Ibid., 10 February 1933, p. 1, 6 April 1937, p. 8, 18 March 1938, p. 8.

123. Ibid., 28 April 1933, p. 5.

124. Rubin, p. 18, OHP; *Reveille,* 24 February 1933, p. 2, 31 March 1933, p. 1, 11 October 1935, p. 5, 8 January 1932, p. 1.

125. Rubin, p. 18, OHP; *Reveille,* 10 December 1935, p. 2, 18 November 1939, p. 2, 29 September 1938, p. 4.

126. *Reveille,* 8 December 1933, p. 1.

127. D'Amico, p. 15, OHP.

128. Gerard, p. 9, OHP.

129. *Reveille,* 9 March 1934, p. 1; Landry, Frances Leggio, interview by Nina Pugh, audiotape recording 4700.1427, 21 April 1983, pp. 3, 4, 8 (the married man was Joe Starring), 2, OHP; Cangelosi, p. 4, OHP; F. Landry, pp. 6, 2, 3, OHP; Purvis, p. 2, OHP.

130. *Reveille,* 7 July 1933, p. 1, 24 March 1936, p. 1, 2 April 1937, p. 5, 2 March 1939, p. 1.

131. Kilbourne, p. 18, OHP; Gerard, p. 20, OHP; *Reveille,* 9 March 1934, p. 5, 19 July 1935, p. 1.

132. Rubin, p. 28, OHP; *Reveille,* 23 October 1934, p. 1.

133. *Reveille,* 2 October 1936, p. 5.

134. Ibid., 3 May 1938, p. 6, 4 May 1938, p. 1, 4 October 1938, p. 1.

135. Ibid., 1 October 1937, p. 6, 23 September 1938, p. 5, 27 October 1938, p. 1.

136. Ibid., 13 September 1938, p. 1; Kay, "The Future of Women Law Professors," 5; *Reveille,* 17 September 1938, pp. 1, 6.

137. Taylor, p. 16, OHP. Alvin Rubin, however, remembered that a fire truck came and took the hat down (Rubin, p. 25, OHP).

138. Rubin, p. 25, OHP.

139. Craig, pp. 16, 17, OHP; Harrison, p. 4, OHP.

140. Craig, p. 12, OHP; *Reveille*, 28 September 1938, pp. 1, 5, 29 September 1938, p. 1, 4 October 1938, p. 2, 7 October 1938, p. 1.

5. THE FORTIES: WORLD WAR II AND POSTWAR CHALLENGES

1. Flory, "Editorial: The Law School," 155; *Bulletin* (1940–41), 253.

2. *Reveille*, 18 April 1940, p. 1; Fordham to Hebert, 1 March 1940, in Personnel Files; Fordham to Gene F. Tarver, 10 September 1973, in Personnel Files.

3. *Reveille*, 22 October 1935, p. 1, 17 April 1936, p. 8; Craig, pp. 80–81, OHP; Clyde W. Thurmon, "Basic Procedures for Examination of Title to Real Property in Louisiana," *Institute on Mineral Law* 8 (1961): 72.

4. Minutes, 27 October 1941; *Bulletin* (1941), 170; Paul M. Hebert, "Editorial: The Law School," *Louisiana Law Review* 4 (1941): 107; *Bulletin* (1941), 58; *Reveille*, 22 September 1940, p. 5; *Bulletin* (1941), 55.

5. *Reveille*, 17 October 1940, p. 1; *Bulletin* (1941), p. 3.

6. *Reveille*, 10 March 1941, p. 1, 9 May 1940, p. 1, 21 May 1940, p. 1; Frank James Price, *Troy H. Middleton: A Biography* (Baton Rouge: Louisiana State University Press, 1974), 129.

7. Price, *Middleton*, 13; Dakin, Melvin, interview by Susie Crews, audiotape recording 4700.0008, November 16, 1978, p. 15, OHP.

8. Dakin, p. 15, OHP; Soderbergh *Tower, Tablet, and Tree*, iv: "[L]egion posts and universities kept their distances except, intermittently, on patriotic occasions. Given this pattern, LSU's relationship with the Legion must be viewed as unique. With the blessings of President Thomas D. Boyd and his faculty a Legion enclave, David J. Ewing Post 58, was admitted into the University environment in 1920"; Dakin 700.0008, pp. 3, 39, OHP (Smith and Pipkin made genuinely cosmopolitan appointments: "All of that would necessarily result in resentments building up against old regimes who were concerned with conserving things as they were, although they realized these new developments had to come. Still in all, they were still in the process of accommodating them, and sometimes accommodation comes very dearly"); Charles Hyneman and Mel Dakin, interview by Jack Fiser, audiotape recording 4700.0458, 21 December 1981, pp. 7, 11, 12, OHP.

9. Minutes, 17 November, 1 December 1941.

10. Malone, Wex S., interview by Nina Pugh, audiotape recording 4700.1433, 28 March 1983, p. 28, OHP; Minutes, 17 November 1941.

11. Minutes, 23 March 1942.

12. Hebert, "Editorial: The Law School," 107, 109. The students Corwin was visiting were Robert J. Harris and Donald H. Morrison (*Reveille*, 6 February 1941, p. 5). *Reveille*, 14 February 1941, p. 1, 29 March 1941, p. 1.

13. *Reveille*, 28 August 1940, p. 1.

14. Ibid., 13 February 1940, p. 1, 28 August 1940, p. 5C, 29 July 1941, p. 5; Board of Supervisors

of Louisiana State University and Agricultural and Mechanical College Minutes, 9 August 1939, in Hill Memorial Library, Louisiana State University, Baton Rouge; V9, p. 19.

15. Minutes, 1 December 1941; *Reveille*, 11 February 1941, p. 5, 1 March 1941, p. 4. That topic was the subject at the Missouri Valley Forensic Association debates. LSU's debaters included Carmouche, Jere Hudson, Arnold Abalon, and Ed Glusman. *Reveille*, 29 March 1941, p. 1.

16. *Reveille*, 6 March 1941, p. 2, 17 June 1941, p. 1.

17. Ibid., 7 March 1940, p. 5.

18. Ibid., 17 January 1940, p. 1.

19. Ibid., 21 September 1940, p. 2, 1 October 1940, p. 1, 20 May 1941, p. 2.

20. Frost, *The LSU College of Engineering*, II, 113, citing *Reveille*, 9 December 1941; Litton, Dupre, interview by Nina Pugh, audiotape recording 4700.1431, 26 October 1983, pp. 5, 6, OHP.

21. Minutes, 3 January, 26 January, 3 March 1942; *Law School Bulletin* (1945–46), 6; Minutes, 27 April, 13 April 1942; Litton, p. 5, OHP.

22. Sullivan, "Paul Macarius Hebert," ii; *Bulletin* (1942), 7; Henry G. McMahon, "Editorial: The Law School," *Louisiana Law Review* 4 (1942): 419; Dale E. Bennett, "Editorial: The Law School," *Louisiana Law Review* 5 (1942): 99; Minutes, 15 July 1942; *Bulletin* (1943), 12, 16 and (1942), 257.

23. *Reveille*, 8 December 1942, p. 2; Soderbergh, *Tower, Tablet, and Tree*, 88; *Reveille*, 10 November 1942, p. 5; Bennett, Dale, interview by Nina Pugh, audiotape recording 4700.1386, 19 April 1983, p. 19, OHP; Minutes, 23 September 1942, p. 16 September 1943.

24. Barham, Mack, interview by Nina Pugh, audiotape recording 4700.1385, 13 June 1984, p. 1, OHP; *Reveille*, 13 October 1942, p. 2; Minutes, 15 July 1942; Landry, Frances Leggio, interview by Nina Pugh, audiotape recording 4700.1427, 21 April 1983, pp. 9, 10, OHP.

25. Frost, *The LSU College of Engineering*, II, 114.

26. *Bulletin* (1942), 170; ibid. (1943), 167; ibid. (1942), 171.

27. McMahon, "Editorial: The Law School," 419; *Reveille*, 19 April 1941, p. 8.

28. McKeithen, John J., interview by Nina Pugh, audiotape recording 4700.1435, 23 September 1983, p. 2, OHP, 3. The student was John Dixon, who graduated from Tulane Law School after his distinguished war service and become chief justice of the Louisiana Supreme Court. See Robert G. Pugh, "Proceedings on the Retirement of Honorable John A. Dixon, Jr.," 562 So.2d (1990): lv; McKeithen, pp. 4, 6, OHP.

29. McKeithen, pp. 2, 7, OHP; Litton, pp. 1, 2, 3, OHP.

30. Innes, Martha Caldwell, interview by Nina Pugh, audiotape recording 4700.1415, 22 June 1984, p. 3, OHP; Minutes, 16 September 1943; *Reveille*, 11 May 1943, p. 3; Purvis, Frank, Jr., interview by Nina Pugh, audiotape recording 4700.1453, 4 November 1983, p. 17, OHP.

31. Bennett, p. 21, OHP; *Reveille*, 19 February 1943, p. 1, 12 February 1943, p. 8, 23 February 1943, p. 5, 19 October 1956, p. 1.

32. Ratcliff, Betty Ann Gremillion, interview by Nina Pugh, audiotape recording 4700.1455, 26 January 1984, pp. 2, 4, 10, OHP.

33. Dale E. Bennett, "Editorial: The Law School," *Louisiana Law Review* 6 (1944): 70.

34. Ibid.; Malone, p. 25, OHP; *Bulletin* (1946), 7; Minutes, 21 March 1946; Paul M. Hebert, "Editorial: The Law School," *Louisiana Law Review* 7 (1946): 123, 124.

35. Hebert, "Editorial: The Law School" (1946): 123, 125; McMahon to Harrison, 30 April 1948, in Personnel Files; Genie Taylor Harrison, *Turnip Greens in the Bathtub* (Baton Rouge: Land and Land Printers, 1981), v.

36. Minutes, 3 April 1946; Hebert, "Editorial: The Law School" (1946), 123, 125; Rubin, p. 4, OHP; LSU Law article.

37. Minutes, 21 February 1947; Personnel Files.

38. *Bulletin* (1949), 6; Minutes, 16 September 1948; Paul M. Hebert, "Editorial: The Law School," *Louisiana Law Review* 9 (1949): 278, 280; *Bulletin* (1948), 7; Hebert, "In Memoriam: Henry George McMahon," 162; *Bulletin* (1948), 8.

39. Hebert, "Editorial: The Law School" (1949), 278, 279; Minutes, 30 March 1948; Hebert, "Editorial: The Law School" (1949), 278, 280; Hebert to Reynard, 13 April 1948, in Personnel Files.

40. Harrison, Milton, interview by Nina Pugh, audiotape recording 4700.1412, 22 March 1983, p. 29, OHP; Personnel Files.

41. Minutes, 27 July 1948; Hebert, "Editorial: The Law School" (1949), 278, 280.

42. Hebert, "Historical Sketch," 146; Beverly Gordon Womack, "Editorial: Growth of the Law Library Book Collection," *Louisiana Law Review* 6 (1945): 264; Hebert, "Editorial: The Law School" (1946), 123, 125.

43. *Bulletin* (1949), 30; Hebert, "Editorial: The Law School" (1949), 278, 280; Personnel Files; Hebert, "Editorial: The Law School" (1946), 123, 125; *Louisiana Law Review* 9 (1949): advertisement after p. 306.

44. Hebert, "Historical Sketch," 146; *Baton Rouge Morning Advocate*, 20 June 1975, p. 3B; *The Civilian*, 14 January 1980, p. 1; Paul M. Hebert, "Dedication," *Louisiana Law Review* 35 (1975): v, vi; Milton M. Harrison to Kate Wallach, 16 July 1949, in Personnel Files.

45. Personnel Files; Ernst Rable, "Private Laws of Western Civilizations: Part I, The Significance of Roman Law," *Louisiana Law Review* 10 (1949): 1; "Part II, The French Civil Code," ibid., 10 (1950): 107; "Part III, The German Code," ibid., 10 (1950): 265; "Part IV, Civil Law and Common Law," ibid., 10 (1950): 431; "Part V, The Law in the World," ibid., 10 (1950): 449.

46. Edwards, Edwin, interview by Nina Pugh, audiotape recording 4700.1404, 2 March 1988, pp. 1, 2, OHP.

47. Minutes, 30 November 1948.

48. Lenoir, "Historical Sketch of the Southern University Law School," 157; Harrison, p. 22, OHP.

49. Minutes, 6 August 1946, 11 September 1946; *Bulletin* (1947), 219.

50. Minutes, 1 July, 12 September 1947; Hebert, "Editorial: The Law School" (1946), 123; Minutes, 12 September 1947.

51. Frost, *The LSU College of Engineering*, II, 124; Minutes, 17 September, 16 December, 23 September, 30 September 1947.

52. Hebert, "Editorial: The Law School" (1946), 123, 125; Minutes, 23 February 1948.

53. Harrison, p. 11, OHP; Meyers, William, interview by Nina Pugh, audiotape recording 4700.1437, 1 March 1984, pp. 7, 15, OHP; Blanche, Fred A., Jr., interview by Nina Pugh, audiotape recording 4700.1389, 31 March 1984, p. 1, OHP.

54. Hebert, "Editorial: The Law School" (1946), 123, 124; Harrison, pp. 12, 13, OHP.
55. Minutes, 2 February, 13 February, 3 April 1946; Meyers, pp. 17, 18, OHP.
56. Meyers, pp. 27, 29, 31, OHP.
57. Minutes, 3 April 1946; "Historical Sketch of the Committee on Bar Admissions of the Supreme Court of Louisiana," 72, 73.
58. Minutes, 1 May 1946, 14 October, 28 October 1947, 6 May, 8 August 1946.
59. Meyers, pp. 2, 11, OHP.
60. Ibid., 2.
61. Ibid., 20; Pugh, Robert G., Sr., interview by Nina Pugh, audiotape recording 4700.1452, 9 June 1983, p. 5, OHP, 2.
62. William L. Prosser, Review of *The Famous Case of Myra Clark Gaines* by Nolan B. Harmon, *Louisiana Law Review* 7 (1946): 157, 158.
63. Minutes, 15 December 1947.
64. Hebert, "Editorial: The Law School" (1949), 278.
65. Long, Gillis, interview by Nina Pugh, audiotape recording 4700.1432, 8 November 1984 pp. 1, 3–4, 7, 31–32, OHP.
66. Henry G. McMahon, "In Memoriam: Ira S. Flory," *Louisiana Law Review* 11 (1950): 1; Personnel Files; Litton, p. 6, OHP.
67. *Bulletin* (1949–50), 7.
68. Ibid., 9–11, 17–21.

6. THE FIFTIES: RETURN TO NORMALCY

1. Minutes, 2 March 1953; McDonald, Jesse, interview by Nina Pugh, audiotape recording 4700.1434, 16 February 1985, p. 4, OHP; Odom, Huntington, interview by Nina Pugh, audiotape recording 4700.1442, 5 June 1984, p. 4, OHP; Politz, Henry A., letter addendum, interview by Nina Pugh, audiotape recording 4700.1448, 1 July 1986, OHP.
2. Because he demanded of students the precise word or words from the appropriate Civil Code provision.
3. Politz, letter addendum, OHP.
4. Politz, p. 18, OHP.
5. Minutes, 6 November 1951.
6. See McMahon, "In Memoriam," 1; Personnel Files; *Reveille*, 19 September 1950, p. 1; Conversation of author with Warren Mengis, professor, LSU Law School, 12 October 2001.
7. George W. Pugh, "Historical Approach to the Doctrine of Sovereign Immunity," *Louisiana Law Review* 13 (1953): 476; Paul M. Hebert, "Editorial: The Law School," ibid., 169, 171; *Reveille*, 10 July 1952, p. 3; Minutes, 6 February 1956; Paul M. Hebert, "Editorial: The Law School," *Louisiana Law Review* 15 (1954): 158, 159; Paul M. Hebert, "Editorial: The Law School," *Louisiana Law Review* 17 (1956): 191, 194; Lee Hargrave and Frank L. Maraist, "Dedication: George Willard Pugh," *Louisiana Law Review* 54 (1994): 489.
8. Minutes, 20 November 1950; *Reveille*, 2 October 1950, p. 1; Minutes, 10 March, 8 April, 17

March 1952; Hebert, "Editorial: The Law School" (1953): 169, 172; *Reveille*, 10 June 1952; *Baton Rouge Advocate*, 15 March 1998, p. 12A; Long, Gillis, interview by Nina Pugh, audiotape recording 4700.1432, 8 November 1984, p. 8, OHP; Morial, Ernest N., interview by Nina Pugh, audiotape recording 4700.1441, 13 June 1984, p. 25, OHP.

9. Hebert, "Editorial: The Law School" (1953), 169, 171; *Reveille*, 20 October 1953, p. 3; Minutes, 7 May 1953; Paul M. Hebert, "Editorial: The Law School and Legal Education," *Louisiana Law Review* 14 (1953): 3, 4; Minutes, 11 October 1954, 11 August 1955; Dakin, Melvin G., interview by Nina Pugh, audiotape recording 4700.1397, 18 February 1986, p. 13, OHP.

10. *Reveille*, 5 March 1952, p. 4.; Wex S. Malone, Review of *The Law of Torts* by Harper and James, *Louisiana Law Review* 17 (1957): 877; *Reveille*, 12 September 1957, p. 4E.

11. Minutes, 27 February, 5 March, 19 March, 16 April, 17 September 1956.; *AALS Directory of Law Teachers* (1974), 479; Minutes, 27 March 1969; Jaro Mayda, *François Geny and Modern Jurisprudence* (Baton Rouge: Louisiana State University Press, 1978); Minutes, 14 May 1973.

12. Minutes, 7 January, 25 March, 28 October 1957, 6 January 1958; *Reveille*, 19 March 1958, p. 3.; Minutes, 17 June 1958; Milton M. Harrison, "Editorial: The Law School," *Louisiana Law Review* 19 (1958): 145, 147; Athanassios N. Yiannopoulos, "Brokerage, Mandate, and Agency in Louisiana: Civilian Tradition and Modern Practice," *Louisiana Law Review* 19 (1959): 777.

13. *Reveille*, 27 October 1950, p. 1.; Harrison, "Editorial: The Law School" (1958), 145, 148, 149; Minutes, 8 December 1952; *Reveille*, 10 June 1952, p. 3; Harrison, "Editorial: The Law School," 150; Hebert, "Editorial: The Law School" (1954), *Louisiana Law Review* 16 (1955): 83, 86.

14. Hebert, "Dedication" (1975), vii; *Reveille*, 13 September 1951, p. 7A, 24 October 1956, p. 2.

15. *Reveille*, 22 April 1952, p. 4; Minutes, 26 September 1955; Craig, Frank S., Jr., interview by Nina Pugh, audiotape recording 4700.1395, 28 June 1984, p. 34, OHP.

16. Personnel Files; Minutes, 23 March, 11 May 1953, 16 May 1965; Cangelosi, Theo F., interview by Nina Pugh, audiotape recording 4700.1391, 19 January 1984, p. 18, OHP.

17. William E. Trice, "Eulogy: Charles A. Reynard," *Louisiana Law Review* 19 (1959): 245; *Reveille*, 4 February 1959, p. 3A; Wex S. Malone, "Eulogy: Charles A. Reynard," *Louisiana Law Review* 19 (1959): 248; Charles A. Reynard, "Governmental Regulation of Individual Employment Conditions in the United States," *Louisiana Law Review* 19 (1959): 253; Charles A. Reynard, "Developments in Constitutional Law," *Louisiana Law Review* 19 (1959): 364.

18. Minutes, 16 March 1959.; Reynard, "Developments in Constitutional Law," 352.

19. Index to Articles, *Louisiana Law Review* 13 (1953): iii, vii.

20. Minutes, 28 November 1950, 27 September 1954, 12 March 1951, 8 March 1954, 25 April 1955.

21. Ibid., 3 December 1952, 8 February 1954, 7 February, 21 February, 28 February 1955, 6 December 1954, 18 May 1953.

22. Harrison, Milton, interview by Nina Pugh, audiotape recording 4700.1412, 22 March 1983, p. 29, OHP; Lazarus, Carlos, interview by Nina Pugh, audiotape recording 4700.1430, 20 May 1983, p. 8, OHP.

23. Minutes, 9 February 1953. Dean Hebert announced her retirement at a faculty meeting; ibid., 20 July 1973.

24. *Reveille*, 6 November 1951, p. 1; Minutes, 4 May 1959, 14 December 1953, 29 October 1956 (p. 4).

25. Minutes, 20 November 1950; *Baton Rouge Morning Advocate*, 21 January, 17 January 1951; *Reveille*, 17 January 1951, p. 1.

26. Minutes, 8 August 1951, 10 March 1952; *Reveille*, 8 February 1952, p. 1, 14 May 1954, p. 4.; Paul M. Hebert to President Troy H. Middleton, 2 April 1957, attached to Minutes, 8 April 1957; Milton M. Harrison, "Dedication," *Louisiana Law Review* 18 (1957): v; *Reveille*, 12 September 1957, p. 3A.

27. *Reveille*, 16 June 1959, p. 1; Rubin, Alvin, interview by Nina Pugh, audiotape recording 4700.1457, 15 December 1983, pp. 2, 3, OHP; Lee Hargrave, "Retirement: Professor Milton M. Harrison," *Louisiana Law Review* 43 (1983): ix.

28. Personnel Files. The Mixed Courts of Egypt were imposed by colonial powers and "had exclusive jurisdiction over civil and commercial litigation between natives and foreigners, and between foreigners of different nationalities." Hoyle, *Mixed Courts of Egypt*, 13. The judges were chosen by ability from Egypt and abroad (p. 21). See also Brinton, *The Mixed Courts of Egypt*, 229. Another judge of the district court, Pierre Crabites from Louisiana, served from 1911 to 1936, after which he was appointed to the LSU law faculty. *Reveille*, 24 February 1950, p. 2.

29. *Reveille*, 2 October 1950, p. 1; Minutes, 20 November 1950, 30 November 1953.

30. *Reveille*, 8 February 1952, p. 9.

31. Minutes, 2 March 1953 (p. 2), 9 March, 23 March 1953; Hebert, "Editorial: The Law School and Legal Education," 3, 4; *AALS Directory of Law Teachers* (1961), 97; Memorandum for the Law Faculty, attachment to Minutes, 12 June 1953 (p. 6); Pascal, conversation with author; Lanier, Leah, interview by Nina Pugh, audiotape recording 4700.1429, 25 October 1983, p. 25, OHP; Odom, p. 7, OHP.

32. "Program," *Louisiana Law Review* 17 (1957): 505; Minutes, 14 May, 24 September 1956; Paul M. Hebert, "Statement of Welcome," *Louisiana Law Review* 17 (1957): 509.

33. Paul M. Hebert, "Editorial: The Law School," *Louisiana Law Review* 16 (1955): 83, 85; Minutes, 6 December 1954.

34. Minutes, 16 April 1956.

35. Ibid., 12 March 1951.

36. Ibid., 20 June, 10 September, 29 October 1951; *Reveille*, 18 April 1952, p. 1, 14 April 1954, p. 1; Hebert, "Editorial: The Law School and Legal Education," 3, 5.

37. Minutes, 12 March 1956, 17 March 1958; Walter J. Suthon Jr., "The Dubious Origin of the Fourteenth Amendment," *Tulane Law Review* 28 (1953): 22; *Reveille*, 15 April 1958, p. 1.

38. Minutes, 25 October 1954; Yvon Loussouarn, "The Relative Importance of Legislation, Custom, Doctrine, and Precedent in French Law," *Louisiana Law Review* 18 (1958): 235; *Reveille*, 24 September 1957, p. 1, 7 October 1958, p. 1.

39. *Reveille*, 1 October 1953, p. 1.

40. See Minutes, 6 October, 13 October, 24 November 1952.

41. Memorandum for the Law Faculty, attached to Minutes, 12 June 1953 (p. 2).

42. The others were Philip W. West, Chemistry, and T. Harry Williams, History. They were named on June 1, 1953. http://lsb380.plbio.lsu.edu/undergrad%20research/Boyd.members.

43. Minutes, 30 July 1953, 29 March 1954, 31 October 1955, 3 February 1956; Crawford, William, interview by Nina Pugh, audiotape recording 4700.1396, 1 June 1983, p. 2, OHP.

44. Minutes, 4 August 1954, 6 February 1956, 1 December 1952.

45. Ibid., 10 May 1954, 15 October, 29 October 1951, 19 September 1955.

46. Ibid., 15 September 1952, 5 February, 9 February 1953, 12 June 1953, 8 November 1954, 16 January 1956.

47. *Reveille*, 16 October 1957, p. 1.

48. Minutes, 19 September, 23 September 1957, 20 March 1969.

49. Malone, Wex S., interview by Nina Pugh, audiotape recording 4700.1433, 28 March 1983, pp. 33, 34, OHP.

50. Harrison, p. 44, OHP.

51. Voegelin was LSU's highest-paid academician at the time, with a $10,500-per-academic-year salary. President Middleton was unwilling to recommend a $15,000 salary for him on the grounds that it would establish disparity in the campuswide salary structure. Middleton to Taylor, Hebert, and Williamson, 19 November 1956, in Voegelin Personnel File, LSU Law Archives. Minutes, 30 September 1957.

52. Minutes, 13 January 1958.

53. Ibid., 12 January, 3 February 1958.

54. Ibid., 17 March 1958, Attachment (p. 2).

55. Harrison, "Editorial: The Law School," 145, 147.

56. Minutes, 5 May, 17 June 1958, 7 December 1959.

57. Ibid., 15 December 1958.

58. Ibid., 30 November 1948.

59. *Reveille*, 19 September 1950, p. 7, 28 September 1950, p. 1, 9 October 1950, p. 1; *Board of Supervisors v. Wilson*, 92 F. Supp. 986 (1950); *Reveille*, 10 October 1950, p. 1, 5 January 1951, p. 1; *Board of Supervisors v. Wilson*, 340 U.S. 909 (1951), reh. den. 340 U.S. 939 (1951). The per curiam of the court simply affirmed the lower-court decision and cited *Sweatt v. Painter*, 339 U.S. 629, and *McLaurin v. Oklahoma State Regents*, 339 U.S. 637).

60. *Reveille*, 1 November 1950, p. 1, 18 January 1951, p. 1; Minutes, 4 December 1950; Morial, p. 2, OHP; Minutes, 15 January 1951; *Baton Rouge Morning Advocate*, 17 January 1951.

61. *Reveille*, 14 June 1951, p. 1. They included Fred S. LeBlanc, state attorney general, J. C. Pearce, assistant attorney general, Fred A. Blanche Sr., C. D. Bird, L. W. Brooks, James H. Fuller, Arthur O'Quin, Leander Perez, C. V. Porter, Victor Sachse, R. B. Sadler Jr., H. C. Sevier, A. J. Shepard Jr., Grover Stafford, Oliver P. Stockwell, Wood H. Thompson, John H. Tucker Jr., and W. Scott Wilkinson. *Reveille*, 22 September 1953, pp. 1, 3; Letter by Waldo F. McNeir, *Reveille*, 10 October 1958, p. 4.

62. Minutes, 20 June 1951; Morial, p. 2, OHP; *Reveille*, 13 September 1951, p. 1, 14 March 1952, p. 4; Minutes, 10 September 1951; Ernest N. Morial file, LSU Law Archives.

63. *Reveille*, 2 April 1952, p. 1; *Louisiana Weekly*, 3 May 1952; Morial, pp. 6, 7, OHP.

64. Hebert, "In Memoriam: Henry George McMahon," 162, 167.

65. Minutes, 1 February 1954.

66. La. Acts 1956, No. 15; *Reveille*, 1 November 1956, pp. 1, 5; *Bulletin* (1957–58), 14; Frost, *The LSU College of Engineering*, II, 171; *Reveille*, 17 April 1957, p. 1; *Ludley v. Board of Supervisors*, 150

F. Supp. 900 (E.D. La. 1957); *Reveille,* 14 February 1958, p. 1; *Board of Supervisors v. Ludley,* 252 F.2d. 372 (5th Cir. 1958).

67. *Reveille,* 20 October 1956, p. 2, 31 October 1956, p. 8, 30 October 1956, p. 1.

68. Ibid., 2 November 1956, p. 1, 6 November 1956, p. 8.

69. Ibid., 12 June 1958, p. 1.

70. Minutes, 28 November, 18 December 1950. A later letter to Robert Pascal from McMahon instructed him to vote against the Yale proposal. The draft of a letter was said to have misplaced parentheses, according to "N.V."

71. *AALS Proceedings,* 1950, pp. 22–46.

72. Minutes, 4 December 1951.

73. Ibid., 15 October 1951; *Reveille,* 18 October 1951, p. 5, 6 November 1951, p. 2; Minutes, 29 October 1951.

74. Miller, Ben R., Sr., interview by Nina Pugh, audiotape recording 4700.1438, 17 May 1983, p. 13, OHP; *Clark Hulings (1922–): Master American Painter,* http:/www.tfaoi.com/aa/laa/laa11.htm (10/16/2001); Miller, p. 18, OHP.

75. *Baton Rouge Sunday Advocate Magazine,* 27 February 2000, p. 12.

76. Gottlieb quoted in *The Formal Presentation to the Law School of Oil Portraits of Dean Emeritus Robert Lee Tullis and the Late Professor Ira S. Flory on Saturday, March 28, 1953 at 2 O'Clock P.M.* (Baton Rouge: Louisiana State University Law School Alumni Association, 1953), 9, LSU Law Archives Folder 69; Sachse quoted ibid., 10.

77. Minutes, 9 February 1953, 2 November 1959.

78. *Reveille,* 12 June 1952, p. 1, 18 June 1963, p. 6; Minutes, 6 February 1956 (p. 2), 16 April 1956.

79. Harrison, p. 45, OHP.

80. Minutes, 12 January, 2 March 1953, 28 February 1955, 5 March 1956; *Reveille,* 12 September 1957, p. 7E.

81. Hebert, "Editorial: The Law School and Legal Education," 3, 8.

82. Paul M. Hebert, "Editorial: The Law School," *Louisiana Law Review* 20 (1960): 350; *Reveille,* 20 September 1950, p. 2; Minutes, 12 September 1956.

83. Hebert, "Editorial: The Law School" (1960): 355.

84. *Bulletin* (1959–60), 19.

85. Long, pp. 13, 14, OHP.

86. Politz, p. 26, OHP.

87. *Reveille,* 29 October 1958, p. 1, 4 December 1958, p. 1.

88. Ibid., 30 April 1959, p. 1, 22 September 1959, p. 1, 25 September 1959, p. 1, 6 October 1959, p. 1.

89. Minutes, 6 February 1956.

90. *Reveille,* 9 January 1959, p. 1, 4 October 1962, p. 4.

91. Ibid., 23 September 1953, p. 2.

92. Minutes, 28 November 1950, 22 September 1952, 16 January 1956.

93. Ibid., 12 February 1951; *Reveille,* 19 September 1950, p. 1; Minutes, 5 March, 7 May 1951, 20 October 1952.

94. Crawford, p. 1, OHP; Minutes, 7 January, 14 January 1952, 30 July 1953; *Reveille,* 4 December 1941, p. 1, 12 December 1951, p. 1.

95. Minutes, 14 November 1950, p. 1.

96. Giuseppe Bisconti, *Diritto comparato: scienza e metodo* (1953), biography of author inscribed by Robert A. Pascal; Minutes, 17 September 1956.

97. Minutes, 8 June 1951, 24 November 1952, 15 November 1954; *Reveille,* 18 November 1953, p. 1; Minutes, 4 November, 25 November 1957.

98. Minutes, 6 February 1956; Hebert, "Editorial: The Law School" (1954), 158, 160, 152; Minutes, 6 February 1956; "In Memoriam: Robert Lee Tullis," *Louisiana Law Review* 15 (1955): 507; Paul M. Hebert to Melvin G. Dakin, 28 February 1955, in Melvin G. Dakin Personnel File, LSU Law Archives.

99. *Reveille,* 19 September 1957, pp. 3A, 7B, 28 March 1958, p. 1.

100. Ibid., 15 April 1959, p. 1, 30 April 1959, p. 2.

101. Minutes, 27 April 1953; Harrison, p. 26, OHP; "Historical Sketch of the Committee on Bar Admissions of the Supreme Court of Louisiana," 72, 73; *Reveille,* 13 June 1957, p. 2.

102. Minutes, 22 September, 28 September, 29 September 1958.

103. The references to "Dean" Harrison, who held that position from 1957 to 1959, and to students who graduated in 1957 and 1958 suggest that date.

7. THE SIXTIES: STEADY GROWTH

1. Moore, Henson, interview by Nina Pugh, audiotape recording 4700.1439, 3 March 1984, pp. 1, 2, OHP. See also Schroeder, Leila, interview by Nina Pugh, audiotape recording 4700.1459, 20 June 1984, p. 11, OHP.

2. Moore, pp. 16, 17, 18, OHP; Phillips, James E., Jr., interview by Nina Pugh, audiotape recording 4700.1447, 14 November 1984, p. 5, OHP.

3. Minutes, 15 September 1964; *Reveille,* 6 November 1962, p. 2; Paul M. Hebert, "Editorial: Report of the Dean of the LSU Law School," *Louisiana Law Review* 24 (1964): 354, 361.

4. *Reveille,* 27 January 1928, p. 1; Minutes, 24 October 1960, 16 June 1966.

5. Minutes, 9 August 1963; *Reveille,* 9 December 1964, p. 5, 19 February 1965, p. 5.

6. Minutes, 7 November 1960, 17 January 1969, 29 October 1965, 17 October 1973; *Reveille,* 28 September 1973, p. 5.

7. Minutes, 21 November 1960, 27 March 1974.

8. Ibid., 21 November 1960, 9 October 1961.

9. Ibid., 5 December 1960, 19 October 1964; Paul M. Hebert, "Editorial: Biennial Report of the Law School to the Chancellor, 1964–66," *Louisiana Law Review* 26 (1966): 317, 320.

10. Petition of Mrs. Amelia Canaday, in Minutes, 1 September 1967, 29 February 1968.

11. Ibid., 1 February, 9 May 1960; Paul M. Hebert, "Editorial: The Law School," *Louisiana Law Review* 21 (1961): 393, 400.

12. *Bulletin* (1963–64), 21; Hebert, "Editorial: Report of the Dean of the LSU Law School," 354, 365; *Bulletin* (1965–66), 26–33; ibid. (1970–71), 25–32; Minutes, 12 September 1966.

13. Minutes, 9 August 1963.

14. *Bulletin* (1960–61), 15. The LSAT scale at the time was 200–800, and the median slowly rose to 540 in 1982, when a new scale of 10–50 was adopted. Law School Admission Council, *Law School Admission Test: Sources, Uses, Contents* (Washington, D.C.: Law School Admissions Services, 1982). Hebert, "Editorial: Report of the Dean of the LSU Law School," 354, 362. The higher requirement was phased in gradually—500 required for students entering in 1964–65 and 525 for 1965–66. Minutes, 5 November 1963; *Bulletin* (1964–65), 14, 15. See *Law School Admission Test*, 18; Minutes, 23 November 1964, 16 June, 1 August 1966.

15. Minutes, 27 September 1966; Tate, Al, interview by Nina Pugh, audiotape recording 4700.1464, 9 November 1983, pp. 30–31, OHP.

16. Donnie G. Brunson, Carl H. Hanchey, Patrick A. Juneau Jr., Morris A. Lottinger Jr., Michael R. Mangham, Rogers M. Prestridge, and George B. Ware.

17. Hebert, "Editorial: Biennial Report of the Law School to the Chancellor, 1964–66," 317, 343; Minutes, 29 March, 8 July 1965, 31 March 1964, 27 March 1974 (p. 4).

18. Minutes, 27 September, 5 December 1966, 30 September 1968.

19. Ibid., 19 October 1967 (p. 1); Curriculum Study 1967, memorandum to the faculty, 13 November 1967, in LSU Law Archives.

20. Minutes, 25 March 1968; Memorandum by Curriculum Committee B, 25 March 1968, ibid.

21. Minutes, 28 May 1968.

22. Ibid., 26 May 1968. Not present for the vote were Currier, Smith, A. Tate, and D. Tate. Hebert was present but would vote only in case of a tie. Two faculty members who were present must have abstained to produce a vote of 10 to 6. Rubin to Hebert, 14 June 1968, in Rubin Personnel File, LSU Law Archives.

23. Dakin, Melvin G., interview by Nina Pugh, audiotape recording 4700.1397, 18 February 1986, p. 37, OHP.

24. Minutes, 18 January 1960; Donald H. Wollett, "Race Relations," *Louisiana Law Review* 21 (1960): 85.

25. Minutes, 5 December 1968, 14 May 1969.

26. Ibid., 29 February, 10 September 1968, 27 March 1969.

27. Ibid., 21 March 1961; "Resolution of the Law Faculty," *Louisiana Law Review* 21 (1961): 687; *Reveille*, 3 October 1961, p. 3; Minutes, 1 August, 27 September 1966, attachment; Resolution of the Board of Supervisors, Minutes of the Board of Supervisors, 8 October 1966, Board of Supervisors Records, RG#A0003, Louisiana State University Archives, LSU Libraries, Baton Rouge; "In Memoriam: Harriet Spiller Daggett 1891–1966," *Louisiana Law Review* 27 (1966): 1.

28. Minutes, 7 February 1961; *Reveille*, 16 February 1965, p. 1.

29. *Reveille*, 24 October 1961, p. 1; Paul M. Hebert, "Editorial: The Law School, 1961–62," *Louisiana Law Review* 22 (1962): 404, 408; La. Acts 1974, No. 50.

30. Hardy to President John A. Hunter, 22 January 1964, in Hardy Personnel File, LSU Law Archives.

31. *Reveille*, 24 October 1961, p. 1; Hebert, "Editorial: The Law School, 1971–62," 404, 409; *LSU Law* 3, No. 2 (1986): 5; Hebert, "Editorial: The Law School, 1961–62," 404, 407; *Reveille*, 19 December 1961, p. 5.

32. Minutes, 9 May 1961; Hebert, "Editorial: The Law School, 1961–62," 404, 406; James W. Moore and Thomas S. Currier, "Mutuality and Conclusiveness of Judgments," *Tulane Law Review* 35 (1961): 301; Ray Forrester and Thomas S. Currier, *Cases and Materials on Federal Jurisdiction and Procedure* (2d ed. St. Paul: West, 1962); *Reveille*, 10 October 1962, p. 3; Hebert, "Editorial: Report of the Dean of the LSU Law School" (1964), 354, 355.

33. Minutes, 14 March 1963; *Reveille*, 10 October 1962, p. 3; Hebert, "Editorial: Report of the Dean of the LSU Law School" (1964): 354, 356, 363; David W. Robertson, "The Precedent Value of Conclusions of Fact in Civil Cases in England and Louisiana," *Louisiana Law Review* 29 (1968): 78.

34. Minutes, 9 August, 5 November 1963; Paul M. Hebert, "Editorial: Report of the Dean of the LSU Law School," *Louisiana Law Review* (1964) 24: 354, 355; Paul M. Hebert, "Editorial: Bicentennial Report of the Law School to the Chancellor of Louisiana State University, Main Campus, 1964–66," *Louisiana Law Review* 26 (1966): 317, 325; Russell H. Barrett, *Integration at Ole Miss* (Chicago: Quadrangle Books, 1965), 226 ("There were thirty-nine resignations of faculty members of professorial rank"), 243–54 (Appendix C).

35. Letter to Paul M. Hebert, 1 July 1963, in Currier Personnel File, LSU Law Archives.

36. *Reveille*, 18 June 1964, p. 5, 29 July 1965, p. 5; Hebert, "Editorial: Biennial Report," 317, 325.

37. Hebert, "Editorial: Biennial Report," 317, 325.

38. Ibid., 317, 326; Crawford, William, interview by Nina Pugh, audiotape recording 4700.1396, 1 June 1983, p. 16, OHP.

39. Minutes, 18 April 1967; Hebert, "Editorial: Biennial Report," 317, 328.

40. Crawford, p. 9, OHP; Hebert, "Editorial: Biennial Report," 317, 327.

41. Minutes, 10 February 1966.

42. Ibid., 6 December 1967, 22 February 1968; Dakin, p. 7, OHP; *Reveille*, 23 October 1968.

43. Tate, pp. 18, 19, OHP; Roger A. Stetter, "A Portrait of the Good Lawyer," in *In Our Own Words: Reflections on Professionalism in the Law*, edited by Roger A. Stetter (New Orleans: Louisiana Bar Foundation, 1998), 1.

44. Tate, pp. 28, 56, OHP. Mrs. Molaison was Dean Hebert's secretary.

45. Minutes, 24 February 1969, 8 December 1965, 10 February 1966; Ellis Personnel File, LSU Law Archives; *Baton Rouge Advocate*, 6 February 1994, p. 7E.

46. Minutes, 1 August 1966, 8 April 1968.

47. Ibid., 25 November 1968.

48. Ibid., 15 September 1964, 20 December 1966; 17 June 1967; *LSU Law* 1, No. 1 (1983): 17, 19.

49. Minutes, 7 March 1961, 20 October 1966.

50. Ibid., 1 February, 24 February 1960, 29 October 1965.

51. Ibid., 5 June 1963; Hebert, "Editorial: Report of the Dean of the LSU Law School," 354, 357; *Reveille*, 25 June 1963, p. 1; Leon Sarpy, "Forum Juridicum: A Tribute to Henry George McMahon by the Louisiana State Law Institute," *Louisiana Law Review* 20 (1960): 703; Henry G. McMahon, "The Louisiana Code of Civil Procedure," *Louisiana Law Review* 21 (1960): 1; *Louisiana Law Review* 21 (1960): 168; Hebert, "Editorial: The Law School" (1961), 393.

52. Wex S. Malone et al., "Symposium: Assumption of the Risk," *Louisiana Law Review* 22 (1961): 1–167. A 1982 law review study of *Shepherd's Citations* showed that the Robert E. Keeton

article on assumption of the risk was the most-cited law review article at that time. Hebert, "Editorial: The Law School, 1961–62," 404, 412; Minutes, 21 February 1961; *Reveille,* 14 February 1962, p. 5; Paul M. Hebert, "Dedication," *Louisiana Law Review* 34 (1974): v–x; Minutes, 20 October 1966; *LSU Law* 1, No. 1 (1983): 3.

53. 137 So. 2d 298 (La. 1962); Wex S. Malone, "Ruminations on Dixie Drive It Yourself v. American Beverage Company," *Louisiana Law Review* 30 (1970): 363; Wex S. Malone, "Ruminations on Liability for the Acts of Things," *Louisiana Law Review* 42 (1982): 979.

54. Barham, "A Renaissance of the Civilian Tradition in Louisiana," 357, 375.

55. *Reveille,* 17 May 1962, p. 1, 3 April 1964, p. 5.

56. *LSU Law* 3, No. 1 (1985): 6.

57. Hebert, "Editorial: Biennial Report," 317, 332; A. N. Yiannopoulos, "Usufruct: General Principles," *Louisiana Law Review* 27 (1967): 369; A. N. Yiannopoulos, "Rights of the Usufructuary: Louisiana and Comparative Law," *Louisiana Law Review* 27 (1967): 647; A. N. Yiannopoulos, "Predial Servitudes: General Principles—Louisiana and Comparative Law," *Louisiana Law Review* 29 (1968): 1; A. N. Yiannopoulos, *Civil Law Treatise,* Vol. 2, *Property* (St. Paul: West, 1967), Vol. 3, *Personal Servitudes* (St. Paul: West, 1968); Saul Litvinoff, "Offer and Acceptance in Louisiana Law: A Comparative Analysis," *Louisiana Law Review* 28 (1967): 1 (1967), 28 (1968): 153; Saul Litvinoff, *Civil Law Treatise,* Vol. 6, *Obligations, Book I* (St. Paul: West, 1969).

58. Hebert, "Editorial: The Law School, 1961–62," 404, 412; *Reveille,* 2 February 1962, p. 7B; "Professor George Willard Pugh: Career and Bibliography," *Louisiana Law Review* 54 (1994): 491; George W. Pugh, with Francis C. Sullivan et al., *Cases and Materials on the Administration of Justice* (Mineola, N.Y.: Foundation Press, 1966; 2d ed., 1969); George W. Pugh, "Administration of Criminal Justice in France: An Introductory Analysis," *Louisiana Law Review* 23 (1962): 1; George W. Pugh, "Aspects of the Administration of Justice in the Philippines," *Louisiana Law Review* 26 (1965): 1.

59. Hebert, "Editorial: Biennial Report," 317, 333; Hebert, "Editorial: The Law School, 1961–62," 404, 412; *Reveille,* 30 April 1963, p. 5, 15 December 1964, p. 4; Hebert, "Editorial: Report of the Dean of the LSU Law School," 354; Hebert, "Editorial: Biennial Report," 317, 344; *Reveille,* 25 June 1964, p. 1.

60. *Reveille,* 25 June 1964, p. 3.

61. Hebert Personnel File, LSU Law Archives; *Reveille,* 16 July 1964, p. 7, 19 February 1965, p. 11.

62. Minutes, 8 July 1965; Hebert, "Editorial: Biennial Report," 317, 320; Sarpy, "Forum Juridicum," 621.

63. Minutes, 15 March, 5 April 1966, 17 June 1967, 8 April 1968.

64. Dakin, p. 7, OHP; Melvin G. Dakin and Michael R. Klein, *Eminent Domain in Louisiana: An Analysis of Expropriation Law and Practice* (Indianapolis: Bobbs-Merrill, 1970), ix.

65. Minutes, 19 January 1970.

66. Ibid., 28 October, 7 November 1968.

67. Ibid., 7 November 1968.

68. *Reveille,* 18 September 1969, p. 38, 19 May 1970, p. 5, 16 October 1969, p. 3.

69. Francis C. Sullivan to Lee Hargrave, 17 September 1969.

70. Minutes, 15 September 1964.

71. Ibid., 18 April, 9 October 1961; *Reveille,* 11 April 1962, p. 1, 17 April 1962, p. 1, 20 December 1963, p. 4.

72. Minutes, 10 January 1964, 10 February 1966, 10 January 1964; *Reveille,* 3 December 1964, p. 11.

73. Minutes, Tenured Faculty, 9 April 1968.

74. Minutes, 17 February 1964; Hebert, "Editorial: Biennial Report," 317, 327.

75. Hebert, "Editorial: Report of the Dean of the LSU Law School," 354, 356–57; *Baton Rouge Morning Advocate,* 28 February 1964.

76. Minutes, 24 June 1964; Hebert, "Editorial: Biennial Report," 317, 341; *Reveille,* 30 September 1964, p. 5.

77. *Reveille,* 9 April 1965, p. 1; Minutes, 29 March 1965.

78. Hebert, "Editorial: Report of the Dean of the LSU Law School," 354, 360. The lectures were published in the *Louisiana Law Review* 26 (1966): 189–316.

79. Minutes, 4 April 1960; *Reveille,* 5 December 1962, p. 3A.

80. Greco, Cyrus J., interview by Nina Pugh, audiotape recording 4700.1410, January 25, 1984, p. 6, OHP; Minutes, 21 December 1964. Quotation from Minutes, 29 June 1965.

81. *Reveille,* 1 July 1965, p. 1. The Burden site was donated to LSU by the Burden family and is located at the intersection of Essen Lane and I-10 near the Rural Life Museum.

82. Robert F. Kennon (Class of 1925) was the first LSU law graduate to be elected governor of the state. John McKeithen (Class of 1942) was the second; Edwin W. Edwards (Class of 1949) was the third. McKeithen, John, interview by Nina Pugh, audiotape recording 4700.1435, September 23, 1983, p. 19, OHP.

83. *Baton Rouge Morning Advocate,* 18 October 1966; *Baton Rouge State-Times,* 15 April 1968, p. 7B, 8 October 1968, p. 7A.

84. Minutes, 12 January 1966.

85. Harrison, Milton, interview by Nina Pugh, audiotape recording 4700.1412, 22 March 1983, p. 30, OHP; *LSU Law* 4, No. 1 (1987): 6; Minutes, 24 February 1966.

86. Minutes, 18 April, 19 October 1967; *Reveille,* 22 October 1969, p. 1; *Profile of a Law Center: Louisiana State University, Baton Rouge* (Baton Rouge: LSU Office of Publications, 1970), 4.

87. Hebert, "Editorial: Biennial Report," 317, 319.

88. *Reveille,* 6 November 1973, p. 9.

89. Ibid., 18 September 1969, p. 39.

90. Ibid.; Art. XII, Sec. 7 of the Articles of Incorporation of the Louisiana State Bar Association; "Historical Sketch of the Committee on Bar Admissions of the Supreme Court of Louisiana, Sesquicentennial of the Louisiana Supreme Court," 72, 73.

91. Greco, p. 15, OHP; Pugh, John F., Jr., interview by Nina Pugh, audiotape recording 4700.1451, 24 May 1983, p. 15, OHP.

92. DeBessonet, Cary, interview by Nina Pugh, audiotape recording 4700.1400, 6 April 1984, p. 8, OHP; Pugh, John F., Jr., p. 7, OHP; deBessonet, pp. 1, 7, OHP.

93. Minutes, 20 October 1966.

94. Ibid., 27 September 1966; Crawford, p. 12, OHP.

95. DeBessonet, pp. 3, 4, 12, OHP.
96. *Reveille*, 22 February 1963, p. 3, 8 January 1965, p. 10.
97. Minutes, 18 September 1969; *Reveille*, 17 September 1963, p. 2C; *LSU Bulletin–General Catalogue* (1963–65), 200.
98. Carver, Marshall Hampton, IV, interview by Nina Pugh, audiotape recording 4700.1393, 4 November 1983, pp. 16–7, OHP.
99. Ibid., p. 16; *Reveille*, 26 October 1971, p. 1, 10 April 1970, p. 4.
100. *Reveille*, 17 September 1963, p. 4D.
101. Ibid., 9 March 1965, p. 2, which remarked, "For the benefit of the uninitiated, the real reason the Field House pool is closed has nothing to do with integration, see; it's really because the Alaskan earthquake cracked the foundation of the pool. Get it?" *Reveille*, 4 August 1964, pp. 1, 2, 22 April 1965, p. 1.
102. Ibid., 23 September 1964, p. 1, 30 September 1964, p. 2.
103. Minutes, 27 March, 1 May, 14 May 1969.
104. Ibid., 30 October, 24 November 1970.
105. Ibid., 9 May, 9 October 1961, 23 October, 8 August 1962.
106. Ibid., 10 February 1966, 22 February 1968, 14 April 1970.
107. *Reveille*, 23 October 1964, p. 22, 11 February 1965, p. 1.
108. Former football coach Paul Dietzel was known as "Pepsodent Paul." *Dicta*, LSU Law Archives, Folder 69, p. 3.
109. *Reveille*, 1 November 1961, p. 5.
110. Ibid., 17 January 1962, p. 1.
111. Abell, Edward, interview by Nina Pugh, audiotape recording 4700.1384, 8 November 1989, pp. 9–11, OHP.
112. Dennis, James L., interview by Nina Pugh, audiotape recording 4700.1401, 31 March 1984, pp. 7, 8, 6, 15, OHP; Greco, p. 19, OHP; Moore, p. 3, OHP; Greco, p. 4, OHP.
113. *Reveille*, 19 September 1961, p. 5B, 26 July 1962, p. 1, 3 May 1963, p. 4, 6 July 1965, p. 5.
114. Ibid., 3 November 1964, p. 5.
115. Ibid., 8 May 1963.
116. Ibid., 6 October 1961, p. 5, 15 September 1964, p. 3F, 30 September 1964, p. 5, 13 October 1964, p. 5, 4 December 1964, p. 4.
117. Ibid., 26 February 1965, p. 3.
118. Ibid., 9 April 1965, p. 9.
119. Ibid., 25 September 1963, p. 1, 26 September 1963, p. 1, 2 October 1963, p. 6, 14 November 1963, p. 7.
120. Ibid., 22 October 1963, p. 6, 7 November 1963, p. 3, 27 February 1964, p. 2.

8. 1970–1977: RUNNING HARD TO STAY IN PLACE

1. The figures for the years between are: 1970–71, 163; 1971–72, 164; 1972–73, 238; 1973–74, 291; 1974–75, 254; 1975–76, 285.

2. Dainow, "Dean Hebert and the LSU Law School," 3; *Bulletin* (1970–71), 19; Association of American Law Schools, *Prelaw Handbook: The Only Official Guide to Law Schools* (Washington, D.C.: Association of American Law Schools and the Law School Admission Council, 1972–73), 188, 307; *Reveille,* 13 January 1970, p. 2; Minutes, 19 July 1971.

3. Minutes, 29 October 1971, 8 February 1972; *Reveille,* 11 April 1972, p. 1.

4. La. Acts 1971, No. 12; *LSU Financial Report for the Fiscal Year Ended June 30, 1959* (Baton Rouge: Louisiana State University, 1959), 20; *LSU Financial Report for the Fiscal Year Ended June 30, 1964* (Baton Rouge: Louisiana State University, 1964), 22.

5. Minutes, 28 March 1973; La. Acts 1973, No. 14 ($100,000 from the state general fund; $350,000 from the federal state trust fund); Minutes, 28 June 1973.

6. In a memorandum to an ad hoc committee to consider raising the minimum index, Hebert wrote, "The Board was most reluctant to adopt a numerical limitation and stipulated a condition that the numerical limitation be re-evaluated and raised if additional monies are appropriated for the Law School." Memo, 9 April 1973, LSU Law Archives, Hargrave Papers, Box 1, Folder 1; Minutes, 6 February 1974; Louisiana State University, Hebert Law Center, *Self-Study Report, 1988–94* (Baton Rouge: Paul M. Hebert Law Center, 1994), 245.

7. Minutes, 29 January 1970 (attachment), 3 March 1970 (attachment, p. 12).

8. Ibid., 27 March 1974. The original median score of 500 slowly increased over the years and was 540 in 1981 when the LSAT changed to a different system of scoring (0–60).

9. Ibid., 11 September 1974.

10. *Reveille,* 18 November 1971, p. 9; Minutes, 6 February 1974; Hershman Personnel File, LSU Law Archives.

11. Minutes, 19 July 1971, 8 February 1972.

12. *AALS Directory of Law Teachers* (1974), 442.

13. Minutes, 19 July 1971.

14. The scholarship was also supported by a grant to the LSU Foundation. *Reveille,* 6 May 1970, p. 5.

15. Minutes, 31 March 1976.

16. Ibid., 28 March, 14 May 1973.

17. Ibid., 6 February 1974.

18. Ibid., 5 February, 15 July 1975, 26 September 1973; *Reveille,* 5 March 1974, p. 10.

19. Minutes, 15 May 1975.

20. Ibid., 29 September 1976, 12 January 1977, 19 January, 3 March 1976.

21. Harper Personnel File, LSU Law Archives.

22. Lanier Personnel File, LSU Law Archives; Minutes, 19 July 1971.

23. Letter, 7 November 1975, in Molaison Personnel File, LSU Law Archives.

24. Dean Paul M. Hebert to Chancellor Cecil G. Taylor, 1 February 1974, in Personnel Files.

25. *Reveille,* 9 February 1972, p. 7.

26. Minutes, May 26, 1970; *Reveille,* 2 March 1972, p. 6.

27. George W. Pugh, "Ruminations re Reform of American Criminal Justice (Especially our Guilty Plea System): Reflections Derived from a Study of the French System," *Louisiana Law Review* 36 (1976): 947; George W. Pugh, *Louisiana Evidence Law* (Indianapolis: Bobbs-Merrill,

1971); Carlos Lazarus, trans., *Successions and Donations* by Charles Aubry and Charles Frédéric Rau, in *Louisiana Civil Law Translations,* Vols. 3 and 4 (St. Paul: West, 1969, 1971).

28. Lee Hargrave, "Legal Problems in the Development of Geothermal Energy Resources," in *Proceedings of the Twenty-Sixth Annual Institute on Mineral Law,* edited by Patrick H. Martin (Baton Rouge: Louisiana State University Law Center Institute of Continuing Education, 1979), 224; Thomas A. Harrell, "Legal Impediments to the Development of the Geopressured Resource," *Interstate Oil Compact Commission Committee Bulletin* 20 (1978): 24; Thomas A. Harrell, "Legal Impediments to the Development of the Geopressured Resource," *Proceedings of the Third Geopressured-Geothermal Energy Conference: Held at the University of Southwestern Louisiana, Lafayette, La., Nov. 16–18, 1977* (Lafayette: University of Southwestern Louisiana, 1977).

29. H. Alston Johnson, "La responsabilité civile du fait des préposés en Louisiane," *Revue juridique et politique: indépendance et coopération* 27 (1973): 650; Lee Hargrave, "La condition juridique, politique et sociale de la femme en Louisiane: la femme épousée," *Revue juridique et politique: indépendance et coopération* 28 (1974): 942.

30. Cheney C. Joseph Jr., P. Raymond Lamonica, and Fred Sliman Jr., *Louisiana Law Enforcement Handbook,* 2nd ed. (Baton Rouge: Louisiana District Attorneys Association, 1979); Cheney C. Joseph Jr. and P. Raymond Lamonica, *Louisiana Judge's Benchbook* (Baton Rouge: Advisory Committee on Judges' Benchbook, 1978).

31. A. N. Yiannopoulos, *Louisiana Civil Law Treatise,* Vol. 3, *Personal Servitudes,* 2nd ed. (St. Paul: West, 1978).

32. *LSU and You: A Handbook for the Faculty and Staff of Louisiana State University* (Baton Rouge: Louisiana State University, 1955), 27; La. Acts 1971, No. 26; La. Acts 1978, No. 643.

33. Hebert, "Dedication," *Louisiana Law Review* 33, No. 3: iii–vi; Smith to Hebert, 31 August 1972, in Smith Personnel File, LSU Law Archives.

34. Minutes, 6 February 1974; Paul M. Hebert, "Dedication," *Louisiana Law Review* 34, No. 4 (1974): v–x; *Reveille,* 8 December 1976, p. 15.

35. Paul M. Hebert, "Professor Dale E. Bennett: A Dedication," *Louisiana Law Review* 36, No. 4 (1976): vii, x.

36. *Reveille,* 30 August 1973, p. 13; Minutes, 14 February 1973.

37. Minutes, 11 September 1974.

38. Ibid., 23 October 1974.

39. Ibid., 27 August 1975.

40. *Reveille,* 1 May 1970, p. 1, 28 February 1974, p. 9.

41. Minutes, 26 June 1973; *Reveille,* 23 January 1974, p. 8.

42. Minutes, 6 September (attachment), 4 October 1972, 14 March 1973.

43. Ibid., 11 September 1974; P. Michael Hebert, Curriculum Study, 1974, p. 3, in LSU Law Archives, Hargrave Papers, Box 1, Folder 1.

44. Dainow, "Dean Hebert and the LSU Law School," 3; Minutes, 27 March 1974.

45. Minutes, 19 January 1970, 11 September 1974.

46. Ibid., 14 April 1970, 9 March 1971.

47. Ibid., 10 May 1976.

48. Ibid., 17 September, 24 November 1970. For an example of faculty reluctance to allow overloads, see ibid., 14 December 1970, denying the petition of Van Mayhall.

49. Ibid., 30 October 1970, 17 October 1968, 20 April 1971, 6 September 1972; *Reveille*, 5 November 1971, p. 7.

50. Minutes, 16 March, 1 June 1971.

51. Ibid., 19 July 1971, 20 July 1973.

52. Ibid., 22 March 1972.

53. Ibid., 19 July 1971.

54. Ibid., 27 March 1974; *Reveille*, 12 February 1974, p. 8. The definition of a public body subject to the open-meetings law includes "any other state . . . authorities . . . where such body possesses policy making, advisory, or administrative functions, including any committee or subcommittee of any of these bodies enumerated in this paragraph." La. R. S. 42:4.2. Minutes, 6 September 1962.

55. Minutes, 6 September 1962.

56. *Bulletin* (1973–74), 10; Minutes, 6 September, 15 November 1972.

57. Minutes, 26 May 1970.

58. Ibid., 14 February 1973; *AALS Directory of Law Teachers* (1977), 739.

59. *Reveille*, 10 February 1972, p. 1, 14 March 1972, p. 7, 26 April 1972, p. 5.

60. Ibid., 13 March 1970, p. 1; George W. Hardy III, "Highlights of the Mineral Code Recommendations: A Guide to the More Important Suggested Changes and Elaborations," *Louisiana Law Review* 32 (1972): 543.

61. Minutes, 10 May 1976.

62. Kate Wallach, *Louisiana Legal Research Manual* (Baton Rouge: LSU Institute of Continuing Education, 1972); Kate Wallach, *Research in Louisiana Law* (Baton Rouge: Louisiana State University Press, 1958); Kate Wallach, *Bibliographical History of Louisiana Civil Law Sources* (Baton Rouge: Louisiana State Law Institute, 1955); Hebert, "Dedication" (1975), v.

63. *Reveille*, 13 February 1970, p. 7; Minutes, 3 March, 26 May 1970; *Reveille*, 17 February 1970, p. 3.

64. Minutes, 11 September 1974, 5 February 1975.

65. Ibid., 14 March, 20 July 1973.

66. "In Memoriam: Beverly Denbo Walker," *Louisiana Law Review* 32 (1972): 495.

67. *Reveille*, 29 April 1970, p. 5.

68. Minutes, 14 May 1973 (attachment: Eubanks to Tarver, 22 March 1973).

69. Ibid., 20 July 1973.

70. Joseph, Mary Terrell, interview by Nina Pugh, audiotape recording 4700.1421, 21 June 1984, pp. 2, 4, OHP; Drew, Jean Talley, interview by Nina Pugh, audiotape recording 4700.1402, 14 August 1984, p. 4, OHP.

71. *Reveille*, 12 October 1971, p. 9, 28 April 1972, p. 3.

72. Ibid., 7 April 1970, p. 5; 8 April 1970, p. 7.

73. Ernst, Jerusha Stewart, interview by Nina Pugh, audiotape recording 4700.1405, 1 June 1983, p. 11, OHP; Masthead, *Louisiana Law Review* 36 (1975): 57; Masthead, ibid., 37 (1977): 615; *Reveille*, 29 September 1976, p. 8.

74. *Reveille,* 2 April 1970, p. 6, 12 February 1970, p. 1, 17 February 1970, p. 1, 19 February 1970, p. 1, 28 July 1970, p. 1.

75. Ibid., 28 October 1969, p. 3, 10 March 1970, p. 6, 31 October 1969, p. 3.

76. Ibid., 7 November 1969, p. 1, 25 November 1969, p. 1, 3 December 1969, p. 1; *SGA v. LSU,* 264 So. 2d 916 (La. 1972).

77. *Reveille,* 19 December 1969, p. 1, 8 January 1970, p. 1, 9 January 1970, pp. 1, 3, 24 February 1970, pp. 1, 5, 10 March 1970, p. 1, 12 March 1970, p. 1.

78. Ibid., 21 September 1971, p. 1, 7 April 1972, p. 2, 12 October 1973, p. 1, 19 October 1973, p. 1.

79. Ibid., 15 November 1973, p. 1.

80. Ibid., 9 March 1972, p. 1, 18 January 1972, p. 1, 19 January 1972, p. 1, 4 May 1972, p. 4.

81. Ibid., 13 March 1974, p. 1; *Baton Rouge Morning Advocate,* 14 March 1974, p. 1-B.

82. *Reveille,* 15 March 1974, p. 1, 21 March 1974, p. 1, 28 March 1974, p. 1.

83. Burglary is defined in the Louisiana Criminal Code as the unauthorized entering of any structure, watercraft, or movable with the intent to commit a felony or theft therein. La. R. S. 14:60–62. Minutes, 1 June 1971; *Baton Rouge Sunday Advocate,* 9 May 1971, p. 4-B; *Baton Rouge Morning Advocate,* 14 May 1971.

84. *Baton Rouge Morning Advocate,* 4 August 1976.

85. Among these groups were the American Legion Nicholson Post 38, the Deux Dux conservative Catholic organization, and Babs Minhinnette of the Taxpayer's Education Association. She called it a "flagrant insult to patriotic Christian taxpayers who are forced to contribute their hard-earned money to this University only to have it used as a forum for anti-Christian productions which mock and debase everything that the majority of Louisiana people hold dear . . . namely God, decency, goodness, patriotism and law." *Reveille,* 5 April 1972, p. 1.

86. Ernst, p. 11, OHP.

87. *Reveille,* 8 October 1971, p. 1.

88. "The Devil and Tom Harrell (A Morality Play); or, The Devil Made Me Do It," script, 27, LSU Law Archives, Hargrave Papers, Box 1, Folder 1.

89. *Reveille,* 18 March 1970, p. 5.

90. Ibid., 14 October 1976, p. 13.

91. Ibid., 8 March 1974, p. 1.

92. Ibid., 19 April 1974, p. 6.

93. Minutes, 27 August 1975; Letters from Dean Hebert to Chancellor Cecil Taylor, 16 January, 7 March, 4 April 1974, Personnel Files.

94. See Sullivan, "Paul Macarius Hebert"; *Baton Rouge Morning Advocate,* 4 February 1977, p. 1.

95. Stockwell, Oliver P., II, interview by Nina Pugh, audiotape recording 4700.1462, 12 December 1983, p. 17, OHP; Minutes, Board of Supervisors, 3 February 1978, p. 16.

9. RUMINATIONS AND CONCLUSIONS

1. Wex Malone thought that LSU was very strong in legal reform, respectably strong in teaching, and weak in research. Malone, Wex S., interview by Nina Pugh, audiotape recording

4700.1433, 28 March 1983, p. 41, OHP. Alvin Rubin said that LSU did a fairly good job of teaching and a creditable job in law reform, but that faculty scholarship horizons were narrow. Rubin, Alvin, interview by Nina Pugh, audiotape recording 4700.1457, 15 December 1983, p. 7, OHP.

2. Charles L. Black, *Structure and Relationship in Constitutional Law*, Edward Douglass White Lectures (Baton Rouge: Louisiana State University Press, 1969).

3. Christopher L. Blakesley, "The Impact of a Mixed Jurisdiction on Legal Education, Scholarship, and Law," in *Louisiana: Microcosm of a Mixed Jurisdiction*, ed. Vernon V. Palmer (Durham, N.C.: Carolina Academic Press, 1999), 65–66.

4. Symeon C. Symeonides, "The Louisiana Judge: Judge, Statesman, Politician," ibid., 103.

5. Daggett et al., "A Reappraisal Appraised," 12.

6. Daggett, *The Community Property System of Louisiana with Comparative Studies;* Smith, *Some Phases of Fair Value and Interstate Rates.*

7. Crabites, "Louisiana Not a Civil Law State," 51.

8. Beutel, "The Place of Louisiana Jurisprudence in the Legal Science of America," 70.

9. Malone, pp. 37, 38, OHP.

10. McKeithen, John, interview by Nina Pugh, audiotape recording 4700.1435, 23 September 1983, p. 3, OHP; Paul R. Baier, "Chief Justice John Dixon: Twenty Years in Retrospect," *Tulane Law Review* 65 (1990): 1.

11. Morgan, Cecil, interview by Nina Pugh, audiotape recording 4700.1440, 3 June 1983, p. 45, OHP.

12. Rubin, p. 17, OHP; Edwards, Edwin, interview by Nina Pugh, audiotape recording 4700.1404, 2 March 1988, p. 2, OHP.

13. Harrison, Milton, interview by Nina Pugh, audiotape recording 4700.1412, 22 March 1983, p. 24, OHP.

BIBLIOGRAPHY

PUBLISHED SOURCES

Books and Articles

Association of American Law Schools. *Directory of Teachers in Member Schools: Teachers' Directory.* St. Paul: West, 1923–55.
———. *American Bar Association Approved Law Schools: Directory of Teachers.* St. Paul: West, 1956.
———. *Directory of Law Teachers in Law Schools in the United States.* 2 vols. St. Paul: West, 1968–69.
———. *Directory of Law Teachers.* 17 vols. St. Paul: West, 1970–87.
———. *The AALS Directory of Law Teachers.* 14 vols. to date. St. Paul: West, 1988–.
———. *Prelaw Handbook: The Only Official Guide to Law Schools.* Washington, D.C.: Association of American Law Schools and the Law School Admission Council, 1972–73.
Aubry, Charles. *Cours de droit civil français.* Translated by Carlos E. Lazarus. Civil Law Translations 3 and 4. St. Paul: West, 1969, 1971.
Baade, Hans W. "Marriage Contracts in French and Spanish Louisiana: A Study in 'Notarial' Jurisprudence." *Tulane Law Review* 53 (1978): 3–92.
Baier, Paul R. "Chief Justice John Dixon: Twenty Years in Retrospect." *Tulane Law Review* 65 (1990): 1–14.
Baker, Newman Freece. *Legal Aspects of Zoning.* Chicago: University of Chicago Press, 1927.
———. "Some Legal Aspects of Impeachment in Louisiana." *Southwestern Political and Social Science Quarterly* 10 (1930): 359–87.
Barham, Mack E. "A Renaissance of the Civilian Tradition in Louisiana." *Louisiana Law Review* 33 (1973): 357–89.

Barrett, Russell H. *Integration at Ole Miss.* Chicago: Quadrangle Books, 1965.
Bennett, Dale E. "Editorial: The Law School." *Louisiana Law Review* 5 (1942): 99–101.
———. "Editorial: The Law School." *Louisiana Law Review* 6 (1944): 70–72.
Beutel, Frederick K. "The Place of Louisiana Jurisprudence in the Legal Science of America." *Tulane Law Review* 4 (1929): 70–72.
———. "The Pressure of Organized Interests as a Factor in Shaping Legislation." *Southern California Law Review* 3 (1929): 10–37.
———. "The Necessity of a New Technique of Interpreting the N.I.L.: The Civil Law Analogy." *Tulane Law Review* 6 (1931): 1–22.
———. "Common Law Judicial Technique and the Law of Negotiable Instruments: Two Unfortunate Decisions." *Tulane Law Review* 9 (1934): 64–77.
———. *Toward an Experimental Definition of the Criminal Mind.* Philadelphia: University of Pennsylvania Press, 1942.
———. *Experimental Jurisprudence and the Scienstate.* Bielefeld: Gieseking, 1975.
Biographical and Historical Memoirs of Louisiana. Edited by Allen Johnson. 1892. Rprt., Baton Rouge: Claitor's, 1975. Vol. 1.
Bisconti, Giuseppe. *Diritto comprato: scienza e metodo* (1953). Biography of author inscribed by Robert A. Pascal.
Black, Charles L., Jr. *Structure and Relationship in Constitutional Law.* Edward Douglass White Lectures. Baton Rouge: Louisiana State University Press, 1969.
Blakesley, Christopher L. "The Impact of a Mixed Jurisdiction on Legal Education, Scholarship, and Law." In *Louisiana: Microcosm of a Mixed Jurisdiction*, edited by Vernon V. Palmer. Durham, N.C.: Carolina Academic Press, 1999.
Bonomo, Alfred J. *Lectures on the Civil Code of Louisiana by Hon. Eug. D. Saunders.* New Orleans: E. S. Upton Printing, 1925.
Brinton, Jasper Yeates. *The Mixed Courts of Egypt.* Rev. ed. New Haven: Yale University Press, 1968.
Brosman, Paul. "The Statutory Presumption." *Tulane Law Review* 5 (1930): 16; 6 (1931): 178.
———. "The First Hundred Years." *Tulane Law Review* 22 (1948): 543–46.
Carleton, Mark T. "Newton Crain Blanchard." In *The Louisiana Governors: From Iberville to Edwards*, edited by Joseph G. Dawson III. Baton Rouge: Louisiana State University Press, 1990. Pp. 198–204.
Cowan, Thomas A. *The American Jurisprudence Reader.* Dobbs Ferry, N.Y.: Oceana, 1956.

———. *Essays in the Law of Torts.* New Brunswick, N.J.: Rutgers University Press, 1961.

Crabites, Pierre. "Louisiana Not a Civil Law State." *Loyola Law Journal* 9 (1928): 51–52.

———. "The Capitulations Are in Harmony with the Present State of Egypt." *Tulane Law Review* 5 (1931): 245–54.

———. *Unhappy Spain.* Baton Rouge: Louisiana State University Press, 1937.

———. *Americans in the Egyptian Army.* London: G. Routledge and Sons, 1938.

Daggett, Harriet S. "A Comparison of the German Community Property System with That of Louisiana." *Tulane Law Review* 4 (1929): 27–57.

———. "The Wife's Action for a Separation of Property." *Tulane Law Review* 5 (1930): 55–72.

———. *The Community Property System of Louisiana with Comparative Studies.* Baton Rouge: Louisiana State University Press, 1931.

———. "Trends in Louisiana Law of the Family." *Tulane Law Review* 9 (1934): 89–103.

———. "Is Joint Control of Community Property Possible?" *Tulane Law Review* 10 (1935): 589–603.

Daggett, Harriet S., Joseph Dainow, Paul M. Hebert, and Henry George McMahon. "A Reappraisal Appraised: A Brief for the Civil Law of Louisiana." *Tulane Law Review* 12 (1937): 12–41.

Dainow, Joseph. "Unrestricted Testation in Quebec." *Tulane Law Review* 10 (1936): 401–405.

———. "Dean Hebert and the LSU Law School." *L'Avocat* (1977): 3–4.

———. "Dean Hebert and the LSU Law School: Excerpts from an Article Written for *L'Avocat* by Joseph Dainow, Emeritus Professor of Law and Director Emeritus, Center of Civil Law Studies." *Law Center Notes* (March 1978): 4.

Dakin, Melvin G., and Michael R. Klein. *Eminent Domain in Louisiana: An Analysis of Expropriation Law and Practice.* Indianapolis: Bobbs-Merrill, 1970.

Dargo, George. *Jefferson's Louisiana: Politics and the Clash of Legal Traditions.* Cambridge: Harvard University Press, 1975.

Dart, Henry Plauché. "The History of the Supreme Court of Louisiana." *Louisiana Law Reports* 133 (1914): xxx–lxi.

Dawson, Joseph G. III, ed. *The Louisiana Governors: From Iberville to Edwards.* Baton Rouge: Louisiana State University Press, 1990.

Dictionary of American Biography. New York: Scribner's, 1957. Vol. 8.

Duplantier, Adrian G. "The Law Schools." *Louisiana Law Reports* 245 (1963): 43–47.

Dyer, John P. *Tulane: The Biography of a University 1834–1965.* New York: Harper & Row, 1966.

Eakin, Sue, ed. *Little Hu: The Boy Who Planned to Be Governor.* Winnfield, La.: Louisiana Political Museum and Hall of Fame, 1997.

"Editorial: The Association of American Law Schools and the Standards of Legal Education in the South." *Tulane Law Review* 4 (1930): 236–37.

Ellis, C. W. "The Louisiana Bar, 1813–1913." *Louisiana Law Reports* 133 (1914): lxvi–lxxx.

Ferri, Enrico. *Criminal Sociology.* Translated by Kelly and John Lisle. 1917. Rprt., New York: Agathon Press, 1967.

Flory, Ira S. "Editorial: The Law School." *Louisiana Law Review* 2 (1939): 155–56.

Foote, Henry S. *The Bench and Bar of the South and Southwest.* 1876. Rprt., Buffalo: William S. Hein, 1994.

The Formal Presentation to the Law School of Oil Portraits of Dean Emeritus Robert Lee Tullis and the Late Professor Ira S. Flory on Saturday, March 28, 1953, at 2 O'Clock P.M. Baton Rouge: Louisiana State University Law School Alumni Association, 1953.

Forrester, Ray, and Thomas S. Currier. *Cases and Materials on Federal Jurisdiction and Procedure.* 2d ed. St. Paul: West, 1962.

Frost, Dan R. *The LSU College of Engineering.* Baton Rouge: Louisiana State University College of Engineering, 2000. Vol. 2.

Gaspard, Elizabeth. "The Rise of the Louisiana Bar: The Early Period, 1813–1839." *Louisiana History* 28 (1987): 183–97.

Greenburg, Leonard. "Must Louisiana Resign to the Common Law?" *Tulane Law Review* 11 (1937): 598–601.

Groner, Samuel B. "Louisiana Law: Its Development in the First Quarter-Century of American Rule." *Louisiana Law Review* 8 (1948): 350–82.

Gumbo, The. Yearbook issued by the students of the Louisiana State University and Agricultural and Mechanical College. Baton Rouge: Louisiana State University Student Government Association. Published annually.

Haas, Edward F. "Louisiana's Legal Heritage: An Introduction." In *Louisiana's Legal Heritage,* edited by Edward F. Haas. Pensacola, Fla.: Perdido Bay Press, 1983. Pp. 1–6.

Hair, William Ivy. *The Kingfish and His Realm: The Life and Times of Huey P. Long.* Baton Rouge: Louisiana State University Press, 1991.

Hall, A. Oakey. *The Manhattaner in New Orleans; or, Phases of "Crescent City" Life.*

Edited by Henry A. Kmen. 1851. Baton Rouge: Louisiana State University Press, 1976.

Hall, Jerome. *Readings in Jurisprudence*. Indianapolis: Bobbs-Merrill, 1938.

———. *Theft, Law and Society*. Boston: Little, Brown, 1935.

Hardy, George W. III. "Highlights of the Mineral Code Recommendations: A Guide to the More Important Suggested Changes and Elaborations." *Louisiana Law Review* 32 (1972): 542–99.

Hargrave, Carolyn H., and W. Lee Hargrave. *A History of Graduate Education at Louisiana State University*. Baton Rouge: Louisiana State University Graduate School, 1976.

Hargrave, Lee. "La condition juridique, politique et sociale de la femme en Louisiane: la femme épousée." *Revue juridique et politique: indépendance et coopération* 28 (1974): 942–56.

———. "Legal Problems in the Development of Geothermal Energy Resources." In *Proceedings of the Twenty-Sixth Annual Institute on Mineral Law*, edited by Patrick H. Martin. Baton Rouge: Louisiana State University Law Center Institute of Continuing Education, 1979.

———. "Retirement: Professor Milton M. Harrison." *Louisiana Law Review* 43 (1983): ix–xi.

———. *The Louisiana State Constitution: A Reference Guide*. Westport, Conn.: Greenwood Press, 1991.

Hargrave, Lee, and Frank L. Maraist. "Dedication: George Willard Pugh." *Louisiana Law Review* 54 (1994): 489–90.

Harper, Fowler V. Review of *Hugo L. Black: A Study in the Judicial Process* by Charlotte Williams. *Louisiana Law Review* 11 (1951): 498.

Harrell, Thomas A. "Legal Impediments to the Development of the Geopressured Resource." *Interstate Oil Compact Commission Committee Bulletin* 20 (June 1978): 24.

———. "Legal Impediments to the Development of the Geopressured Resource." In *Proceedings of the Third Geopressured-Geothermal Energy Conference: Held at the University of Southwestern Louisiana, Lafayette, La., Nov. 16–18, 1977*. Lafayette, La.: University of Southwestern Louisiana, 1977.

Harrison, Genie Taylor. *Turnip Greens in the Bathtub*. Baton Rouge: Land and Land Printers, 1981.

Harrison, Milton M. "Editorial: The Law School." *Louisiana Law Review* 19 (1958): 145–50.

———. "Dedication." *Louisiana Law Review* 18 (1957): n.p.

Hart, W. O. *Fragments of Louisiana Jurisprudence: Twelve Lectures Delivered to the Students in the Law Department of the Louisiana State University.* Baton Rouge: Daily State Publishing, State Printers, 1908.

Hatcher, William B. *Edward Livingston: Jeffersonian Republican and Jacksonian Democrat.* Baton Rouge: Louisiana State University Press, 1940.

Hebert, Paul M. "The Origin and Nature of Maritime Liens." *Tulane Law Review* 4 (1930): 381–408.

———. "Editorial: The Law Review and the Law School." *Louisiana Law Review* 1 (1938): 157–60.

———. "Editorial: The Law School." *Louisiana Law Review* 4 (1941): 107–109.

———. "Editorial: The Law School." *Louisiana Law Review* 7 (1946): 123–26.

———. "Editorial: The Law School." *Louisiana Law Review* 9 (1949): 278–81.

———. "Editorial: The Law School." *Louisiana Law Review* 13 (1953): 169–72.

———. "Editorial: The Law School and Legal Education." *Louisiana Law Review* 14 (1953): 3–10.

———. "Editorial: The Law School." *Louisiana Law Review* 15 (1954): 158–62.

———. "Editorial: The Law School." *Louisiana Law Review* 16 (1955): 83–88.

———. "Editorial: The Law School." *Louisiana Law Review* 17 (1956): 191, 194.

———. "Statement of Welcome." *Louisiana Law Review* 17 (1957): 509–12.

———. "Editorial: The Law School." *Louisiana Law Review* 20 (1959–60): 350–56.

———. "Editorial: The Law School, 1960–1961." *Louisiana Law Review* 21 (1961): 393–401.

———. "Editorial: The Law School 1961–62." *Louisiana Law Review* 22 (1962): 404–17.

———. "Historical Sketch of the LSU Law School." *Louisiana Law Reports* 245 (1963): 137–51.

———. "Editorial: Report of the Dean of the LSU Law School." *Louisiana Law Review* 24 (1964): 350–74.

———. "Editorial: Bicentennial Report of the Law School to the Chancellor of Louisiana State University, Main Campus, 1964–66." *Louisiana Law Review* 26 (1966): 317–48.

———. Foreword. *The 1965 Bailey Lectures. Louisiana Law Review* 26 (1966): 189–316.

———. "In Memoriam: Henry George McMahon." *Louisiana Law Review* 27 (1967): 161–69.

———. "Dedication." *Louisiana Law Review* 33, No. 3 (1973): iii–vi.

———. "Dedication." *Louisiana Law Review* 34, No. 4 (1974): v–x.

———. "Dedication." *Louisiana Law Review* 35, No. 5 (1975): v–viii.

———. "Professor Dale E. Bennett: A Dedication." *Louisiana Law Review* 36, No. 4 (1976): vii–xi.

"Historical Sketch of the Committee on Bar Admissions of the Supreme Court of Louisiana." *Louisiana Law Reports* 245 (1963): 72–73.

Hood, John T., Jr. "The Louisiana Lawyer." *Louisiana Law Review* 18 (1958): 661–70.

Hoyle, Mark S. *Mixed Courts of Egypt*. London: Graham and Trotman, 1991.

Hug, Walter, and Gordon Ireland. "The Progress of Comparative Law." *Tulane Law Review* 6 (1931): 68–82.

Hughes, Thomas Welburn. *An Illustrated Treatise on the Law of Evidence*. Chicago: Callahan, 1907.

"In Memoriam: Harriet Spiller Daggett, 1891–1966." *Louisiana Law Review* 27 (1966): 1–4.

Ireland, Gordon. "Constitutional Amendments: Power of Conventions." *Tulane Law Review* 6 (1931): 75–82.

———. "The Use of Decisions by United States Students of Civil Law." *Tulane Law Review* 8 (1934): 358–75.

———. "Louisiana's Legal System Reappraised." *Tulane Law Review* 11 (1937): 585–98.

———. *Boundaries, Possessions, and Conflicts in Central and North America and the Caribbean*. Cambridge: Harvard University Press, 1941.

Ireland, Gordon, and Jesús de Galindez. *Divorce in the Americas*. Buffalo: Dennis, 1947.

Johnson, H. Alston. "La responsabilité civile du fait des préposés en Louisiane." *Revue juridique et politique: indépendance et coopération* 27 (1973): 650–74.

Joseph, Cheney C., Jr., P. Raymond Lamonica, and Fred Sliman Jr. *Louisiana Law Enforcement Handbook*. 2nd. ed. Baton Rouge: Louisiana District Attorneys Association, 1979.

Joseph, Cheney C. Jr., and P. Raymond Lamonica. *Louisiana Judge's Benchbook*. Baton Rouge: Advisory Committee on Judges' Benchbook, 1978.

Kay, Herma Hill. "The Future of Women Law Professors." *Iowa Law Review* 77 (1991): 5–18.

Kelly, Joseph I. "The Gaian Fragment." 6 Ill. L. Rev. 561 (1911).

———. "The *Titanic* Death Liability." 7 Ill. L. Rev. 137 (1912).

Law School Admission Council. *Law School Admission Test: Sources, Uses, Contents*. Washington, D.C.: Law School Admissions Services, 1982.

Lenoir, A. A. "Historical Sketch of the Southern University Law School." *Louisiana Law Reports* 245 (1963): 157–58.

Levasseur, Alain A. *Louis Casimir Elisabeth Moreau-Lislet: Foster Father of Louisiana Civil Law*. Baton Rouge: Louisiana State University Law Center Publications Institute, 1996.

Litvinoff, Saul. "Offer and Acceptance in Louisiana Law: A Comparative Analysis. Part 1." *Louisiana Law Review* 28 (1967): 1–80.

———. "Offer and Acceptance in Louisiana Law: A Comparative Analysis. Part 2." *Louisiana Law Review* 28 (1968): 153–210.

———. *Civil Law Treatise*. Vol. 6, *Obligations, Book I*. St. Paul: West, 1969.

Louisiana State Bar Association. *Report of the Louisiana State Bar Association*. 34 vols. New Orleans: Louisiana State Bar Assocation, 1898–1941.

Loussouarn, Yvon. "The Relative Importance of Legislation, Custom, Doctrine, and Precedent in French Law." *Louisiana Law Review* 18 (1958): 235–70.

Malone, Wex S. Review of *The Law of Torts* by Harper and James. *Louisiana Law Review* 17 (1957): 877–80.

———. "In Memoriam: Charles A. Reynard." *Louisiana Law Review* 19 (1959): 248–51.

———. "Ruminations on Dixie Drive It Yourself v. American Beverage Company." *Louisiana Law Review* 30 (1970): 363–93.

———. "Ruminations on Liability for the Acts of Things." *Louisiana Law Review* 42 (1982): 979–1009.

Malone, Wex S., et al. "Symposium: Assumption of the Risk." *Louisiana Law Review* 22 (1961): 1–167.

Maraist, Frank L. "In Memoriam: F. Hodge O'Neal." *Louisiana Law Review* 51 (1991): 939–41.

Masthead, *Louisiana Law Review* 36 (1975): 57.

Mayda, Jaro. *François Geny and Modern Jurisprudence*. Baton Rouge: Louisiana State University Press, 1978.

McKeag, Edwin C. *Mistake in Contract: A Study in Comparative Jurisprudence*. 1905. Rprt., New York, AMS Press, 1968.

McMahon, Henry George. "The Exception of No Cause of Action in Louisiana." *Tulane Law Review* 9 (1934): 17–63.

———. "Parties Litigant in Louisiana." *Tulane Law Review* 10 (1935): 489–536.

———. "Editorial: The Law School." *Louisiana Law Review* 4 (1942): 419–21.

———. "In Memoriam: Ira S. Flory." *Louisiana Law Review* 11 (1950): 1–3.

———. "The Louisiana Code of Civil Procedure." *Louisiana Law Review* 21 (1960): 1–52.

Mississippi College Law Review (1998). Mississippi College School of Law, Jackson.

Moore, James W., and Thomas S. Currier. "Mutuality and Conclusiveness of Judgments." *Tulane Law Review* 35 (1961): 301–30.

Morgan, Cecil. *The First Constitution of the State of Louisiana*. Baton Rouge: Louisiana State University Press, 1975.

Murchison, Kenneth M. "The Judicial Revival of Louisiana's Civilian Tradition: A Surprising Triumph for the American Experience." *Louisiana Law Review* 49 (1988): 1–37.

O'Neal, F. Hodge. "An Appraisal of the Louisiana Law of Partnership." *Louisiana Law Review* 9 (1949): 307–69.

Palmer, Vernon V., ed. *Louisiana: Microcosm of a Mixed Jurisdiction*. Durham, N.C.: Carolina Academic Press, 1999.

Parkman, Francis. *LaSalle and the Discovery of the Great West*. Boston: Little, Brown, 1905.

Pleasant, John R. "Remarks by Mr. John R. Pleasant, Law Class of '28." In *The Formal Presentation to the Law School of Oil Portraits of Dean Emeritus Robert Lee Tullis and the Late Professor Ira S. Flory on Saturday, March 28, 1953, at 2 O'Clock P.M.* Baton Rouge: Louisiana State University Law School Alumni Association, 1953.

Price, Frank James. *Troy H. Middleton: A Biography*. Baton Rouge: Louisiana State University Press, 1974.

"Proceedings of the Golden Anniversary Celebration of the Louisiana State University Law School." *Louisiana Law Review* 17 (1957): 505–508.

"Professor George Willard Pugh: Career and Bibliography." *Louisiana Law Review* 54 (1994): 491–95.

Profile of a Law Center: Louisiana State University, Baton Rouge. Baton Rouge: LSU Office of Publications, 1970.

Prosser, William L. Review of *The Famous Case of Myra Clark Gaines* by Nolan B. Harmon. *Louisiana Law Review* 7 (1946): 157–60.

Pugh, George W. "Historical Approach to the Doctrine of Sovereign Immunity." *Louisiana Law Review* 13 (1953): 476–94.

———. "Administration of Criminal Justice in France: An Introductory Analysis." *Louisiana Law Review* 23 (1962): 1–28.

———. "Aspects of the Administration of Justice in the Philippines." *Louisiana Law Review* 26 (1965): 1–24.

———. *Louisiana Evidence Law.* Indianapolis: Bobbs-Merrill, 1971.

———. "Ruminations re Reform of American Criminal Justice (Especially Our Guilty Plea System): Reflections Derived from a Study of the French System." *Louisiana Law Review* 36 (1976): 947–71.

Pugh, George W., with Francis C. Sullivan et al. *Cases and Materials on the Administration of Justice.* Mineola, N.Y.: Foundation Press, 1966; 2d ed. 1969.

Pugh, Robert G. "Proceedings on the Retirement of Honorable John A. Dixon, Jr." *West Louisiana Cases* 562 So.2d (1990): liii–lxxiii.

Rable, Ernst. "Private Laws of Western Civilizations: Part I. The Significance of Roman Law." *Louisiana Law Review* 10 (1949): 1–14.

———. "Private Laws of Western Civilizations: Part II. The French Civil Code." *Louisiana Law Review* 10 (1950): 107–19.

———. "Private Laws of Western Civilizations: Part III. The German Code." *Louisiana Law Review* 10 (1950): 265–75.

———. "Private Laws of Western Civilizations: Part IV. Civil Law and Common Law." *Louisiana Law Review* 10 (1950): 431–49.

———. "Private Laws of Western Civilizations: Part V. The Law in the World." *Louisiana Law Review* 10 (1950): 449–60.

"Resolution of the Law Faculty," *Louisiana Law Review* 21 (1961): 687–90.

Reynard, Charles A. "Governmental Regulation of Individual Employment Conditions in the United States." *Louisiana Law Review* 19 (1959): 253–72.

———. "Developments in Constitutional Law." *Louisiana Law Review* 19 (1959).

Roalfe, William R. *John Henry Wigmore: Scholar and Reformer.* Evanston: Northwestern University Press, 1977.

Robertson, David W. "The Precedent Value of Conclusions of Fact in Civil Cases in England and Louisiana." *Louisiana Law Review* 29 (1968): 78–99.

Ruffin, Thomas E. *Under Stately Oaks: A Pictorial History of LSU.* Baton Rouge: Louisiana State University Press, 2002.

Sarpy, Leon. "Forum Juridicum: A Tribute to Henry George McMahon by the Louisiana State Law Institute." *Louisiana Law Review* 20 (1960): 703–13.

Scott, Henry W. *Distinguished American Lawyers.* New York: Charles L. Webster, 1891.

Semmes, Thomas J. "The Civil Law as Transplanted in Louisiana: A Paper Read Before the American Bar Association at Saratoga Springs, N.Y., August 10th, 1882." *Report of the Annual Meeting of the American Bar Association.* Philadelphia: E. C. Markley and Son, 1883.

Smith, James Barclay. *Some Phases of Fair Value and Interstate Rates.* Baton Rouge: Louisiana State University Press, 1931.

———. *Studies in the Adequacy of the Constitution.* Los Angeles: Parker and Baird, 1939.

Smith, J. Denson. "Impossibility of Performance as an Excuse in French Law: The Doctrine of Force Majeure." *Yale Law Journal* 45 (1936): 452–67.

Smithers, William W. Preface to Enrico Ferri, *Criminal Sociology.* 1917. Rprt., New York: Agathon Press, 1967.

Soderbergh, Peter A. *Tower, Tablet, and Tree: LSU and the American Legion.* Baton Rouge: Boyd-Ewing Post 58, American Legion, 1983.

Suthon, Walter J., Jr. "The Dubious Origin of the Fourteenth Amendment." *Tulane Law Review* 28 (1953): 22.

Stetter, Roger A. "A Portrait of the Good Lawyer." In *In Our Own Words: Reflections on Professionalism in the Law,* edited by Roger A. Stetter. New Orleans: Louisiana Bar Foundation, 1998.

Stevens, Robert. *Law School: Legal Education in America from the 1850s to the 1980s.* Chapel Hill: University of North Carolina Press, 1983.

Stumberg, George W. *Principles of Conflict of Laws.* 1937. Rprt., Brooklyn: Foundation Press, 1963.

———. *Cases on Conflict of Laws.* St. Paul: West, 1956.

———. *Guide to the Law and Legal Literature of France.* Washington, D.C.: U.S. Government Printing Office, 1931.

Sullivan, Francis C. "Highlights of the Professional and Academic Careers of Paul Macarius Hebert." *Louisiana Law Review* 37, Supplement (1977): i–xvii.

———. "Paul Macarius Hebert." *Louisiana Law Review* 37, Supplement (1977): i–ii.

Symeonides, Symeon C. "The Louisiana Judge: Judge, Statesman, Politician." In *Louisiana: Microcosm of a Mixed Jurisdiction,* edited by Vernon V. Palmer. Durham, N.C.: Carolina Academic Press, 1999. Pp. 89–103.

"The Association of American Law Schools and the Standards of Legal Education in the South." Editorial. *Tulane Law Review* 4 (1930): 236–37.

Thurmon, Clyde W. "Basic Procedures for Examination of Title to Real Property in Louisiana." *Institute on Mineral Law* 8 (1961): 72–87.

Trice, William E. "Eulogy: Charles A. Reynard." *Louisiana Law Review* 19 (1958): 245–47.

Tullis, Robert Lee. "Louisiana's Legal System Reappraised." *Tulane Law Review* 12 (1937): 113–19.

Updegraff, Clarence M. *Arbitration and Labor Relations.* 3rd ed. Washington, D.C.: Bureau of National Affairs, 1970.

Verrall, Harold E., and Gail Boreman Bird. *Cases and Materials on California Community Property.* St. Paul: West, 1983.

Wallach, Kate. *Louisiana Legal Research Manual.* Baton Rouge: Louisiana State University Institute of Continuing Education, 1972.

———. *Research in Louisiana Law.* Baton Rouge: Louisiana State University Press, 1958.

———. *Bibliographical History of Louisiana Civil Law Sources.* Baton Rouge: Louisiana State Law Institute, 1955.

Wheaton, Carl C. *Cases on Federal Procedure.* Chicago: Callaghan, 1921.

Wigmore, John Henry. "Louisiana: The Story of Its Jurisprudence." *American Law Review* 22 (1888): 890–902.

Wilkerson, Marcus M. *Thomas Duckett Boyd: The Story of a Southern Educator.* Baton Rouge: Louisiana State University Press, 1935.

Williams, T. Harry. *Huey Long.* New York: Alfred A. Knopf, 1969.

Wollett, Donald H. "Race Relations." *Louisiana Law Review* 21 (1960): 85–108.

Womack, Beverly Gordon. "Editorial: Growth of the Law Library Book Collection." *Louisiana Law Review* 6 (1945): 264–67.

Yiannopoulos, Athanassios N. "Brokerage, Mandate, and Agency in Louisiana: Civilian Tradition and Modern Practice." *Louisiana Law Review* 19 (1959): 777–812.

———. "Rights of the Usufructuary: Louisiana and Comparative Law." *Louisiana Law Review* 27 (1967): 668–755.

———. "Usufruct: General Principles." *Louisiana Law Review* 27 (1967): 369–422.

———. "Predial Servitudes: General Principles—Louisiana and Comparative Law." *Louisiana Law Review* 29 (1968): 1–45.

———. *Louisiana Civil Law Treatise.* Vol. 2, *Property.* St. Paul: West, 1967; Vol. 3, *Personal Servitudes.* St. Paul: West, 1968. 2nd ed. 1978.

Newspapers and Magazines

Baton Rouge Morning Advocate.

Civilian, The. Published by the Louisiana State University Student Bar Association.

Louisiana State University Alumni News. Also published variously as *Alumnus* and *Louisiana State University Quarterly.*

LSU Law. Published by the Paul M. Hebert Law Center, Louisiana State University, 1983–.
New Orleans Times-Picayune.
Reveille (also published at various times as *Daily Reveille* and *Summer Reveille*).
Shreveport Journal.
Whangdoodle, The.

Public Documents

Biennial Report of the President (1935–37). Baton Rouge: Louisiana State University, 1937.
Board of Supervisors v. Wilson, 92 F. Supp. 986 (1950).
Board of Supervisors v. Ludley, 252 F. 2d. 372 (5th Cir. 1958).
Documents and Minutes of the General Faculty of the University of Texas: Report of the Special George W. Stumberg Memorial Resolution Committee Filed Jan. 14, 1965. Austin: University of Texas, n.d.
Law School Bulletin. Baton Rouge: Louisiana State University, 1906–.
La. Acts. 1884, No. 43.
La. Acts 1908, No. 227.
La. Acts 1924, No. 113.
La. Const. (1845), Art. 137.
La. Const. (1879), Art. 230.
Louisiana Constitution of 1921. Baton Rouge: Thos. J. Moran's Sons, 1955.
Louisiana State University Law Register 1977. Baton Rouge: Louisiana State University Law Center, 1977.
Louisiana State University and Agricultural and Mechanical College. *A Survey Report by a Commission of the American Council on Education*. Washington, D.C.: American Council on Education, 1940.
LSU and You: A Handbook for the Faculty and Staff of Louisiana State University. Baton Rouge: Louisiana State University, 1955.
Louisiana State University System. *Financial Report for the Fiscal Year Ended June 30, 1959*. Baton Rouge: Louisiana State University, 1959.
———. *Financial Report for the Fiscal Year Ended June 30, 1964*. Baton Rouge: Louisiana State University, 1964.
Louisiana State University, Paul M. Hebert Law Center. *Self-Study Report, 1988–94*. Baton Rouge: Paul M. Hebert Law Center, 1994.

BIBLIOGRAPHY

Ludley v. Board of Supervisors, 150 F. Supp. 900 (E.D. La. 1957).
SGA v. LSU, 264 So.2d 916 (La. 1972).

Other

Clark Hulings (1922–): Master American Painter. <http:/www.tfaoi.com/aa/laa/laa11.htm> (10/16/2001)
Social Security Death Index. Familytreemaker.com.
http://www.westegg.com/inflation/infl.cgi, Jan. 28, 2002.

UNPUBLISHED SOURCES

Manuscripts

Board of Supervisors of Louisiana State University. . . . Minutes. Hill Memorial Library, Louisiana State University, Baton Rouge.
Flory, Ira S., to United States Attorney General John G. Sargent, January 6, 1928, LSU Law School Archives, Box 58.
Hebert, P. Michael. Curriculum Study, 1974. LSU Law School Archives, Hargrave Papers, Box 1, Folder 1.
Lile, William Minor, Dean of the University of Virginia Law Department, to Professor Ira S. Flory, 25 February 1925. Lee Hargrave Personal Papers.
Memorandum by Curriculum Committee B to Law School Dean and Faculty Concerning Civil Law, 25 March 1968. Lee Hargarve Personal Papers.
Minutes of the LSU Law School Faculty. Chancellor's Office, Paul M. Hebert Law Center, Louisiana State University, Baton Rouge.
Official Transcript 10743. Student Records, Paul M. Hebert Law Center. Louisiana State University, Baton Rouge.
Personnel Files. Hebert Law Center. Louisiana State University, Baton Rouge.
Stumberg, George W. "Government in Louisiana During the French and Spanish Regimes." Senior thesis, Louisiana State University, 1909.

Other

Various interviews by Nina Pugh and others. LSU Law School Oral History Series. T. Harry Williams Center for Oral History Collection, LSU Libraries, Baton Rouge.

INDEX OF NAMES

Abadie, James F., 206, 210
Abbott, Hirschel T., Jr., 219
Abell, Edward C., Jr., 207
Abney, Marguerite, 98
Adams, Gregory B., 262
Aguilar, Juan F., 262
Aleman, Roberto, 116
Alexander, John Bentley, 241
Allen, Durrelle L., Jr., 243
Allen, Lyndon B., 97
Allen, Oscar K., 65, 66
Anderson, Charles, 239
Anderson, Lawrence R., 206
Apperson, Priscilla F., 194
Armstrong, Barbara Nachtrieb, 103
Armstrong, Willie, 243
Arruebarrena, Dian T., 262
Ashmun, John, 5
Atkinson, Thomas W., 59, 64

Babin, James L., 166
Bacon, Aubrey, 113
Bagner, Hans G., 194
Bagni, Bruce N., 220
Baiamonte, Joseph J., 202, 233
Baier, Paul R., 217, 223
Bailey, George J., 95
Bailey, James J., 111, 134, 195, 262
Bailey, Kenneth J., 97, 110
Baker, John S., Jr., 219
Baker, Newman Freece, 48, 55–57, 87, 110

Banfield, Kenneth, 99, 103
Baranco, Juanita P., 236, 243
Barham, Charles E., 98
Barham, Mack E., 125, 188, 233, 261
Barnett, C. A., 210
Baudoin, Jean-Louis, 194, 226
Bauer, Theo W., 55
Beck, Mrs. William D., 163
Behymer, E. Hugh, 93
Belanger, Homer, 97
Benjamin, Judah Philip, 4, 5, 28
Bennett, Dale Elmer: advisor on ALI's Model Penal Code, 134–35, 251; joins faculty, 79–80; helps draft Louisiana Criminal Code, 110, 116, 134; and Louisiana Code of Criminal Procedure, 135; and numerical grading, 146, 228; on Dean Beutel, 70; on Dean Hebert, 73; on Huey Long and *Whangdoodle* incident, 67; and post-WWII accelerated program, 116–17; retirement of, 225; mentioned, 19, 62, 86, 88, 94, 105, 106, 113, 119, 124, 142, 155–57, 160, 164, 174–75, 190, 192, 208, 225, 226, 231
Bennett, J. M., 102
Benoit, Carroll A., 22
Benton, Fred, Sr., 13
Bentson, Lloyd, 218
Berrigan, Helen G., 261
Berry, Albert T., 239
Beutel, Frederick K.: and civil-law analogies in negotiable-instruments law, 69; joins

315

INDEX OF NAMES

faculty, 67–68, 74, 79–88; resignation of, 71–72; and social science and law, 69; student impressions of, 69–70; mentioned, 92–93, 95–96, 117, 143, 194, 253, 254, 263
Beychok, Shelley, 161
Biddle, Francis, 110
Bilbe, George L., 227, 262
Bird, Cecil, 38
Bird, Mary Herron, 36, 38, 199
Bird, Thomas, 38
Bisconti, Giuseppe, 164
Blackshear, David A.: joins faculty, 27–28; Flory on, 27; student impressions of, 28; mentioned, 16, 37, 39
Blakesley, Christopher L., 220, 249–50
Blanchard, Jean Antoine, 102, 103
Blanchard, Newton C., 16, 27
Blanche, Fred A., 54, 124, 261
Blass, William J., 97, 261
Blum, Thomas R., 191, 202
Bockrath, Joseph T., 219–20
Bodenheimer, Bert, 95
Bodenheimer, G. M., 99
Boland, Gary Lee, 232
Bonnette, Michael J., 236
Boone, John, 53
Borah, Wayne G., 95, 261
Bordelon, Maxwell, 99
Boyd, Annie, 9
Boyd, Thomas D.: and admission of women, 9; early expansion of university under, 9–10; resignation of, 59; mentioned, 8, 12, 14, 18, 51, 52, 55, 74, 108
Bradford, Donald E., 210
Brady, James J., 204, 261
Breaux, John B., 201, 261
Breaux, Joseph A., 12
Breazeale, H. Payne, 55
Bronson, William, 95
Brooks, Thomas Overton, 53, 261
Broussard, Andre C., 210
Broussard, J. F., 37

Broussard, Jerome A., 159
Brown, Daniel Scott, 210
Brown, James, 2
Brumfield, Alva, 210
Bryan, William Jennings, 27
Bugea, James, 88, 96–97, 135
Burden, John C., Jr., 157
Burgess, Jack, 112
Burns, Odis Herschel, 46, 48, 57
Burton, Cleve, 126

Caffery, Patrick Thomson, 261
Caire, Agna, 243
Caldwell, Jack C., 128
Campbell, Hodges B., 59
Campbell, John T., 46, 55
Campbell, Richard, 142
Campbell, Sarah J., 243
Cangelosi, Theodore F., 80, 95, 101, 111, 136, 158
Cannon, Raymond L., 236
Carmouche, Eddie, 111
Carpenter, John T., 55
Carriere, Ike, 54
Carriere, Oliver P., 99
Carver, M. Hampton, 202
Cavanaugh, Karl W., 170, 206
Centola, Lawrence J., Jr., 239
Chamallas, Martha, 219–20, 240, 262
Champagne, Sidney A., 128, 199, 220–21
Chandler, Walter, 54
Chaney, Bailey E., 186
Chappuis, Richard D., Jr., 209
Charles, Pierre S., 152
Charmatz, Jan Paul, 133, 140–41
Chastain, Merritt B., 175
Chinn, Bob, 100
Chretien, David M., 236
Claiborne, Ian, 152
Clark, Charles E., 91
Clark, Daniel, 126
Clark, David S., 219–20

INDEX OF NAMES

Clayton, Marshall, 161
Clifford, Donald F., Jr., 227
Cohen, Harry, 174, 194
Colby, Leavenworth, 82, 86, 93–94, 105
Cole, Evelyn, 116
Cole, Luther F., 128, 211, 261
Collins, Robert F., 152–53, 191, 235, 261
Colomb, Paul H., 237
Cooks, Sylvia R., 236, 243
Coon, J. Norman, 55
Correro, Anthony J., 206
Corwin, Edward S., 110
Cotton, Albert H., 119
Cotton, Davis, 54, 55
Courville, Cindy, 243
Cowan, Thomas Anthony, 82–83, 87–88, 96, 105–106
Crabites, Pierre: joins faculty, 82, 83–84; on his students, 84; mentioned, 68, 88, 105
Craig, Frank S., Jr.: on Dean Beutel's resignation, 71; on Professor Cowan, 83; mentioned, 97, 103, 135
Craighead, Craig, 84
Craighead, Jean G., 84, 97, 103, 238
Crane, Richard G., 239
Crawford, William E.: translation of French Code of Civil Procedure, 223; mentioned, 164, 182, 197
Crepeau, Paul A., 227
Crowe, William L., 227
Cueto-Rua, Julio C., 219
Curet, Louis D., 128
Currie, J. Hector, 181, 206, 216, 224, 254
Currier, Thomas S., 180, 205–06
Curry, Robert L., III, 163
Cutshaw, Leila Obier, 191

Daggett, Damon Devan, 46, 96
Daggett, David, 5
Daggett, Harriet Spiller: Leadership Day featured speaker, 138; and Daggett Memorial Fountain, 199; declining health of, 135, 178;

joins faculty, 46–47; appointment to federal judiciary urged, 85; Hulings's portrait of, 157; idiosyncratic grading of, 258; and International Congress of Comparative Law, 85; and Mid-Century White House Conference on Children and Youth, 134; "Most Intelligent Coed," 55; opposition to extra classes, 146; retirement of, 178; twenty-year anniversary, 135; started Yale J.S.D. tradition, 47; mentioned, 52, 57, 61, 62, 68, 74, 76-77, 80, 83, 86, 96, 98, 100, 103, 105, 106, 107, 110–11, 113, 119, 121–22, 130, 133, 137, 149, 155–57, 251
Dainow, Joseph: represents LSU in American Society of Comparative Law, 142; on civil law versus common law, 254; extra classes, 146; joins faculty, 86–87; Fulbright grant/ Guggenheim Fellowship, 188; on Dean Hebert, 73; retirement of, 225; mentioned, 68, 88, 92, 96, 105–06, 113, 117, 119, 121–22, 131, 135, 140, 141, 149, 155–57, 175, 176, 187, 191, 201, 203, 208, 215, 230, 235, 245
Dakin, Melvin G.: joins faculty, 118; and Louisiana expropriation law, 183, 191; consultant to Louisiana Tax Commission and Louisiana Public Service Commission, 135; on Beutel's resignation, 71; retirement of, 225; mentioned, 73, 88, 92, 108, 119, 130, 132–33, 147, 155–57, 197, 209, 216
Dameron, Claiborne, 102
D'Amico, Sam, 70, 100–01
Dannel, Dennis J., 236
Darsey, Glen, 53
Daspit, Alice Greenburg, 82, 86, 93, 106, 120
Dauphin, William M., Jr., 236
David, René, 19, 142
Davis, James D., 210
Davis, Ronald L., 51
Dawkins, Benjamin C., Jr., 95, 101, 261
Day, Winston R., 213, 219–20
De Kerstrat, Grivart Françoise, 227
DeBessonet, Cary, 201, 262

317

INDEX OF NAMES

Decuir, Winston, 236
Denbo, Beverly, 97
Dennis, James L., 207, 261
Derr, Jacque D., 238
Diamond, Alfreda Sellers, 262
Dickson, Lance E., 234, 262
Dixon, John A., 256–57
Doherty, Rebecca F., 261
Domengeaux, Jerome E., 193
Doré, Hugo, 33
Dozier, Gilbert L., 202
Drehr, Gladys, 234
Drestler, Claus Jurgen, 182
Drew, Jean Talley, 237
Dry, Elton, 210
Dué, Paul H., 206
Duhon, Bernard F., 241
Duncan, Nora K., 238
Duncan, Norma Mayo, 135
Dupree, Tom, 54
Duval, Stanwood R., Jr., 261

Easterly, Ernest S., III, 262
Edwards, Edwin W.: and law school funding, 213–14; on post-WWII faculty, 121; mentioned, 126, 260
Edwards, Francis, 111
Ehmke, Horst, 143
Eisenhower, Dwight David, 116
Elam, E. J., 34
Elkins, Gary, 242
Ellis, Frederick W., 175, 176, 185, 230, 247
Ensminger, Art, 239
Eubanks, Cecil L., 236
Evans, Melvin, 99, 101

Farrar, Edgar H., 16–17
Fenet, Robert W., 236
Ferri, Enrico, 18
Fitzgerald, John R., 201
Fleming, Walter Lynwood, 17, 21
Flory, Ira Samuel: acting dean, 67, 73; Dean Hebert on, 28; death of, 131–32; joins faculty, 28; Flory Trials, 210–11, 243–44; on 1924 library collection campaign, 43–44, 51; on Blackshear, 27; Order of Coif, 115, 127; salary concerns, 51–52; student impressions of, 28; "two-stack" grading, 258; and university committee service, 45; YMCA moonlighting, 50; mentioned, 29, 37, 38, 48, 55, 57, 61–63, 70, 74, 81, 86–88, 94, 96, 100, 105–06, 112–13, 119–20, 124, 138, 216, 249, 251
Flory, Mrs. I. S., 28
Foot, Henry S., 1
Ford, Gerald, 226
Fordham, Jefferson B., 106–107, 109, 110, 113, 117, 142, 143, 227
Forrester, William Ray, 180
Foster, Bonnie, 243
Foster, Murphy J., 217
Fournet, John B., 95, 141, 178, 261
French, Arden O., 124
Frey, Fred C., 44, 53, 108
Fuller, James R. "Yank," 54
Fuller, Wilbur C., 236
Fulmer, Mary, 98
Fussell, Howard R., 191

Gahagan, Russell E., 56
Gaharan, Phillip S., 21
Garrett, David I., 123
Garrett, J. David, 238
Garrett, John, 154
Garro, Alejandro, 262
Garsaud, Marcel, Jr., 227
Gary, Leon, 168, 211
Gellhorn, Walter, 142
Gerard, Richard E., 67, 87–88, 101
Germain, Claire M., 262
Gervey, John G., 141
Ghetti, Michelle Ward, 262
Gibbens, Daniel G., 227
Girod, Clinton S., 43
Givens, Lloyd, 236

Goff, A. K., Jr., 111
Gold, Leo, 49
Goldman, Solomon S., 157
Golson, Gordon, 95
Gordon, Jack M., 261
Gordon, Kenneth E., Jr., 202
Gore, Roy Cletis, 46, 48, 50, 52, 56, 57, 61–63, 80, 105
Gottlieb, Lewis, 158
Grafton, Hoye, 55
Gravel, Camille F., 256
Gray, Ernestine S., 236, 237, 243
Gray, Gammiel B., 153, 209, 236, 237
Gray, James A., II, 218, 232, 237
Greco, Cyrus A., 97, 196
Green, Leon, 91
Greenburg, Leonard, 76, 82, 86
Griffith, Ordell, 221
Grymes, John R., 3
Gueno, Harry Williams, 32
Guidry, Kirby J., 175
Guillory, Robert K., 163
Gunby, A. A., 16

Hackman, Gordon, 209
Hair, Mansford T., 36
Hair, William Ivy, 60
Hall, A. Oakley, 5
Hall, Jerome: and International Congress of Comparative Law, 85; joins faculty, 80–81; mentioned, 76, 77, 86, 88, 194, 250, 252
Hall, Luther E., 27
Hall, Pike, Jr., 261
Hall, William M., 95, 101, 105
Hamilton, Leo C., 237
Hamiter, Joe B., 53, 261
Hanchey, Ben R., 239
Hardin, A. Edward, 244
Hardy, George W., III: implements graduate program in marine resources law, 192; as mineral code reporter, 179, 251; mentioned, 170, 173, 176, 190, 215–16, 225–26, 230, 231, 233

Hargrave, W. Lee: and 1973 Constitutional Convention, 222, 247, 251, 259; and 1974 Tunis IDEF conference, 224; address to Mineral Law Institute, 223; grade statistics, 259; "Hard Ass Index," 259; joins faculty, 183; and Vietnam legal reform program, 192–93; mentioned, 175–76, 178, 191
Harper, Fowler Vincent: and 1937 International Congress of Comparative Law, 85; joins faculty, 84–85; mentioned, 82, 86, 105, 133
Harper, Peggy, 120, 221
Harrell, Thomas A., 140, 218, 223, 244
Harris, Rufus C., 78
Harris, Thomas H., 10
Harrison, Genie Taylor, 118
Harrison, Milton M.: deanship, 139–40; joins faculty, 88, 117–18; and new-building committee, 197–98; on Dean Beutel, 70–71; on Professor Cotton, 119; on Professor Cowan, 83; on student attendance, 147–48; and post-WWII students, 123; mentioned, 90, 130, 150, 162, 179, 183, 214–15, 222, 230, 251
Harrison, Robert, 210
Hart, William O., 16, 44
Harvey, Eldon T., 211
Havard, William C., 170, 211
Hawkins, Melvin L., 237, 243
Hawkland, William D.: as Bailey Lecturer, 195; mentioned, 158, 263
Hawthorne, Frank W.: on Dean Tullis, 21; mentioned, 53, 261
Hebert, P. Michael: and 1970s curriculum study, 228; mentioned, 206, 218
Hebert, Paul Macarius: and AALS report debate, 177; 1962 illness of, 190; anti-Catholic sentiment against, 108; changes since Dean Beutel, 159; and *Civil Code Rally Songs*, 166–67; and class sections, 146; and curricula, 145, 148; deanship, 72–73, 109, 138–39; death of, 247, 251, 254, 263; during desegregation years, 153–54; Development Memo-

randa #1 and #2, 175–76; and establishment of Louisiana State Law Institute, 79; joins faculty, 72–73; and fiftieth anniversary of law school, 141; and Florence Molaison, 222; historical sketch of law school, 41; naming of law center after, 247; and new-building drive, 196–97; judge at Nuremberg Trials, 119; on civil law versus common law, 254; on clinical programs, 229–30; on Dean Beutel's resignation, 72; on Dean McMahon's leadership during desegregation, 153; on graduation rate, 160; on Flory, 28; on McMahon as student, 53; on "package courses," 170–71; on Tullis, 20; on separate commencement, 205; organization and administration under, 246–47; and law school philosophy, 14; private law practice, 138, 144–45; president of 1929 senior class, 55; Rubin on, 139–40; student impressions of, 200; and STUD investigation, 207–08; and Tidelands litigation, 196–97; and Vietnam faculty deferments, 183; WWII military service of, 113; mentioned, 56, 68, 70, 76, 80, 83, 87, 88, 92, 96, 97, 101, 106–09, 111, 113, 115–19, 121, 125, 129, 178, 186, 202, 215, 222

Henry, Robert Llewellyn, Jr.: first common-law faculty member, 18; interest in LSU football, 32; student recruiting in *Reveille*, 33; mentioned, 21, 37, 39, 83, 140

Herget, G. Caldwell, 54–55, 157
Herold, Sidney L., 99
Hersbergen, Ronald L., 217, 219, 220
Hershman, Marc, 216
Hickman, John A., 95
Higgins, Archibald T., 95, 99
Hilpert, Elmer E., 86
Hirsch, Aubrey, 100
Hodges, Campbell Blackshear, 59, 107–08, 112
Holder, Horace, 95
Holliday, James S., Jr., 206
Hood, John T., Jr., 10, 226
Hope, Robert, 55

Howell, Boatner Roland, 35, 36
Howerton, Huey Blair, Jr., 140, 155–56
Hubert, Leon D., Jr., 165, 187
Hughes, Albert T., 101
Hughes, Evans Charles, 27
Hughes, Thomas Welburn, 25–26, 34, 39
Hulings, Clark (artist), 157–58
Humphrey, Hubert H., 99, 100, 195
Hunter, Edwin K., 210
Hunter, John A., 196, 246
Hynes, John W., 73

Ireland, Gordon: and 1937 International Congress of Comparative Law, 85; joins faculty, 81–82; mentioned, 76, 80, 86, 105
Irving, Steven M., 240, 242

Jalowicz, Herbert F., 143
James, Fleming, Jr., 133
James, Robert G., 261
Jaworski, Leon, 232
Jeanclos, Raymond, 164
Jefferson, William J., 237
Jenkins, Diane A., 238
Jenkins, Louis E., 238
Jennings, Robert B., 50, 98
Jensen, Mary Brandt, 262
Jewell, J. P., 95
Joffrion, Winston K., 55
Johnson, Anthony J., 243
Johnson, Bernette Joshua, 153, 209, 236, 261
Johnson, Fred, 53
Johnson, James M., 207
Johnson, Michael T., 226
Johnston, Douglas, 195
Johnston, H. Alston, III: and 1974 Tunis IDEF conference, 224; joins faculty, 217–18; mentioned, 19, 202, 205, 206
Johnston, J. Bennett, 237, 261
Jones, Alva, 112
Jones, Alvin, 243
Jones, Henry Craig, 44

INDEX OF NAMES

Jones, Robert B., 54
Jones, Sam H., 108
Jones, W. Carruth, 95
Jones, Ward T., 98
Joseph, Cheney C.: joins faculty, 216–17; helps produce *Louisiana Judge's Benchbook* and *Louisiana Law Enforcement Handbook*, 224
Joseph, Mary Terrell, 237
Juergensmeyer, Julian C., 226
Juneau, Patrick A., Jr., 161, 210–11

Kane, Susan, 234
Kean, Eileen Murphy, 120
Kean, R. Gordon, 186
Kelly, David S., 238
Kelly, Joseph Ignatius: first regular faculty member, 17–18; on shortcomings of two-year curriculum, 22; mentioned, 20, 25, 32, 39
Kelly, Susan R., 238
Kelly, William G., Jr., 164
Kennedy, Kemble K., 55, 56, 63–67, 77–79
Kennon, Robert F., 53, 211, 260
Kerameus, K. D., 227
Kernan, William F., 12
Kilbourne, Richard H., 101, 241
Kimball, Catherine D., 261
Kimball, George A., 206
Kimmell, David C., 239
Kitchens, Graydon K., Jr., 205
Kizer, Roland, 54–55
Klein, Michael R., 175, 178, 183, 185
Kleinpeter, Robert L. "Buck," 142, 210
Kline, William F., 162
Knight, H. Gary, 185, 192, 223, 247

Laborde, John, 116
Laclavere, Suzanne, 103
Lafleur, Catherine L., 262
Lamonica, P. Raymond: joins faculty, 217–18; helps produce *Louisiana Judge's Benchbook* and *Louisiana Law Enforcement Handbook*, 224
Landry, Frances Leggio, 85, 98, 101, 114
Landry, Jules, 50
Landry, Paul B.: on Dean Beutel's resignation, 71; on James Barclay Smith, 50; mentioned, 81
Landry, Wilfred J., Jr., 112
Lane, Horace, 115
Lane, Margaret Taylor, 120
Lanier, Leah Devall, 141, 208, 221–22
Lanier, Walter I., 107, 111
Lassalle, Leo J., 104
Lastrapes, Henry, Jr., 102
LaVern, John F., 239
Lawson, Warner, Jr., 227
Lazarus, Abigail, 243
Lazarus, Carlos Enrique: joins faculty, 109–10; completes translation of Aubry and Rau treatise, 223; mentioned, 96, 133, 138, 175, 179, 215, 251
Leach, Anthony Claude, Jr., 261
Lear, Elmo C., 164
Leavall, Jerome F., 226
LeBlanc, Peggy, 243
LeBlanc, Sam, 142
Lebowitz, Leon, 141
Leche, Richard W., 60, 73, 92, 106
Lee, Richard E., 211
Leigh, Thomas W., 53, 158, 178
L'Enfant, Howard W., Jr., 185, 206, 219, 226, 247
LeSage, Joe C., Jr., 164
Lessley, George Pote, 32
LeStage, Henry Oscar, Jr., 99
LeVan, N. Gerald, 217, 247
Levasseur, Alain A.: and Aix-en-Provence study program, 232; associate director of Center of Civil Law Studies, 224; joins faculty, 220–21
Levin, A. Leo, 227

INDEX OF NAMES

Lewis, Hoffman, 36
Lewis, J. Bradley, 229
Limpens, Jean, 143
Lindsay, Wendell G., 206, 207
Lindsey, Coleman, 53
Linh, Tran Van, 193
Litton, Dupre G., 115
Litvinoff, Saul: director of Center of Civil Law Studies, 224; obligations research, 189, 224, 252; mentioned, 175, 182, 193
Liuzza, B. Roy, 166–67
Livingston, Edward, 3–4
Lloyd, C. Jerre, 195
Lombard, Homer, 112
Long, Earl K., 73, 136, 155, 196
Long, Frank, 34
Long, Gillis William: on LSU education, 127; on Professor Shestack, 133; mentioned, 160–61, 164, 197, 211, 261
Long, Huey P.: 1935 LSU expansion goals of, 69; AALS criticisms of, 78; appointment of Dean Beutel, 67; campus visits, 101; censorship of *Reveille*, 60; effect of death on LSU probation investigation, 77–78; and Law School, 7; Long era, 59–61; mentioned, 48, 63-66, 73, 79. *See also* Kennedy, Kemble K.; *Whangdoodle* incident
Long, Julius, 7
Long, Ralph, 242
Long, Russell: on J. Denson Smith, 102; and Order of the Coif, 116; mentioned, 80, 100, 102, 112, 115, 207, 261
Long, Speedy O., 239, 261
Loret, Joseph Arthur, 47–48, 56, 61–63, 85, 94
Lottinger, Morris L., Jr., 174
Loussouarn, Yvon, 143
Lowery, Richard, 161
Lyles, William Murray "Buffalo," 31
Lyons, Charleton, 211

Macleod, Henry Rhoderich, 32
Madden, Ragan, 111
Madison, John M., 157
Magbee, Byron D., 238
Magruder, Allan Bowie, 3
Makar, John, 100, 112
Malmstrom, Abe, 143
Malone, Wex Smathers: 1976 AALS Prosser award, 225; AALS presidency/executive committee, 187–88; and restatement (2d) of the Law of Torts, 135; ALI membership, 138; Boyd professorship, 187; chairman of law faculty committee, 109; joins faculty, 87; influence on Louisiana tort law, 187–88; and Myra Clark Gaines case, 126; and no-fault car insurance concept, 133; on Dean Beutel, 70–71; on civil law versus common law, 254; retirement of, 225; mentioned, 73, 94, 97, 105, 110, 113, 117, 119, 121–22, 127, 129, 142, 155–57, 175, 194, 216, 251, 252
Mangham, Marston Arthur, 31
Maraist, Frank L.: *Civil Code Rally Songs*, 166–67, 176; mentioned, 219, 223
Marsh, John S., 233
Marks, Paul, Jr., 202
Martin, Clift, 36
Martin, Patrick L., 220–21
Martin, Virginia L., 126
Matox, Mary, 222
Matthews, George, 210
Matthews, Orin F., 55
Mayda, Jaro, 134
Mayeaux, Donald L., 175, 191
McCain, Wilbur T. "Brandy," 116
McCann, Dayton, 102
McClendon, Charles, 206
McCormick, Charles T., 115
McCoy, Kenneth D., Jr., 206
McCrery, James O., 261
McDougal, Myres S., 195
McGivney, Eugene J., 10–11, 31
McGough, Lucy, 250
McIntosh, Phillip L., 262
McKeag, Edwin Corwin, 25, 39

INDEX OF NAMES

McKeever, Kent, 262
McKeithen, John J.: on Alvin Rubin, 115; on Dean Hebert, J. Denson Smith, and Wex Malone, 115; refusal to abandon old law school, 197; and Tidelands litigation, 196–97; mentioned, 211, 256, 260
McKenzie, W. Shelby, 186
McKinnis, E. Drew, 164
McMahon, Henry George: Boyd professorship, 187; city-parish attorney of Baton Rouge, 120; deanship, 139; appointed to Commission on International Rules of Judicial Procedure, 138; and Louisiana Code of Civil Procedure, 133, 135; and numerical grading, 169; on hats-and-canes tradition, 209; mentioned, 53, 68, 86, 88, 95–96, 105–106, 113, 117, 119, 120–121, 129, 145–46, 152, 155–57, 163, 208, 210, 215, 251
McManis, Charles R., 220–21
McNeir, Waldo F., 155
McSween, Harold Barnett, 128, 261
Mengis, Warren: and desegregation, 153; on Flory's evidence class, 131–32; mentioned, 128
Mentz, Henry A., 261
Mersky, Roy, 234
Meunier, Jean, 103
Meyers, William M., 124, 125, 126
Middleton, Beverly, 111
Middleton, Troy H.: on Robert Lee Tullis, 20; mentioned, 73, 108, 139, 153, 155, 162, 178
Millar, Robert W., 86
Miller, Ben R., Jr.: says 1927 class "one of best ever," 54–55; on LSU education and Dean Flory, 44; mentioned, 45, 157, 158, 174, 186
Miller, Minos D., Jr., 213–14
Mims, Samuel Stewart, 31
Minor, Donald R., 237, 243
Mitchell, Bessie, 120
Mitchell, Lansing I., 261
Mizell, Walter H., 219
Molaison, Florence H., 114, 184, 208, 221–22

Moncure, Effie, 98
Monroe, Frank A., 7
Monroe, James: Long selection as LSU president, 59–60; mentioned, 73
Moore, Henson William, III, 168, 209, 211, 261
Morgan, Cecil: on 1912 students, 33; on Tulane and LSU law schools, 260
Morgan, D. D., 36
Morgan, Earl A., 112, 233–34
Morgan, Turner B., 111
Morial, Ernest, 133, 152–53, 208, 235
Morrison, deLesseps S., 101, 111, 211
Morrison, Phoebe, 103
Morse, Wayne, 67
Moyse, Hermann: WWI service and honors, 37–38; mentioned, 11, 32, 33
Murchison, Kenneth M., 220–21
Murov, Mark G., 240
Murrell, James R., III, 178
Murrill, Paul W., 222
Myers, Sidney, 111

Naranjo, Lourdes, 243
Neibel, John B., 227
Newman, Raleigh C., 205, 206
Nicholson, J. W., 36–37
Nicholson, Joanna W., 243
Noble, W. O. "Bulldog," 116

Odom, Frederick M., 95
Odom, John, Jr., 230, 238
O'Meara, Margaret A., 191
O'Neal, F. Hodge, 96, 97, 110, 195, 227, 262
O'Neill, Charles Austin, Jr., 53–54
Oppenheim, Leonard, 135
O'Quin, Leo, 35
O'Quinn, Claude, 96, 97
Osakwe, Christopher, 227

Parker, John M., 41, 59
Parker, John V., 261
Pascal, Robert Anthony: urges abolishing

law-review student editorial staff, 234; on civil law versus common law, 254–55; on curricula and grading, 146–49, 169, 188–89; joins faculty, 133; Fulbright grants, 188–89; mentioned, 74, 91, 117, 119, 121, 129, 155–56, 164, 175, 178, 180, 195, 201, 208, 232, 244
Patin, Charles L., Jr., 236
Patterson, Michael, 239
Payne, Lutrill Amos, 152
Pearson, Richard N., 227
Penney, Norman, 195
Pepper, Horace, 116
Percy, Jean L., 115
Perez, Leander H., Jr., 128
Perkins, Mary Bird, 38, 98, 199
Perkins, Paul Dorsey, 38, 199
Perkins, Robert "Rocky" (artist), 158
Peters, Walter, 112
Pettway, James R., 206
Phelps, Paul C., 95
Phillips, Tom, 210
Phillips, W. M., 51
Picou, Cynthia, 262
Pierce, Judy, 243
Pipkin, Charles W., 47, 60, 85, 99, 100
Pitcher, Mrs. Charlie Holcomb, 103
Pitcher, Sargent, Jr., 112, 115, 242
Plaeger, Frederick J., II, 241
Plant, Marcus L., 226
Politz, Henry A.: award of Ph.T. degree to wife of, 162–63; *Civil Code Rally Songs*, 166–67; on 1950s faculty, 129–31, 227, 261
Politz, Mrs. Marie, 162–63
Polozola, Frank J., 261
Ponder, Amos Lee, 33, 71, 95, 261
Ponder, Elven E., 186
Porteous, G. Thomas, 261
Porterfield, John, 242
Porterie, Gaston L., 261
Pos, Anton G., 182
Posner, Harvey, 115
Pound, Roscoe, 85, 91, 96

Powell, Thomas Reed, 99
Powers, Brunette, 86
Prejean, Frederick, 243
Prescott, Amelie Ellis, 52
Prescott, Arthur T.: and establishment of law school, 14; first faculty, 17; mentioned, 20, 21, 23, 37, 46, 50
Prestridge, Rogers M., 201–02, 209
Prevost, John B., 3
Price, Frank J., 108
Price, Karen Lee, 243
Propst, Gordon M., 239
Prosser, William L., 87, 97
Pugh, George W.: selected for worldwide comparative study of judicial administration, 189; on faculty, 132, 136, 183; and grade statistics, 259; and "journalistic" faculty minutes, 186–87; *Louisiana Evidence Law* treatise, 223; and numerical grading, 169–70; mentioned, 127, 128, 130, 160, 175, 180, 192, 197, 210, 215, 230, 231, 232, 251
Pugh, John F., Jr., 202
Pugh, Robert G., 126, 137
Pugh, Thomas B., 210
Pugliese, Giovanni, 194
Purvis, G. Frank, 50, 67, 116

Quick, Charles W., 226
Quienalty, Charley, 166

Rabel, Ernst, 121
Rainach, Willie M., 154
Ratcliff, Betty Ann Gremillion, 116
Rault, Gerald A., Jr., 217, 230
Rausch, Joseph W., 210
Ray, Gail E. H., 237, 243
Read, Elaine Goodale, 18
Reddoch, James W., 201, 239, 240
Reed, Albert G., 21
Reed, Rex, 165
Reynard, Charles A.: and 1960 curriculum

INDEX OF NAMES

committee, 148; eulogy on, 136; mentioned, 119, 130–31, 155–57, 160, 216
Roberts, Helen "Ginger," 244
Roberts, Robert, Jr., 50, 53–54
Robertson, David W., 166, 173, 180, 183, 207, 225, 262
Robichaux, John F., 204
Roddy, Floyd A., 209
Rogers, Jack J., 164
Rogers, Wynne G., 95
Roland, Robert L., 186
Romero, Clarence E., 126
Rostow, Eugene V., 141
Roundtree, Gordon E., 206
Roy, Anthony J., 53
Rubin, Alvin B.: adjunct, 118, 123; associate professor, 136; deanship consideration, 139–40; joins faculty, 118; on Dean Hebert, 139–40; on Thomas Cowan, 83; mentioned, 103, 112, 133, 174, 176, 186, 203, 210, 219, 261
Rush, Richard O., 114
Russell, Sera H., 243
Ryland, B. Dexter, 209

Sachse, Harry R., 166
Sachse, Victor A., 53–54, 158
Sadler, Buck, 210
Sanders, Henry, 191
Sanders, Joe W., 81, 111, 261
Sargent, John G., 27
Sarpy, Leon, 187
Saunders, E. D., 12, 16
Scharff, Moses C., 22
Schill, Golda, 52
Schmidt, Gustavus, 5–6
Schmitthoff, Clive M., 194
Schonekas, Kyle, 244
Schrumpf, Oliver, 242
Schulingkamp, Oliver P., 94
Schwing, Charles E., 31
Seago, John E., 240
Seavey, Warren A., 85

Segura, Perry, 198, 223
Shaw, John M., 261
Shaw, Robert B., 164
Shaw, William M., 112, 154, 238
Sherman, William T., 74, 108
Shestack, Jerome J., 132, 137, 155–57
Shieber, Benjamin M., 175, 181–2, 184, 192, 197, 202–03, 214, 226, 231, 232
Shows, Pat, 210
Shuey, John M., 97
Simmer, Helen M., 163
Simoneaux, Frank P., 166
Sims, Vernon J., 56
Slack, J. Stewart, 152
Slaughter, Midge, 243
Slidell, John, 5
Smith, Arthur J., 229
Smith, J. Denson: comparison of Denson exam to D-Day, 123; on civil law versus common law, 254; and numerical grading, 169; retirement of, 225; mentioned, 56, 68, 74, 80, 83, 86–88, 93, 95, 100, 103, 105–06, 110, 112–14, 117, 119, 121–22, 129–31, 143, 155–57, 175, 180, 190, 191, 197, 208, 215, 242, 251
Smith, James Barclay, 49–50, 57, 61–64, 76, 79–80, 88, 102, 105
Smith, James Monroe, 59, 60, 66, 71–74, 89, 90, 92, 100, 106, 108
Smith, Joe L., 236
Smith, Munroe, 25
Smith, T. B., 227
Smitherman, James E., 11, 158
Soileau, David E., 218
Sorley, Louis, 10
Sorola, Diane, 243
Sotela, Dean Regelio, 190
Spaht, Katherine Shaw: wins American Association of University Women scholarship, 238; revision of Louisiana community-property system, 223; mentioned, 217–18, 243, 251
Spaht, Paul H., 202, 238

325

Spence, Hardy, 209
Spence, James T., 115
Spies, Frederick K., 226
Sponsler, Thomas H., 227
St. Paul, John, 6
Stagg, Tom, 157
Stein, Peter G., 227
Stelly, Arthur, 52
Stetter, Roger A., 217
Stevens, Robert, 5
Stewart, Ashton, 49
Stewart, Jerusha (Judy), 238
Stewart, Samuel Mims, 31
Stickman, Chris, 243
Stockwell, Oliver, 55, 157, 247
Stoke, Harold W., 108, 119, 121, 123, 138
Story, Joseph, 5
Strickland, Leslie Clyde, 45
Strickland, Theodore C., 164
Stulb, Joseph G., Jr., 112
Stumberg, George Wilfred: joins faculty, 29–30; on effects of codification of law, 30; university committee service, 45; mentioned, 31, 39, 44–46, 57, 166
Stumbert, Charles H., 29–30
Sullivan, Francis C., 175, 183, 192, 222, 232, 245, 263
Suthon, Walter J., Jr., 143
Sutton, Bobby D., Jr., 205, 206
Symeonides, Symeon C., 250

Tabony, August H., 241–42
Taintor, Charles W., II, 83, 85, 86, 87, 105
Tate, Albert C.: joins faculty, 184; offer to replace Dean McMahon, 184; on Dean Beutel's resignation, 71; on *Whangdoodle* incident, 66–67; and open admissions, 174–75; member of the "Uncommittee," 175; mentioned, 126, 188, 193, 218, 239, 261
Tate, Donald J., 182, 192
Tauzin, Wilbert Joseph (Billy), II, 201, 261
Taylor, B. B., Jr., 21, 84, 85, 88, 96, 99, 101, 103

Tete, William T.: joins faculty, 185; on civil law versus common law, 254; mentioned, 183, 202–03, 206, 223
Theis, William H., 217
Thurman, Samuel D., 227
Thurmon, Clyde W., 95, 107
Town, A. Hays, 158
Trelease, Frank J., 227
Trice, William E., 136
Trimble, James T., 261
Tritico, Lila M., 240–41
Trosclair, Frank, Jr., 210
Tucker, Col. John H., Jr.: donates Civil Law Collection, 199; on WWI, 37; first president of Louisiana State Law Institute, 79; on Dean Tullis, 21; Tucker Lectures, 227; mentioned, 141, 158
Tucker, John Randolph, Jr., 21, 26, 37, 79
Tucker, Patricia, 88
Tulane, Paul, 6
Tullis, Robert Lee: 1913 *Gumbo* coverage, 34; 1918 student impressions of, 38–39; and AALS report on Long, 78–79; as dean, 20, 25, 32, 34–35, 37–39, 45, 50–51, 53, 55, 61; dean emeritus, 67; Dean Hebert on, 20; emphasis on law studies over military or sports, 11, 55; emphasis on public service, 21; and end of prohibition, 20; end of Tullis era, 63–67; joins faculty, 19–20; and intellectual rigor of civil-law education, 248–49; and Louisiana Legislative Reference Bureau, 21; on student grammar and spelling, 39; Middleton on, 20; and Order of the Coif, 114–15, 131; political ambitions of, 50–51; "Tensas Terror," 21; university committee service, 45; mentioned, 22, 42, 43–44, 47–48, 57, 62, 73–74, 80, 82, 94–96, 99, 105, 161, 205, 210, 251, 254
Tunc, André, 143
Turner, Roscoe, 122, 151
Tyson, Ralph E., 236, 261–62

INDEX OF NAMES

Updegraff, Clarence Milton, 29, 38

Van Hecke, Maurice T., 141
Veal, William R., 164
Veron, Earl E., 262
Verrall, Harold Earl, 48–49, 57
Vetter, Bernard K., 262
Vialet, Nell, 138
Viator, James E., 262
Vliet, R. Dale, 227
Voegelin, Eric, 134, 145, 148, 250

Waddlington, Walter, III, 191
Wade, Sparky, 104
Walker, Beverly Denbo, 97, 234
Walker, Charles, 97
Walker, Kathleen, 111
Wallach, Kate: president of AALL, 189; *Research in Louisiana Law*, 135, 233; retirement of, 233; mentioned, 120–21, 137, 218, 221, 234, 262
Walsh, Scallan, 50
Walter, Donald E., 262
Warden, Karl P., 227
Ware, E. O., 52
Ware, G. Bradford "Bumpy," 201
Ware, Winsome, 52
Watson, Warren O., 53
Webb, Gwendolyn, 98
Weber, Dudley L., 22
Weimar, John J., 261
Wells, Sam, 100
West, Elmer Gordon, 115, 210, 262
Westly, John, 6
Whatley, William G., 178
Wheaton, Crumbie, 29, 37, 38
Whipple, Keith M., 166
White, Darrel D., 239
White, Edward Douglass, 34
White, John S., Jr., 141

Whitten, Leon H., 166
Wiggins, Leo, 243
Wigmore, John Henry: on early Louisiana bar, 2–3; on Livingston, 4; mentioned, 18, 75–76, 86–87
Wilkerson, Marcus M.: on tradition of "Hog Law," 24–25; mentioned, 9
Wilkinson, William Scott, 36
Willet, Darrel V., Jr., 191
Williams, Goodwin W., 26–27, 39
Williams, Harry T., 7, 65
Williams, Robert, 112
Wilson, Evelyn E., 262
Wilson, Hugh E., 55
Wilson, John W., 209
Wilson, Roy S., 151–52
Wimberly, Guy, 96, 103, 104
Wimbish, Paul R., 174
Wirtz, William Willard, 142, 195
Wisdom, John Minor, 110
Wollett, Donald H., 136, 169, 177, 180
Womack, Beverly Gordon, 120
Woods, Vernon, 100

Yancey, Benjamin W., 136, 185
Yancey, Clarence, 50
Yeager, Charles, 242
Yiannopoulos, Athanassios N.: Chair in Comparative Law, 186; joins faculty, 134; publications, 189, 224; reporter for revision of civil-code property articles, 224; summer programs, 231–32; mentioned, 175, 193, 215, 250, 252
Yntema, Hessel E., 141
York, Rudy, 243

Zainey, Jay C., 262
Zatzkis, Ralph J., 239
Zaunbrecher, Christopher L., 238
Zimmerman, Bernard J., 217
Zimmerman, Harry R., 206

SUBJECT INDEX

Audubon Sugar School, 9

Bailey Lectures, 134, 195
Baton Rouge Citizens Council, 142–43
Black American Law Students Association (BALSA), 243

Center for Civil Law Studies, 191, 224
Civil Code Rally Songs, 166–67
Civil law/common law "non-debate," 252–55
Council on Legal Opportunity (CLEO), 177, 232, 235–37

Desegregation of the LSU Law School: AALS-Yale proposal, 155–57; alternative admission criteria, 177–78, 213; Black American Law Students Association, 243; and circumvention of *Brown* decision, 153–54; Council on Legal Opportunity (CLEO), 177, 232, 235–37; first black faculty member, 218; "head start" program, 177; Louisiana Council on Campus Minorities, 236; "more thorough" character investigation, 152–53; the "Negro problem," 122; and recruitment, 236; and Roscoe Turner, 122, 151–52; and Roy S. Wilson, 151–52; and Southern University Law School, 6; mentioned, 142, 143, 151–57, 181, 203–04
Dicta, 206

Edward Douglass White Law Society, 34, 56

Edward Douglass White Lectures, 99, 142, 194, 227

Francis X. Martin Law Club, 55

"Hog Law," 24–25

Institute of Advanced Civil Law Studies, 191

L'Avocat, 243–44
Louisiana Constitution: conventions, 16, 50, 107, 222, 247, 251, 259; drafting of initial 1811 constitution, 3; and University of Louisiana, 8
Louisiana Judicial College, 182
Louisiana Judicial Council, 132
Louisiana Law School, 5–6
Louisiana State Law Institute: compiled civil codes and revised statutes, 117; concept by James Smith, 49; Daggett as acting director, 113; design and plan of, 251; established, 79; J. Denson Smith as director, 80; and Louisiana criminal code, 110; and mineral code, 179, 251; and non-profit corporation statute, 110; revision of property law, 224; mentioned, 21, 54, 134, 140, 141, 190, 225, 233, 249, 250
Louisiana State University and Agricultural and Mechanical College: 1901–04 enrollment, 9; 1920 oil and gas severance tax financing, 41, 59–60; 1970s organizational

changes, 245–46; Communist investigations, 154–55; founding of law school, 6, 8; Long era of growth, 60; State Seminary of Learning, 8; Pentagon Barracks, 9, 41–42

LSU Alumni Association: *Louisiana State Quarterly*, 26, 27, 34; mentioned, 157, 228

LSU Law Club, 63

LSU Law School

—buildings: 1925 move to Thomas D. Boyd Hall, 42; 1936 new building, 88–92; 1970s new building, 195–99; chemistry-building basement home, 11, 41; early student boarding options, 11; Hill Memorial Library home, 11; Leche Hall, 92; name change, 11; "old" building problems, 195–96; naming of Hebert Law Center, 247; special committee for new building, 158–59

—class attendance requirements: attendance rules, 147–48; discretionary exceptions, 148; early attendance rules, 11; elimination and reinstatement of 1967 rule, 178, 231

—classes and curricula: 1906 first classes and curricula, 10, 12, 14–15, 16; 1912–13 three-year curriculum, 23; 1916 one-year college prerequisite, 23; 1918 war courses, 38; 1919 undergraduate recommendations, 24; 1923 two-year college prerequisite, 42; 1929 requirements, 44; 1930 requirements, 45; 1931–32 curriculum, 61–62; 1936–37 dramatically new curriculum, 75; 1942 trimester system, 114; 1950s curriculum, 143–46; 1952–53 reinstitution of three-year undergraduate requirement, 146; 1958 curriculum, 148–50; 1960s experiments, 148–49, 169–78; 1970s tinkering, 227–31; 1974 comprehensive study, 228; alternate four-year curriculum, 75–76, 143; bar exam requirement, 12–13, 43, 110, 199, 229; LL.B. changed to J.D., 174–75; change to three-year curriculum, 23; civil code courses, 22; clinical programs, 150, 229–30; combined degree, 170; continuing legal education, 232; diploma privilege, 12, 24, 166, 199; effects of World War II on, 107–08, 112–13, 143–46; elimination of joint B.A.-J.D., 214; ethics requirement, 23, 174; fifty- versus sixty-minute class period debate, 228; fifteen-hour rule, 229; and football team, 55, 206–07; four-year program, 75–76; legal writing, 230; MBA-J.D., 233; mission and curriculum, 175–76; "package courses," 149, 170–71, 230; part-time/night courses, 171; post-WWII accelerated program, 116–17; proposed reading list and public speaking course, 132; separate civil-law and common-law curricula, 148–49, 175–78, 186; tri-semester system, 114

—enrollment: 1904, 9; 1908–09, 31–33; 1918–19, 29; 1937, 76; 1940s, 106, 116; 1950s, 146, 159–60; mid-1950s, 146; 1960s, 168–69, 171–72, 200; 1970s, 212–14, 237; peak post-WWII, 127

—faculty: 1906, 13; 1927 faculty stability, 48; 1930s "frantic innovation," 73–79; 1937 staffing difficulties, 76; 1940s, 106; 1950s, 129–34; 1958 segregation-committee investigation of Communists, 155; 1960s, 172, 178–86; 1970s, 215, 263; bureaucracy, 138; close-knit nature of, 137–38, 200; Dean Hebert on full-time professorships, 141; deliberations, 229; emeritus, 224–25; executive committee, 226; first minority member of, 218; founding members, 17; governance and organization of, 73–75, 245–47; inbreeding index, 216; and Korean crisis, 163–64; national faculty, 257–58; and open admissions debate, 173–74, 212–15; recruitment challenges, 214–15; retirements, 225; retirement system, 131, 134, 224; Rubin on Dean Hebert as faculty executive, 139–40; salaries, 52, 131, 169, 171; scholarship, 186–90; search for foreign-law professors, 134; meetings of, 231; transition, 262–64; visiting professors and lecturers, 121, 140–43, 193–95, 226–27

—grading system/promotions: 1912–13 promotion rates, 24; 1915–16 promotion rates, 24; 1920s bar passage, 43; 1930 change to letter grades, 45, 169; 1933 grade averages, 101; 1970s bar passage, 245; 1970s faculty committee study, 227–28; 1970s grading debate, 214; anonymous grading, 231; attrition rates, 160, 171–73; first quantitative admissions index, 173; "flunk-out" rate, 258–59; hard versus soft graders, 258; law school index study, 214–15; letter grades, 45, 143, 227–28; LSAT, 150–51; minimum-courses passage per semester, 24; numerical grades, 44, 146, 169–70, 227–28; posting of grades with names, 163; readmissions, 124, 173; trial exams, 124, 127, 163; under Beutel, 70

—law library: 1922 holdings, 41; 1924 holdings, 43; 1929 holdings, 44; 1930–31 holdings, 61, 93–94; 1937 holdings, 73; 1945 holdings, 120, 189; 1954 holdings, 135; 1960s holdings, 169, 189–90; 1970s holdings, 233; Daspit-Colby years, 93–94; effect on AALS admission, 43–44; foreign-law collection, 140–41; initial holdings, 11–12; restriction to LSU law students, 135; Wallach years, 120–21, 135, 137, 189, 190–93, 218, 221, 233, 234, 262

—law review: 1930 revival of, 68, 96; eligible students, 137; and end of war emergency, 123; and faculty symposia, 136–37; mentioned, 126, 132, 133, 141–42, 164, 177, 180, 182, 185, 187, 205–06, 218, 220, 234–35, 238, 251

—miscellaneous: renaming of "law department" to "law school," 11; "boutique" nature of law school, 248; early law-reform efforts, 134; education philosophy, 13–14; English and grammar deficiencies, 22–23, 39, 44, 147; feminization, 209; G.I. Bill, 123, 259; independent status, 247; placement of graduates, 187; summer programs, 23, 125, 171, 177, 231–32; Tullis on separate bar examining committees, 34–35; war impact, 37–38, 123–24, 163, 192–93, 238–40

—tuition and fees: 1906, 10; 1908, 10–11; 1914–15, 35; 1930s, 61; 1949–50, 128; 1950s, 166; 1968, 200

LSU Medical School, 13
LSU Press, 61, 133–35, 142, 194
Loyola University Law School, 6

Mineral Law Institute, 158, 179, 190

Order of the Coif, 109, 114, 140, 166, 187, 193, 216

Pearl Harbor attack, 112–13
Phi Alpha Delta, 209, 238
Phi Delta Phi, 55, 164, 166–67, 209
Poopsheets, 244–45
Public service, law school graduates in, 53–54, 111–12, 211, 260–62

Reveille: 1906 approval of law course and hiring of faculty, 10; 1922 move to Highland campus, 41–42; and 1957 Hollywood film productions, 165; on anonymous grading, 231; call for law school, 9–10; and Cohn-Turner fashion, 210; on Dean Hebert's private law practice, 138; on Dean Henry's tea time, 19; and desegregation, 151–54, 203–04; and Flory Trials, 244; and hats-and-canes tradition, 209; and Hill Memorial Library law school, 11; Long-era censorship of, 60; and moot court cases, 16–17, 38–39, 52–53, 95, 111, 210; and Nixon-Humphrey election, 183; and Ole Miss week, 239; and ombudsman office, 241; on Dean Flory, 29; on Professor Stumberg, 21; on Roland Howell, 36; on parking inconveniences, 201, 244; and recruiting law students, 32–34; and refugee students, 88; reserved football seating debate, 161–62; Saturday/holiday classes, 147, 205; and twenty-fifth law review anniversary, 206; on women in law school, 52; mentioned, 27, 37–38, 164, 166, 179, 188, 194, 238, 244–45

School of Banking of the South, 158, 224
Sea-grant college program, 185, 192, 216
Southern Law Review Conference of 1959, 166
Southern Review, 60–61
Southern University Law School, 6, 122
State Seminary of Learning, 8
Student life: 1906–19, 31–37; 1908–09 schedules, 22; 1909 accomplishments and foibles, 32; 1920s, 52–56; 1930s, 98–104; 1914–17 class officers, 35–36; 1940s, 124–28; 1950s, 159–67; 1960s, 199–210; 1961 freshman smoker, 209–10; 1970s, 237–45; Alumni-Senior Parade, 36; Assault and Flattery Show, 244, 250; Barristers' Ball, 162, 244; the *Civilian*, 244; Coed Law Club, 98; coed regulations, 239–40; contrast 1906 to 1976, 259–61; Dean Henry's tea time, 19; "The Devil and Tom Harrell (A Morality Play); or, The Devil Made Me Do It," 244; draft registration, 107–08; early dress code, 32; prohibition, 20, 52; exceptions for military obligations, 202; female students, 36, 52, 61, 237–41; goldfish gulping, 88; hats-and-canes tradition, 163, 209; married students, 238; impact of war on, 37–38, 112–16, 119, 123, 125, 168, 192–93, 238–39; Long censorship efforts, 60; military veterans, 124–25; part-time studies, 171; parking, 201, 244, 239; Ph.T. (Putting Hubby Through) degree, 162; poopsheets, 244–45; Saigon Bar Association, 202; Society for Transmission of Unmutated Descendants (STUD), 207–08; streaking, 245; Women in Law, 243

Tidelands Law Institute, 158
Tulane University: faculty compared with early LSU law faculty, 10; effect of LSU on, 13; founding and early years of, 5–8; preceded by Louisiana Law School/University of Louisiana, 5–6
Tullis Moot Court: student eligibility, 137; mentioned, 59, 94–95, 111, 127, 165, 174, 210, 238, 243

University of Louisiana, 6

Whangdoodle incident, 64–66. *See also* Kennedy, Kemble K.

Printed in the USA
CPSIA information can be obtained
at www.ICGtesting.com
LVHW041203151223
766489LV00003B/203